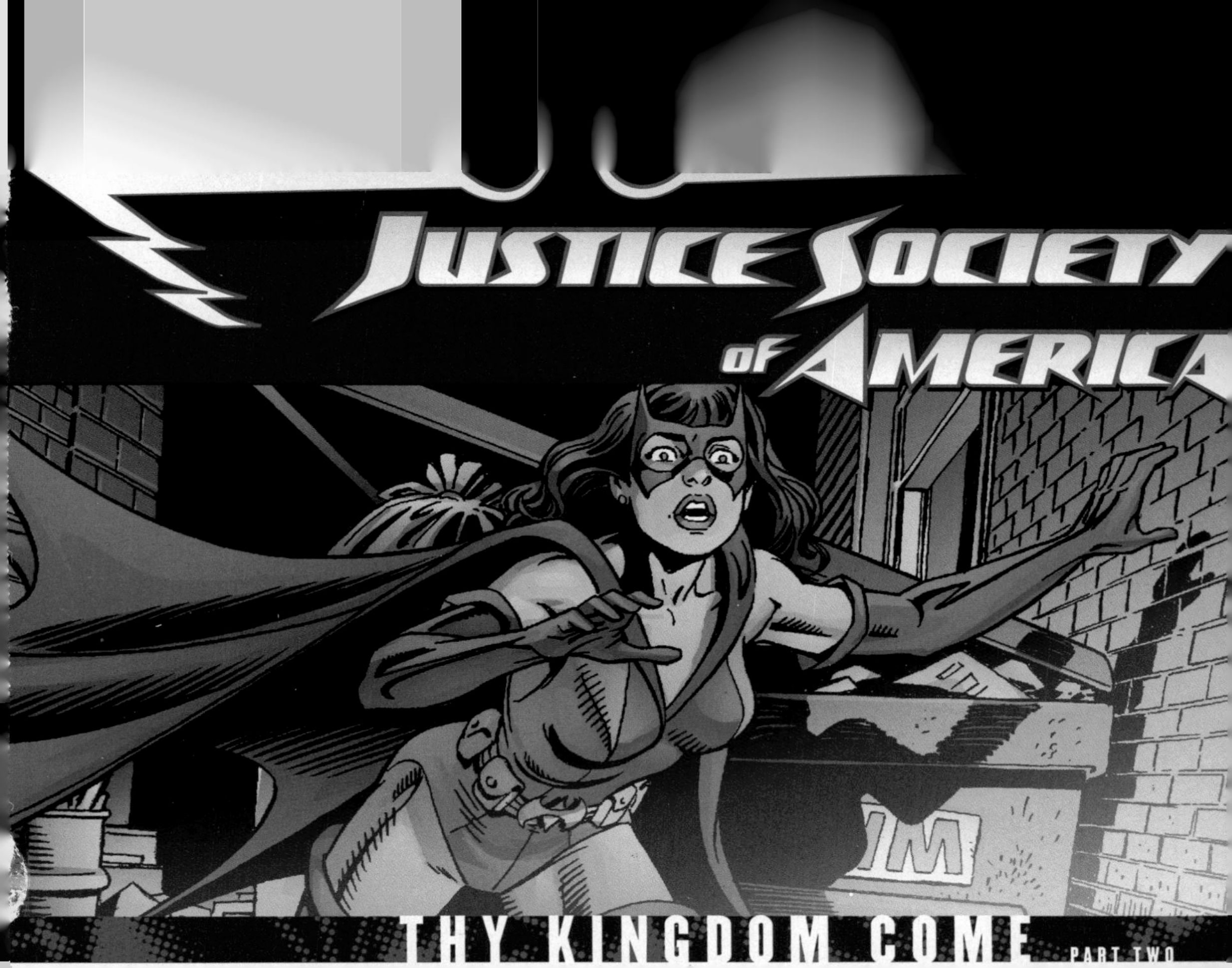
JUSTICE SOCIETY
of AMERICA
THY KINGDOM COME PART TWO

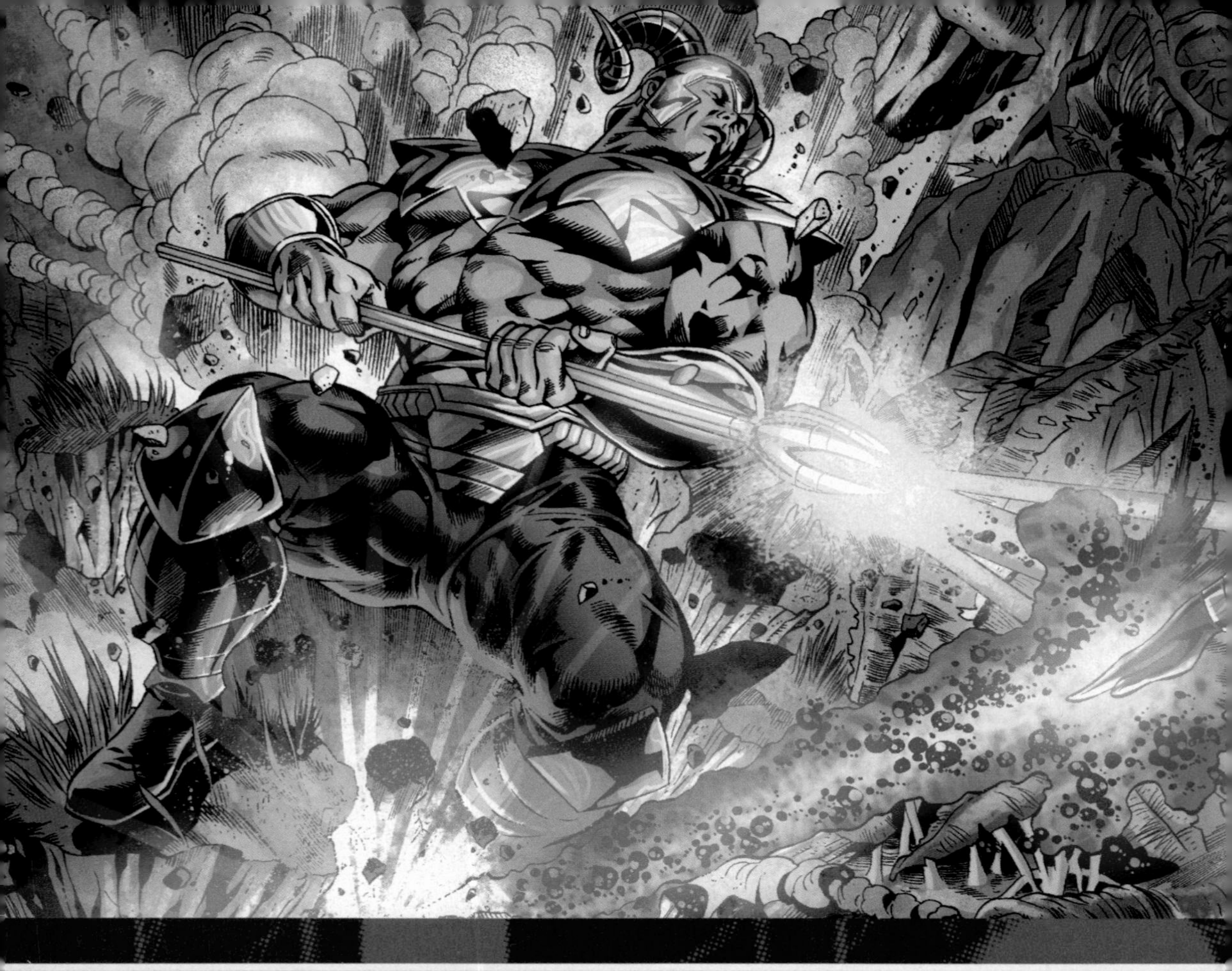

DAN DIDIO SENIOR VP-EXECUTIVE EDITOR **MICHAEL SIGLAIN** EDITOR-ORIGINAL SERIES **HARVEY RICHARDS** ASSISTANT EDITOR-ORIGINAL SERIES
ANTON KAWASAKI EDITOR-COLLECTED EDITION **ROBBIN BROSTERMAN** SENIOR ART DIRECTOR **NADINA SIMON** ART DIRECTOR **PAUL LEVITZ** PRESIDENT & PUBLISHER
GEORG BREWER VP-DESIGN & DC DIRECT CREATIVE **RICHARD BRUNING** SENIOR VP-CREATIVE DIRECTOR **PATRICK CALDON** EXECUTIVE VP-FINANCE & OPERATIONS
CHRIS CARAMALIS VP-FINANCE **JOHN CUNNINGHAM** VP-MARKETING **TERRI CUNNINGHAM** VP-MANAGING EDITOR **AMY GENKINS** SENIOR VP-BUSINESS & LEGAL AFFAIRS
ALISON GILL VP-MANUFACTURING **DAVID HYDE** VP-PUBLICITY **HANK KANALZ** VP-GENERAL MANAGER, WILDSTORM **JIM LEE** EDITORIAL DIRECTOR-WILDSTORM
GREGORY NOVECK SENIOR VP-CREATIVE AFFAIRS **SUE POHJA** VP-BOOK TRADE SALES **STEVE ROTTERDAM** SENIOR VP-SALES & MARKETING
CHERYL RUBIN SENIOR VP-BRAND MANAGEMENT **ALYSSE SOLL** VP-ADVERTISING & CUSTOM PUBLISHING **JEFF TROJAN** VP-BUSINESS DEVELOPMENT, DC DIRECT **BOB WAYNE** VP-SALES

Cover by Alex Ross

JUSTICE SOCIETY OF AMERICA: THY KINGDOM COME PART TWO

DC Comics, 1700 Broadway, New York, NY 10019 | A Warner Bros. Entertainment Company | Printed in USA | First Printing. ISBN: 978-1-4012-1914-7 SC ISBN: 978-1-4012-1943-8

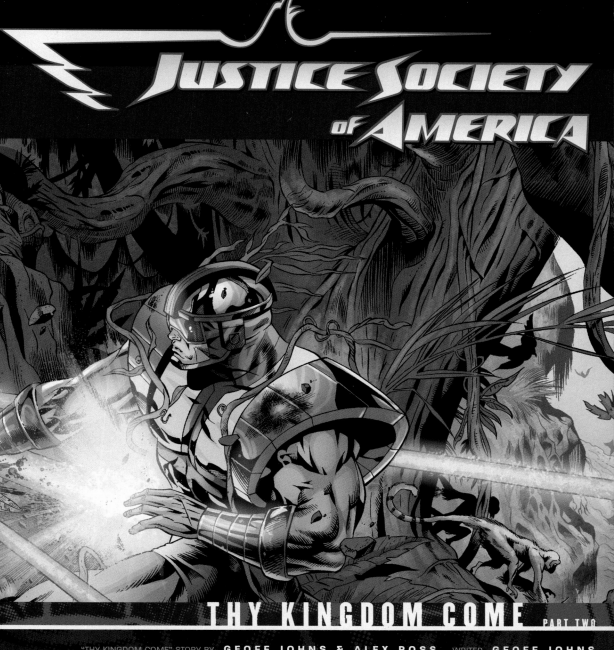

JUSTICE SOCIETY of AMERICA

THY KINGDOM COME PART TWO

"THY KINGDOM COME" STORY BY **GEOFF JOHNS & ALEX ROSS**   WRITER **GEOFF JOHNS**

PENCILLERS **DALE EAGLESHAM**   **FERNANDO PASARIN**   **JERRY ORDWAY**

PAINTED KINGDOM COME SEQUENCES BY **ALEX ROSS**

INKERS **PRENTIS ROLLINS**   BOB WIACEK   RICHARD FRIEND   REBECCA BUCHMAN
JOHN STANISCI   MICK GRAY   KRIS JUSTICE   NATHAN MASSENGILL

COLORISTS **ALEX SINCLAIR**   **HI-FI**   LETTERER **ROB LEIGH**

CAST OF CHARACTERS

 **GREEN LANTERN** Engineer Alan Scott found a lantern carved from a meteorite known as the Starheart. Fulfilling the lamp's prophecy to grant astonishing power, Scott tapped into the emerald energy and fought injustice as the Green Lantern. His ring can generate a variety of effects and energy constructs, sustained purely by his will.

 **THE FLASH** The first in a long line of super-speedsters, Jay Garrick is capable of running at velocities near the speed of light. A scientist, Garrick has also served as mentor to other speedsters, and to many heroes over several generations.

 **WILDCAT** A former heavyweight boxing champ, Ted Grant, a.k.a. Wildcat, prowls the mean streets defending the helpless. One of the world's foremost hand-to-hand combatants, he has trained many of today's best fighters — including Black Canary, Catwoman, and the Batman himself.

 **HAWKMAN** Originally Prince Khufu of ancient Egypt, the hero who would become known as Hawkman discovered an alien spacecraft from the planet Thanagar, powered by a mysterious antigravity element called Nth metal. The unearthly energies of the metal transformed his soul, and he and his love Princess Chay-Ara were reincarnated over and over for centuries. Currently he is Carter Hall, archaeologist and adventurer.

 **POWER GIRL** Once confused about her origins, Karen Starr now knows she is the cousin of an alternate-Earth Superman — who gave his life in the Infinite Crisis. Her enhanced strength and powers of flight and invulnerability are matched only by her self-confidence in action, which sometimes borders on arrogance.

 **MR. TERRIFIC** Haunted by the death of his wife, Olympic gold medal-winning decathlete Michael Holt was ready to take his own life. Instead, inspired by the Spectre's story of the original Mr. Terrific, he rededicated himself to ensuring fair play among the street youth using his wealth and technical skills to become the living embodiment of those ideals. He now divides his time between the JSA and the government agency known as Checkmate.

 **HOURMAN** Rick Tyler struggled for a while before accepting his role as the son of the original Hourman. It hasn't been an easy road — he's endured addiction to the Miraclo drug that increases his strength and endurance, and nearly died from a strange disease. Now, after mastering the drug, he uses a special hourglass that enables him to see one hour into the future.

 **LIBERTY BELLE** Jesse Chambers is the daughter of the Golden Age Johnny Quick and Liberty Belle. Originally adopting her father's speed formula, Jesse became the super-hero known as Jesse Quick. After a brief period without powers, Jesse has returned — now taking over her mother's role. As the new Liberty Belle, Jesse is an All-American Powerhouse.

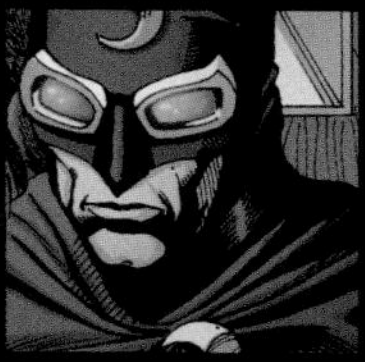

DR. MID-NITE A medical prodigy, Pieter Anton Cross refused to work within the limits of the system. Treating people on his own, he came into contact with a dangerous drug that altered his body chemistry, enabling him to see light in the infrared spectrum. Although he lost his normal sight in a murder attempt disguised as a car accident, his uncanny night vision allows him to protect the weak under the assumed identity of Dr. Mid-Nite.

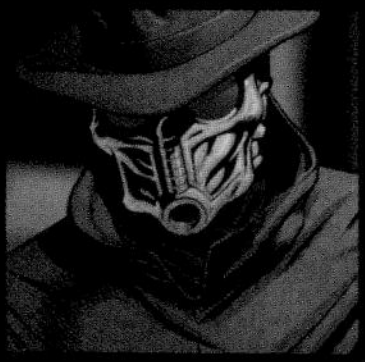

SANDMAN Sandy Hawkins was the ward of original Sandman Wesley Dodds, and he is the nephew of Dodds's lifelong partner, Dian Belmont. After a bizarre accident, Hawkins was able to transform himself into a pure silicon or sand form. Recently, he has been experiencing prophetic dreams. He also carries a gas mask, gas guns and other equipment.

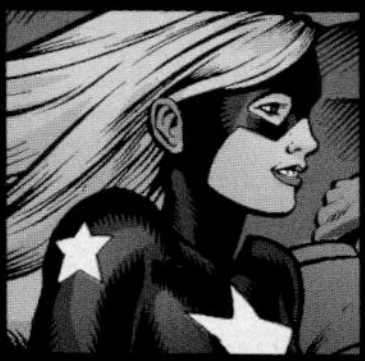

STARGIRL When Courtney Whitmore discovered the cosmic converter belt that had been worn by the JSA's original Star-Spangled Kid (her stepfather, Pat Dugan, was the Kid's sidekick Stripesy), she saw it as an opportunity to cut class and kick some butt. Now called Stargirl, she divides her time between her adventures with the JSA and bickering/teaming up with Pat — who sometimes monitors Courtney from his S.T.R.I.P.E. robot.

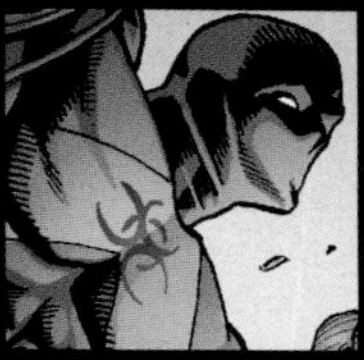

DAMAGE Grant Emerson has had a difficult life. Growing up, he was the victim of an abusive foster father. Then later, after discovering his explosive powers, he accidentally blew up half of downtown Atlanta. Last year, he was almost beaten to death by the super-speed villain known as Zoom. Grant has worn a full-face mask as Damage ever since.

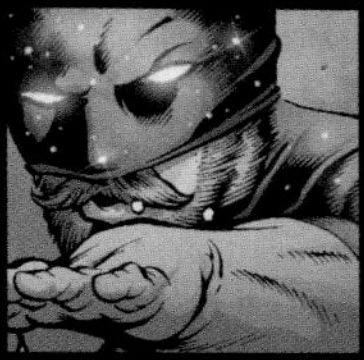

STARMAN A mysterious new Starman recently appeared in Opal City, saving its citizens numerous times. He apparently suffers from some form of schizophrenia, and hears voices in his head. Voluntarily residing in the Sunshine Sanitarium, Starman will occasionally leave and use his gravity-altering powers to fight crime.

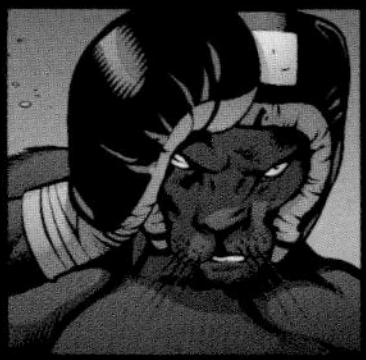

WILDCAT II Tommy Bronson is the newly discovered son of original Wildcat Ted Grant. But it's not quite "like father, like son" here. For one thing, Tom doesn't want to be a fighter like his dad. And second, this new Wildcat has the ability to turn into a feral creature, with enhanced agility and animalistic senses...

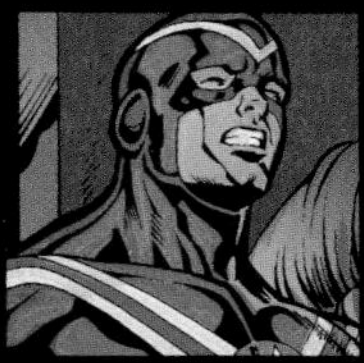

CITIZEN STEEL The grandson of the original Steel, Nathan Heywood is a former football hero who has suffered numerous tragedies. First, an injury and infection required his leg to be amputated. Then, a vicious attack by the Fourth Reich wiped out most of his family. But during the attack, a bizarre incident left him with metal-like skin and superhuman strength.

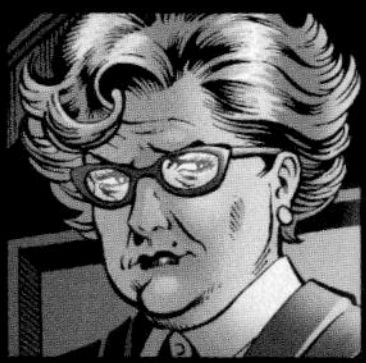

MA HUNKEL Abigail Mathilda "Ma" Hunkel was one of the first female super-heroes of the Golden Age. Wearing colorful long johns and a cooking pot with eye-holes on her head, she was known as the original Red Tornado — fighting local criminals in her New York neighborhood. Now in her eighties, Ma is the current custodian of the Justice Society Museum.

PREVIOUSLY...

The Justice Society of America is back, bigger and better than ever. Formed by Green Lantern, the Flash, and Wildcat and led by new team leader Power Girl, the Society continues to welcome new members whose powers stem from the legacies of past heroes: Mr. America, a former FBI special agent and expert profiler of super-villains who inherited the mantle from his murdered partner. Lightning, the electrically powered daughter of Justice League member Black Lightning. Jakeem Thunder, a returning member of the Society who wields the power of the mystical genie Johnny Thunderbolt. Amazing-Man, grandson and heir to the powers of one of the greatest African-American super-heroes in history. Judomaster, an expert fighter who is literally unhittable in combat and seeks vengeance for her father, a slain Yakuza assassin. Lance Corporal David Reid, grandson of Justice Society founder President Franklin Delano Roosevelt and veteran of the wars in Afghanistan and Iraq, capable of concentrated energy blasts.

When the Society's powerful, seemingly schizo-phrenic new Starman accidentally opens a path-way to another universe, the team's most unex-pected addition arrives: the "Kingdom Come" Superman! This aged Man of Steel has seen his Earth fall victim to heroes gone extreme, killing indiscriminately in the name of "justice" under the influence of a brazen anti-hero named Magog.

Torn from his world just as its remaining heroes fell victim to a nuclear strike, Superman has chosen to remain with the Justice Society, aiding in their mis-sion in order to prevent this Earth from suffering the same fate — yet it may already be too late. A mysterious killer is slaughtering metahuman villains who claim their powers are of godlike origin. Mr. America discovers that the murders have been committed in the name of a being called Gog...

JUSTICE SOCIETY OF AMERICA #13 cover A by ALEX ROSS

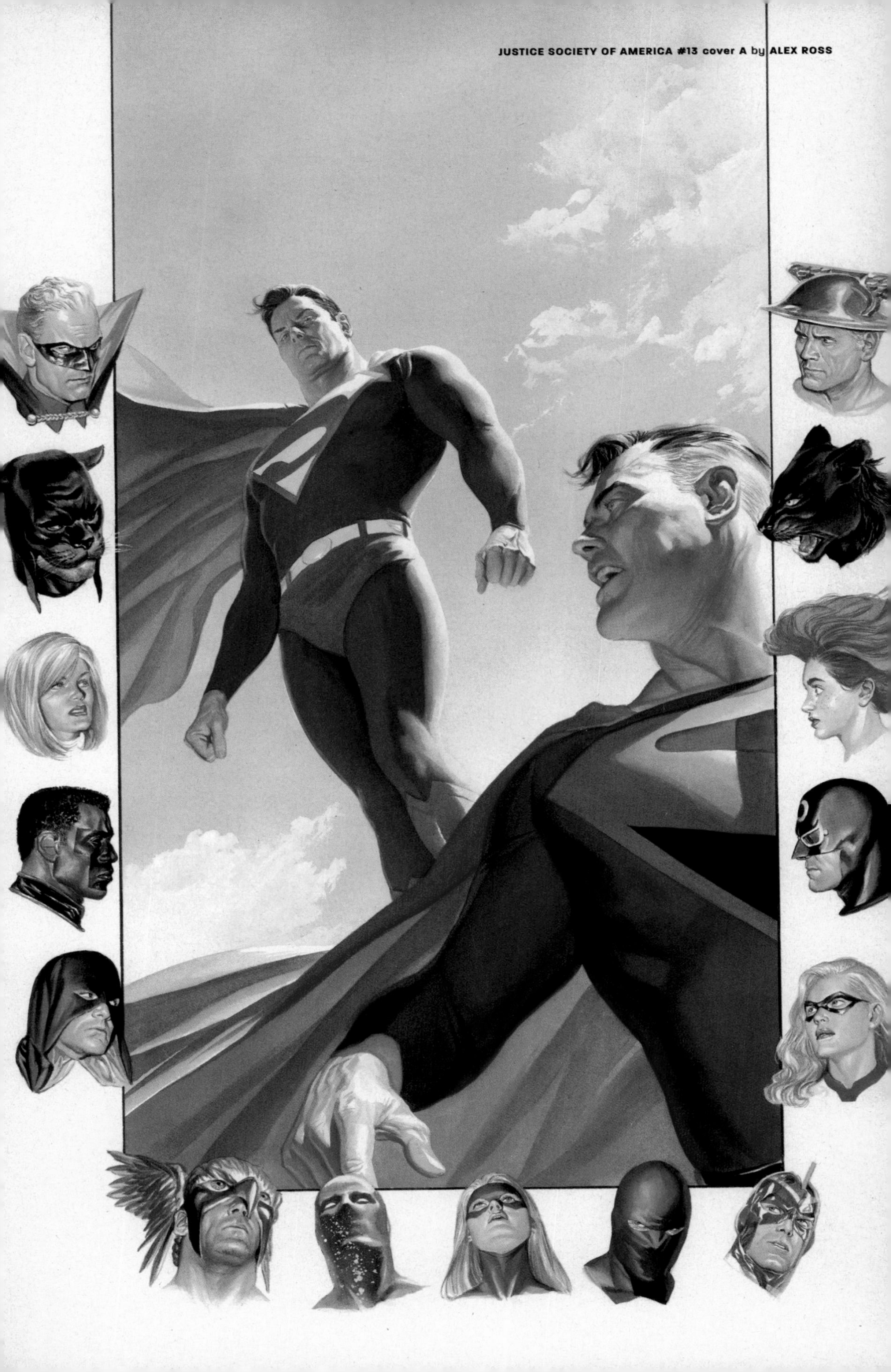

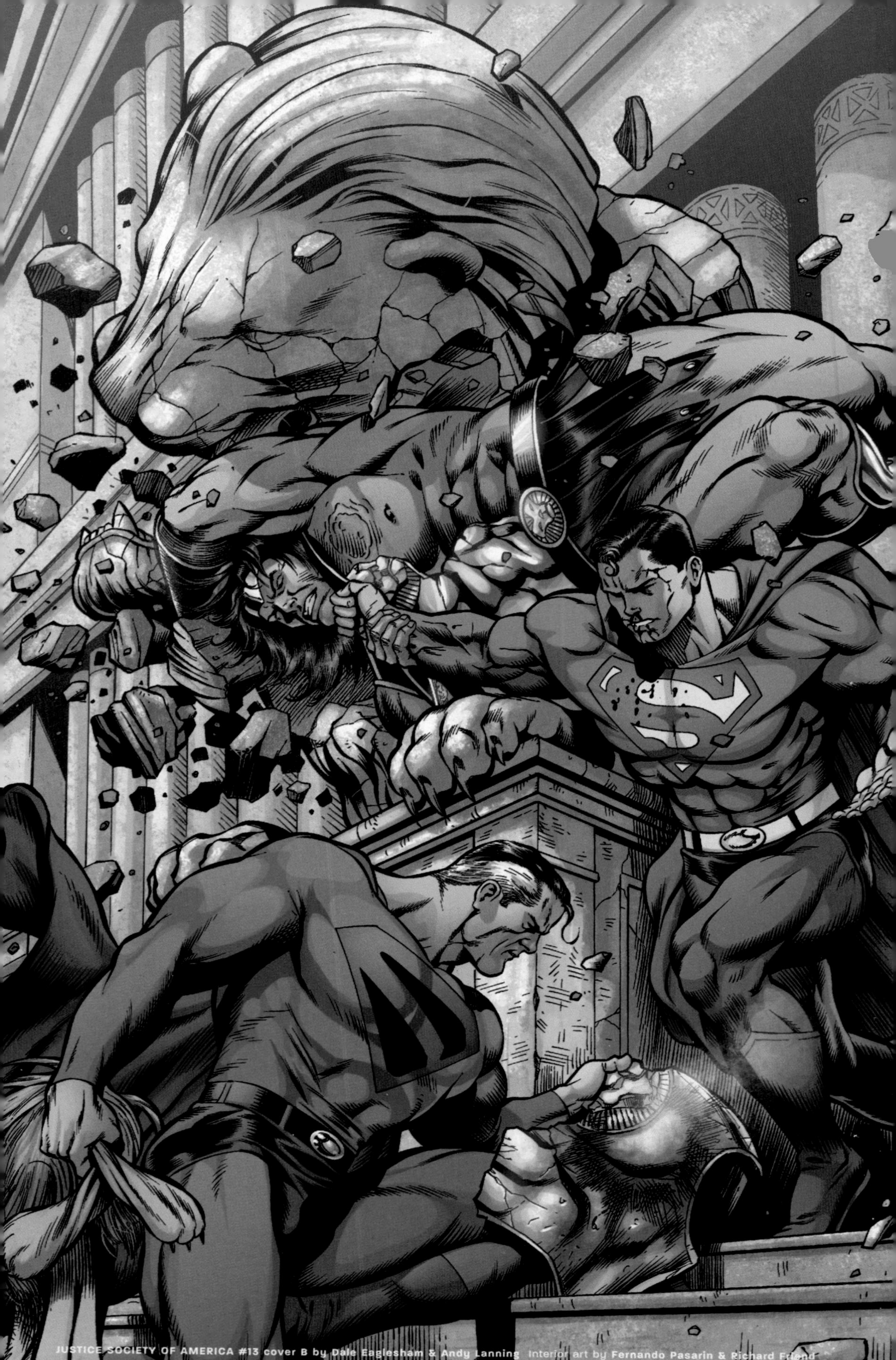

JUSTICE SOCIETY OF AMERICA #13 cover B by Dale Eaglesham & Andy Lanning Interior art by Fernando Pasarin & Richard Friend

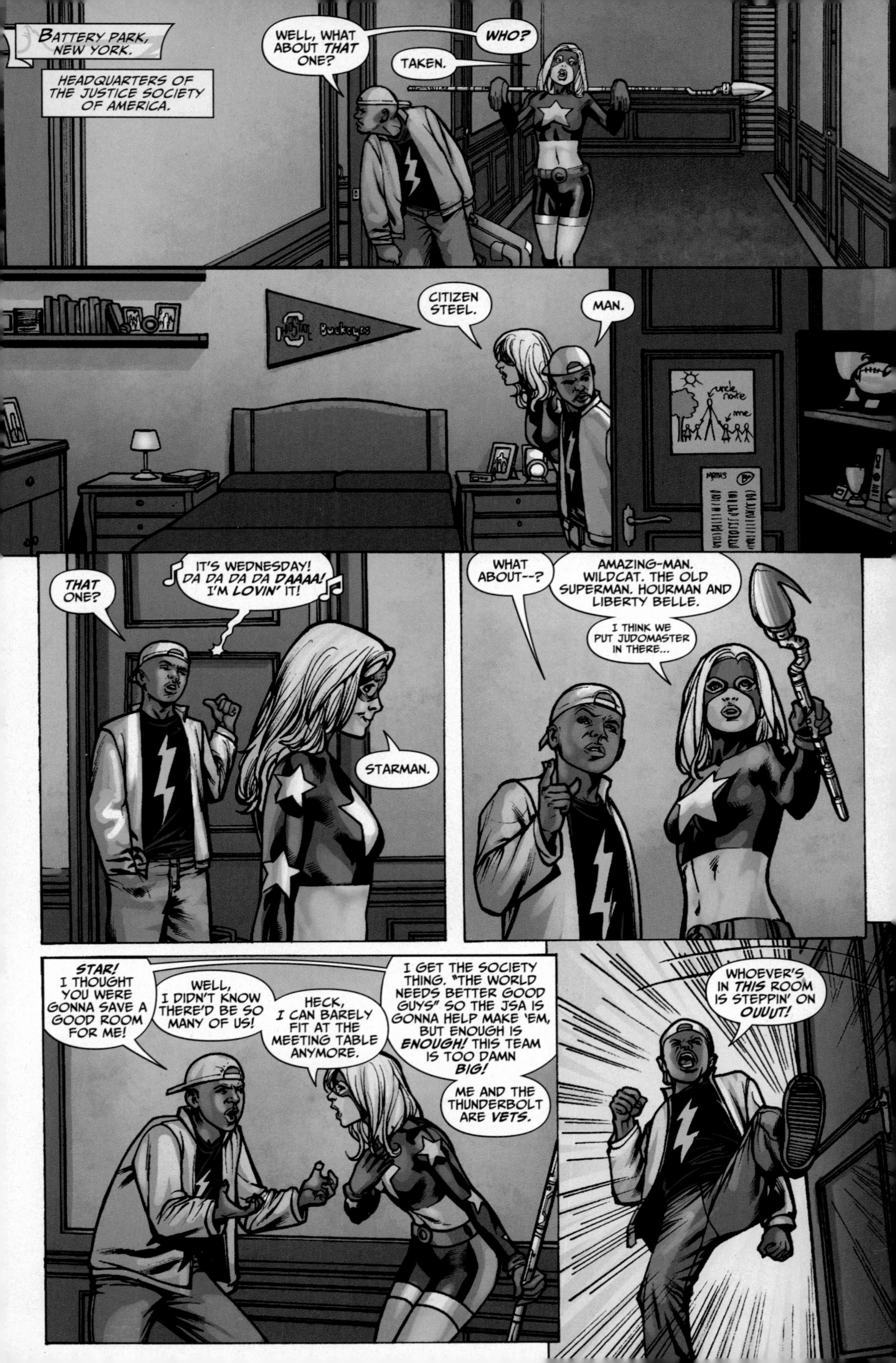
BATTERY PARK, NEW YORK.
HEADQUARTERS OF THE JUSTICE SOCIETY OF AMERICA.
WELL, WHAT ABOUT THAT ONE?
WHO?
TAKEN.
Buckeyes
CITIZEN STEEL.
MAN.
uncle nate
me
THAT ONE?
IT'S WEDNESDAY! DA DA DA DA DAAAA! I'M LOVIN' IT!
STARMAN.
WHAT ABOUT--?
AMAZING-MAN. WILDCAT. THE OLD SUPERMAN. HOURMAN AND LIBERTY BELLE.
I THINK WE PUT JUDOMASTER IN THERE...
STAR! I THOUGHT YOU WERE GONNA SAVE A GOOD ROOM FOR ME!
WELL, I DIDN'T KNOW THERE'D BE SO MANY OF US!
HECK, I CAN BARELY FIT AT THE MEETING TABLE ANYMORE.
I GET THE SOCIETY THING. "THE WORLD NEEDS BETTER GOOD GUYS" SO THE JSA IS GONNA HELP MAKE 'EM, BUT ENOUGH IS ENOUGH! THIS TEAM IS TOO DAMN BIG!
ME AND THE THUNDERBOLT ARE VETS.
WHOEVER'S IN THIS ROOM IS STEPPIN' ON OUUUT!

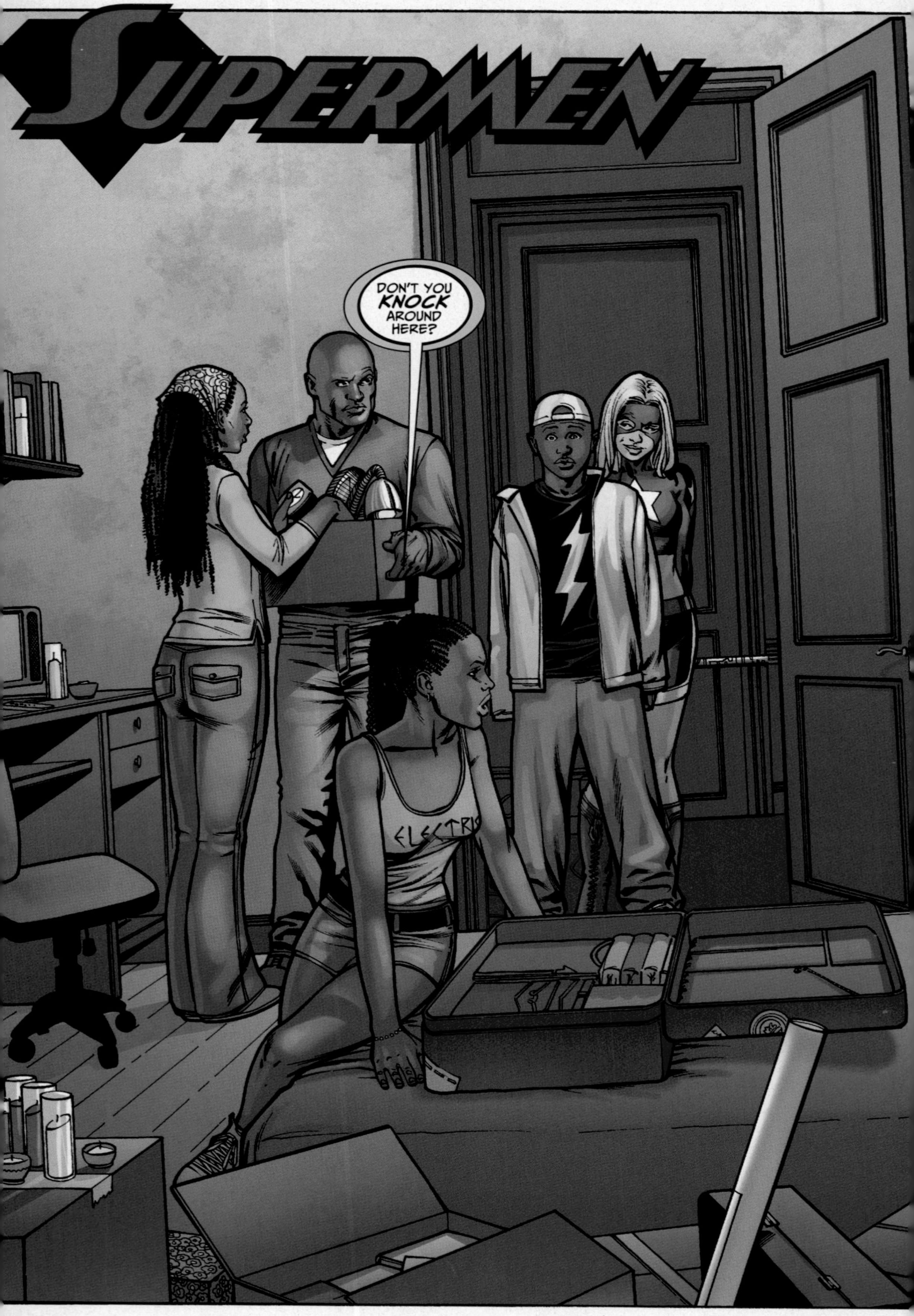
SUPERMEN
DON'T YOU KNOCK AROUND HERE?
ELECTRIC

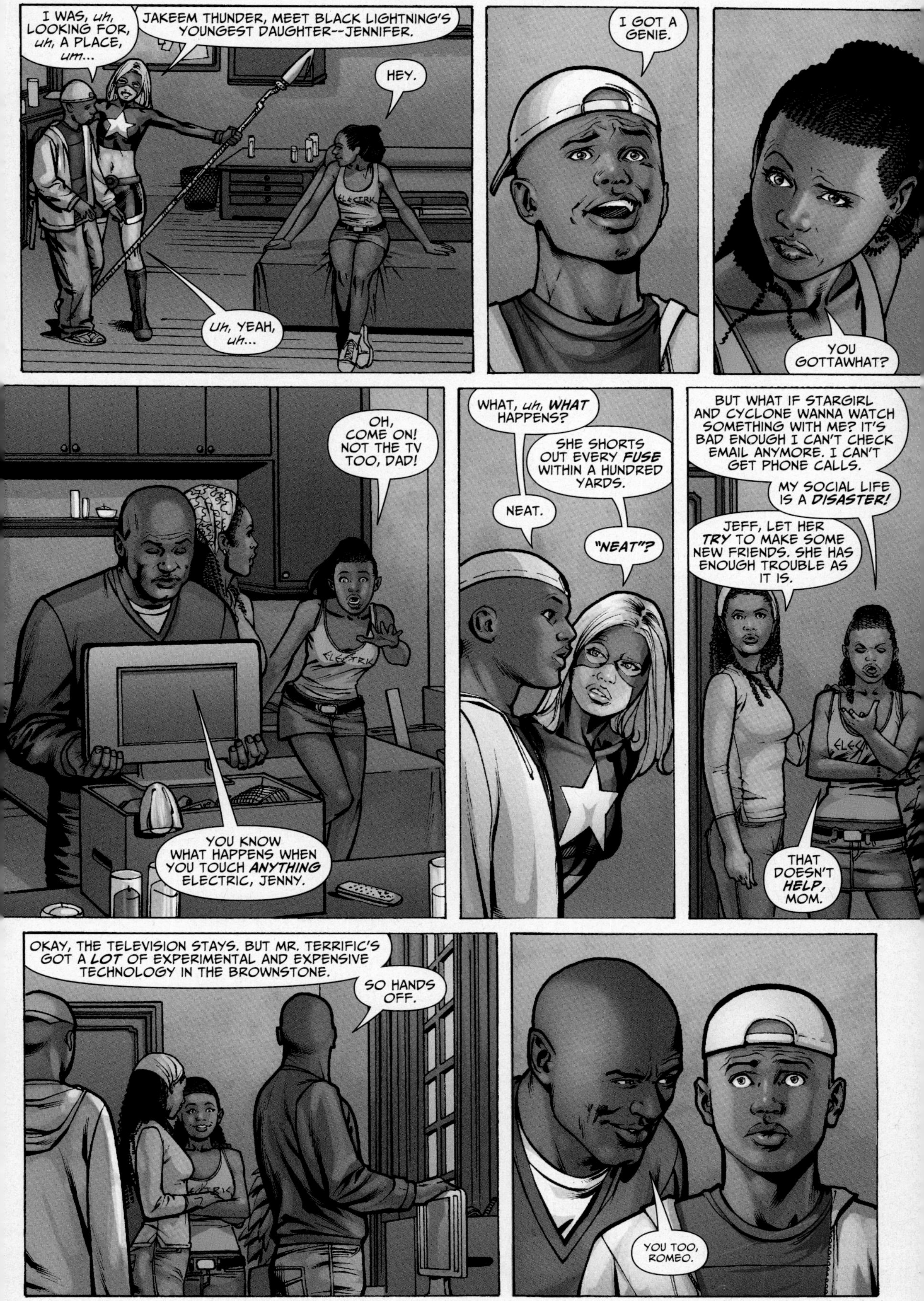
I WAS, uh, LOOKING FOR, uh, A PLACE, um...
JAKEEM THUNDER, MEET BLACK LIGHTNING'S YOUNGEST DAUGHTER--JENNIFER.
HEY.
Uh, YEAH, uh...
I GOT A GENIE.
YOU GOTTAWHAT?
OH, COME ON! NOT THE TV TOO, DAD!
YOU KNOW WHAT HAPPENS WHEN YOU TOUCH ANYTHING ELECTRIC, JENNY.
WHAT, uh, WHAT HAPPENS?
SHE SHORTS OUT EVERY FUSE WITHIN A HUNDRED YARDS.
NEAT.
"NEAT"?
BUT WHAT IF STARGIRL AND CYCLONE WANNA WATCH SOMETHING WITH ME? IT'S BAD ENOUGH I CAN'T CHECK EMAIL ANYMORE. I CAN'T GET PHONE CALLS.
MY SOCIAL LIFE IS A DISASTER!
JEFF, LET HER TRY TO MAKE SOME NEW FRIENDS. SHE HAS ENOUGH TROUBLE AS IT IS.
THAT DOESN'T HELP, MOM.
OKAY, THE TELEVISION STAYS. BUT MR. TERRIFIC'S GOT A LOT OF EXPERIMENTAL AND EXPENSIVE TECHNOLOGY IN THE BROWNSTONE.
SO HANDS OFF.
YOU TOO, ROMEO.

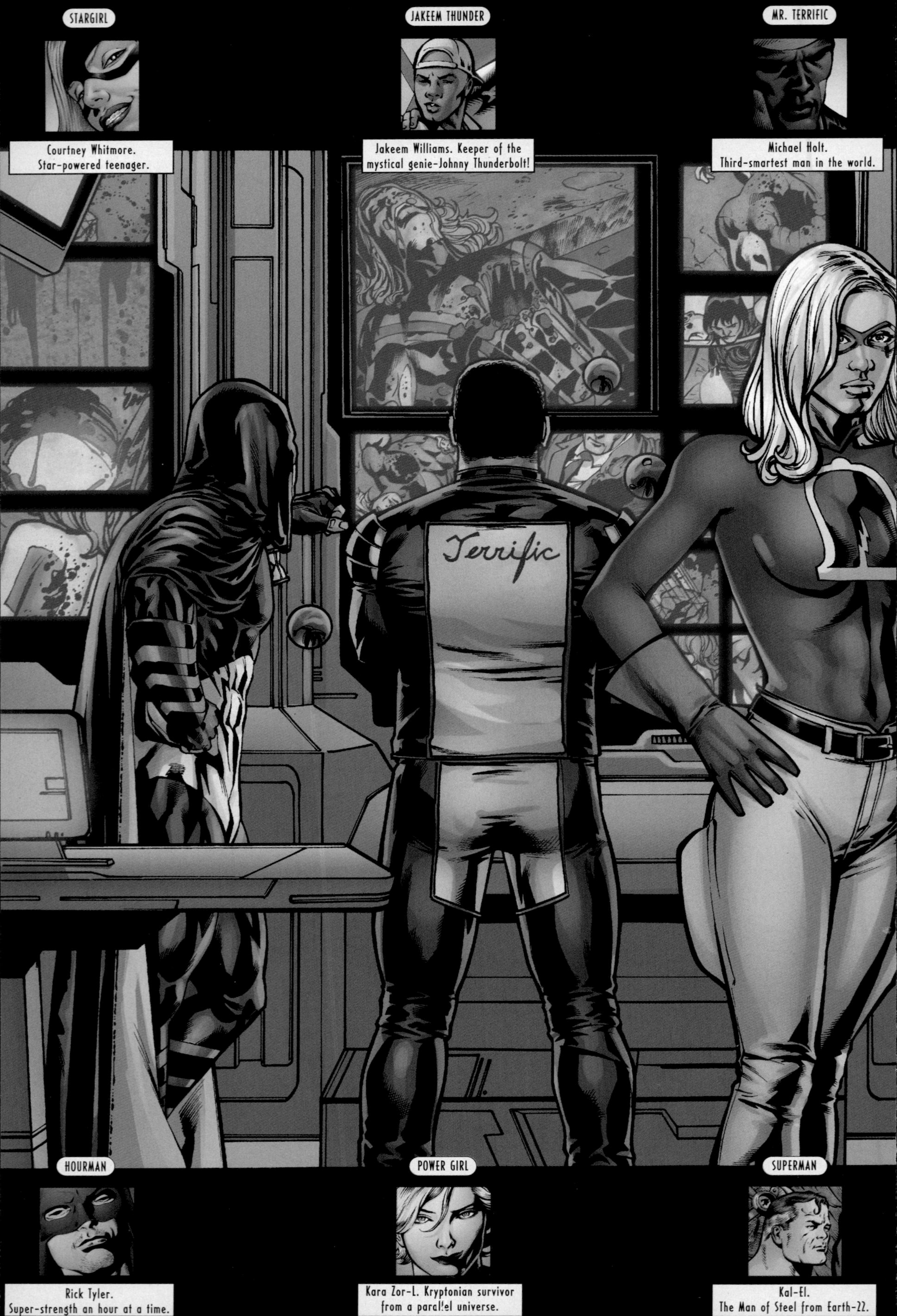

STARGIRL
Courtney Whitmore. Star-powered teenager.
JAKEEM THUNDER
Jakeem Williams. Keeper of the mystical genie–Johnny Thunderbolt!
MR. TERRIFIC
Michael Holt. Third-smartest man in the world.
Terrific
HOURMAN
Rick Tyler. Super-strength an hour at a time.
POWER GIRL
Kara Zor-L. Kryptonian survivor from a parallel universe.
SUPERMAN
Kal-El. The Man of Steel from Earth-22.

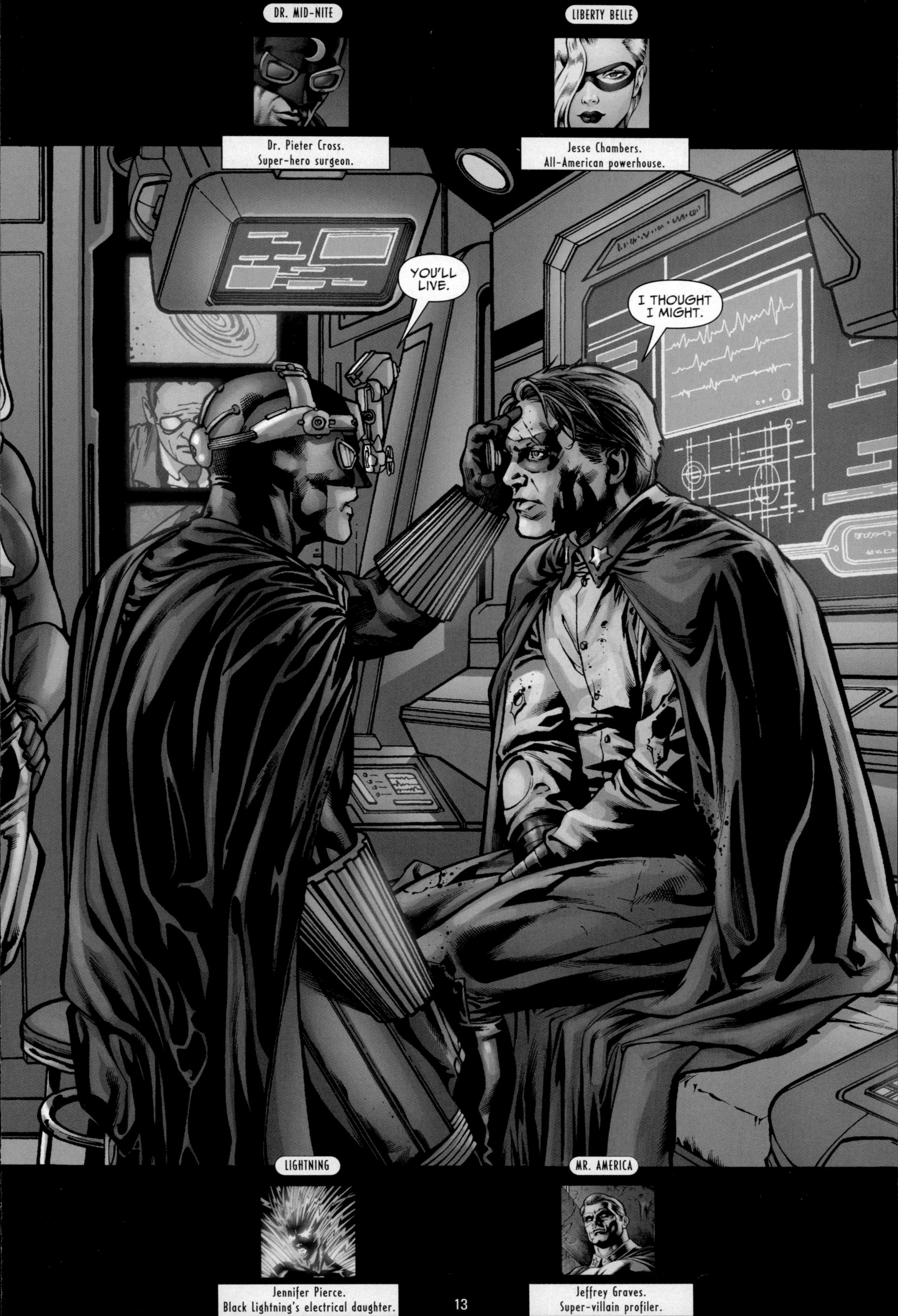
DR. MID-NITE
LIBERTY BELLE
Dr. Pieter Cross.
Super-hero surgeon.
Jesse Chambers.
All-American powerhouse.
YOU'LL LIVE.
I THOUGHT I MIGHT.
LIGHTNING
MR. AMERICA
Jennifer Pierce.
Black Lightning's electrical daughter.
Jeffrey Graves.
Super-villain profiler.

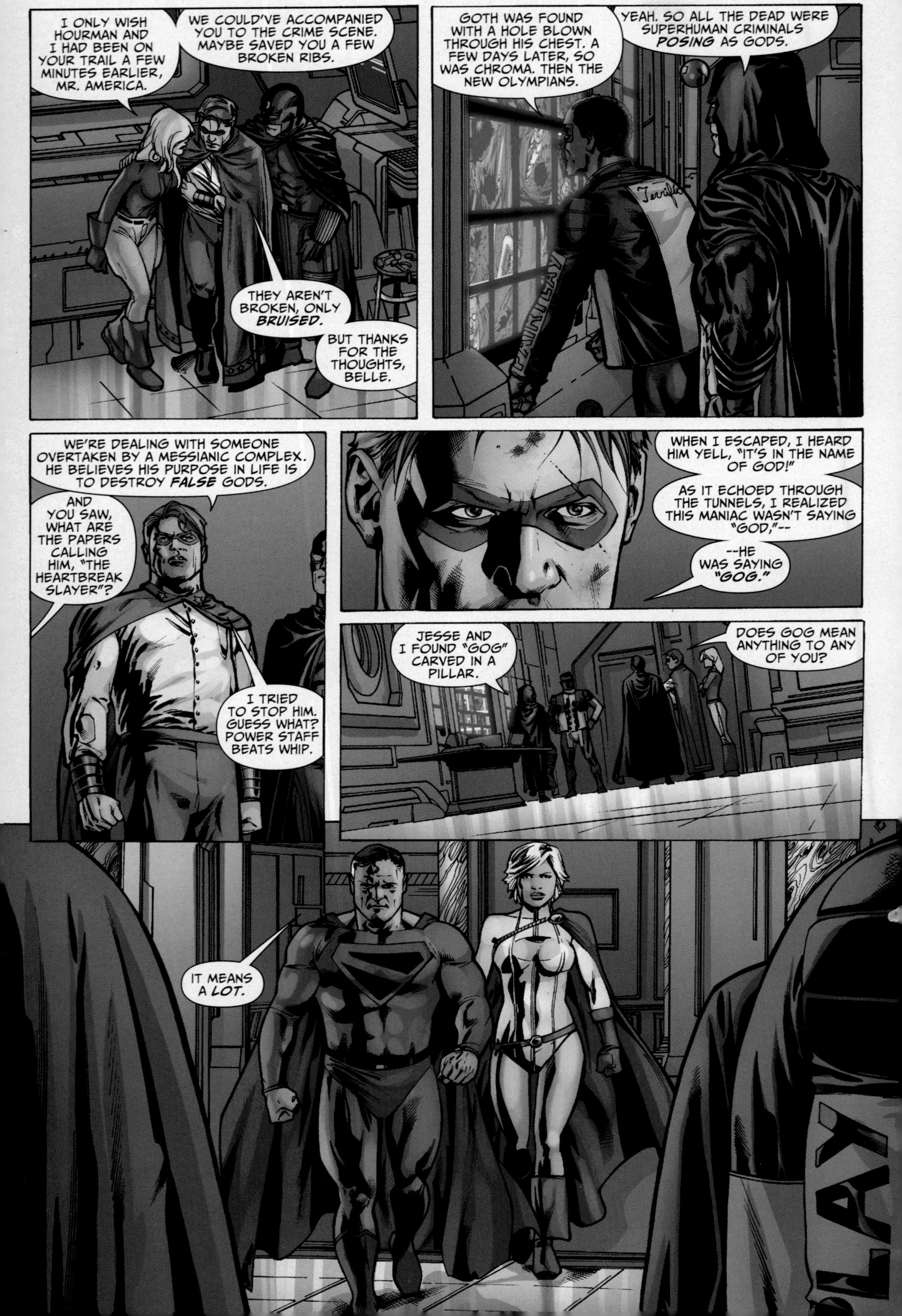

I ONLY WISH HOURMAN AND I HAD BEEN ON YOUR TRAIL A FEW MINUTES EARLIER, MR. AMERICA.
WE COULD'VE ACCOMPANIED YOU TO THE CRIME SCENE. MAYBE SAVED YOU A FEW BROKEN RIBS.
THEY AREN'T BROKEN, ONLY BRUISED.
BUT THANKS FOR THE THOUGHTS, BELLE.
GOTH WAS FOUND WITH A HOLE BLOWN THROUGH HIS CHEST. A FEW DAYS LATER, SO WAS CHROMA. THEN THE NEW OLYMPIANS.
YEAH. SO ALL THE DEAD WERE SUPERHUMAN CRIMINALS POSING AS GODS.
WE'RE DEALING WITH SOMEONE OVERTAKEN BY A MESSIANIC COMPLEX. HE BELIEVES HIS PURPOSE IN LIFE IS TO DESTROY FALSE GODS.
AND YOU SAW, WHAT ARE THE PAPERS CALLING HIM, "THE HEARTBREAK SLAYER"?
I TRIED TO STOP HIM. GUESS WHAT? POWER STAFF BEATS WHIP.
WHEN I ESCAPED, I HEARD HIM YELL, "IT'S IN THE NAME OF GOD!"
AS IT ECHOED THROUGH THE TUNNELS, I REALIZED THIS MANIAC WASN'T SAYING "GOD,"--
--HE WAS SAYING "GOG."
JESSE AND I FOUND "GOG" CARVED IN A PILLAR.
DOES GOG MEAN ANYTHING TO ANY OF YOU?
IT MEANS A LOT.

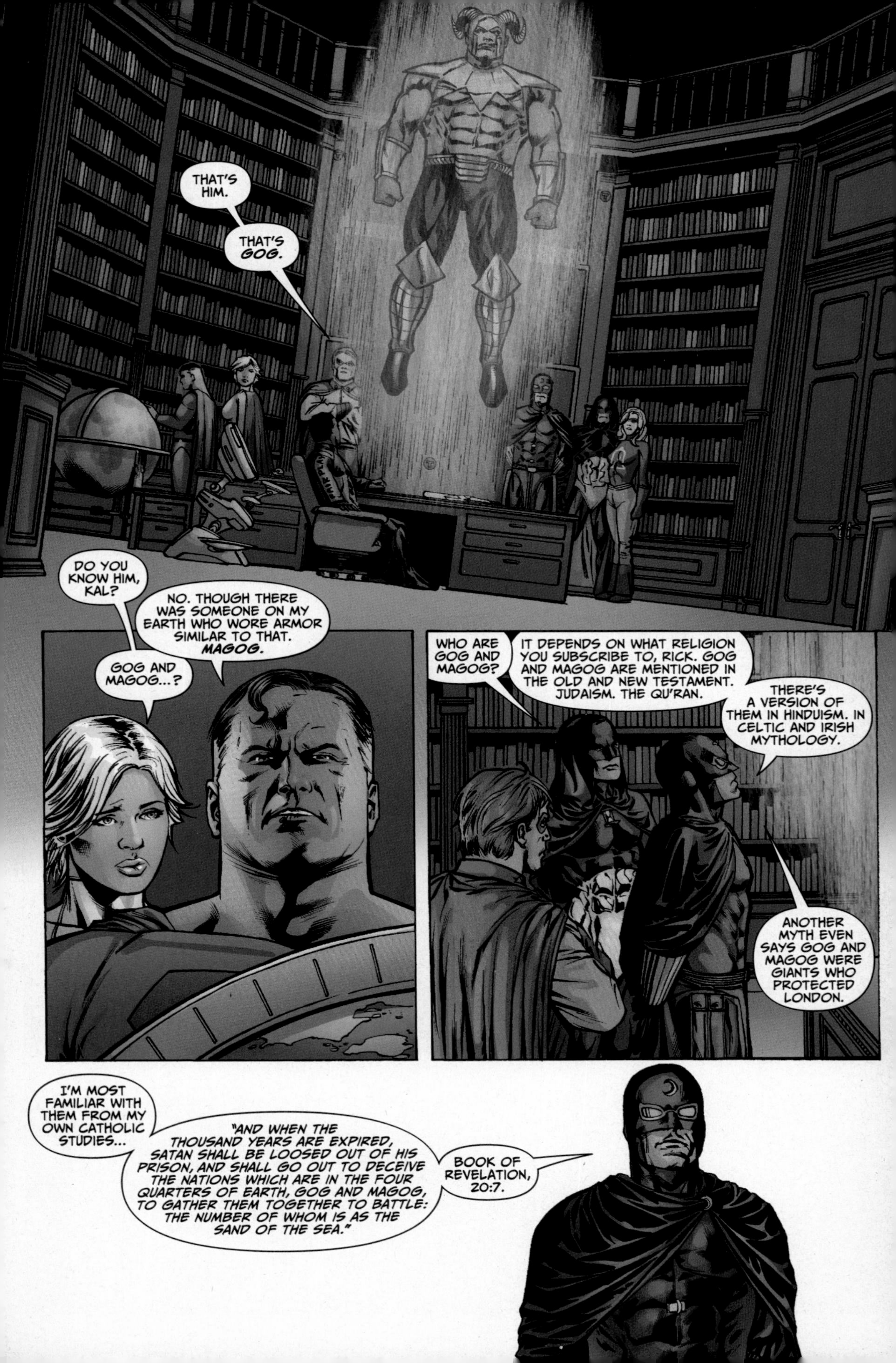
THAT'S HIM.
THAT'S GOG.
DO YOU KNOW HIM, KAL?
NO. THOUGH THERE WAS SOMEONE ON MY EARTH WHO WORE ARMOR SIMILAR TO THAT. MAGOG.
GOG AND MAGOG...?
WHO ARE GOG AND MAGOG?
IT DEPENDS ON WHAT RELIGION YOU SUBSCRIBE TO, RICK. GOG AND MAGOG ARE MENTIONED IN THE OLD AND NEW TESTAMENT. JUDAISM. THE QU'RAN.
THERE'S A VERSION OF THEM IN HINDUISM. IN CELTIC AND IRISH MYTHOLOGY.
ANOTHER MYTH EVEN SAYS GOG AND MAGOG WERE GIANTS WHO PROTECTED LONDON.
I'M MOST FAMILIAR WITH THEM FROM MY OWN CATHOLIC STUDIES...
"AND WHEN THE THOUSAND YEARS ARE EXPIRED, SATAN SHALL BE LOOSED OUT OF HIS PRISON, AND SHALL GO OUT TO DECEIVE THE NATIONS WHICH ARE IN THE FOUR QUARTERS OF EARTH, GOG AND MAGOG, TO GATHER THEM TOGETHER TO BATTLE: THE NUMBER OF WHOM IS AS THE SAND OF THE SEA."
BOOK OF REVELATION, 20:7.

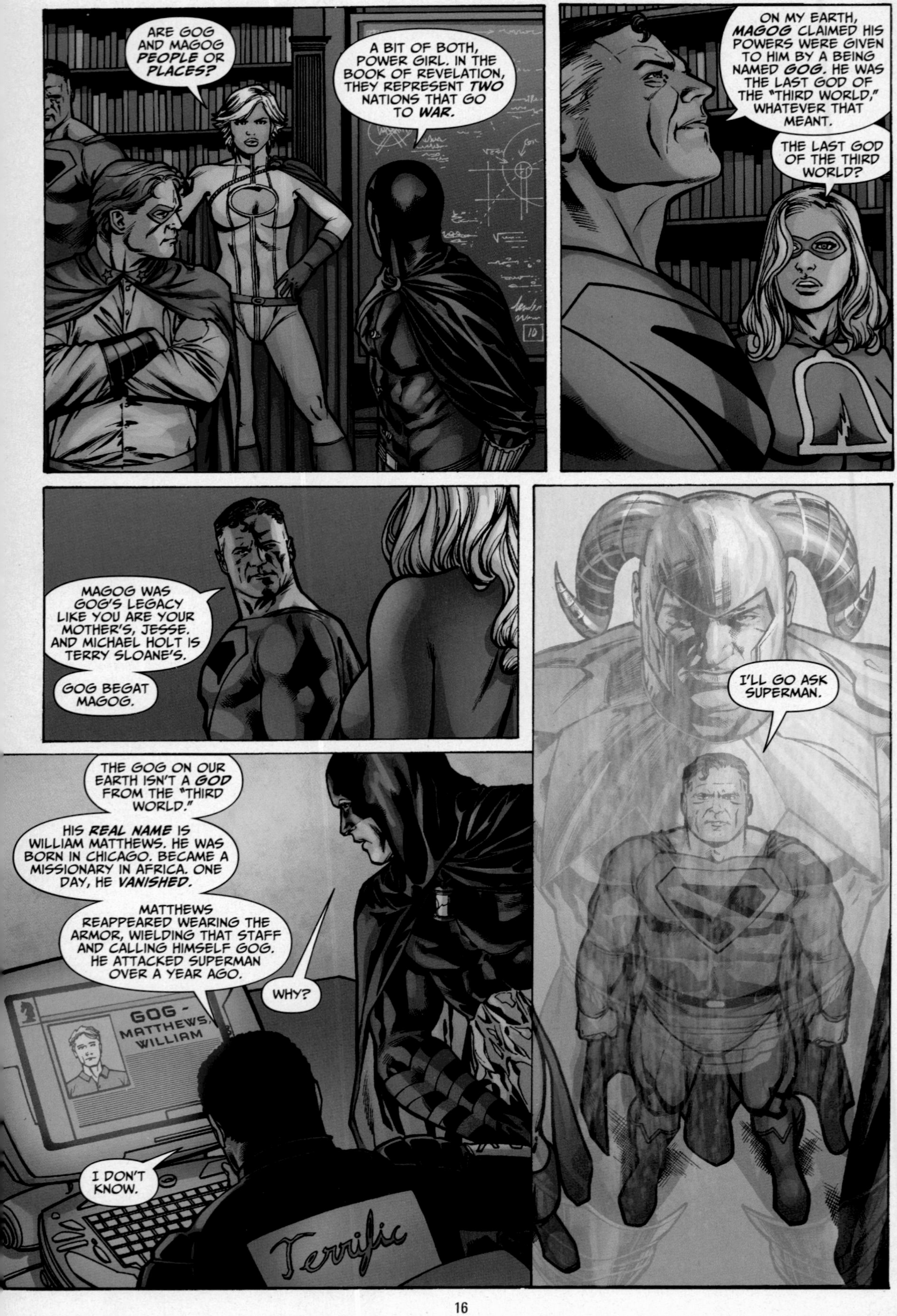

ARE GOG AND MAGOG PEOPLE OR PLACES?
A BIT OF BOTH, POWER GIRL. IN THE BOOK OF REVELATION, THEY REPRESENT TWO NATIONS THAT GO TO WAR.
ON MY EARTH, MAGOG CLAIMED HIS POWERS WERE GIVEN TO HIM BY A BEING NAMED GOG. HE WAS THE LAST GOD OF THE "THIRD WORLD," WHATEVER THAT MEANT.
THE LAST GOD OF THE THIRD WORLD?
MAGOG WAS GOG'S LEGACY LIKE YOU ARE YOUR MOTHER'S, JESSE. AND MICHAEL HOLT IS TERRY SLOANE'S.
GOG BEGAT MAGOG.
I'LL GO ASK SUPERMAN.
THE GOG ON OUR EARTH ISN'T A GOD FROM THE "THIRD WORLD."
HIS REAL NAME IS WILLIAM MATTHEWS. HE WAS BORN IN CHICAGO. BECAME A MISSIONARY IN AFRICA. ONE DAY, HE VANISHED.
MATTHEWS REAPPEARED WEARING THE ARMOR, WIELDING THAT STAFF AND CALLING HIMSELF GOG. HE ATTACKED SUPERMAN OVER A YEAR AGO.
WHY?
GOG - MATTHEWS, WILLIAM
I DON'T KNOW.
Terrific

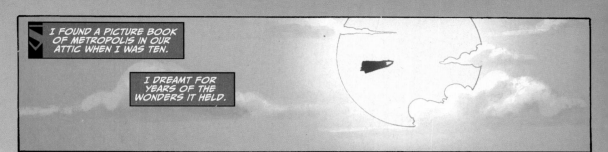

I FOUND A PICTURE BOOK OF METROPOLIS IN OUR ATTIC WHEN I WAS TEN.

I DREAMT FOR YEARS OF THE WONDERS IT HELD.

THEY CALLED IT THE CITY OF TOMORROW.

I CALLED IT THE CITY OF MY TOMORROW.

UNTIL IT ALL WENT SO HORRIBLY WRONG.

...GIVE ME ONE GOOD REASON, OLSEN.

I'M STILL PAYING OFF MY STUDENT LOANS.

WHAT? THE *DAILY PLANET* GAVE YOU A SCHOLARSHIP.

MY WALLET GOT LIFTED ON THE SUBWAY.

YOU RODE YOUR *BICYCLE* TO WORK TODAY!

I, *uh,* I NEVER TELL YOU NOT TO SMOKE!

OLSEN, IF *YOU'RE* NOT LOOKING OUT FOR *MY* BEST INTERESTS, WHY SHOULD I LOOK OUT FOR YOURS?!?

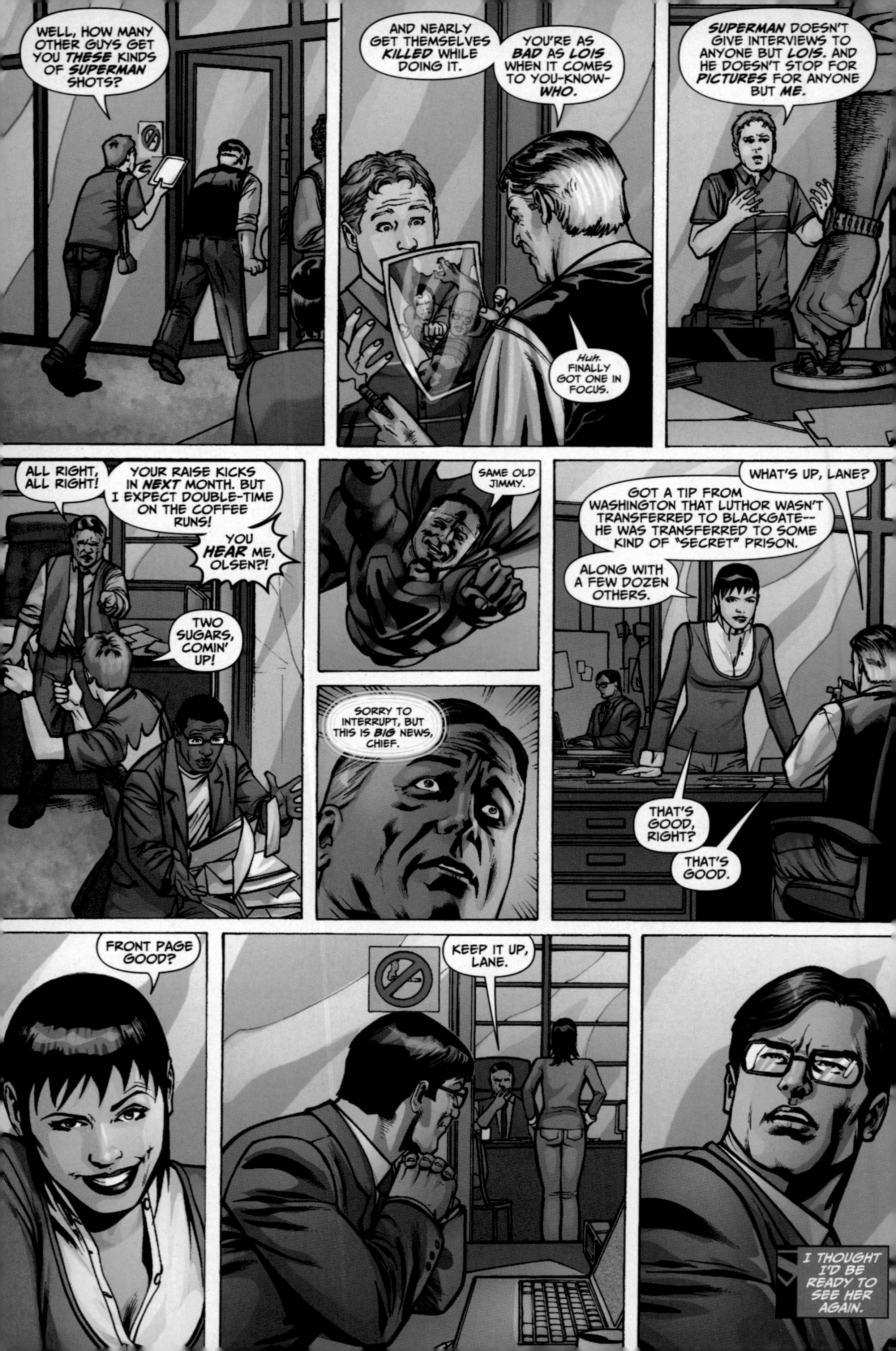
WELL, HOW MANY OTHER GUYS GET YOU THESE KINDS OF SUPERMAN SHOTS?
AND NEARLY GET THEMSELVES KILLED WHILE DOING IT.
YOU'RE AS BAD AS LOIS WHEN IT COMES TO YOU-KNOW-WHO.
Huh. FINALLY GOT ONE IN FOCUS.
SUPERMAN DOESN'T GIVE INTERVIEWS TO ANYONE BUT LOIS. AND HE DOESN'T STOP FOR PICTURES FOR ANYONE BUT ME.
ALL RIGHT, ALL RIGHT!
YOUR RAISE KICKS IN NEXT MONTH. BUT I EXPECT DOUBLE-TIME ON THE COFFEE RUNS!
YOU HEAR ME, OLSEN?!
TWO SUGARS, COMIN' UP!
SAME OLD JIMMY.
SORRY TO INTERRUPT, BUT THIS IS BIG NEWS, CHIEF.
WHAT'S UP, LANE?
GOT A TIP FROM WASHINGTON THAT LUTHOR WASN'T TRANSFERRED TO BLACKGATE-- HE WAS TRANSFERRED TO SOME KIND OF "SECRET" PRISON.
ALONG WITH A FEW DOZEN OTHERS.
THAT'S GOOD, RIGHT?
THAT'S GOOD.
FRONT PAGE GOOD?
KEEP IT UP, LANE.
I THOUGHT I'D BE READY TO SEE HER AGAIN.

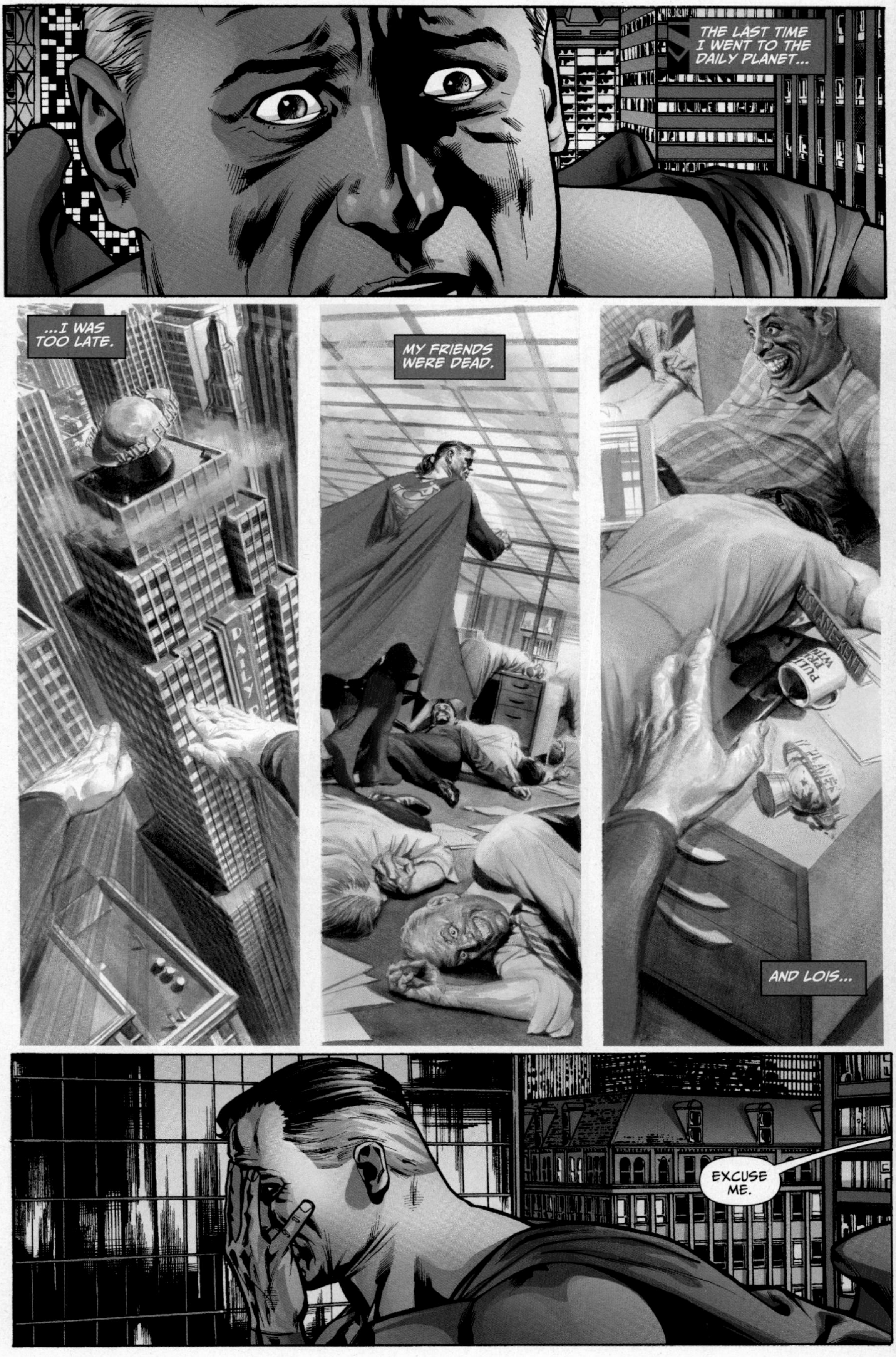
THE LAST TIME I WENT TO THE DAILY PLANET...
...I WAS TOO LATE.
MY FRIENDS WERE DEAD.
AND LOIS...
EXCUSE ME.

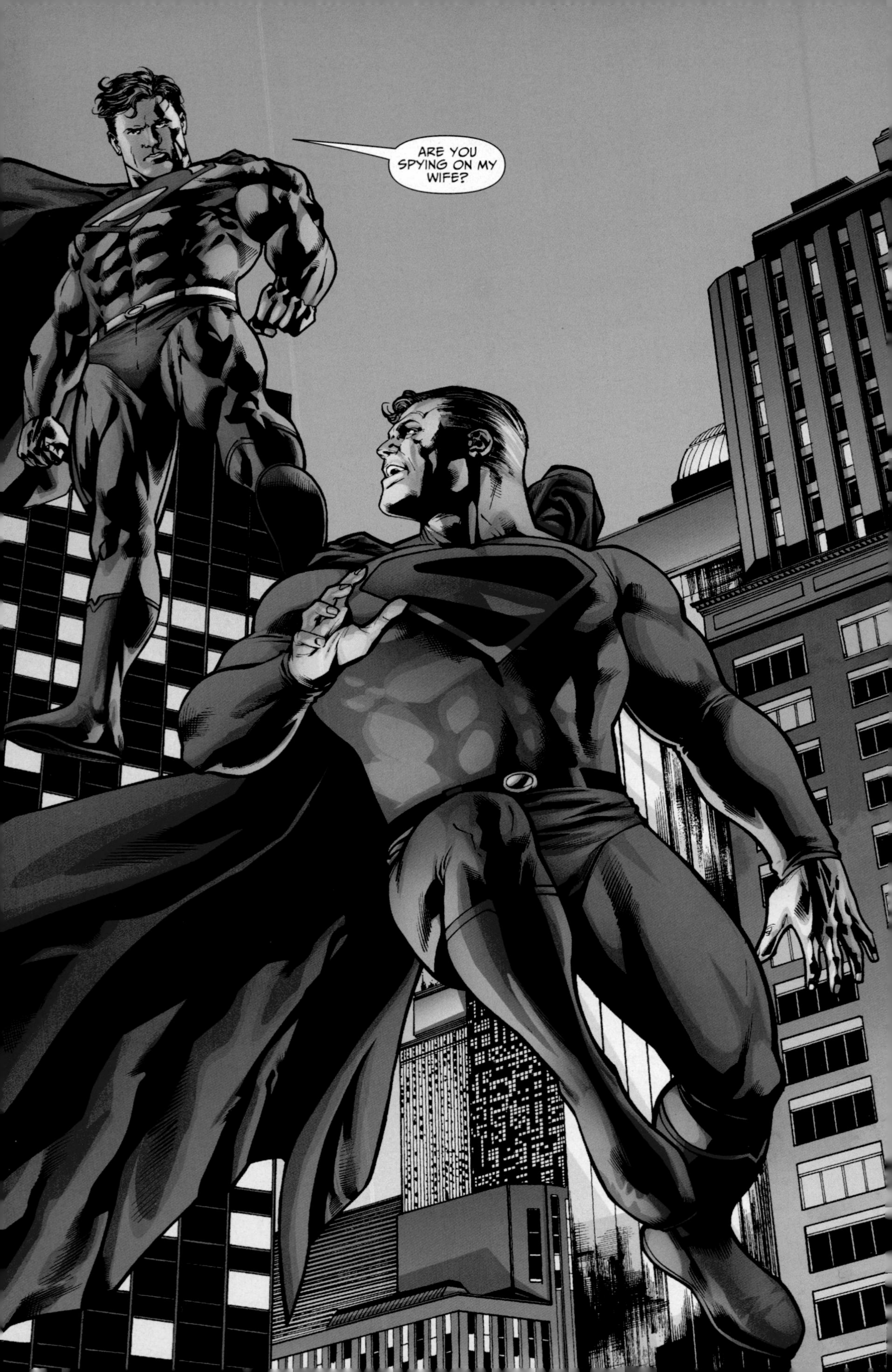
ARE YOU SPYING ON MY WIFE?

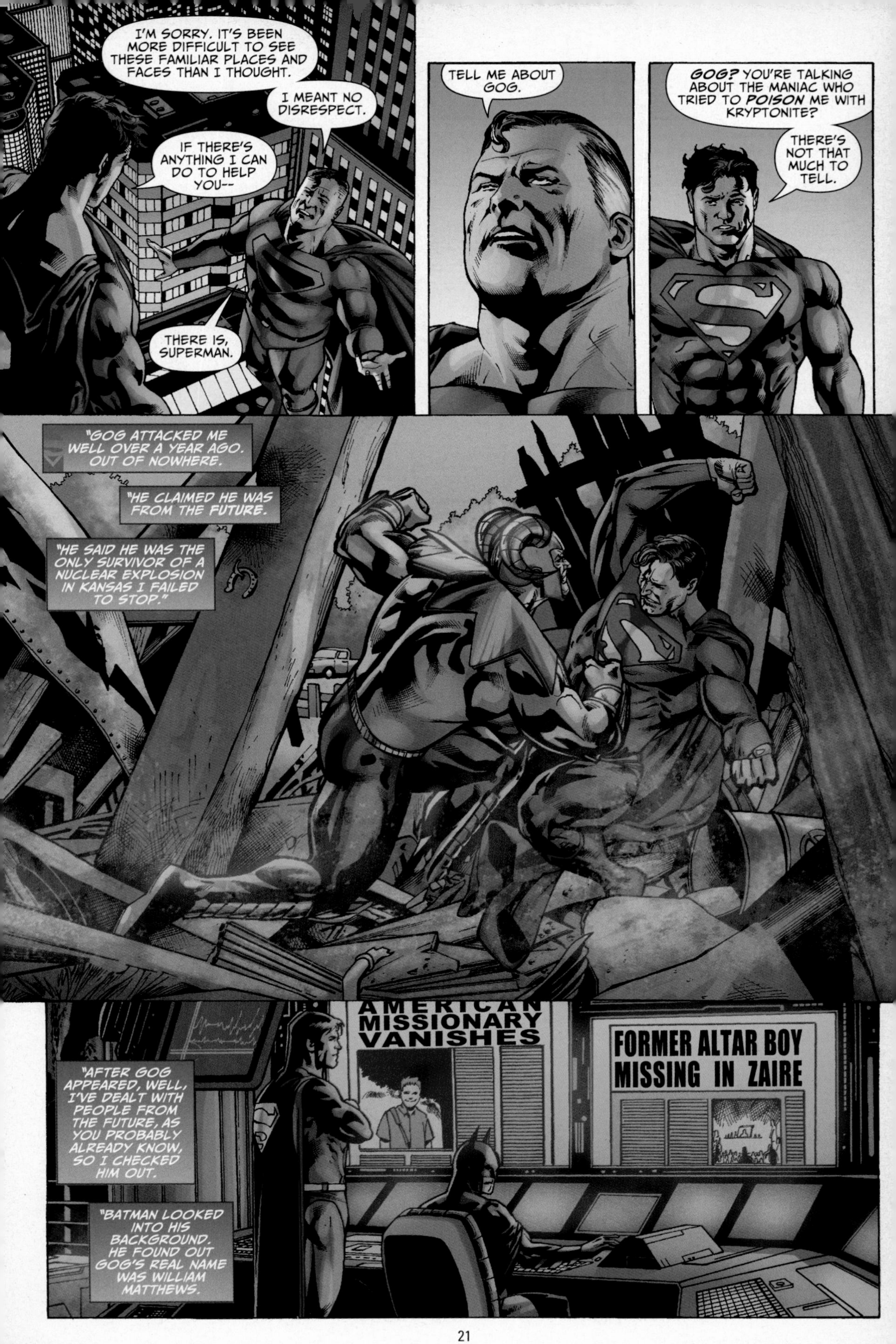
I'M SORRY. IT'S BEEN MORE DIFFICULT TO SEE THESE FAMILIAR PLACES AND FACES THAN I THOUGHT.
I MEANT NO DISRESPECT.
IF THERE'S ANYTHING I CAN DO TO HELP YOU--
THERE IS, SUPERMAN.
TELL ME ABOUT GOG.
GOG? YOU'RE TALKING ABOUT THE MANIAC WHO TRIED TO POISON ME WITH KRYPTONITE?
THERE'S NOT THAT MUCH TO TELL.
"GOG ATTACKED ME WELL OVER A YEAR AGO. OUT OF NOWHERE.
"HE CLAIMED HE WAS FROM THE FUTURE.
"HE SAID HE WAS THE ONLY SURVIVOR OF A NUCLEAR EXPLOSION IN KANSAS I FAILED TO STOP."
AMERICAN MISSIONARY VANISHES
FORMER ALTAR BOY MISSING IN ZAIRE
"AFTER GOG APPEARED, WELL, I'VE DEALT WITH PEOPLE FROM THE FUTURE, AS YOU PROBABLY ALREADY KNOW, SO I CHECKED HIM OUT.
"BATMAN LOOKED INTO HIS BACKGROUND. HE FOUND OUT GOG'S REAL NAME WAS WILLIAM MATTHEWS.

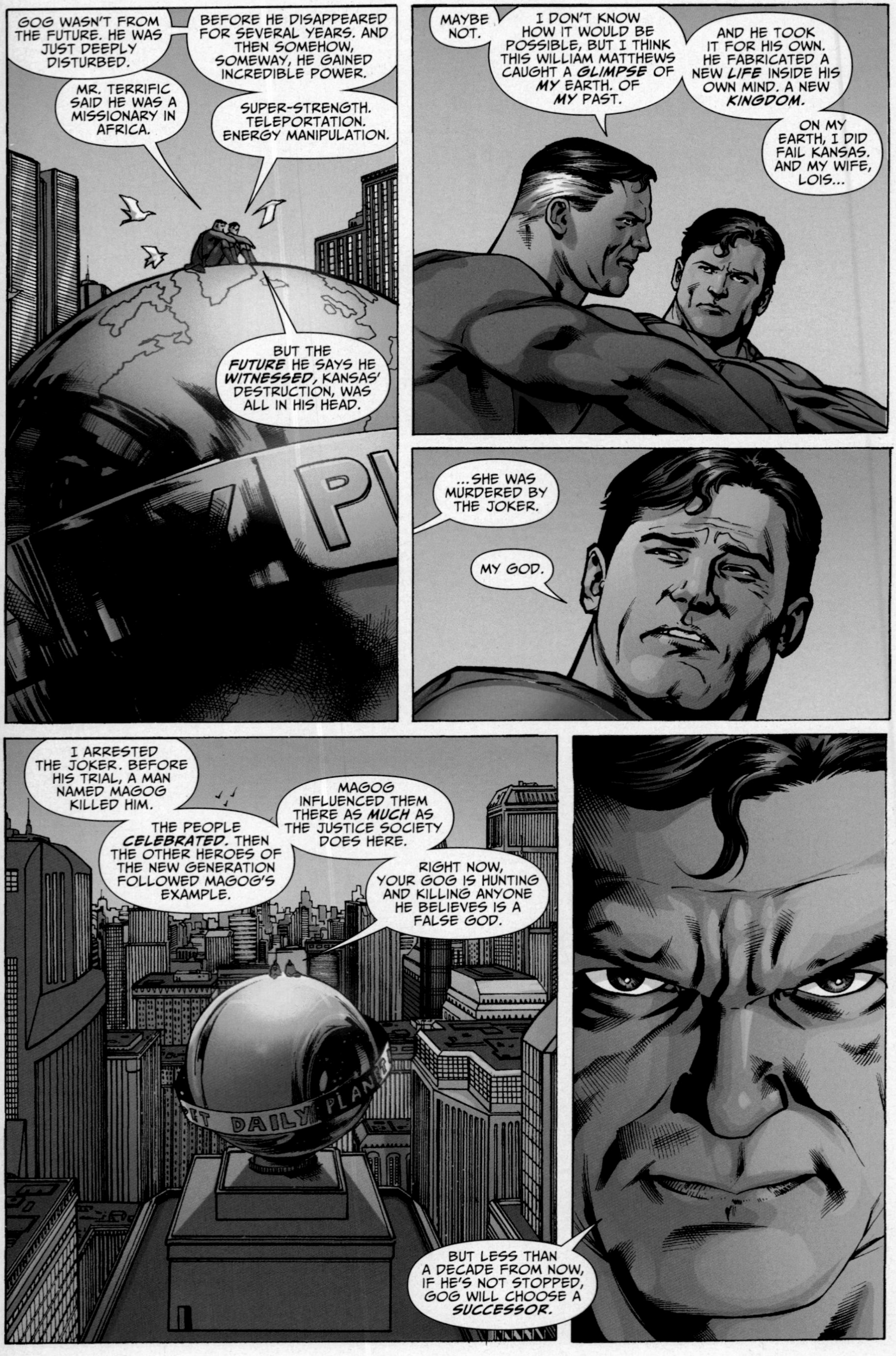
GOG WASN'T FROM THE FUTURE. HE WAS JUST DEEPLY DISTURBED.
BEFORE HE DISAPPEARED FOR SEVERAL YEARS. AND THEN SOMEHOW, SOMEWAY, HE GAINED INCREDIBLE POWER.
MR. TERRIFIC SAID HE WAS A MISSIONARY IN AFRICA.
SUPER-STRENGTH. TELEPORTATION. ENERGY MANIPULATION.
BUT THE FUTURE HE SAYS HE WITNESSED, KANSAS' DESTRUCTION, WAS ALL IN HIS HEAD.
MAYBE NOT.
I DON'T KNOW HOW IT WOULD BE POSSIBLE, BUT I THINK THIS WILLIAM MATTHEWS CAUGHT A GLIMPSE OF MY EARTH. OF MY PAST.
AND HE TOOK IT FOR HIS OWN. HE FABRICATED A NEW LIFE INSIDE HIS OWN MIND. A NEW KINGDOM.
ON MY EARTH, I DID FAIL KANSAS. AND MY WIFE, LOIS...
...SHE WAS MURDERED BY THE JOKER.
MY GOD.
I ARRESTED THE JOKER. BEFORE HIS TRIAL, A MAN NAMED MAGOG KILLED HIM.
THE PEOPLE CELEBRATED. THEN THE OTHER HEROES OF THE NEW GENERATION FOLLOWED MAGOG'S EXAMPLE.
MAGOG INFLUENCED THEM THERE AS MUCH AS THE JUSTICE SOCIETY DOES HERE.
RIGHT NOW, YOUR GOG IS HUNTING AND KILLING ANYONE HE BELIEVES IS A FALSE GOD.
DAILY PLANET
BUT LESS THAN A DECADE FROM NOW, IF HE'S NOT STOPPED, GOG WILL CHOOSE A SUCCESSOR.

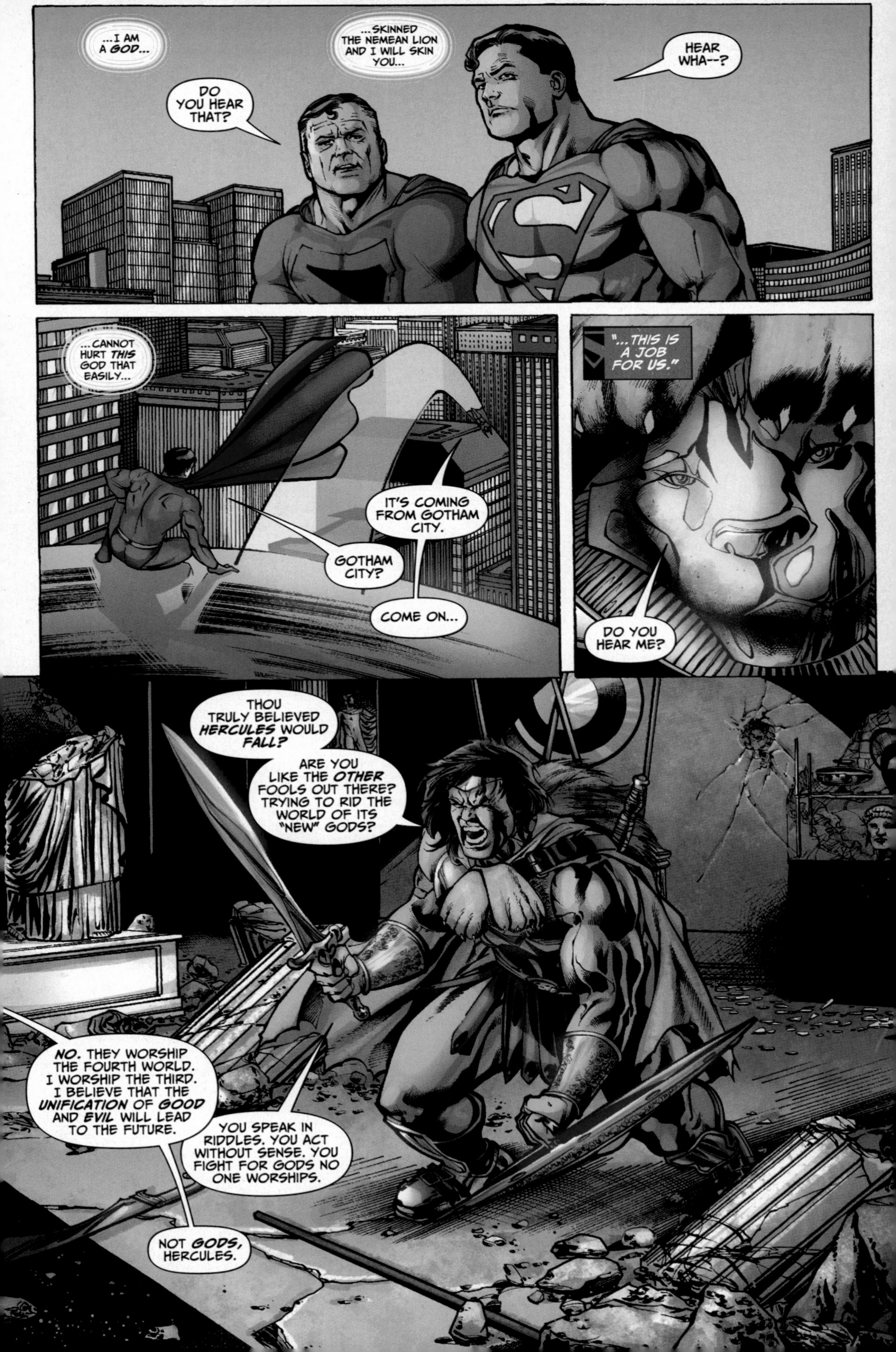
...I AM A GOD...
...SKINNED THE NEMEAN LION AND I WILL SKIN YOU...
DO YOU HEAR THAT?
HEAR WHA--?
...CANNOT HURT THIS GOD THAT EASILY...
IT'S COMING FROM GOTHAM CITY.
GOTHAM CITY?
COME ON...
"...THIS IS A JOB FOR US."
DO YOU HEAR ME?
THOU TRULY BELIEVED HERCULES WOULD FALL?
ARE YOU LIKE THE OTHER FOOLS OUT THERE? TRYING TO RID THE WORLD OF ITS "NEW" GODS?
NO. THEY WORSHIP THE FOURTH WORLD. I WORSHIP THE THIRD. I BELIEVE THAT THE UNIFICATION OF GOOD AND EVIL WILL LEAD TO THE FUTURE.
YOU SPEAK IN RIDDLES. YOU ACT WITHOUT SENSE. YOU FIGHT FOR GODS NO ONE WORSHIPS.
NOT GODS, HERCULES.

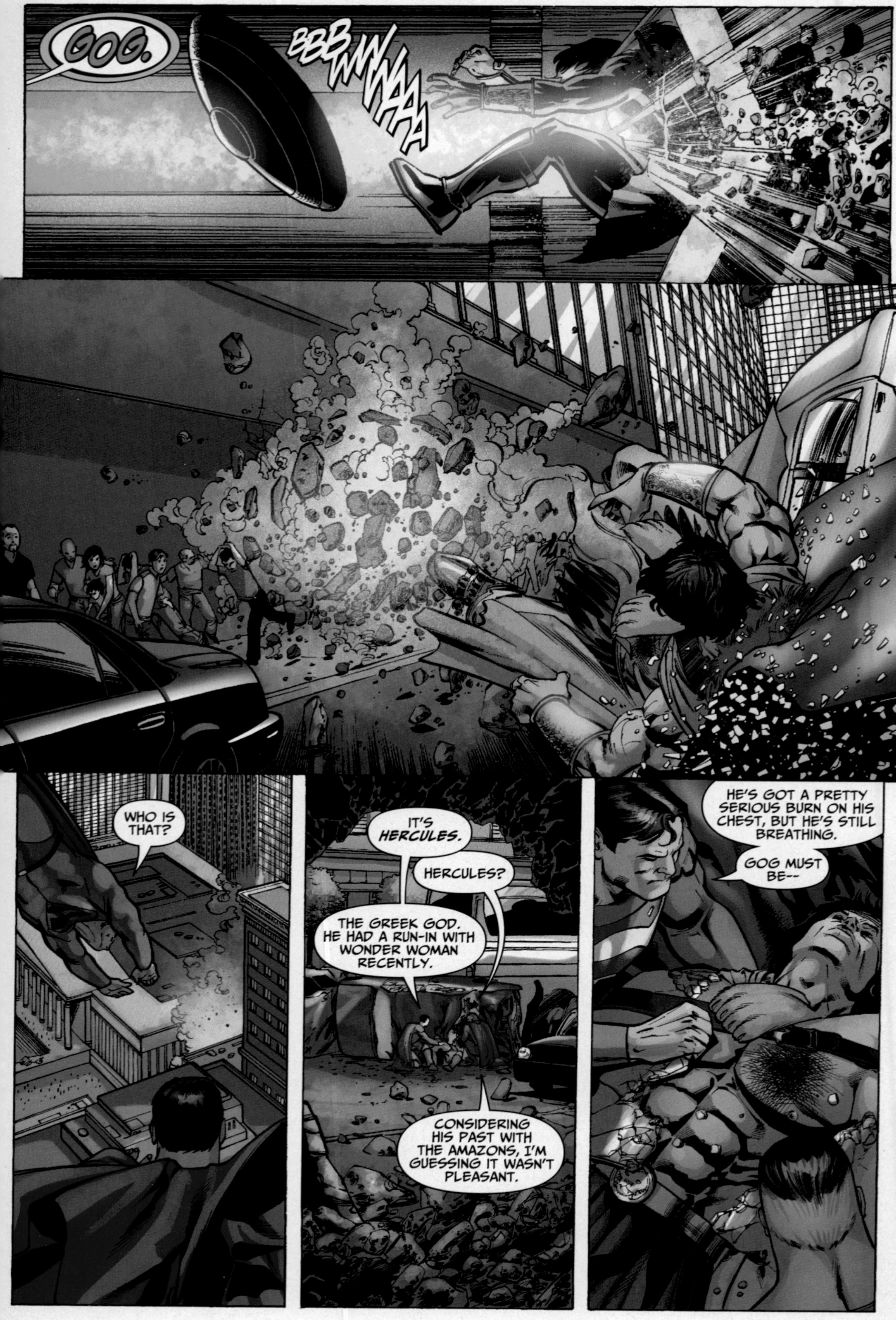
GOG.
BBBWWWAAA
WHO IS THAT?
IT'S HERCULES.
HERCULES?
THE GREEK GOD. HE HAD A RUN-IN WITH WONDER WOMAN RECENTLY.
CONSIDERING HIS PAST WITH THE AMAZONS, I'M GUESSING IT WASN'T PLEASANT.
HE'S GOT A PRETTY SERIOUS BURN ON HIS CHEST, BUT HE'S STILL BREATHING.
GOG MUST BE--

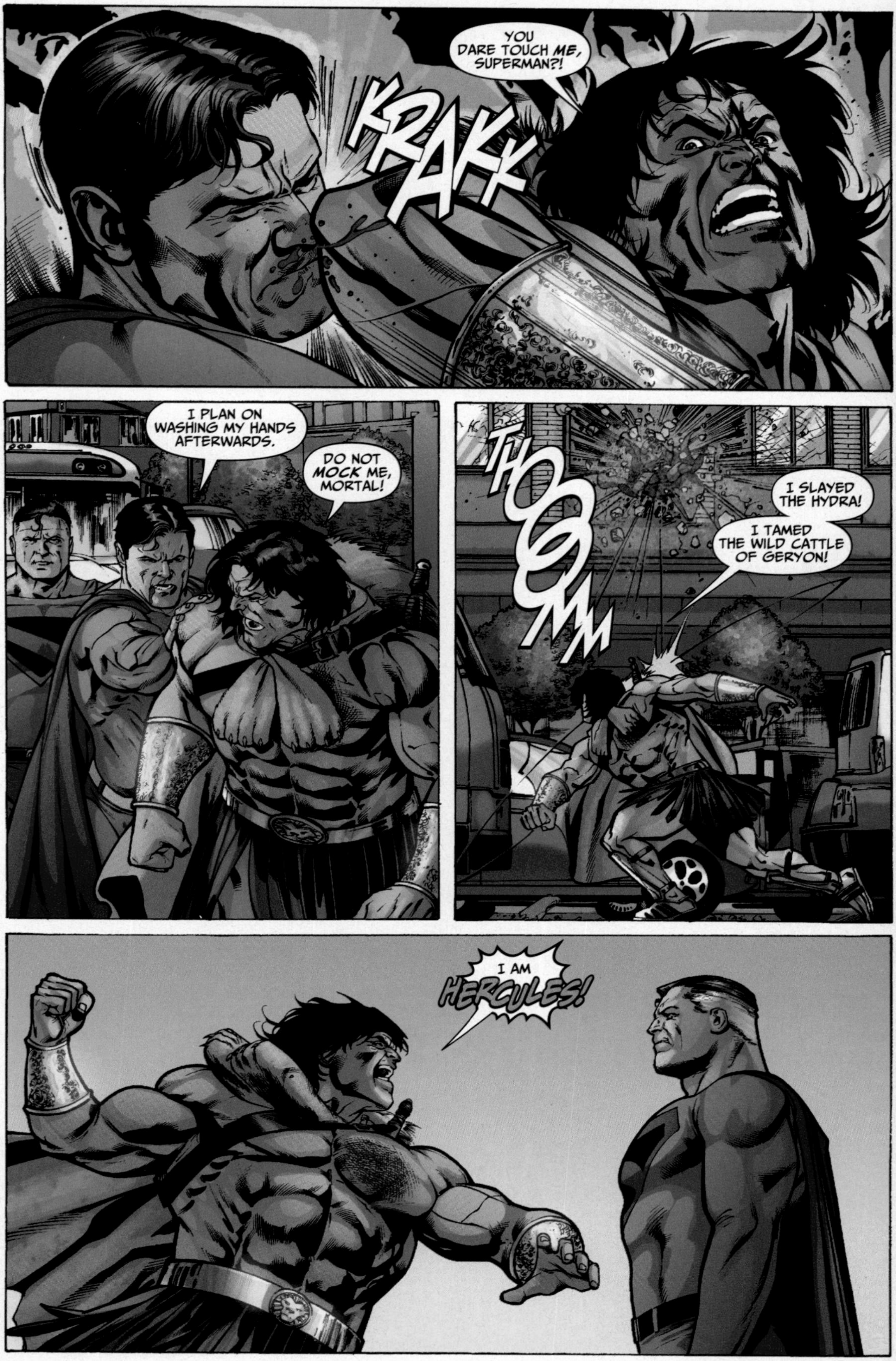
YOU DARE TOUCH ME, SUPERMAN?!
KRAKK
I PLAN ON WASHING MY HANDS AFTERWARDS.
DO NOT MOCK ME, MORTAL!
THOOOMMM
I SLAYED THE HYDRA!
I TAMED THE WILD CATTLE OF GERYON!
I AM HERCULES!

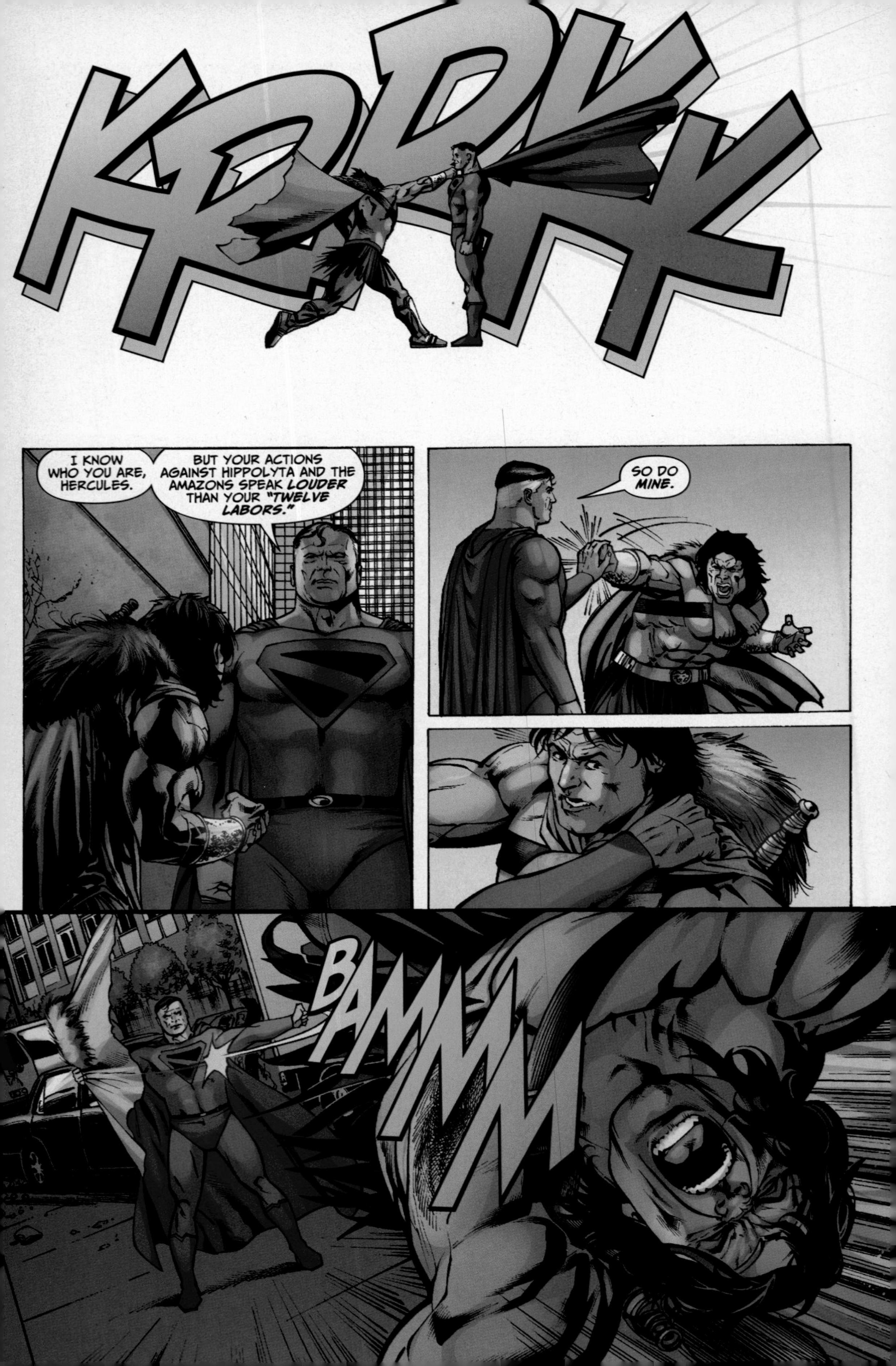

KRAKK
I KNOW WHO YOU ARE, HERCULES.
BUT YOUR ACTIONS AGAINST HIPPOLYTA AND THE AMAZONS SPEAK LOUDER THAN YOUR "TWELVE LABORS."
SO DO MINE.
BAMMM

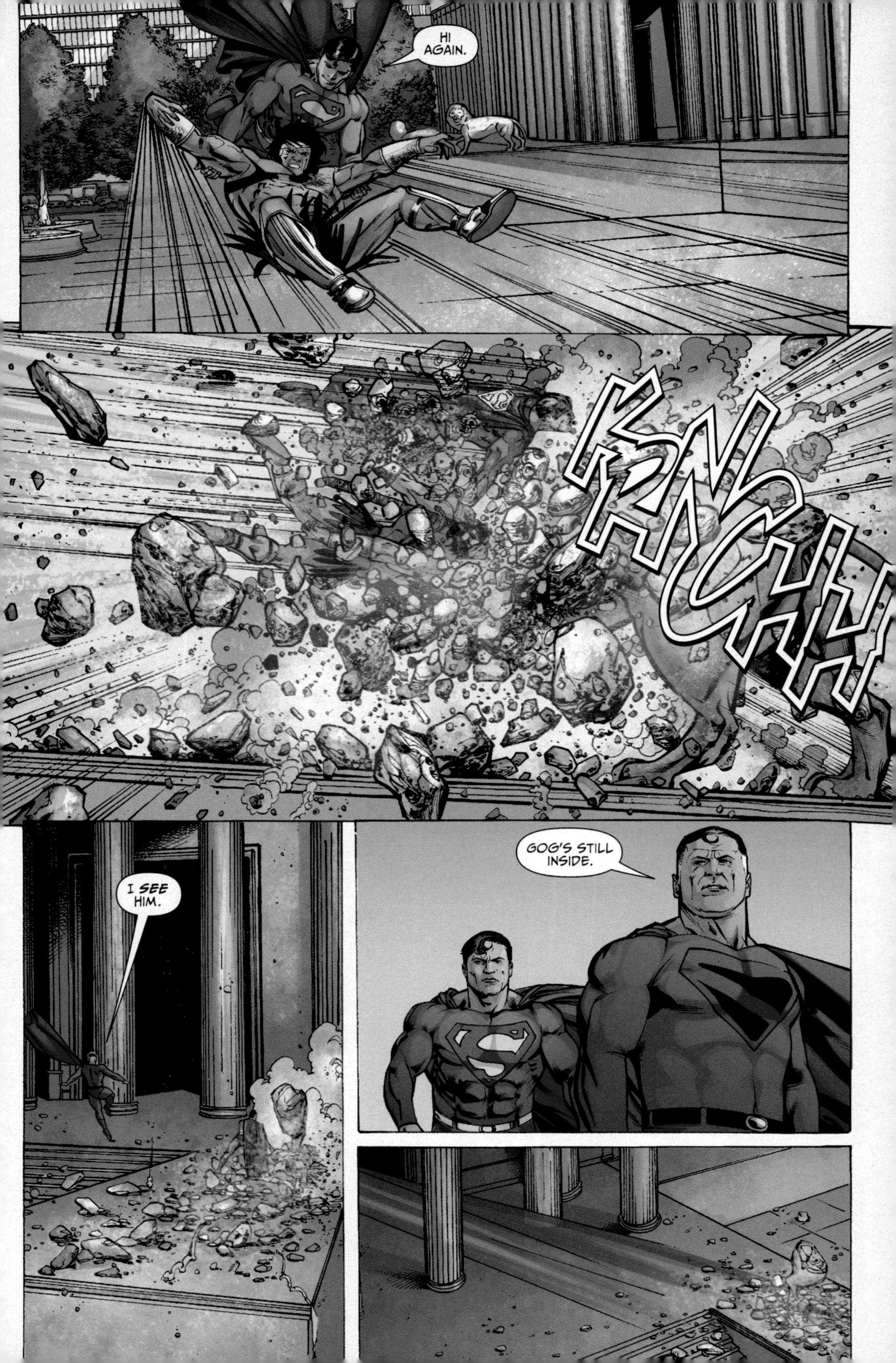
HI AGAIN.
KRNCHCHH
I SEE HIM.
GOG'S STILL INSIDE.

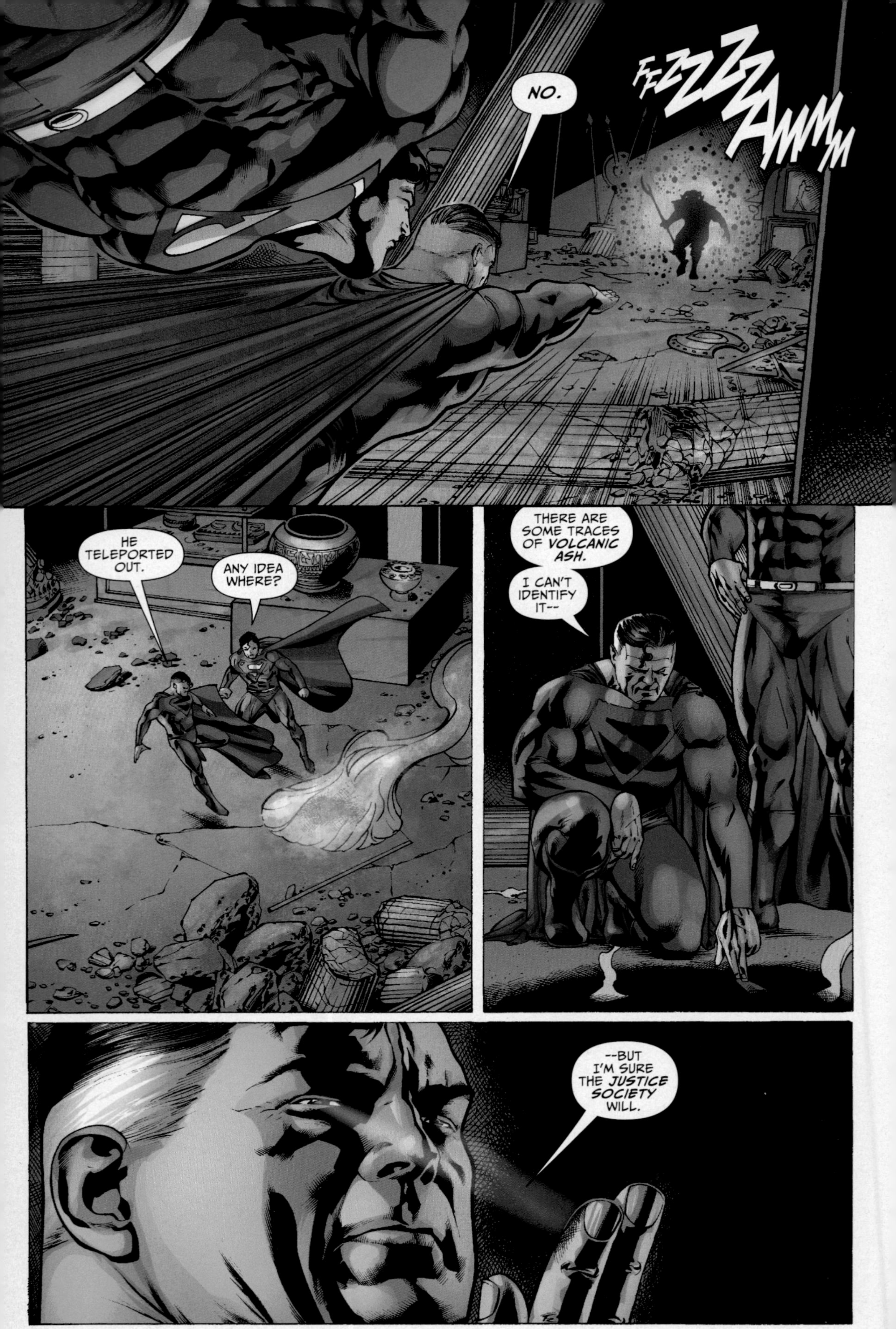
NO.
FFZZZZAMMM
HE TELEPORTED OUT.
ANY IDEA WHERE?
THERE ARE SOME TRACES OF VOLCANIC ASH.
I CAN'T IDENTIFY IT--
--BUT I'M SURE THE JUSTICE SOCIETY WILL.

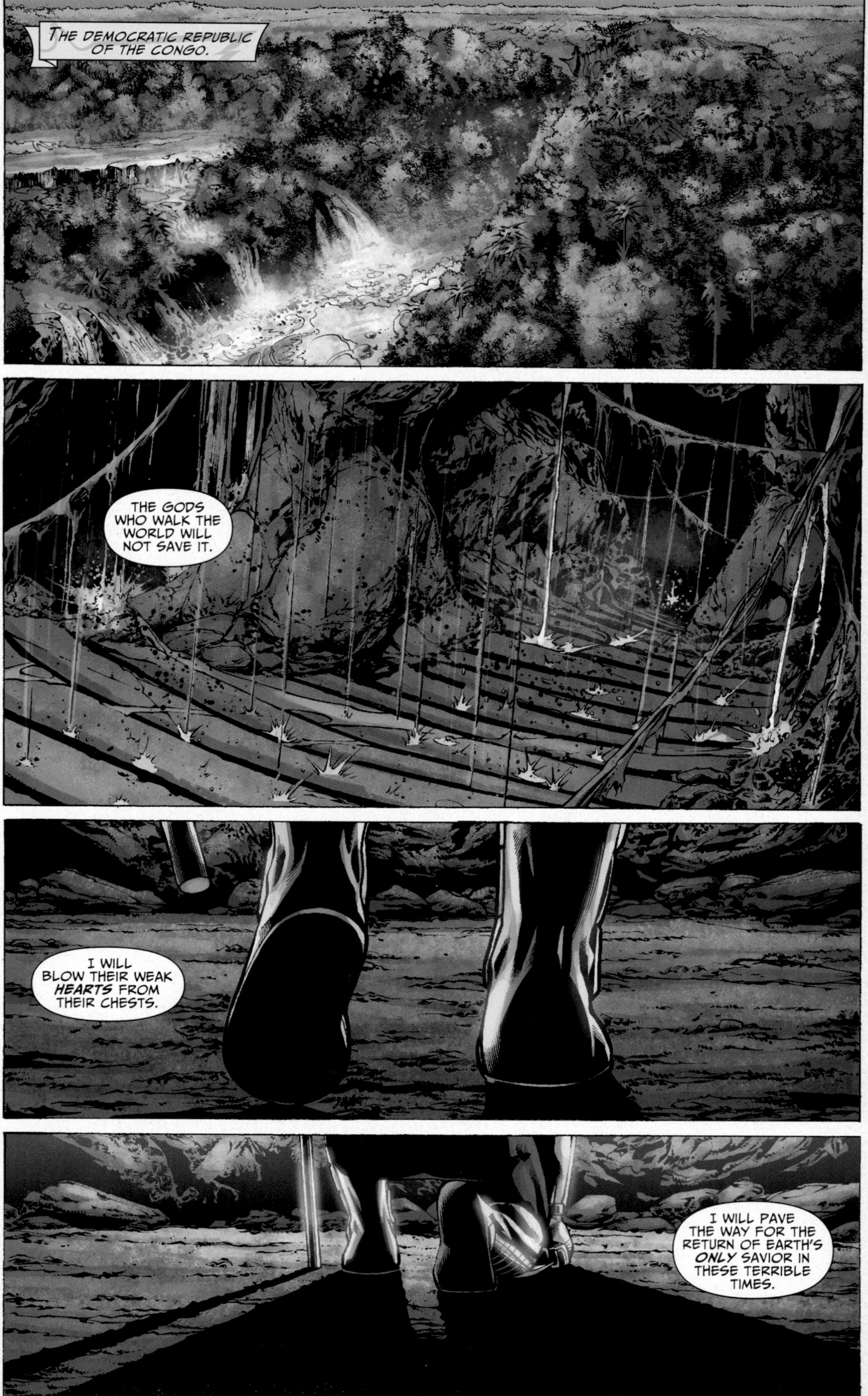
THE DEMOCRATIC REPUBLIC OF THE CONGO.
THE GODS WHO WALK THE WORLD WILL NOT SAVE IT.
I WILL BLOW THEIR WEAK HEARTS FROM THEIR CHESTS.
I WILL PAVE THE WAY FOR THE RETURN OF EARTH'S ONLY SAVIOR IN THESE TERRIBLE TIMES.

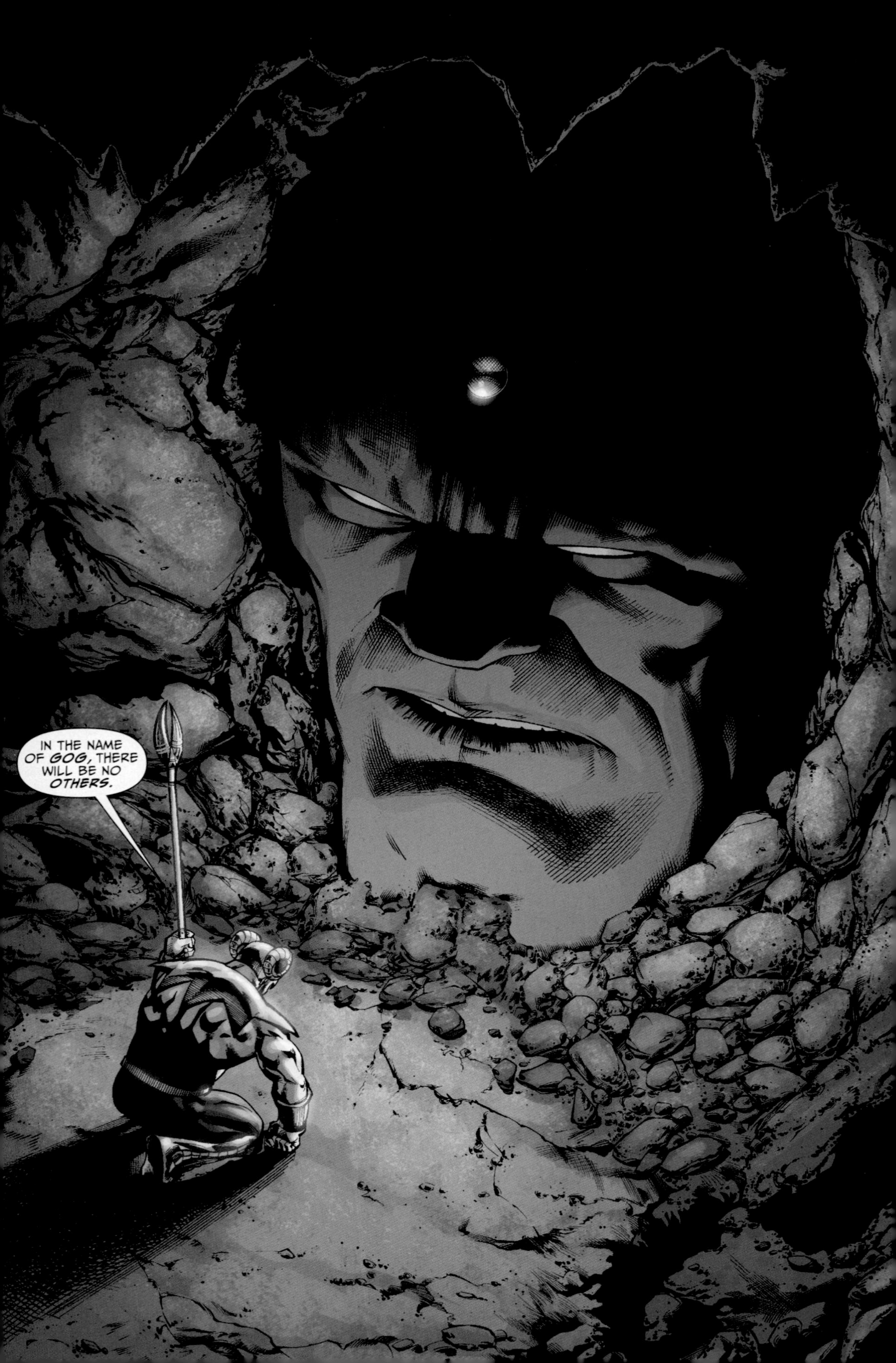
IN THE NAME OF GOG, THERE WILL BE NO OTHERS.

JUSTICE SOCIETY OF AMERICA #14 cover A by Alex Ross

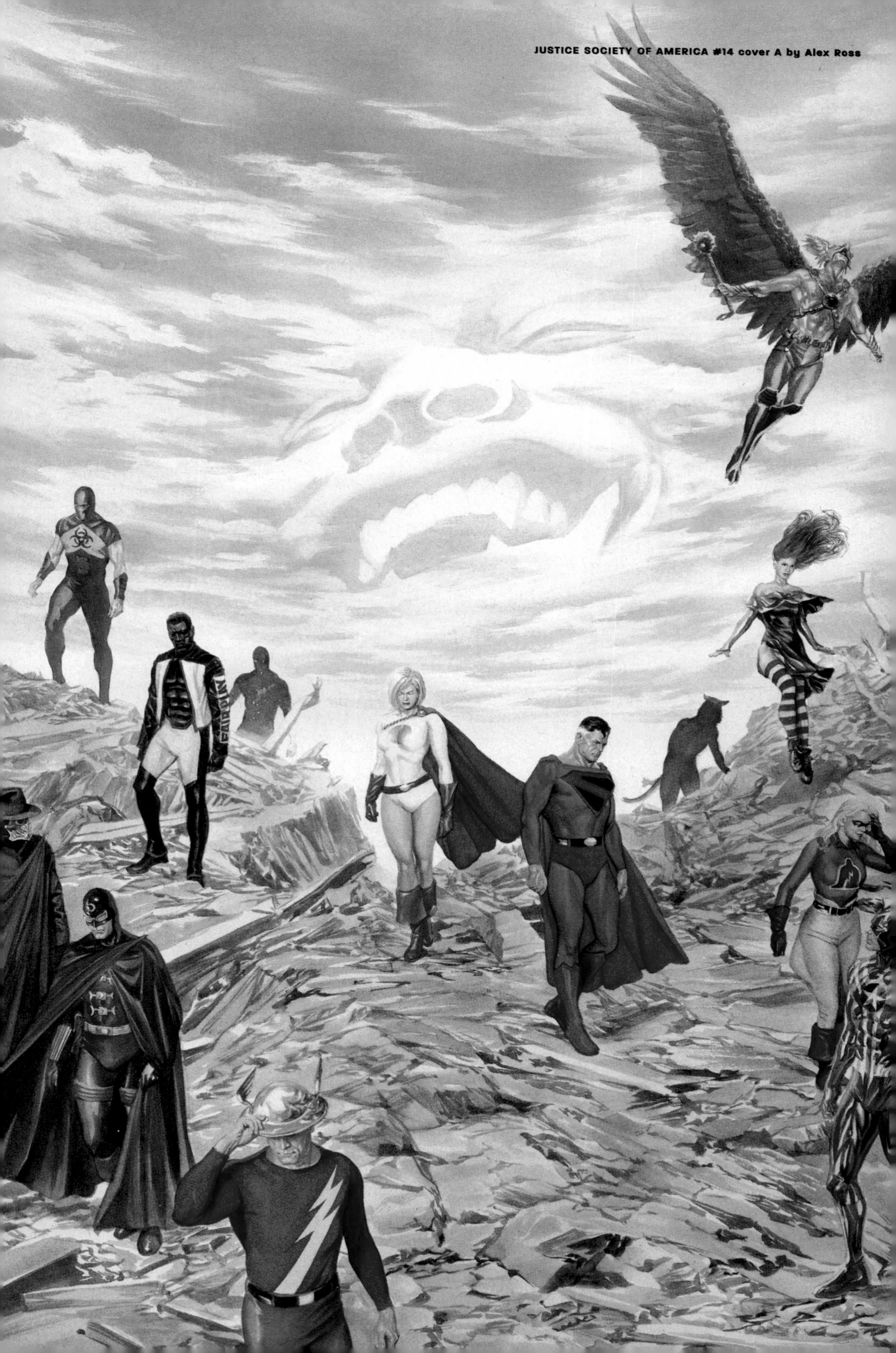

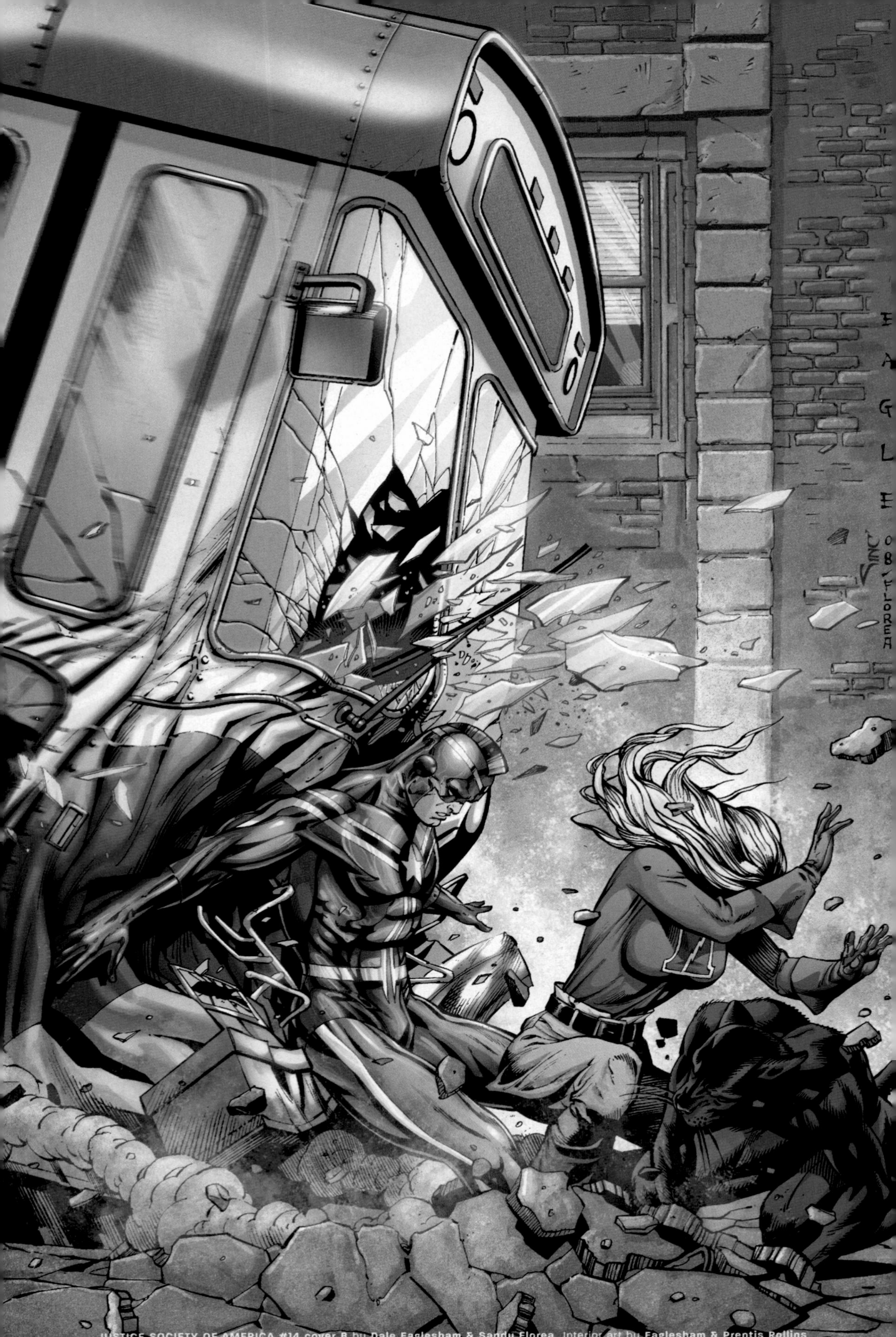
EAGLE

JUSTICE SOCIETY OF AMERICA #14 cover B by Dale Eaglesham & Sandu Florea Interior art by Eaglesham & Prentis Rollins

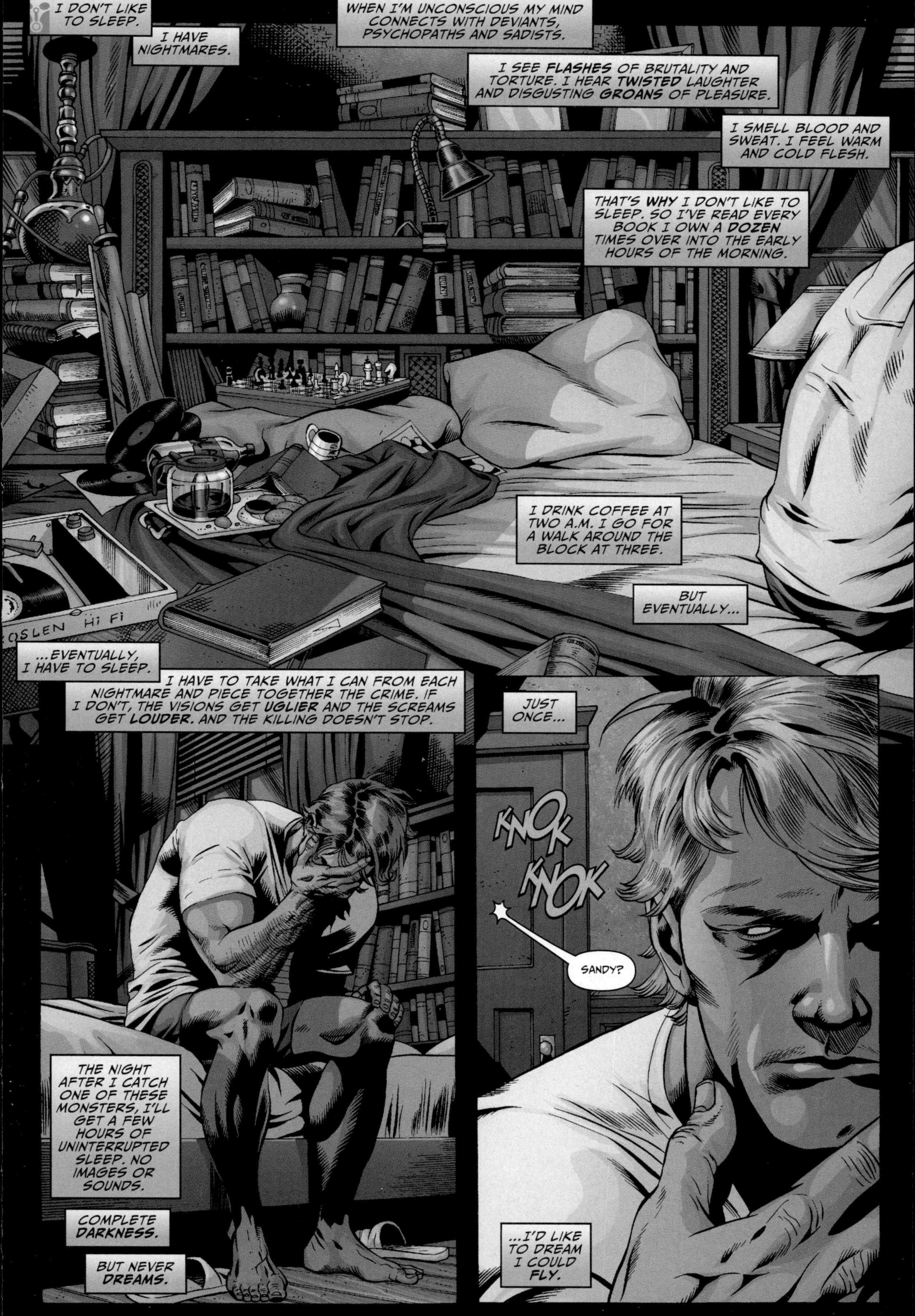

I DON'T LIKE TO SLEEP.
I HAVE NIGHTMARES.
WHEN I'M UNCONSCIOUS MY MIND CONNECTS WITH DEVIANTS, PSYCHOPATHS AND SADISTS.
I SEE FLASHES OF BRUTALITY AND TORTURE. I HEAR TWISTED LAUGHTER AND DISGUSTING GROANS OF PLEASURE.
I SMELL BLOOD AND SWEAT. I FEEL WARM AND COLD FLESH.
THAT'S WHY I DON'T LIKE TO SLEEP. SO I'VE READ EVERY BOOK I OWN A DOZEN TIMES OVER INTO THE EARLY HOURS OF THE MORNING.
I DRINK COFFEE AT TWO A.M. I GO FOR A WALK AROUND THE BLOCK AT THREE.
BUT EVENTUALLY...
OSLEN HI FI
...EVENTUALLY, I HAVE TO SLEEP.
I HAVE TO TAKE WHAT I CAN FROM EACH NIGHTMARE AND PIECE TOGETHER THE CRIME. IF I DON'T, THE VISIONS GET UGLIER AND THE SCREAMS GET LOUDER. AND THE KILLING DOESN'T STOP.
THE NIGHT AFTER I CATCH ONE OF THESE MONSTERS, I'LL GET A FEW HOURS OF UNINTERRUPTED SLEEP. NO IMAGES OR SOUNDS.
COMPLETE DARKNESS.
BUT NEVER DREAMS.
JUST ONCE...
KNOK
KNOK
SANDY?
...I'D LIKE TO DREAM I COULD FLY.

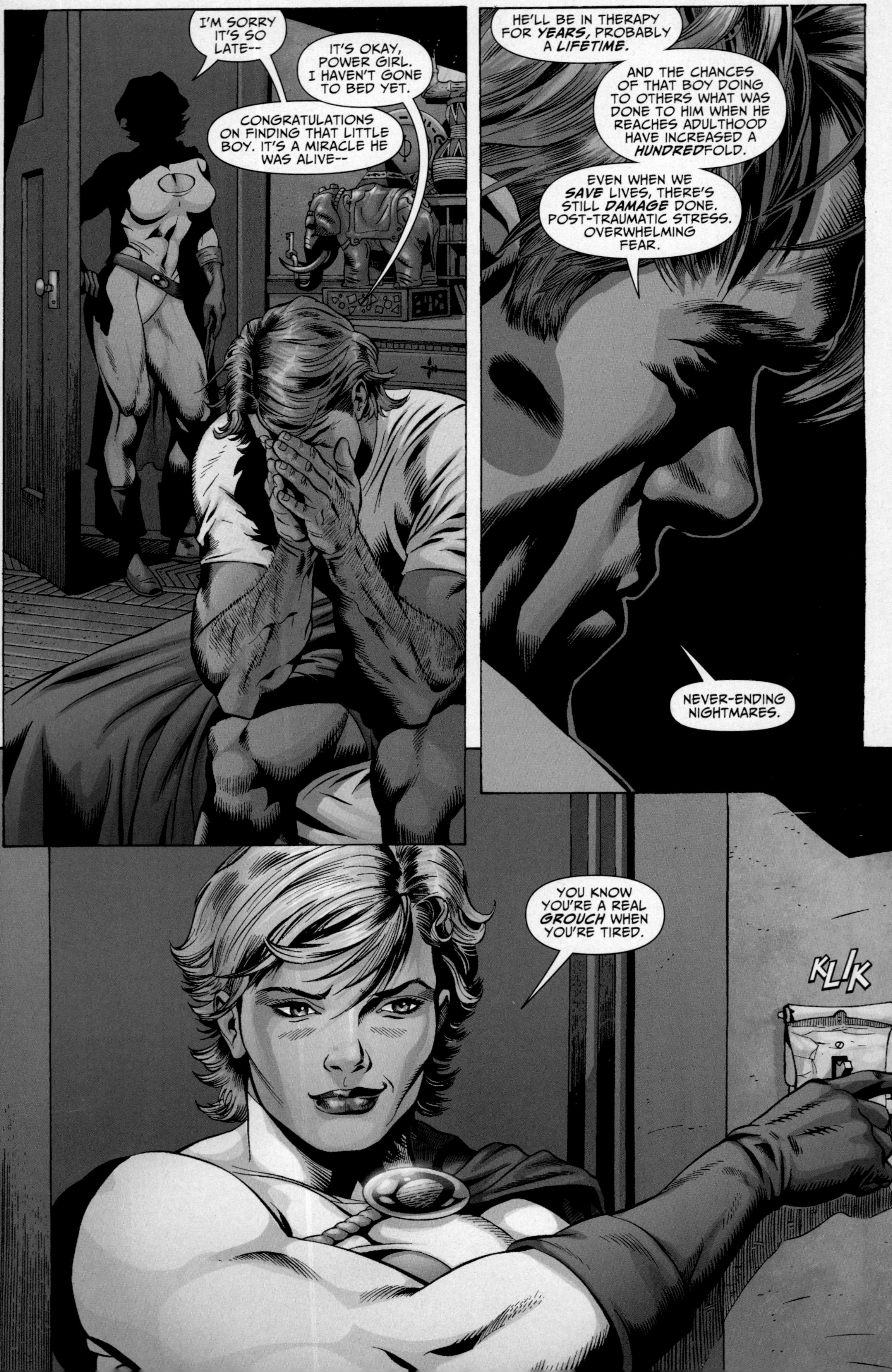
I'M SORRY IT'S SO LATE--
IT'S OKAY, POWER GIRL. I HAVEN'T GONE TO BED YET.
CONGRATULATIONS ON FINDING THAT LITTLE BOY. IT'S A MIRACLE HE WAS ALIVE--
HE'LL BE IN THERAPY FOR YEARS, PROBABLY A LIFETIME.
AND THE CHANCES OF THAT BOY DOING TO OTHERS WHAT WAS DONE TO HIM WHEN HE REACHES ADULTHOOD HAVE INCREASED A HUNDREDFOLD.
EVEN WHEN WE SAVE LIVES, THERE'S STILL DAMAGE DONE. POST-TRAUMATIC STRESS. OVERWHELMING FEAR.
NEVER-ENDING NIGHTMARES.
YOU KNOW YOU'RE A REAL GROUCH WHEN YOU'RE TIRED.
KLIK

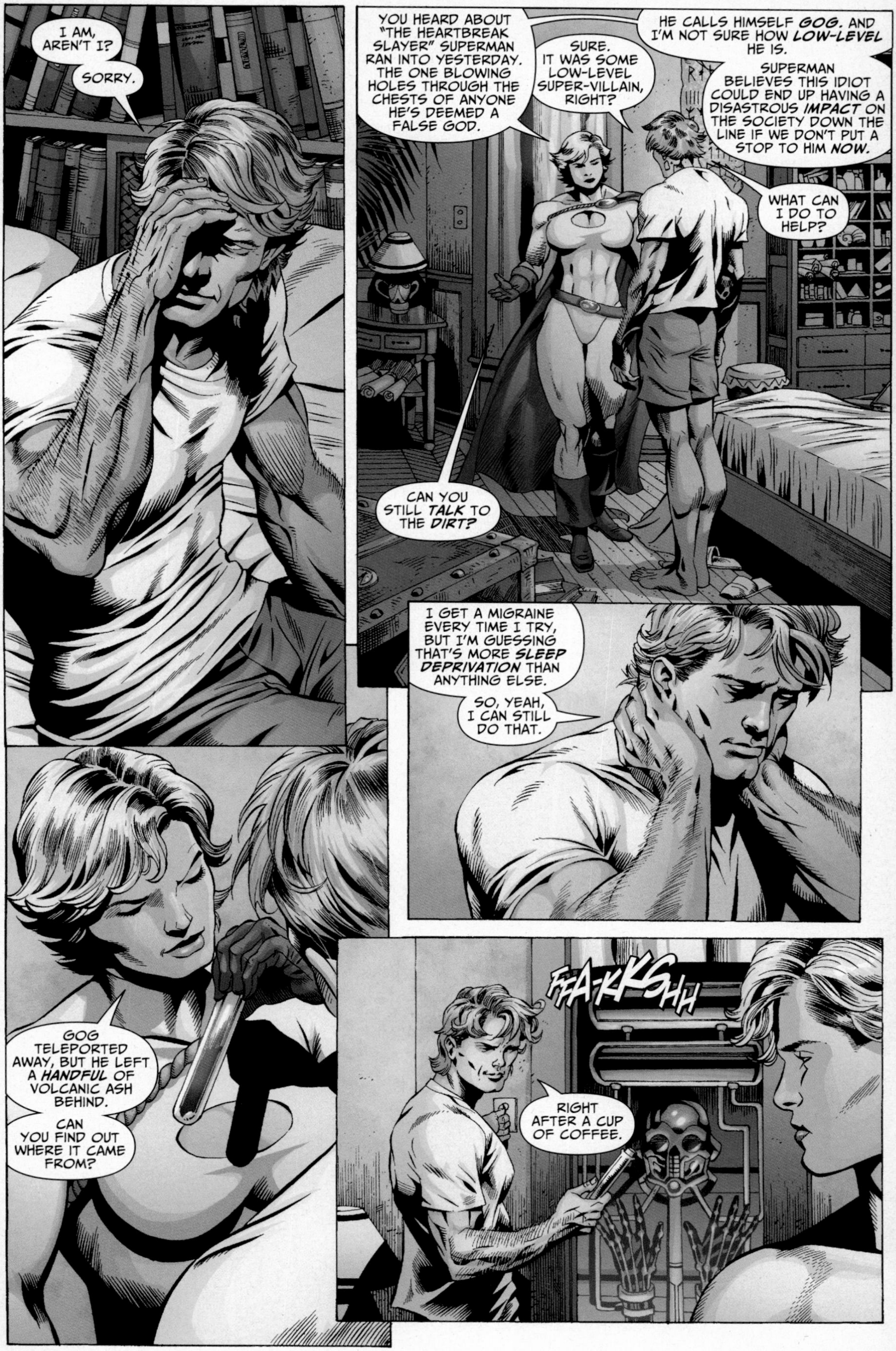
I AM, AREN'T I?
SORRY.
YOU HEARD ABOUT "THE HEARTBREAK SLAYER" SUPERMAN RAN INTO YESTERDAY. THE ONE BLOWING HOLES THROUGH THE CHESTS OF ANYONE HE'S DEEMED A FALSE GOD.
SURE. IT WAS SOME LOW-LEVEL SUPER-VILLAIN, RIGHT?
HE CALLS HIMSELF GOG. AND I'M NOT SURE HOW LOW-LEVEL HE IS.
SUPERMAN BELIEVES THIS IDIOT COULD END UP HAVING A DISASTROUS IMPACT ON THE SOCIETY DOWN THE LINE IF WE DON'T PUT A STOP TO HIM NOW.
WHAT CAN I DO TO HELP?
CAN YOU STILL TALK TO THE DIRT?
I GET A MIGRAINE EVERY TIME I TRY, BUT I'M GUESSING THAT'S MORE SLEEP DEPRIVATION THAN ANYTHING ELSE.
SO, YEAH, I CAN STILL DO THAT.
GOG TELEPORTED AWAY, BUT HE LEFT A HANDFUL OF VOLCANIC ASH BEHIND.
CAN YOU FIND OUT WHERE IT CAME FROM?
FFA-KKSHH
RIGHT AFTER A CUP OF COFFEE.

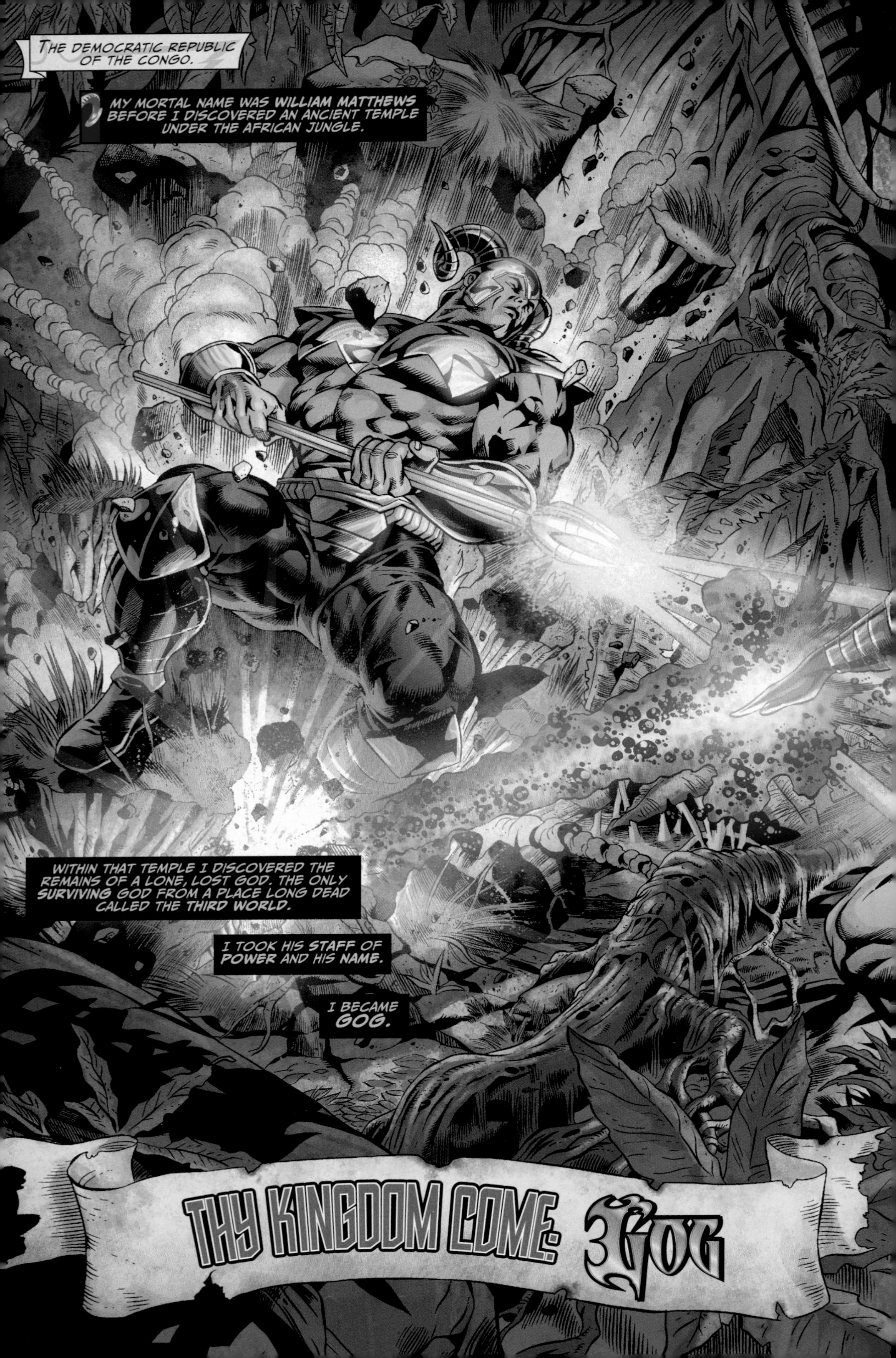
THE DEMOCRATIC REPUBLIC OF THE CONGO.
MY MORTAL NAME WAS WILLIAM MATTHEWS BEFORE I DISCOVERED AN ANCIENT TEMPLE UNDER THE AFRICAN JUNGLE.
WITHIN THAT TEMPLE I DISCOVERED THE REMAINS OF A LONE, LOST GOD. THE ONLY SURVIVING GOD FROM A PLACE LONG DEAD CALLED THE THIRD WORLD.
I TOOK HIS STAFF OF POWER AND HIS NAME.
I BECAME GOG.
THY KINGDOM COME: 3 GOG

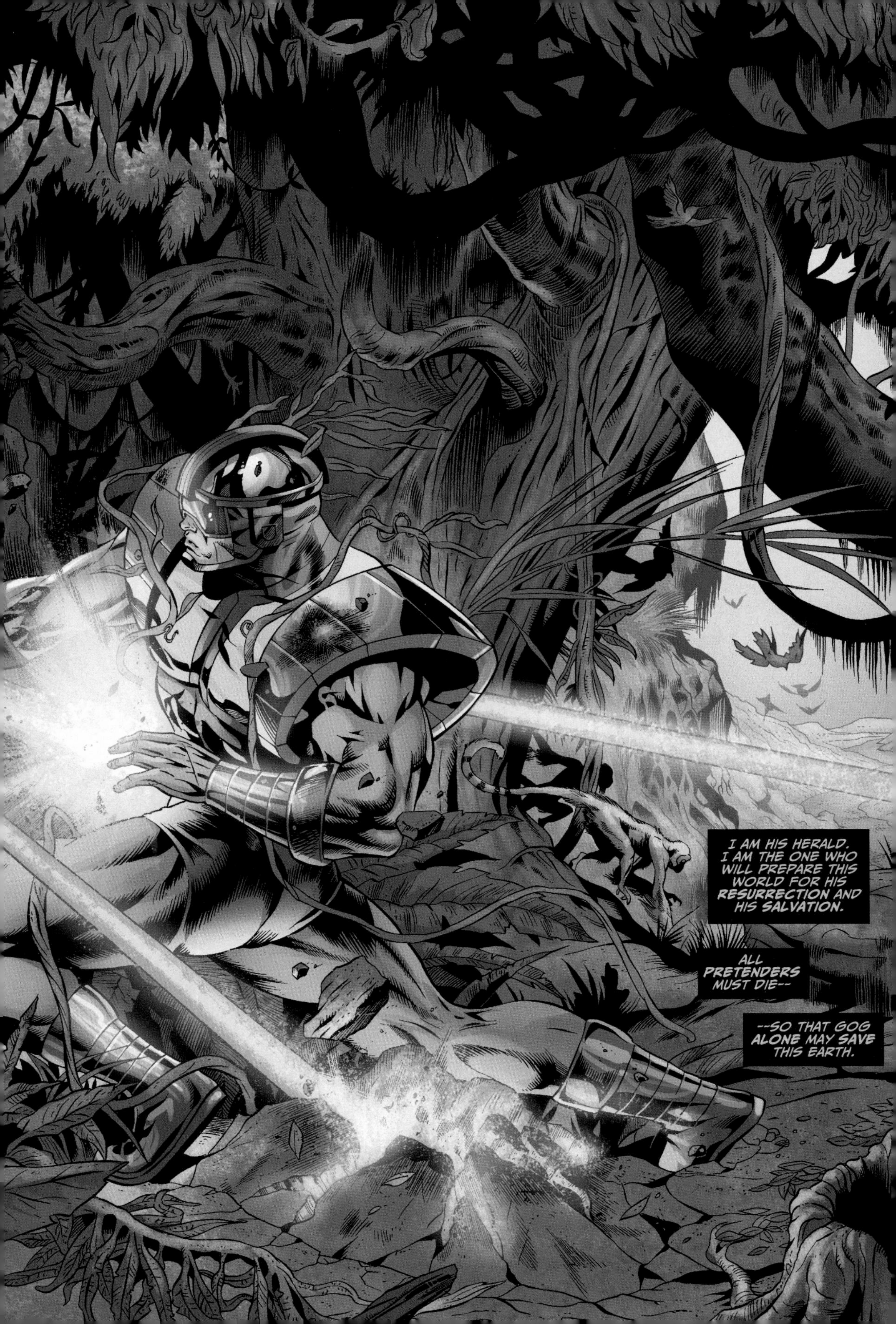
I AM HIS HERALD. I AM THE ONE WHO WILL PREPARE THIS WORLD FOR HIS RESURRECTION AND HIS SALVATION.
ALL PRETENDERS MUST DIE--
--SO THAT GOG ALONE MAY SAVE THIS EARTH.

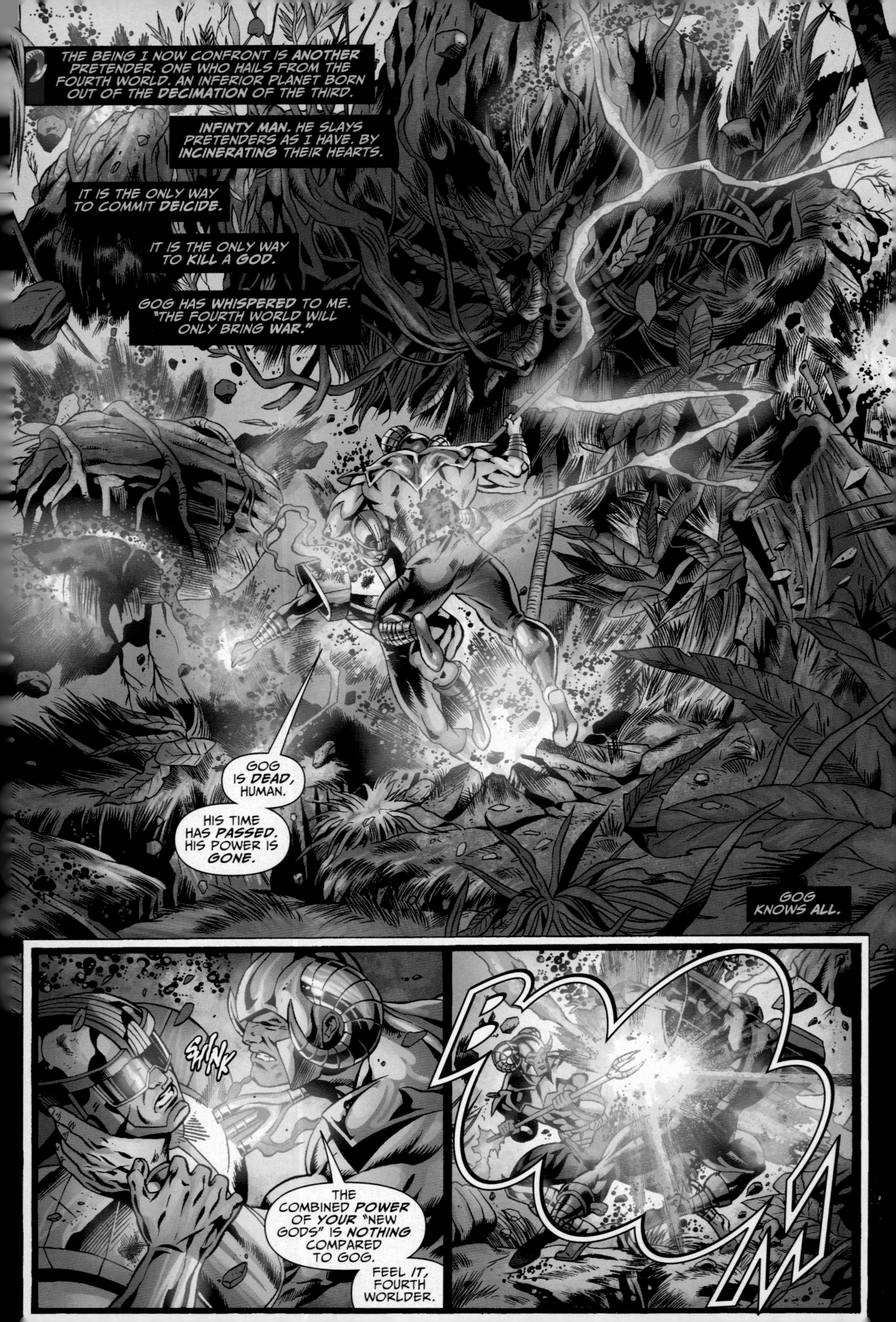

THE BEING I NOW CONFRONT IS ANOTHER PRETENDER. ONE WHO HAILS FROM THE FOURTH WORLD. AN INFERIOR PLANET BORN OUT OF THE DECIMATION OF THE THIRD.
INFINTY MAN. HE SLAYS PRETENDERS AS I HAVE. BY INCINERATING THEIR HEARTS.
IT IS THE ONLY WAY TO COMMIT DEICIDE.
IT IS THE ONLY WAY TO KILL A GOD.
GOG HAS WHISPERED TO ME. "THE FOURTH WORLD WILL ONLY BRING WAR."
GOG IS DEAD, HUMAN.
HIS TIME HAS PASSED. HIS POWER IS GONE.
GOG KNOWS ALL.
SHINK
THE COMBINED POWER OF YOUR "NEW GODS" IS NOTHING COMPARED TO GOG.
FEEL IT, FOURTH WORLDER.

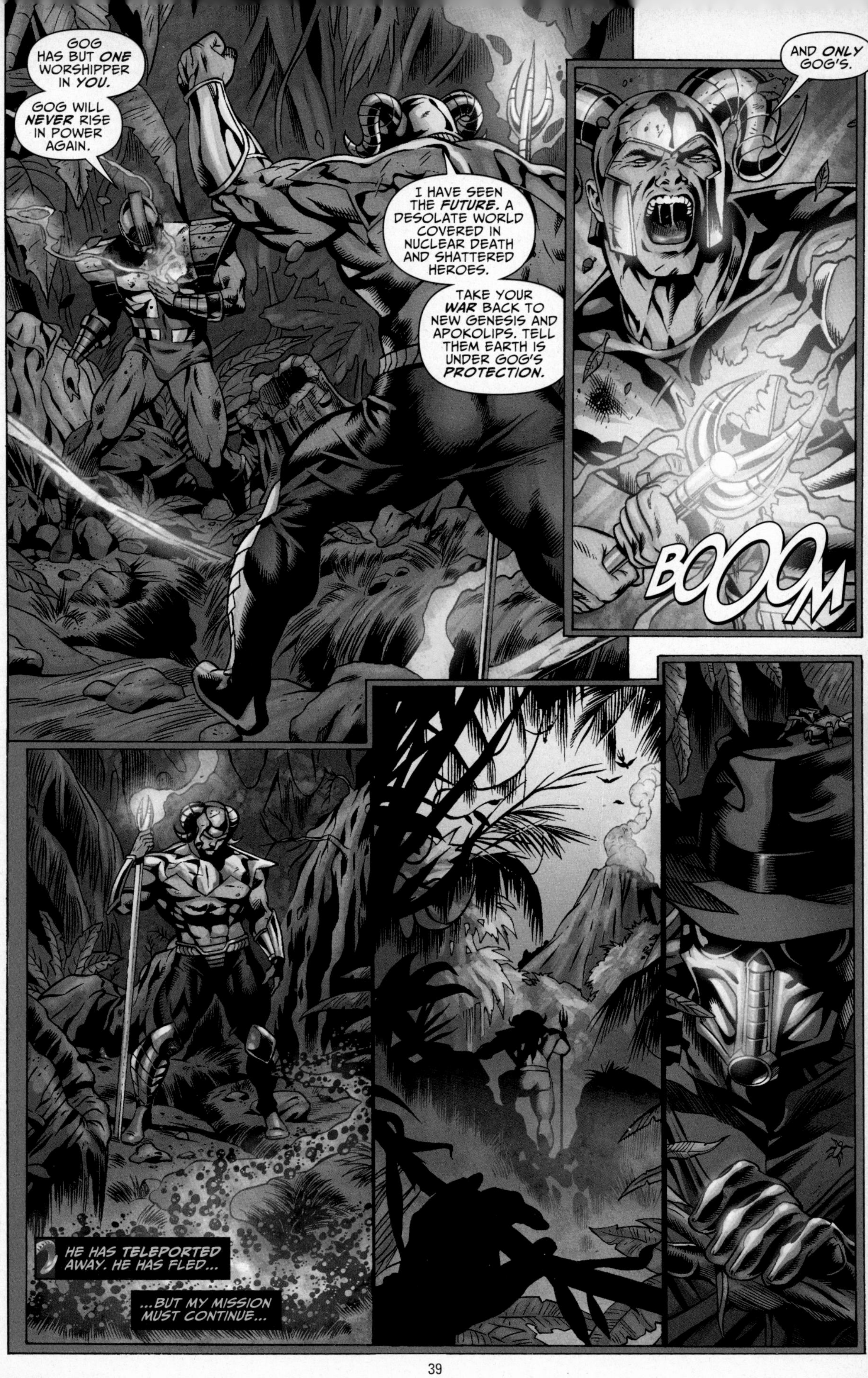
GOG HAS BUT ONE WORSHIPPER IN YOU.
GOG WILL NEVER RISE IN POWER AGAIN.
I HAVE SEEN THE FUTURE. A DESOLATE WORLD COVERED IN NUCLEAR DEATH AND SHATTERED HEROES.
TAKE YOUR WAR BACK TO NEW GENESIS AND APOKOLIPS. TELL THEM EARTH IS UNDER GOG'S PROTECTION.
AND ONLY GOG'S.
BOOOM
HE HAS TELEPORTED AWAY. HE HAS FLED...
...BUT MY MISSION MUST CONTINUE...

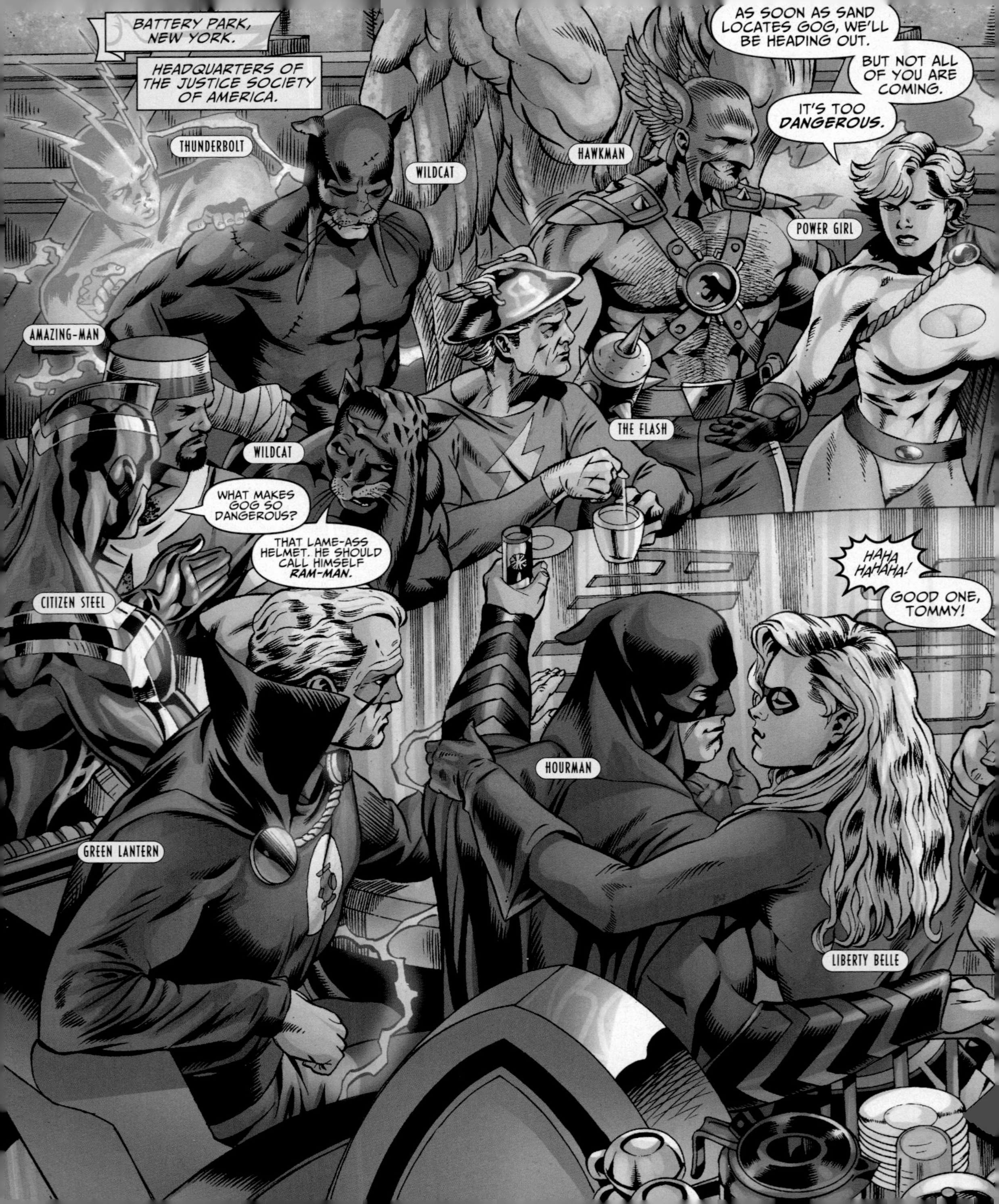
BATTERY PARK, NEW YORK.
HEADQUARTERS OF THE JUSTICE SOCIETY OF AMERICA.
AS SOON AS SAND LOCATES GOG, WE'LL BE HEADING OUT.
BUT NOT ALL OF YOU ARE COMING.
IT'S TOO DANGEROUS.
THUNDERBOLT
WILDCAT
HAWKMAN
POWER GIRL
AMAZING-MAN
THE FLASH
WILDCAT
WHAT MAKES GOG SO DANGEROUS?
THAT LAME-ASS HELMET. HE SHOULD CALL HIMSELF RAM-MAN.
HAHA HAHAHA!
GOOD ONE, TOMMY!
CITIZEN STEEL
HOURMAN
GREEN LANTERN
LIBERTY BELLE

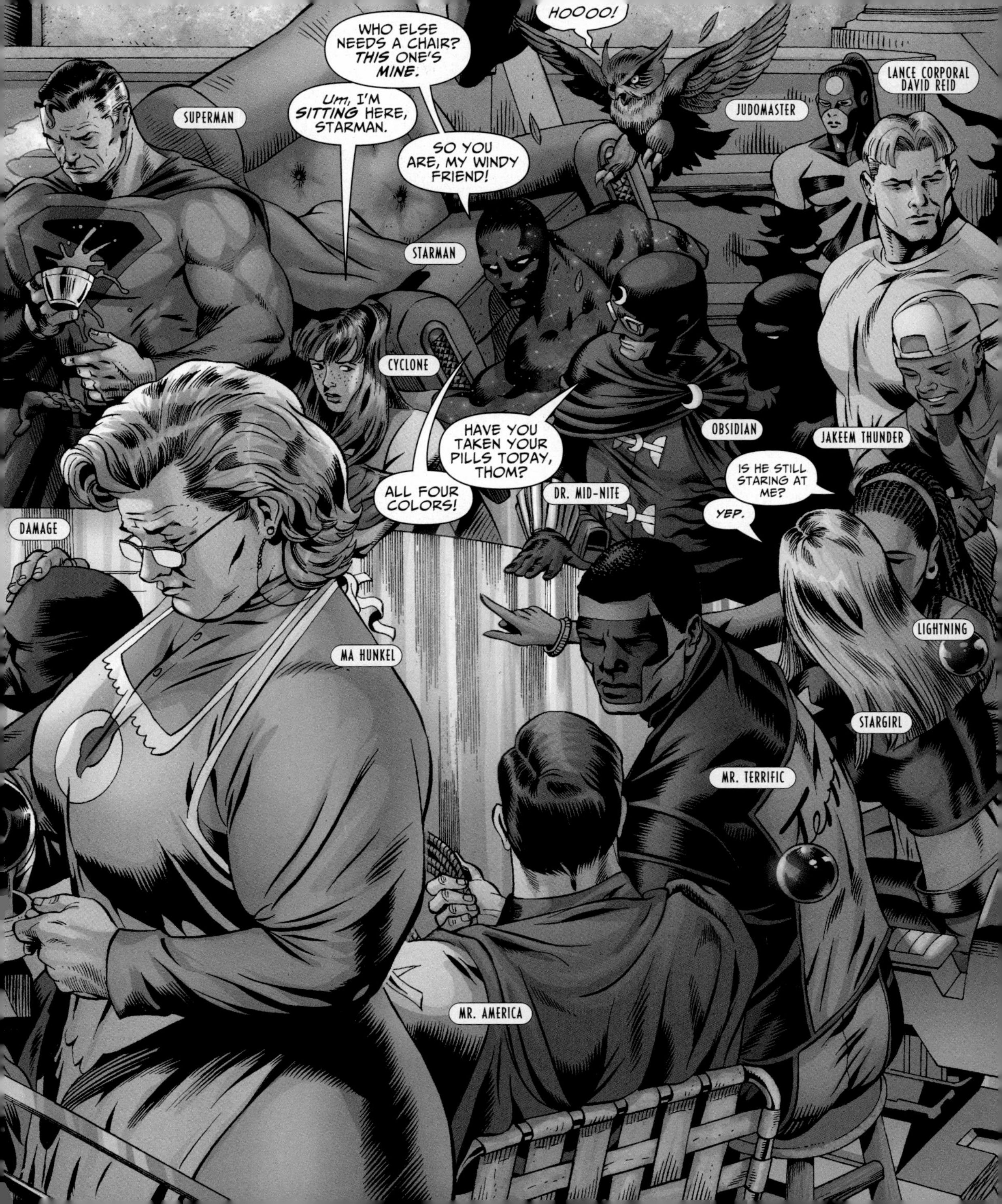
HOOOO!
WHO ELSE NEEDS A CHAIR? THIS ONE'S MINE.
Um, I'M SITTING HERE, STARMAN.
SO YOU ARE, MY WINDY FRIEND!
HAVE YOU TAKEN YOUR PILLS TODAY, THOM?
ALL FOUR COLORS!
IS HE STILL STARING AT ME?
YEP.
SUPERMAN
STARMAN
JUDOMASTER
LANCE CORPORAL DAVID REID
CYCLONE
OBSIDIAN
JAKEEM THUNDER
DR. MID-NITE
DAMAGE
MA HUNKEL
LIGHTNING
STARGIRL
MR. TERRIFIC
MR. AMERICA

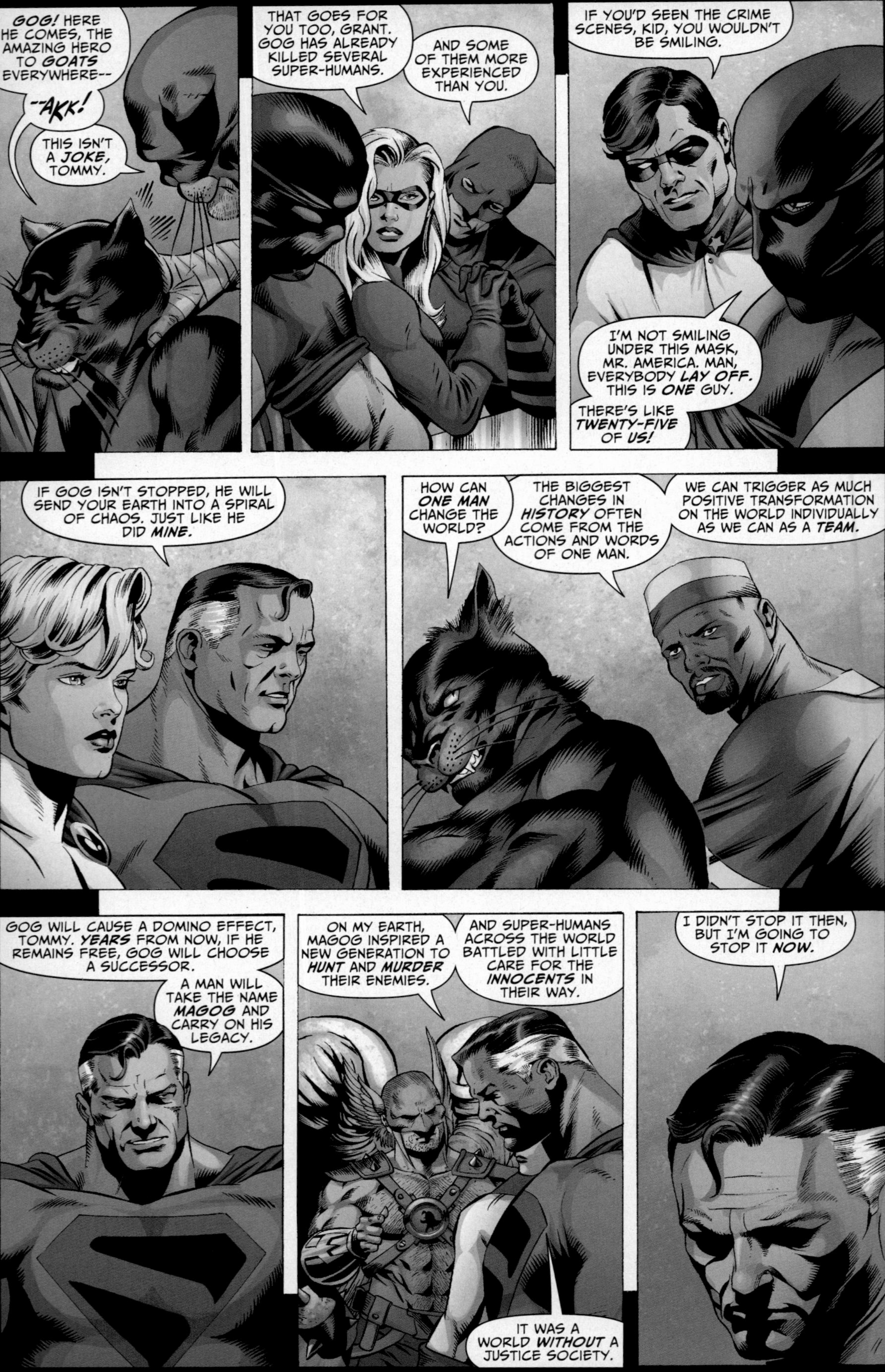
GOG! HERE HE COMES, THE AMAZING HERO TO GOATS EVERYWHERE--
--AKK!
THIS ISN'T A JOKE, TOMMY.
THAT GOES FOR YOU TOO, GRANT. GOG HAS ALREADY KILLED SEVERAL SUPER-HUMANS.
AND SOME OF THEM MORE EXPERIENCED THAN YOU.
IF YOU'D SEEN THE CRIME SCENES, KID, YOU WOULDN'T BE SMILING.
I'M NOT SMILING UNDER THIS MASK, MR. AMERICA. MAN, EVERYBODY LAY OFF. THIS IS ONE GUY.
THERE'S LIKE TWENTY-FIVE OF US!
IF GOG ISN'T STOPPED, HE WILL SEND YOUR EARTH INTO A SPIRAL OF CHAOS. JUST LIKE HE DID MINE.
HOW CAN ONE MAN CHANGE THE WORLD?
THE BIGGEST CHANGES IN HISTORY OFTEN COME FROM THE ACTIONS AND WORDS OF ONE MAN.
WE CAN TRIGGER AS MUCH POSITIVE TRANSFORMATION ON THE WORLD INDIVIDUALLY AS WE CAN AS A TEAM.
GOG WILL CAUSE A DOMINO EFFECT, TOMMY. YEARS FROM NOW, IF HE REMAINS FREE, GOG WILL CHOOSE A SUCCESSOR.
A MAN WILL TAKE THE NAME MAGOG AND CARRY ON HIS LEGACY.
ON MY EARTH, MAGOG INSPIRED A NEW GENERATION TO HUNT AND MURDER THEIR ENEMIES.
AND SUPER-HUMANS ACROSS THE WORLD BATTLED WITH LITTLE CARE FOR THE INNOCENTS IN THEIR WAY.
IT WAS A WORLD WITHOUT A JUSTICE SOCIETY.
I DIDN'T STOP IT THEN, BUT I'M GOING TO STOP IT NOW.

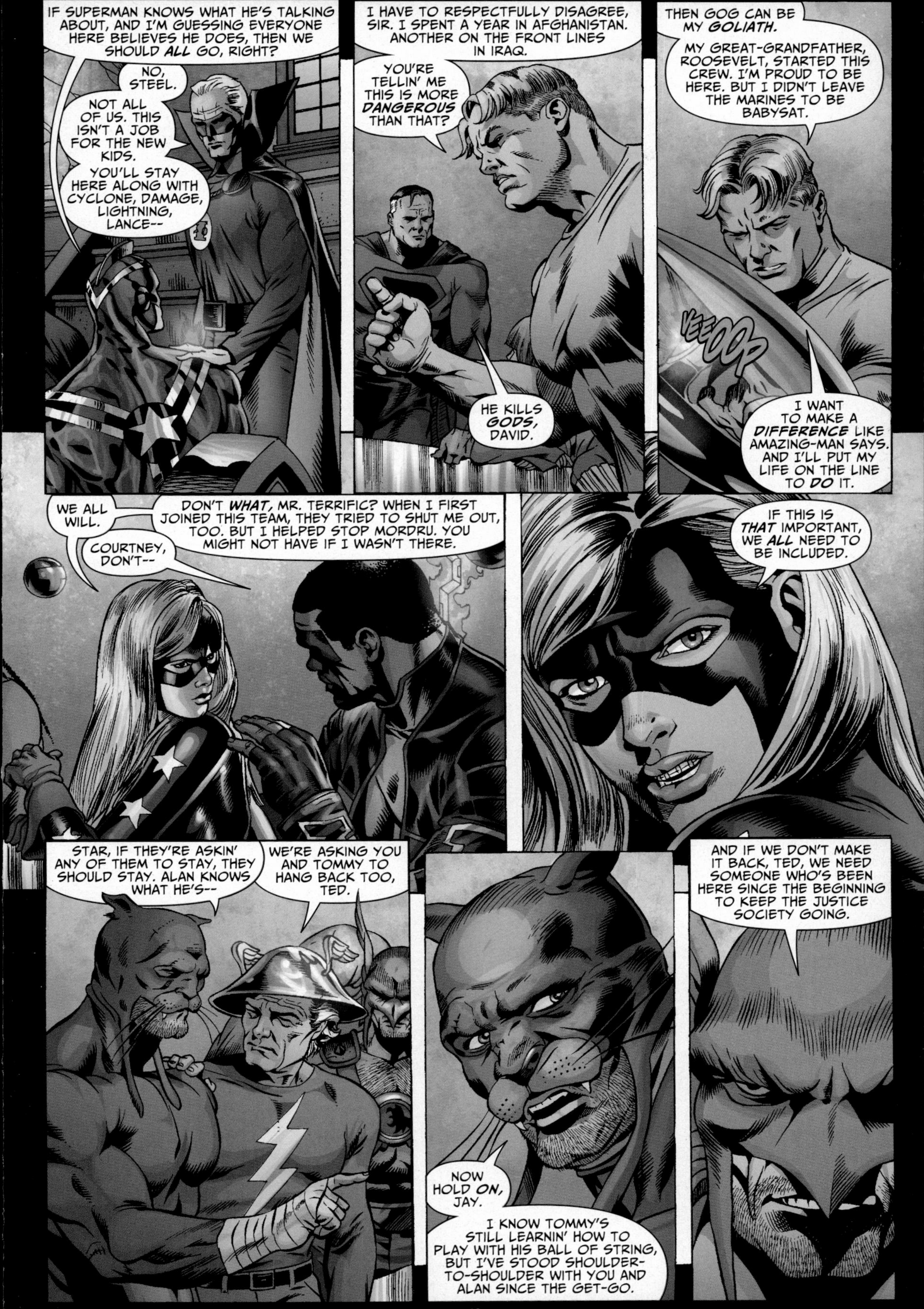

IF SUPERMAN KNOWS WHAT HE'S TALKING ABOUT, AND I'M GUESSING EVERYONE HERE BELIEVES HE DOES, THEN WE SHOULD ALL GO, RIGHT?
NO, STEEL.
NOT ALL OF US. THIS ISN'T A JOB FOR THE NEW KIDS.
YOU'LL STAY HERE ALONG WITH CYCLONE, DAMAGE, LIGHTNING, LANCE--
I HAVE TO RESPECTFULLY DISAGREE, SIR. I SPENT A YEAR IN AFGHANISTAN. ANOTHER ON THE FRONT LINES IN IRAQ.
YOU'RE TELLIN' ME THIS IS MORE DANGEROUS THAN THAT?
HE KILLS GODS, DAVID.
THEN GOG CAN BE MY GOLIATH.
MY GREAT-GRANDFATHER, ROOSEVELT, STARTED THIS CREW. I'M PROUD TO BE HERE. BUT I DIDN'T LEAVE THE MARINES TO BE BABYSAT.
VEEOOP
I WANT TO MAKE A DIFFERENCE LIKE AMAZING-MAN SAYS. AND I'LL PUT MY LIFE ON THE LINE TO DO IT.
WE ALL WILL.
COURTNEY, DON'T--
DON'T WHAT, MR. TERRIFIC? WHEN I FIRST JOINED THIS TEAM, THEY TRIED TO SHUT ME OUT, TOO. BUT I HELPED STOP MORDRU. YOU MIGHT NOT HAVE IF I WASN'T THERE.
IF THIS IS THAT IMPORTANT, WE ALL NEED TO BE INCLUDED.
STAR, IF THEY'RE ASKIN' ANY OF THEM TO STAY, THEY SHOULD STAY. ALAN KNOWS WHAT HE'S--
WE'RE ASKING YOU AND TOMMY TO HANG BACK TOO, TED.
NOW HOLD ON, JAY.
I KNOW TOMMY'S STILL LEARNIN' HOW TO PLAY WITH HIS BALL OF STRING, BUT I'VE STOOD SHOULDER-TO-SHOULDER WITH YOU AND ALAN SINCE THE GET-GO.
AND IF WE DON'T MAKE IT BACK, TED, WE NEED SOMEONE WHO'S BEEN HERE SINCE THE BEGINNING TO KEEP THE JUSTICE SOCIETY GOING.

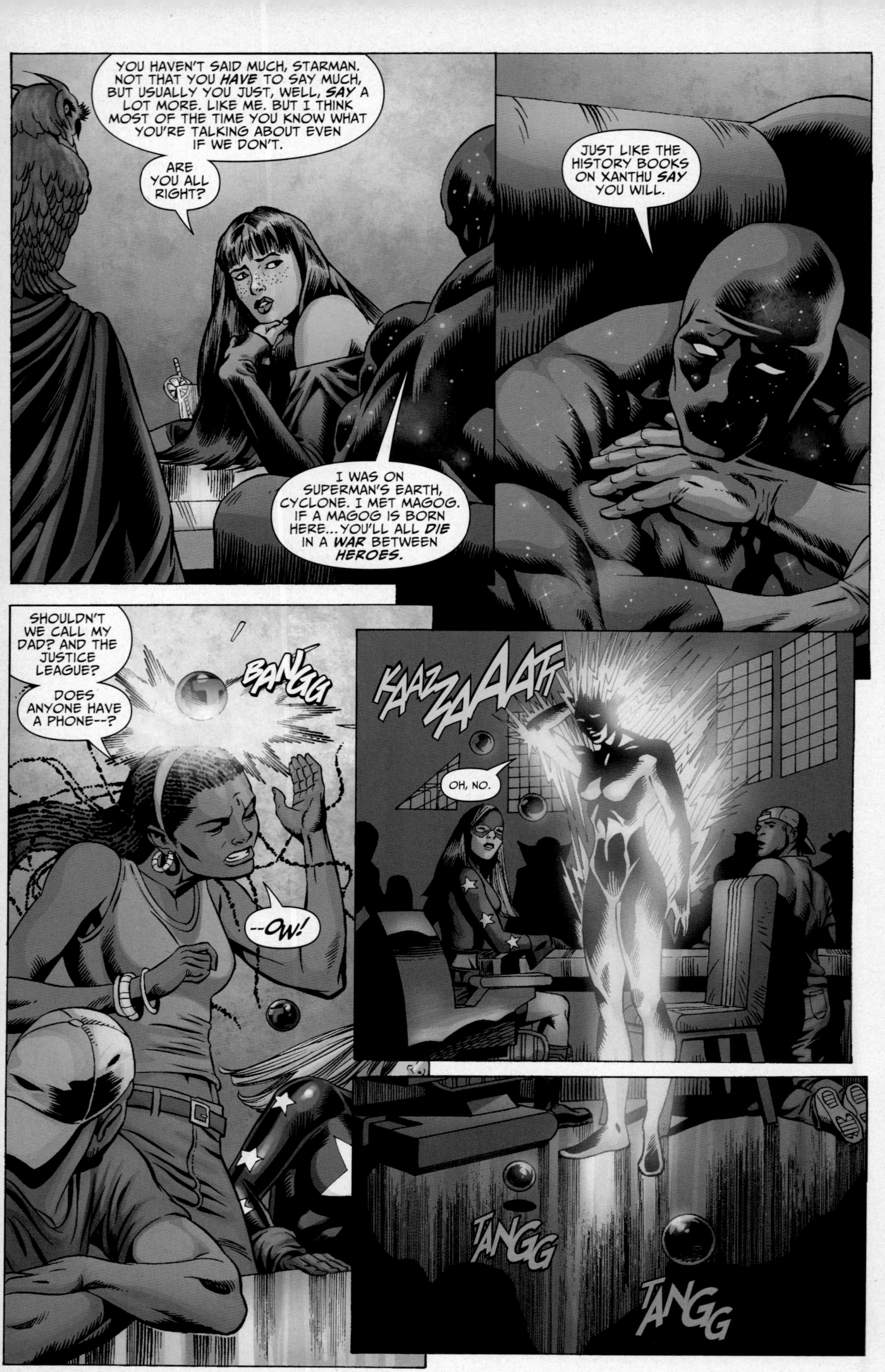
YOU HAVEN'T SAID MUCH, STARMAN. NOT THAT YOU HAVE TO SAY MUCH, BUT USUALLY YOU JUST, WELL, SAY A LOT MORE. LIKE ME. BUT I THINK MOST OF THE TIME YOU KNOW WHAT YOU'RE TALKING ABOUT EVEN IF WE DON'T.
ARE YOU ALL RIGHT?
I WAS ON SUPERMAN'S EARTH, CYCLONE. I MET MAGOG. IF A MAGOG IS BORN HERE...YOU'LL ALL DIE IN A WAR BETWEEN HEROES.
JUST LIKE THE HISTORY BOOKS ON XANTHU SAY YOU WILL.
SHOULDN'T WE CALL MY DAD? AND THE JUSTICE LEAGUE?
DOES ANYONE HAVE A PHONE--?
BANGG
--OW!
KAAZZAAAT
OH, NO.
TANGG
TANGG

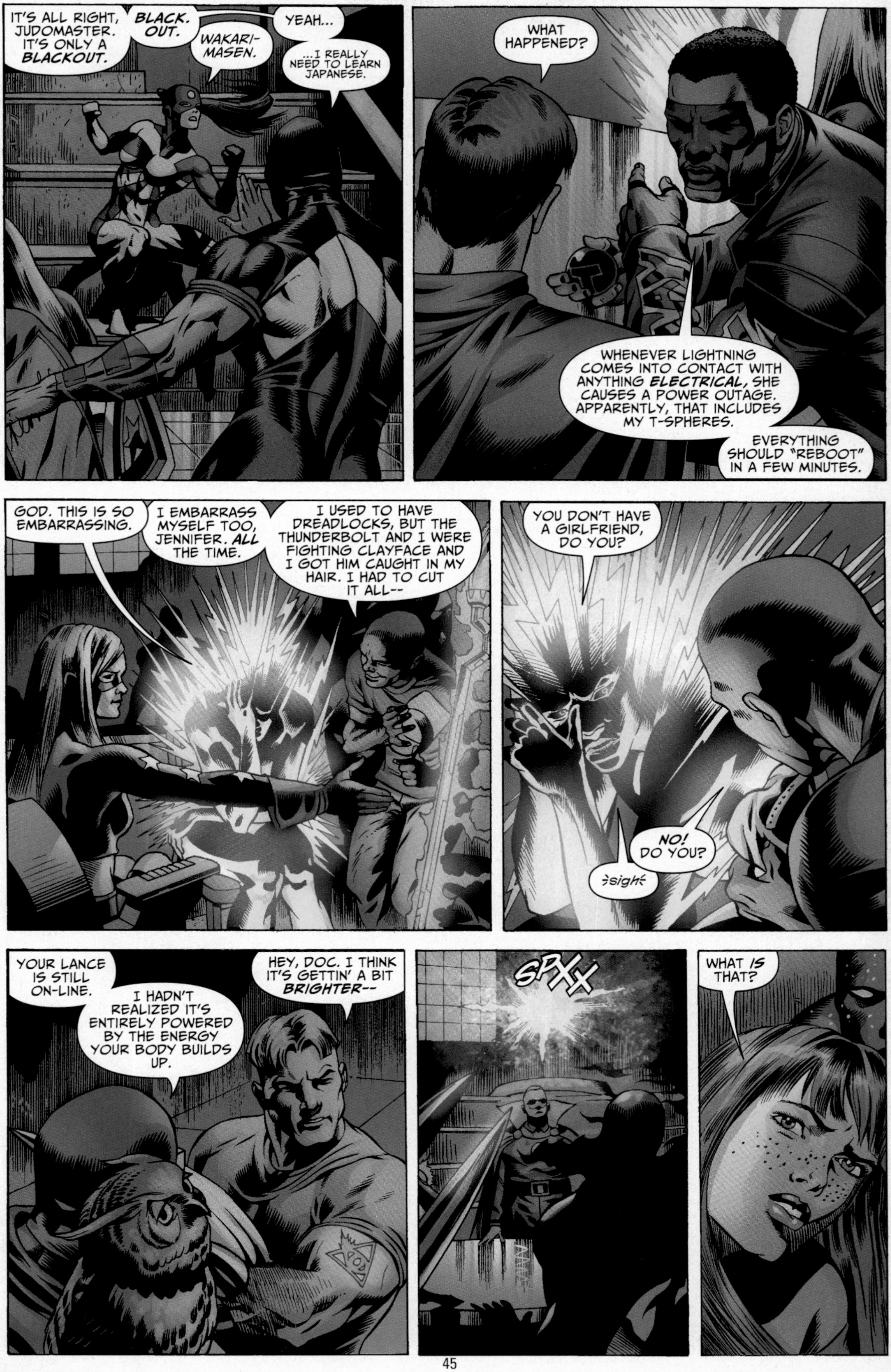

IT'S ALL RIGHT, JUDOMASTER. IT'S ONLY A BLACKOUT.
BLACK. OUT.
WAKARI-MASEN.
YEAH...
...I REALLY NEED TO LEARN JAPANESE.
WHAT HAPPENED?
WHENEVER LIGHTNING COMES INTO CONTACT WITH ANYTHING ELECTRICAL, SHE CAUSES A POWER OUTAGE. APPARENTLY, THAT INCLUDES MY T-SPHERES.
EVERYTHING SHOULD "REBOOT" IN A FEW MINUTES.
GOD. THIS IS SO EMBARRASSING.
I EMBARRASS MYSELF TOO, JENNIFER. ALL THE TIME.
I USED TO HAVE DREADLOCKS, BUT THE THUNDERBOLT AND I WERE FIGHTING CLAYFACE AND I GOT HIM CAUGHT IN MY HAIR. I HAD TO CUT IT ALL--
YOU DON'T HAVE A GIRLFRIEND, DO YOU?
NO! DO YOU?
sigh
YOUR LANCE IS STILL ON-LINE.
I HADN'T REALIZED IT'S ENTIRELY POWERED BY THE ENERGY YOUR BODY BUILDS UP.
HEY, DOC. I THINK IT'S GETTIN' A BIT BRIGHTER--
SPXX
WHAT IS THAT?

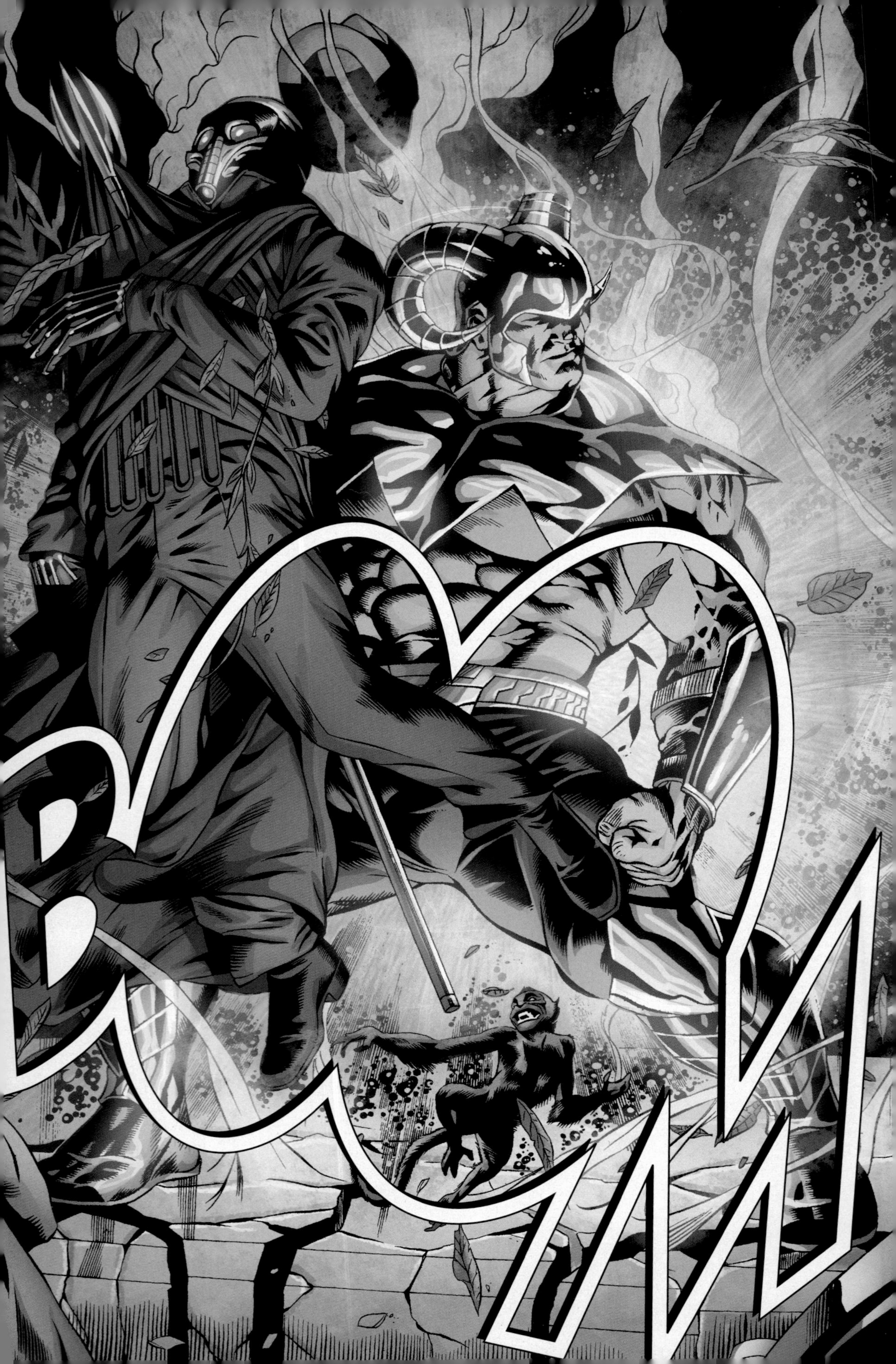
BOOM

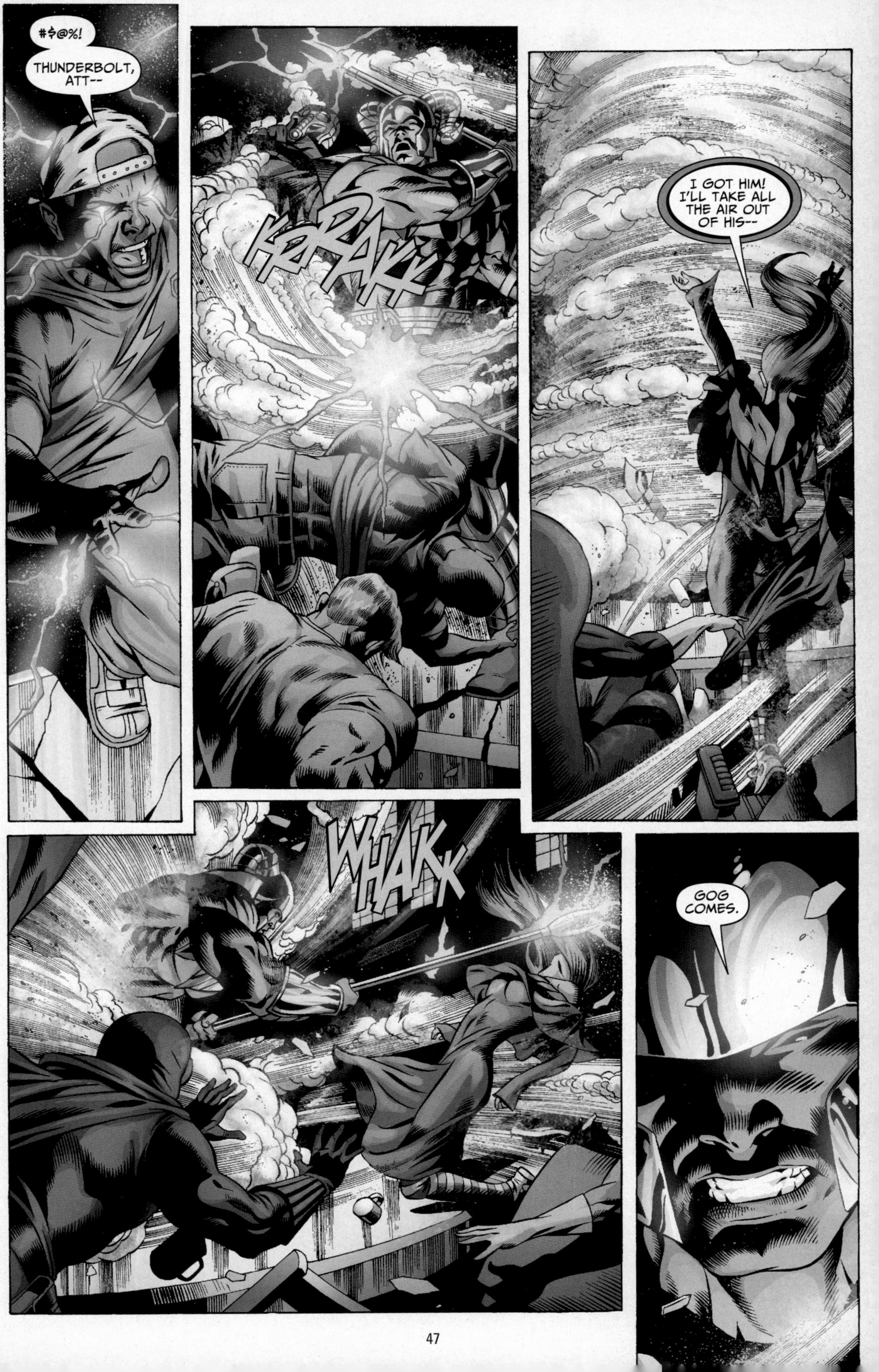
#$@%!
THUNDERBOLT, ATT--
KRAKK
I GOT HIM! I'LL TAKE ALL THE AIR OUT OF HIS--
WHAKK
GOG COMES.

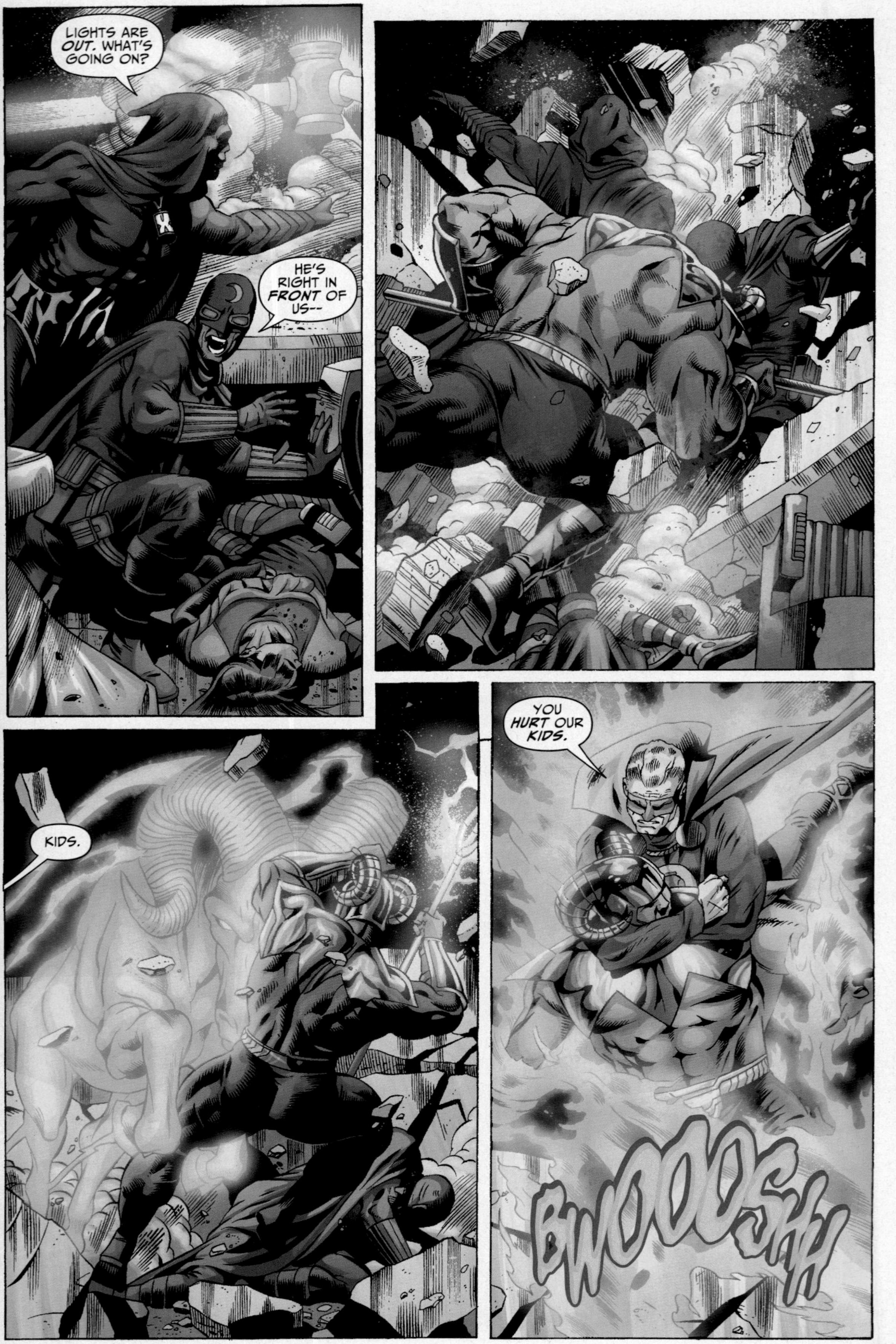
LIGHTS ARE OUT. WHAT'S GOING ON?
HE'S RIGHT IN FRONT OF US--
KIDS.
YOU HURT OUR KIDS.
BWOOOSH

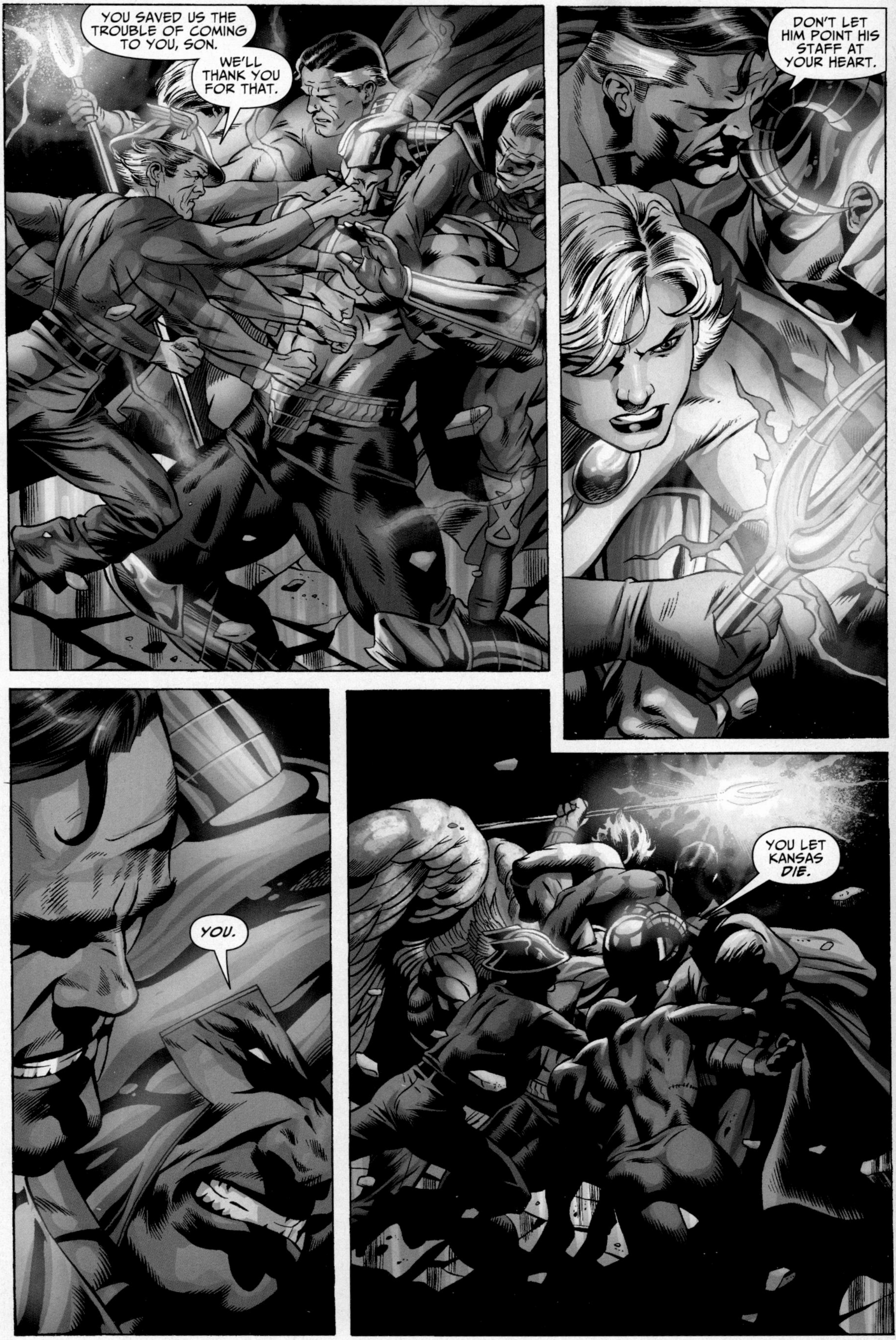
YOU SAVED US THE TROUBLE OF COMING TO YOU, SON.
WE'LL THANK YOU FOR THAT.
DON'T LET HIM POINT HIS STAFF AT YOUR HEART.
YOU.
YOU LET KANSAS DIE.

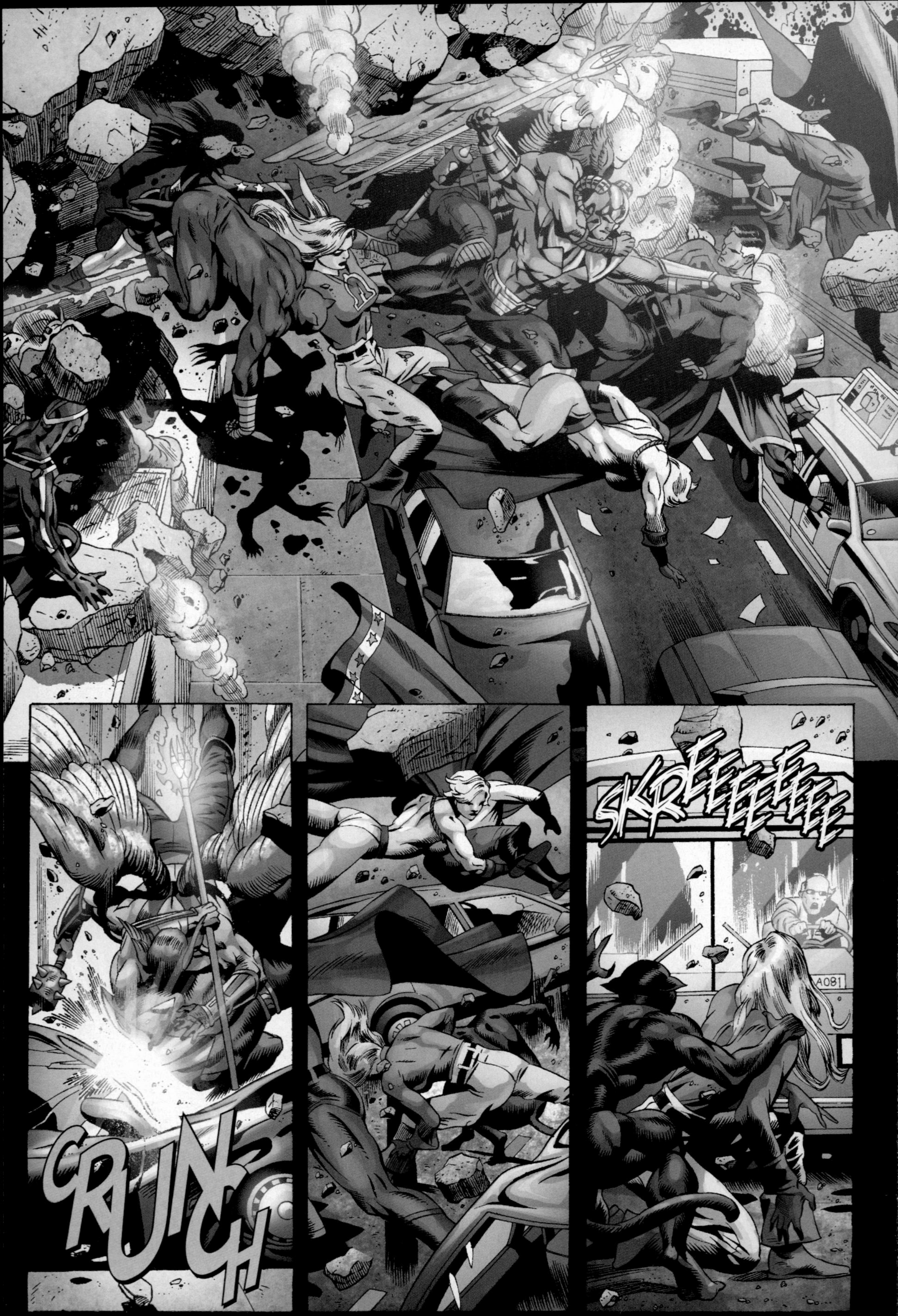

CRUNCH
SKREEEEEEEEEEEE
A081

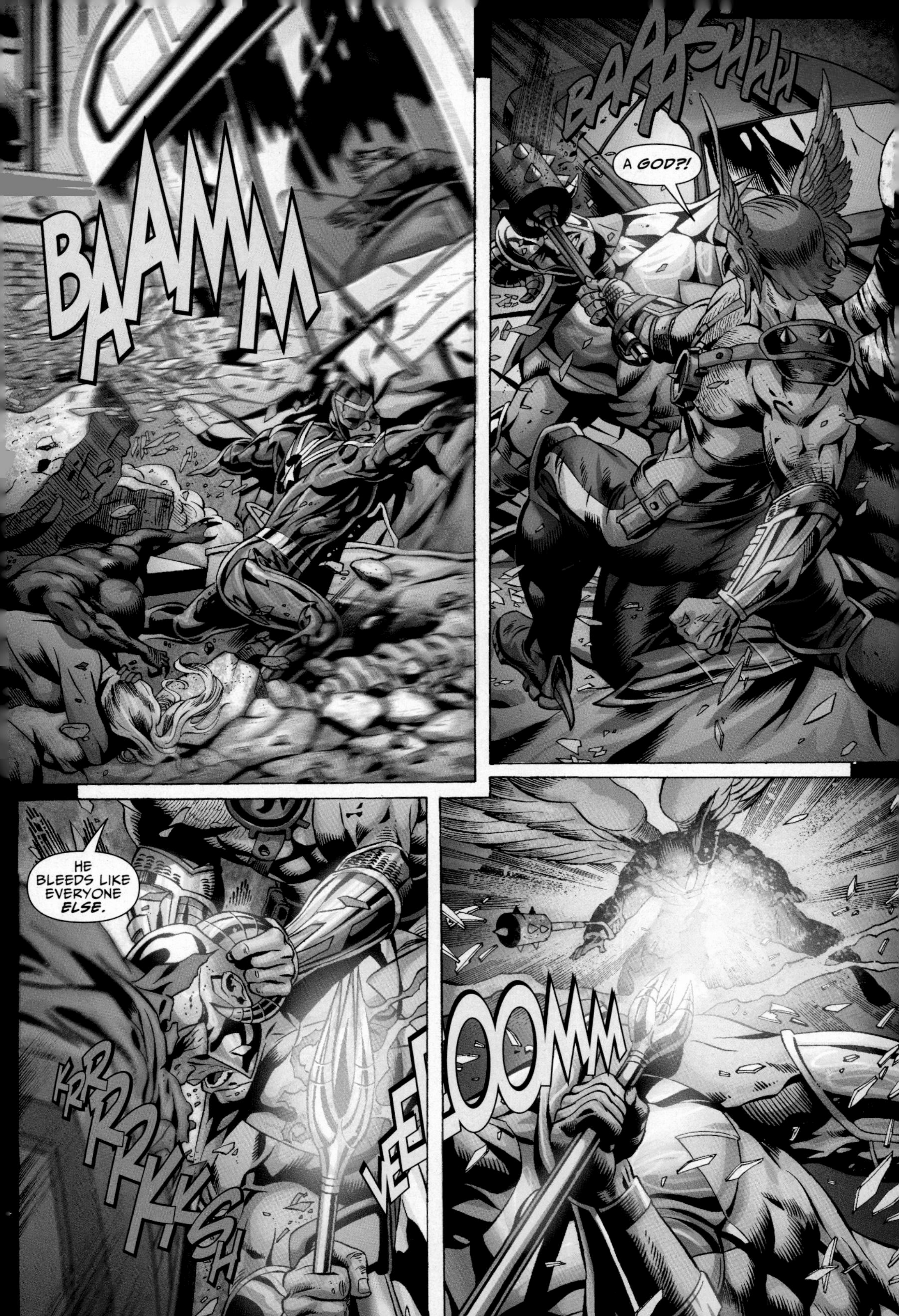
BAAMM
BAAASHHH
A GOD?!
HE BLEEDS LIKE EVERYONE *ELSE.*
KRRRKKSH
VEEZOOMM

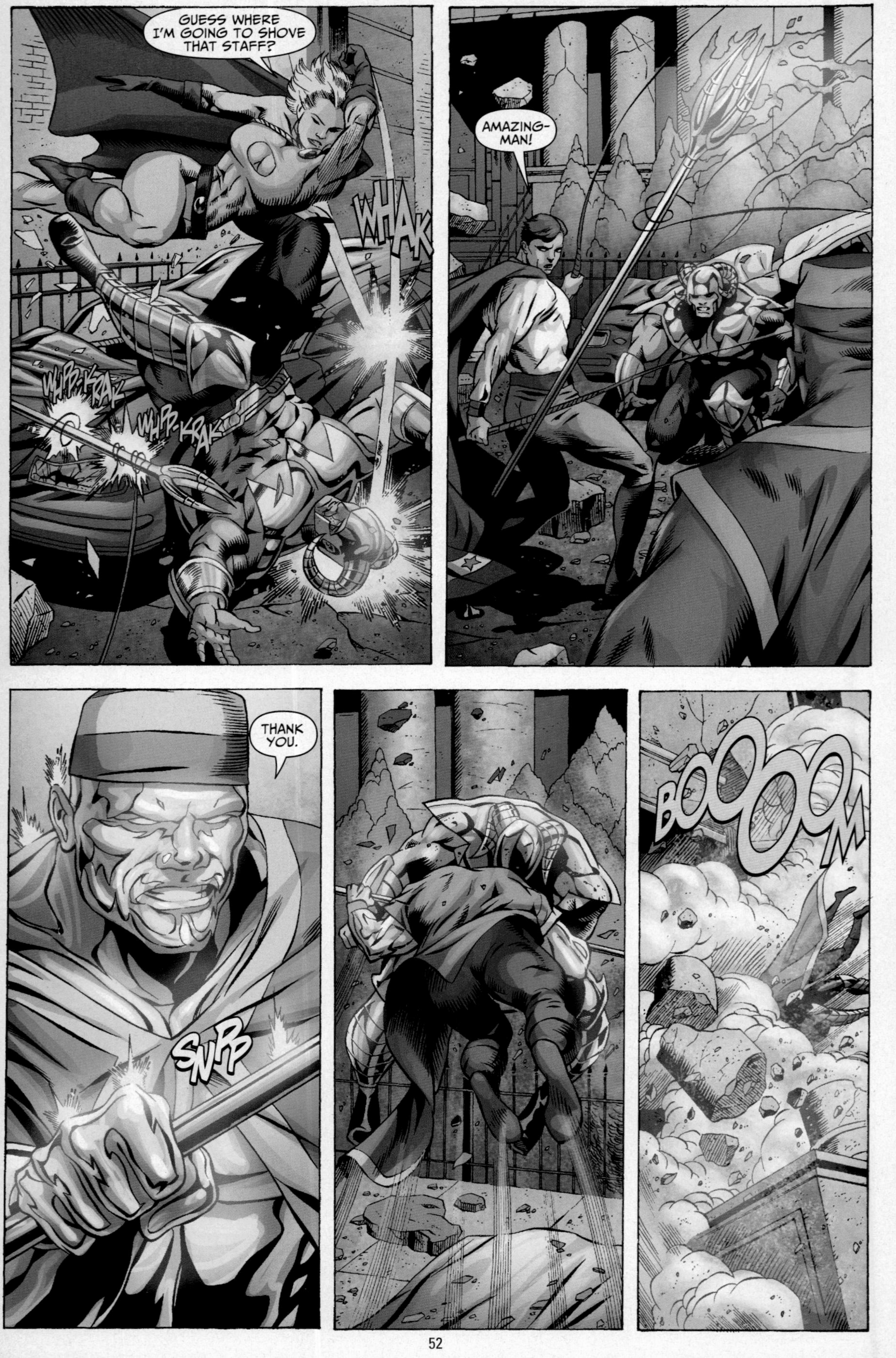
GUESS WHERE I'M GOING TO SHOVE THAT STAFF?
WHAK
WHPP-KRAK
WHPP-KRAK
AMAZING-MAN!
THANK YOU.
SNRP
BOOOOOM

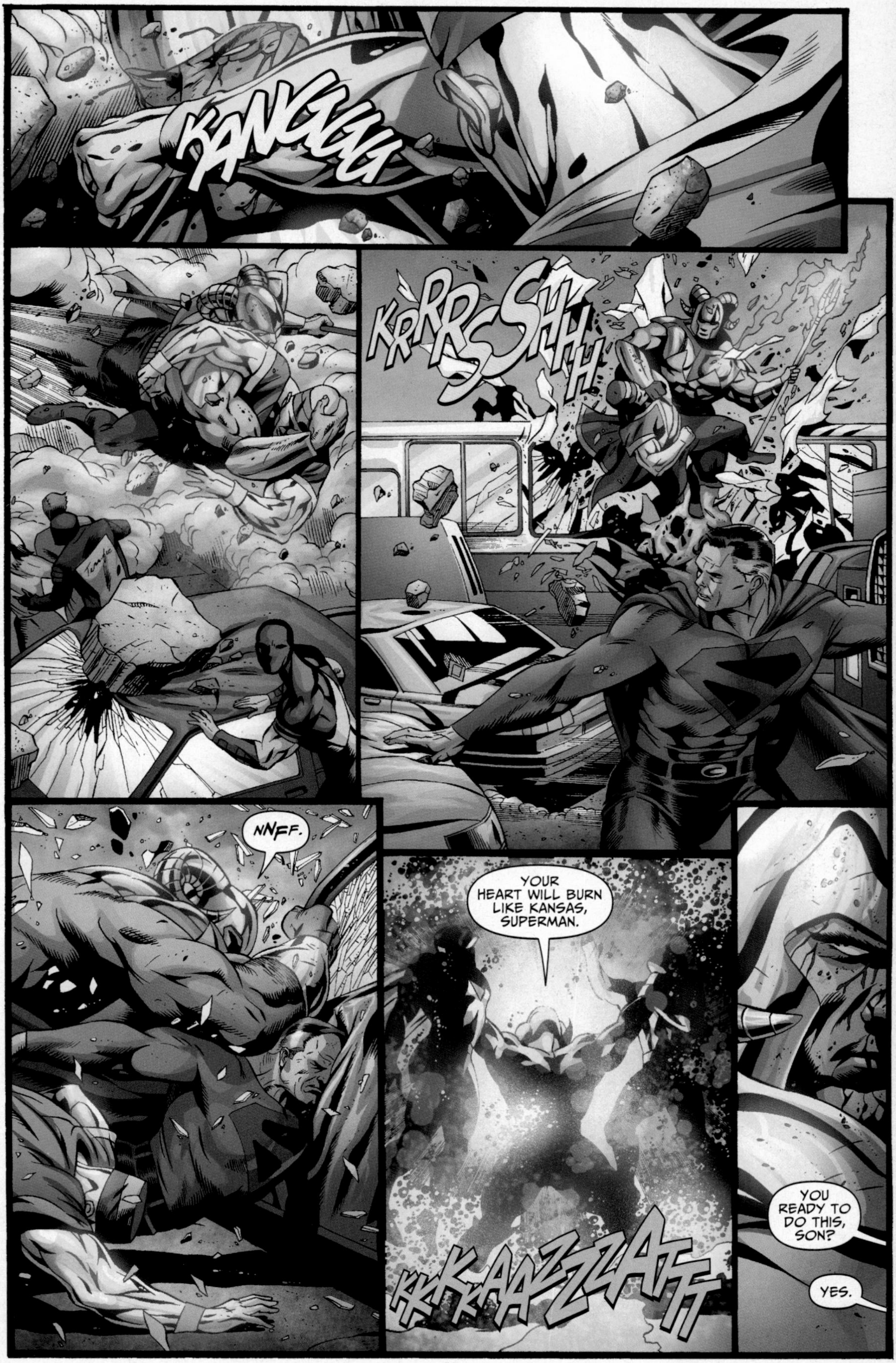
KANGGGG
KRRRSSHHH
NNFF.
YOUR HEART WILL BURN LIKE KANSAS, SUPERMAN.
KKKKAAZZZZAATTT
YOU READY TO DO THIS, SON?
YES.

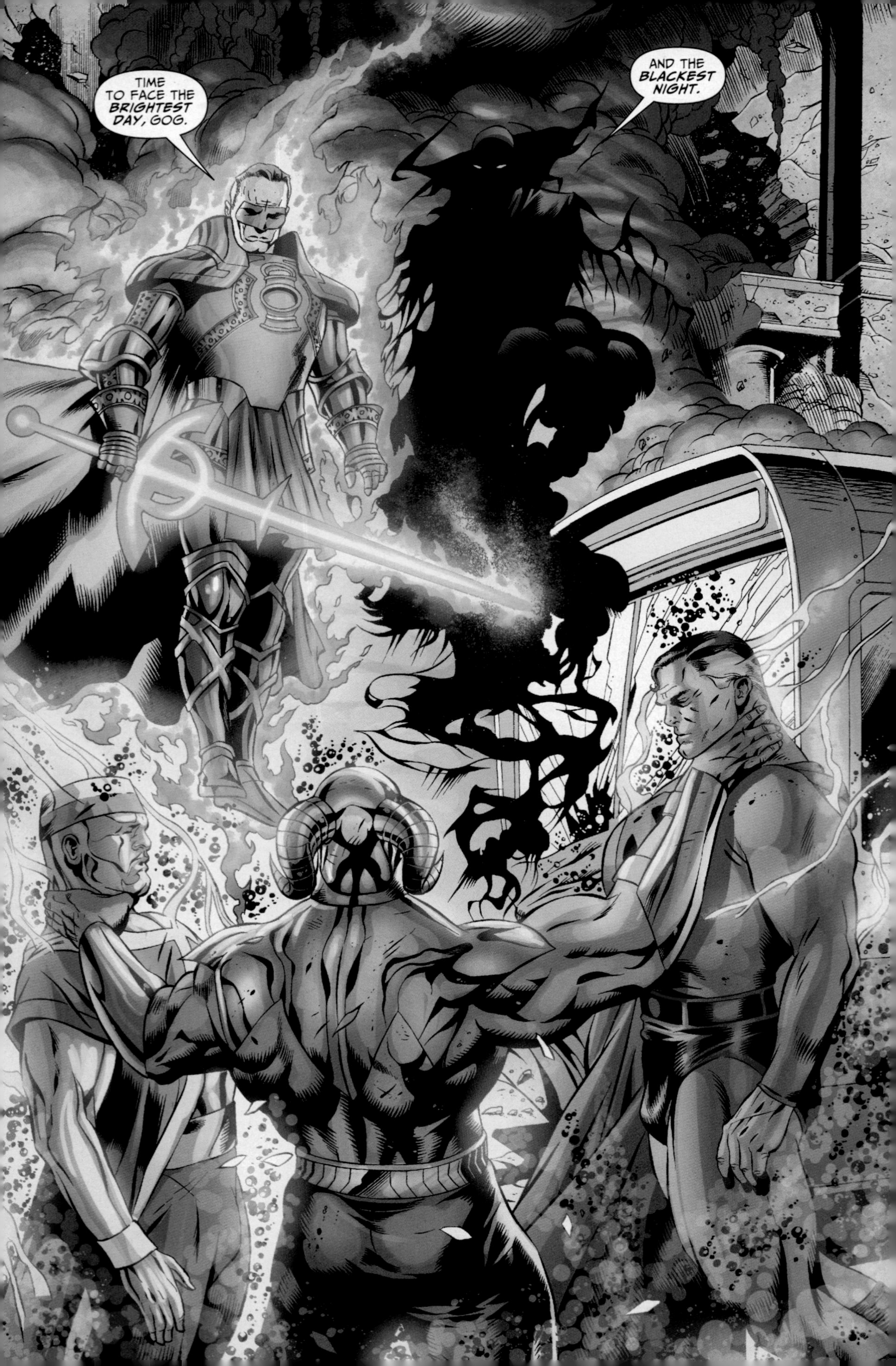
TIME TO FACE THE BRIGHTEST DAY, GOG.
AND THE BLACKEST NIGHT.

JUSTICE SOCIETY OF AMERICA #13 COVER A by Alex Ross

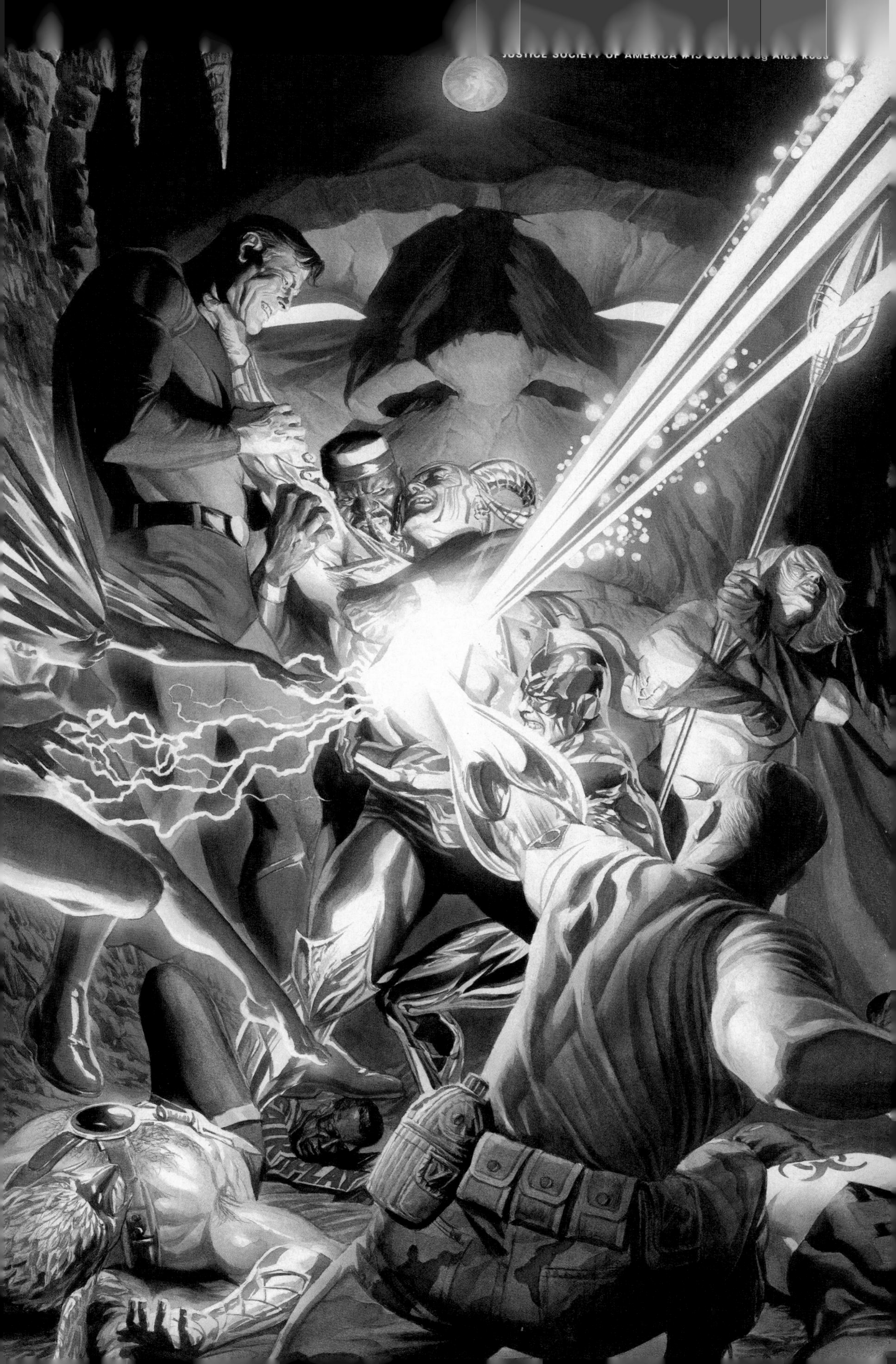

JUSTICE SOCIETY OF AMERICA #15 cover B and interior art by **Dale Eaglesham & Prentis Rollins**

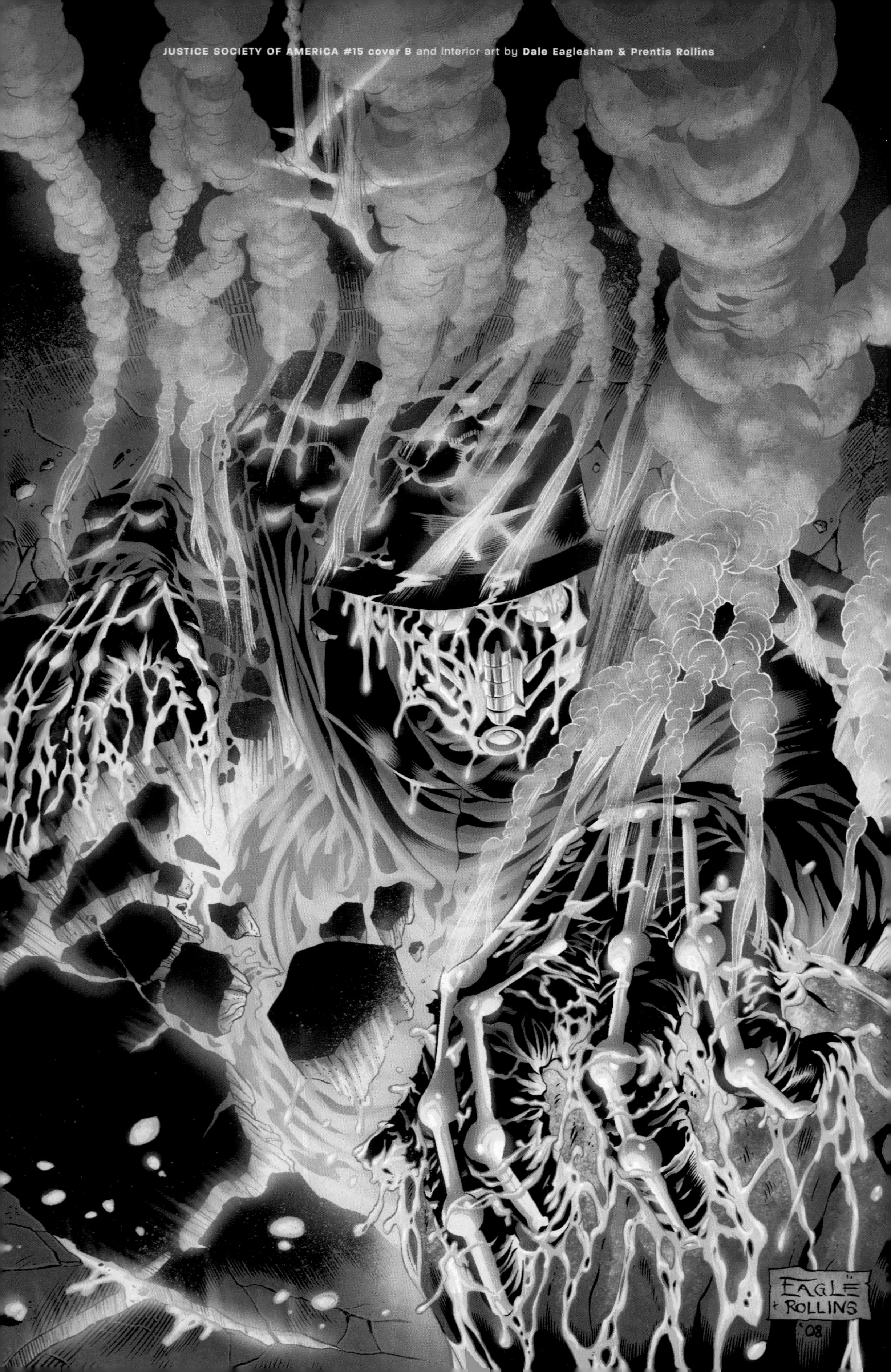
EAGLE
+ ROLLINS
'08

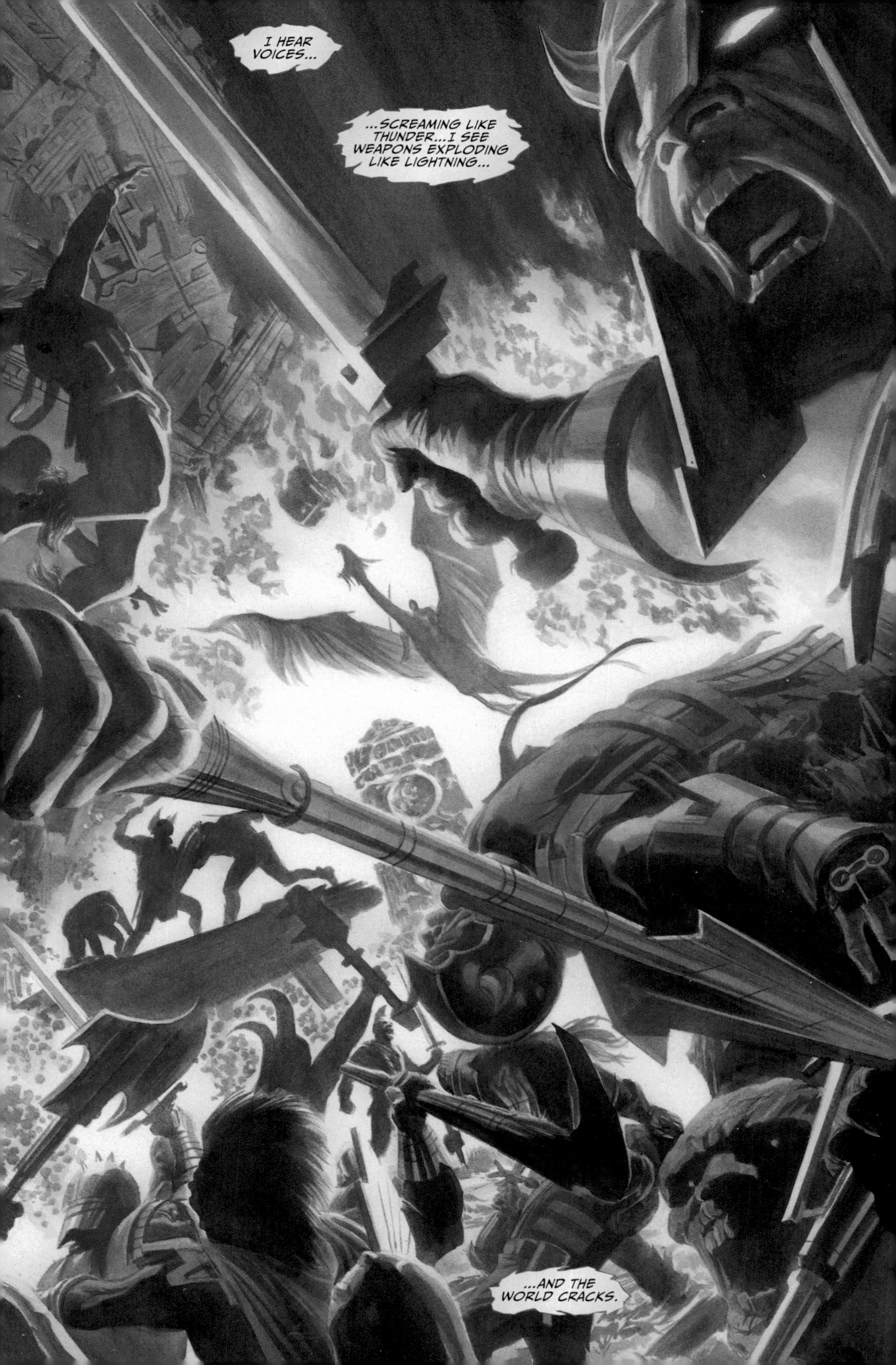
I HEAR VOICES...
...SCREAMING LIKE THUNDER...I SEE WEAPONS EXPLODING LIKE LIGHTNING...
...AND THE WORLD CRACKS.

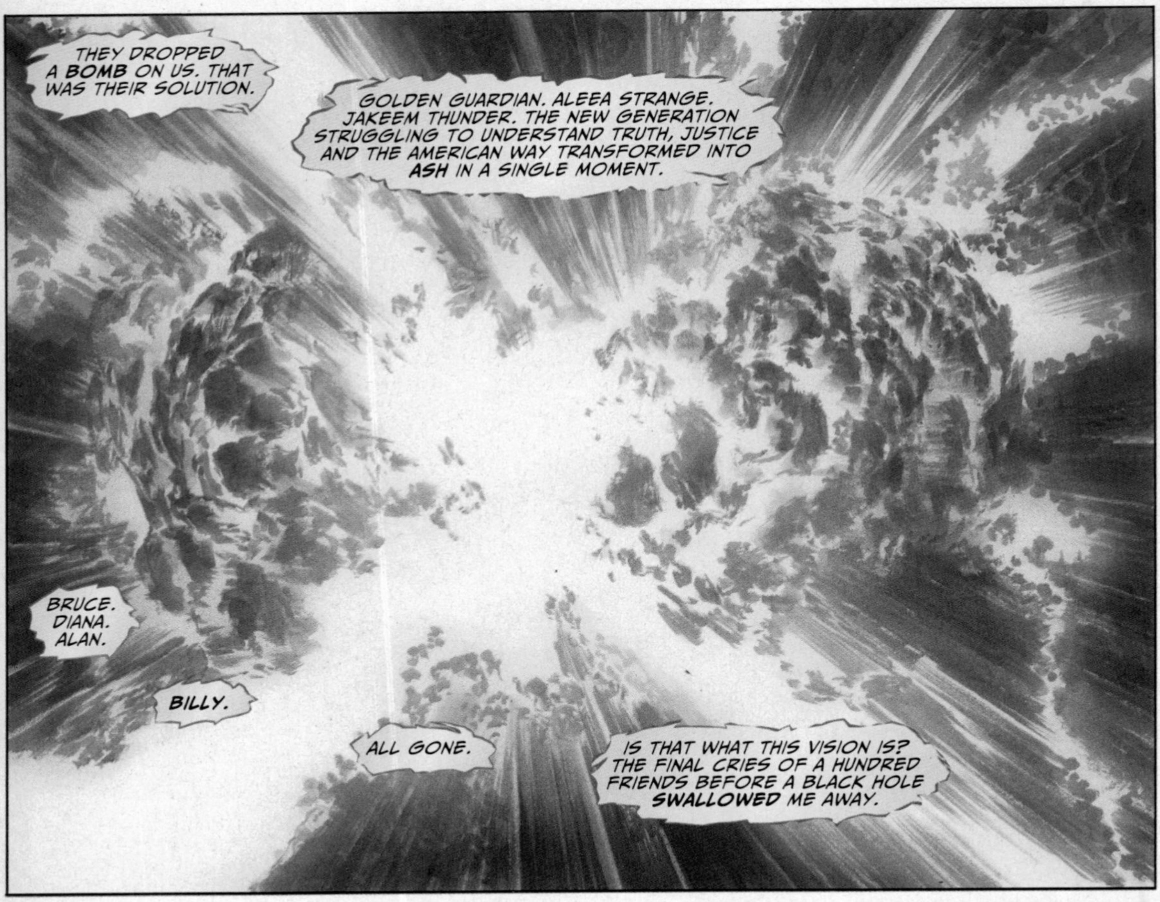
THEY DROPPED A BOMB ON US. THAT WAS THEIR SOLUTION.
GOLDEN GUARDIAN. ALEEA STRANGE. JAKEEM THUNDER. THE NEW GENERATION STRUGGLING TO UNDERSTAND TRUTH, JUSTICE AND THE AMERICAN WAY TRANSFORMED INTO ASH IN A SINGLE MOMENT.
BRUCE. DIANA. ALAN.
BILLY.
ALL GONE.
IS THAT WHAT THIS VISION IS? THE FINAL CRIES OF A HUNDRED FRIENDS BEFORE A BLACK HOLE SWALLOWED ME AWAY.

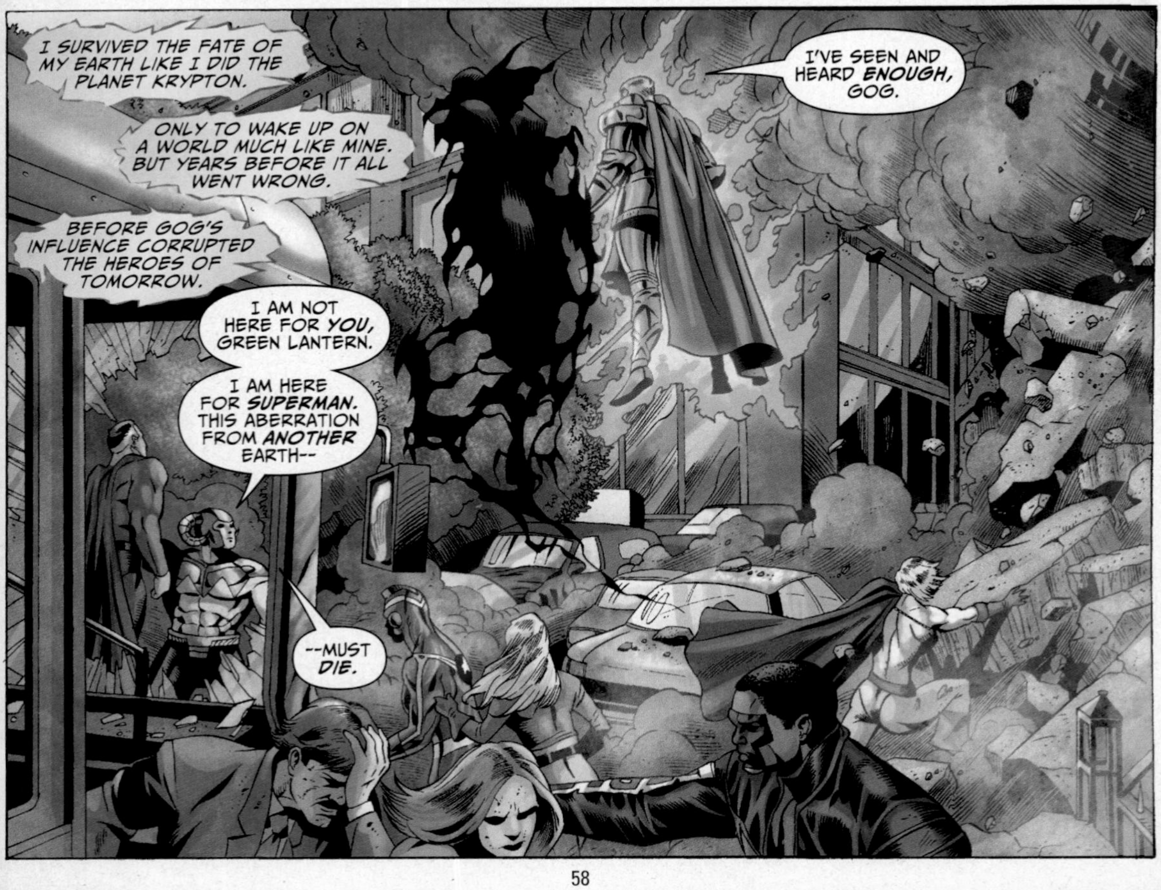
I SURVIVED THE FATE OF MY EARTH LIKE I DID THE PLANET KRYPTON.
ONLY TO WAKE UP ON A WORLD MUCH LIKE MINE. BUT YEARS BEFORE IT ALL WENT WRONG.
BEFORE GOG'S INFLUENCE CORRUPTED THE HEROES OF TOMORROW.
I'VE SEEN AND HEARD ENOUGH, GOG.
I AM NOT HERE FOR YOU, GREEN LANTERN.
I AM HERE FOR SUPERMAN. THIS ABERRATION FROM ANOTHER EARTH--
--MUST DIE.

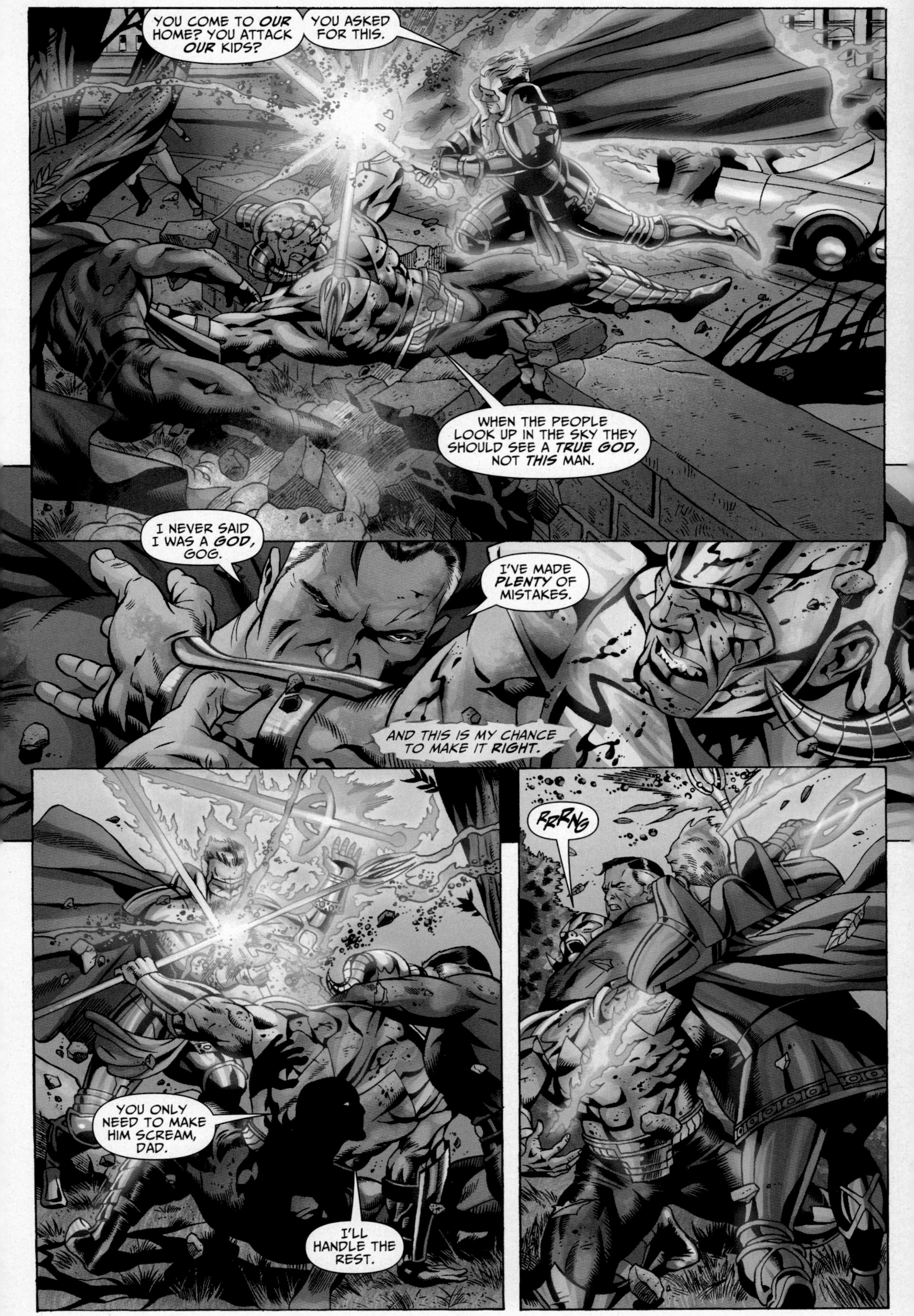
YOU COME TO OUR HOME? YOU ATTACK OUR KIDS?
YOU ASKED FOR THIS.
WHEN THE PEOPLE LOOK UP IN THE SKY THEY SHOULD SEE A TRUE GOD, NOT THIS MAN.
I NEVER SAID I WAS A GOD, GOG.
I'VE MADE PLENTY OF MISTAKES.
AND THIS IS MY CHANCE TO MAKE IT RIGHT.
YOU ONLY NEED TO MAKE HIM SCREAM, DAD.
I'LL HANDLE THE REST.
RRRNG

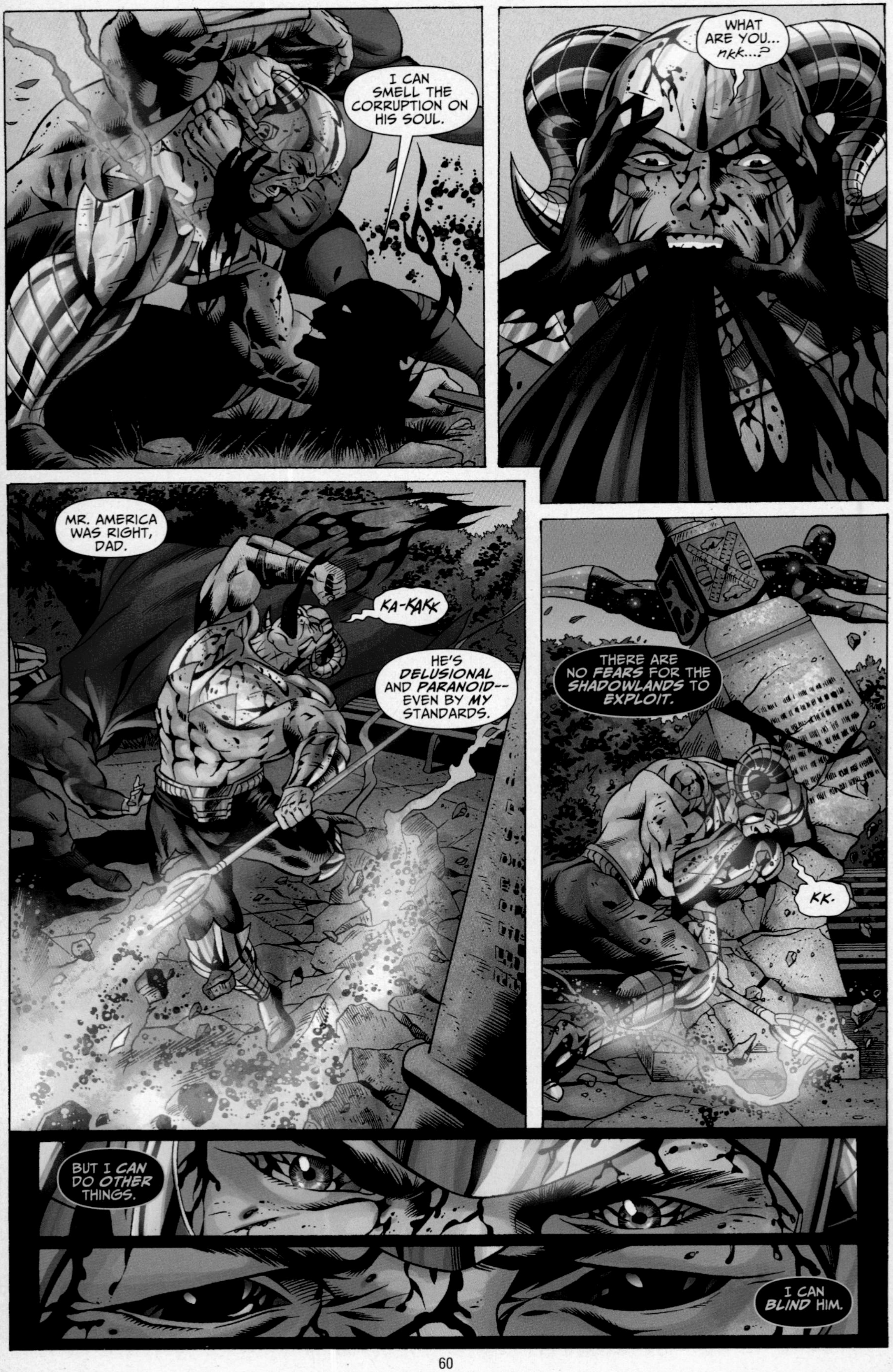
I CAN SMELL THE CORRUPTION ON HIS SOUL.
WHAT ARE YOU... nkk...?
MR. AMERICA WAS RIGHT, DAD.
KA-KAKK
HE'S DELUSIONAL AND PARANOID-- EVEN BY MY STANDARDS.
THERE ARE NO FEARS FOR THE SHADOWLANDS TO EXPLOIT.
KK.
BUT I CAN DO OTHER THINGS.
I CAN BLIND HIM.

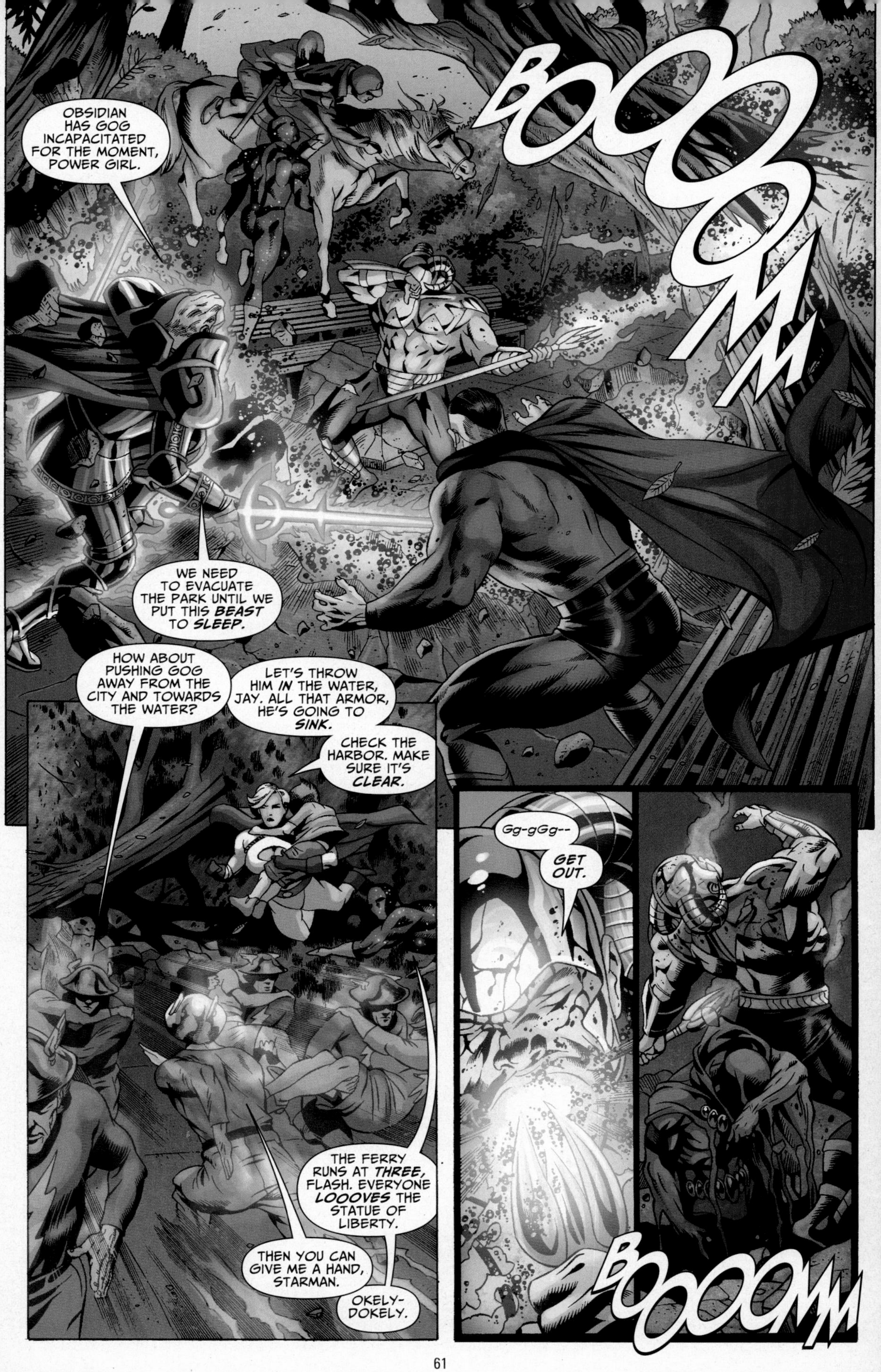
BOOOOMM
OBSIDIAN HAS GOG INCAPACITATED FOR THE MOMENT, POWER GIRL.
WE NEED TO EVACUATE THE PARK UNTIL WE PUT THIS BEAST TO SLEEP.
HOW ABOUT PUSHING GOG AWAY FROM THE CITY AND TOWARDS THE WATER?
LET'S THROW HIM IN THE WATER, JAY. ALL THAT ARMOR, HE'S GOING TO SINK.
CHECK THE HARBOR. MAKE SURE IT'S CLEAR.
THE FERRY RUNS AT THREE, FLASH. EVERYONE LOOOVES THE STATUE OF LIBERTY.
THEN YOU CAN GIVE ME A HAND, STARMAN.
OKELY-DOKELY.
Gg-gGg--
GET OUT.
BOOOOMM

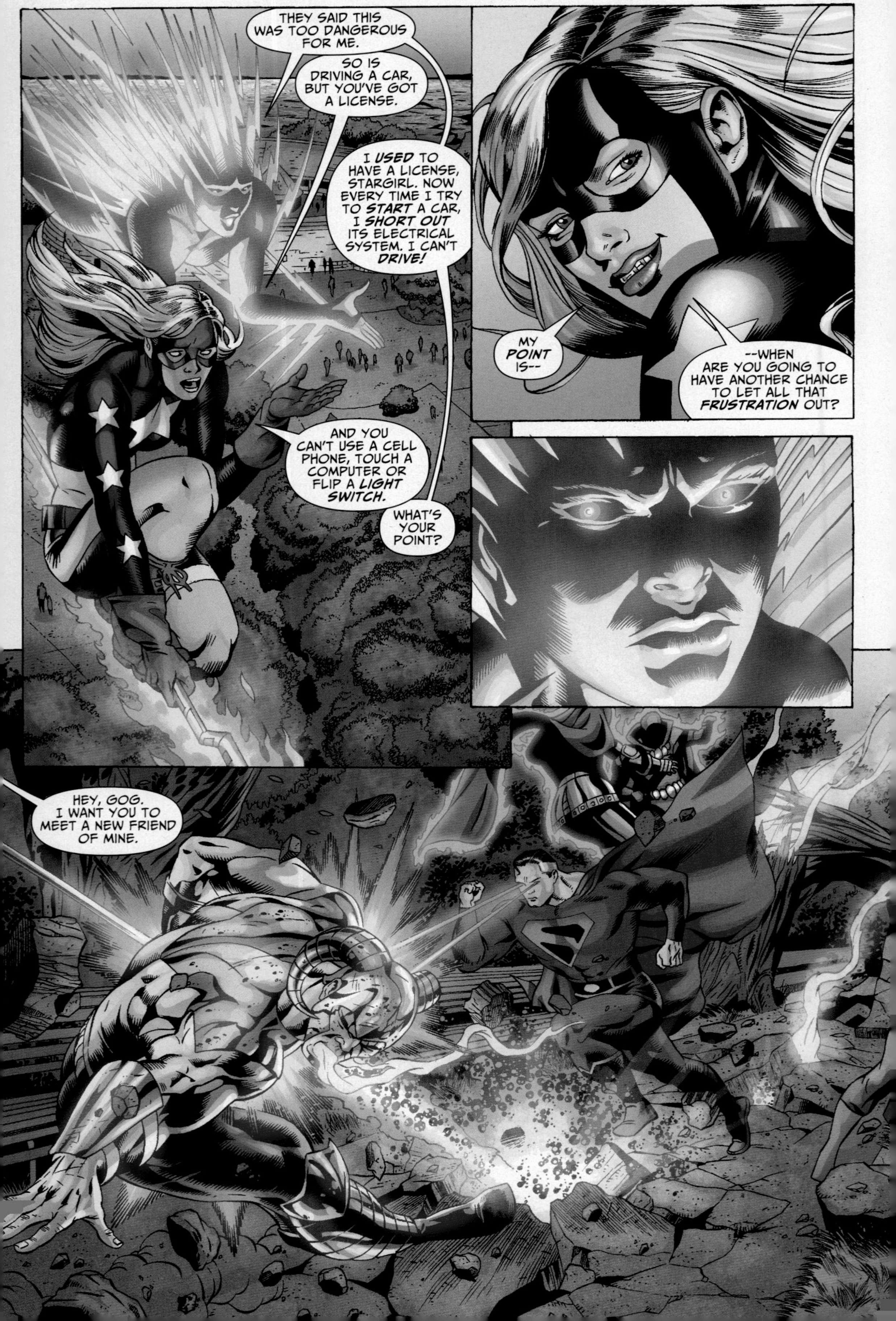

THEY SAID THIS WAS TOO DANGEROUS FOR ME.
SO IS DRIVING A CAR, BUT YOU'VE GOT A LICENSE.
I USED TO HAVE A LICENSE, STARGIRL. NOW EVERY TIME I TRY TO START A CAR, I SHORT OUT ITS ELECTRICAL SYSTEM. I CAN'T DRIVE!
AND YOU CAN'T USE A CELL PHONE, TOUCH A COMPUTER OR FLIP A LIGHT SWITCH.
WHAT'S YOUR POINT?
MY POINT IS--
--WHEN ARE YOU GOING TO HAVE ANOTHER CHANCE TO LET ALL THAT FRUSTRATION OUT?
HEY, GOG. I WANT YOU TO MEET A NEW FRIEND OF MINE.

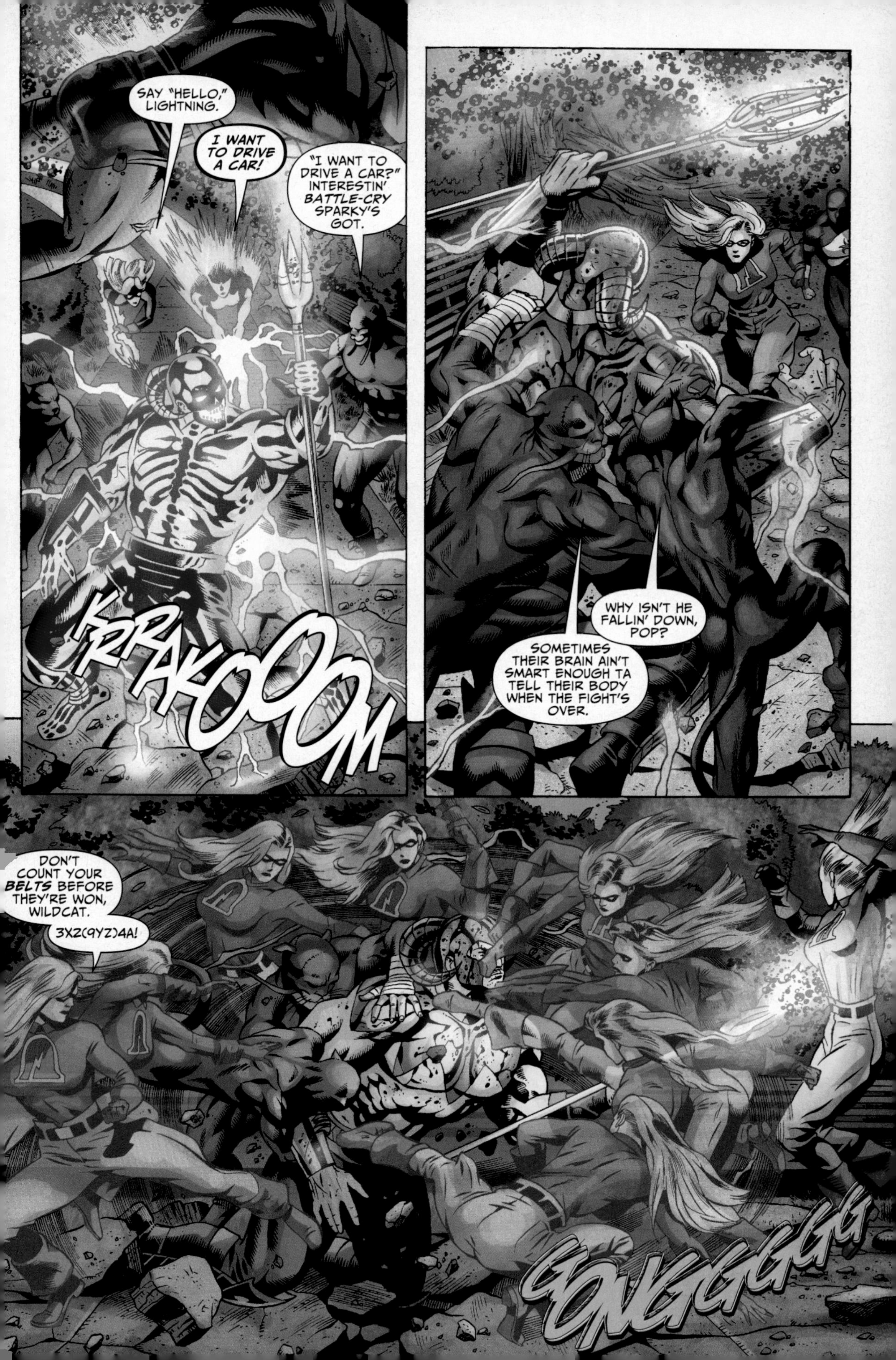
SAY "HELLO," LIGHTNING.
I WANT TO DRIVE A CAR!
"I WANT TO DRIVE A CAR?" INTERESTIN' BATTLE-CRY SPARKY'S GOT.
KRRAKOOOOM
WHY ISN'T HE FALLIN' DOWN, POP?
SOMETIMES THEIR BRAIN AIN'T SMART ENOUGH TA TELL THEIR BODY WHEN THE FIGHT'S OVER.
DON'T COUNT YOUR BELTS BEFORE THEY'RE WON, WILDCAT.
3X2(9YZ)4A!
GONGGGGG

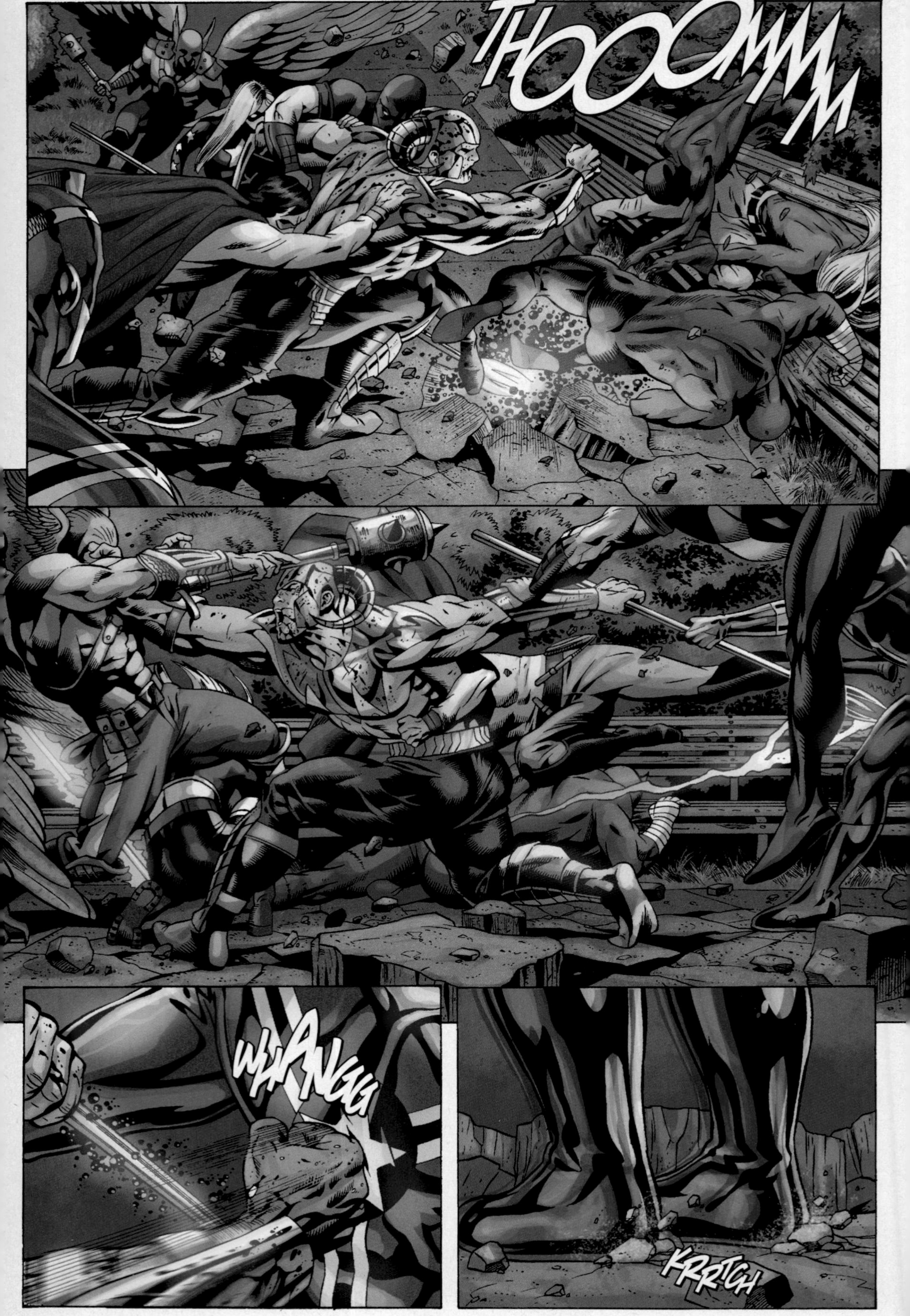
THOOOMMM
WHANGG
KRRTCH

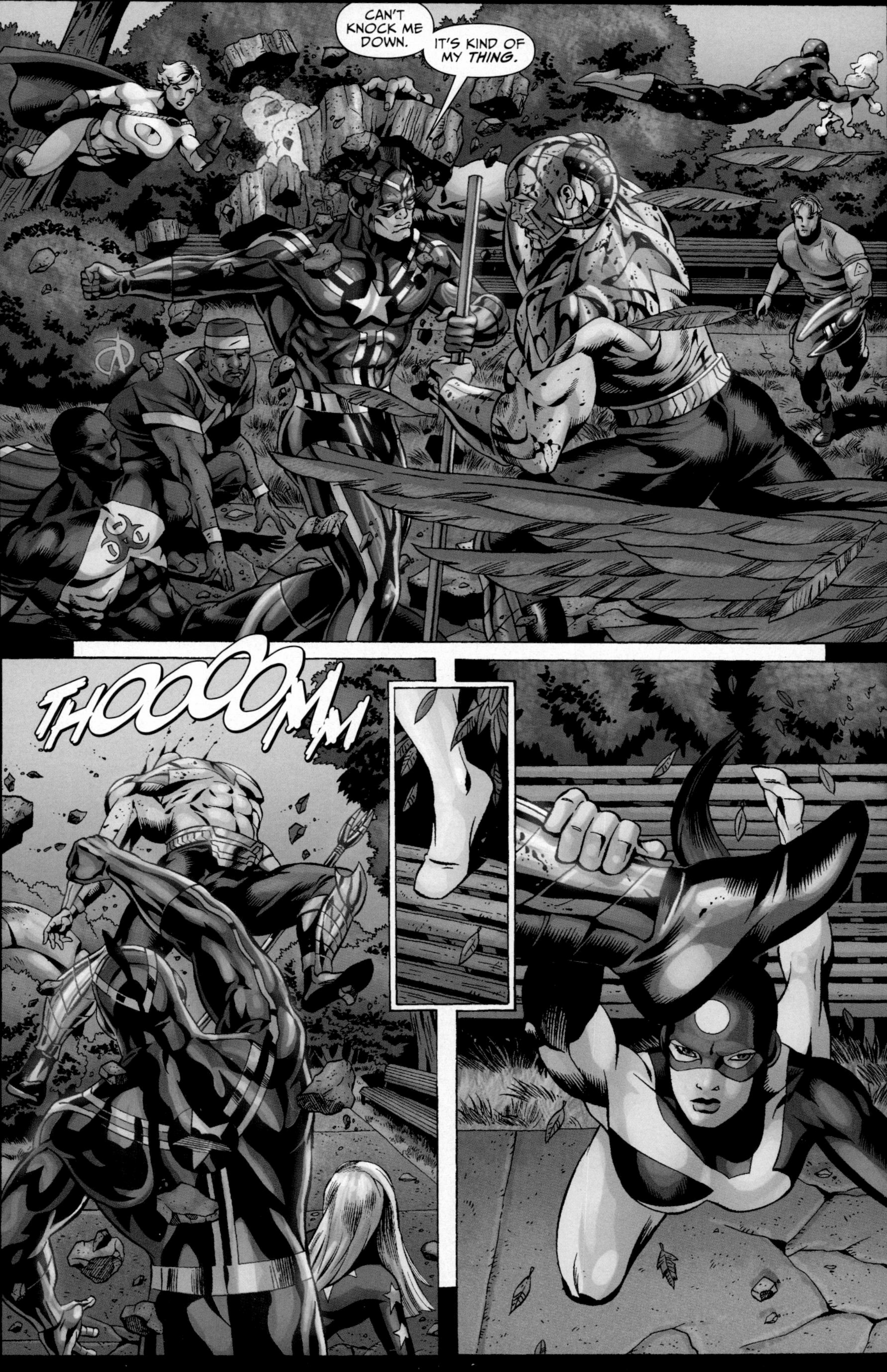
CAN'T KNOCK ME DOWN.
IT'S KIND OF MY THING.
THOOOOMM

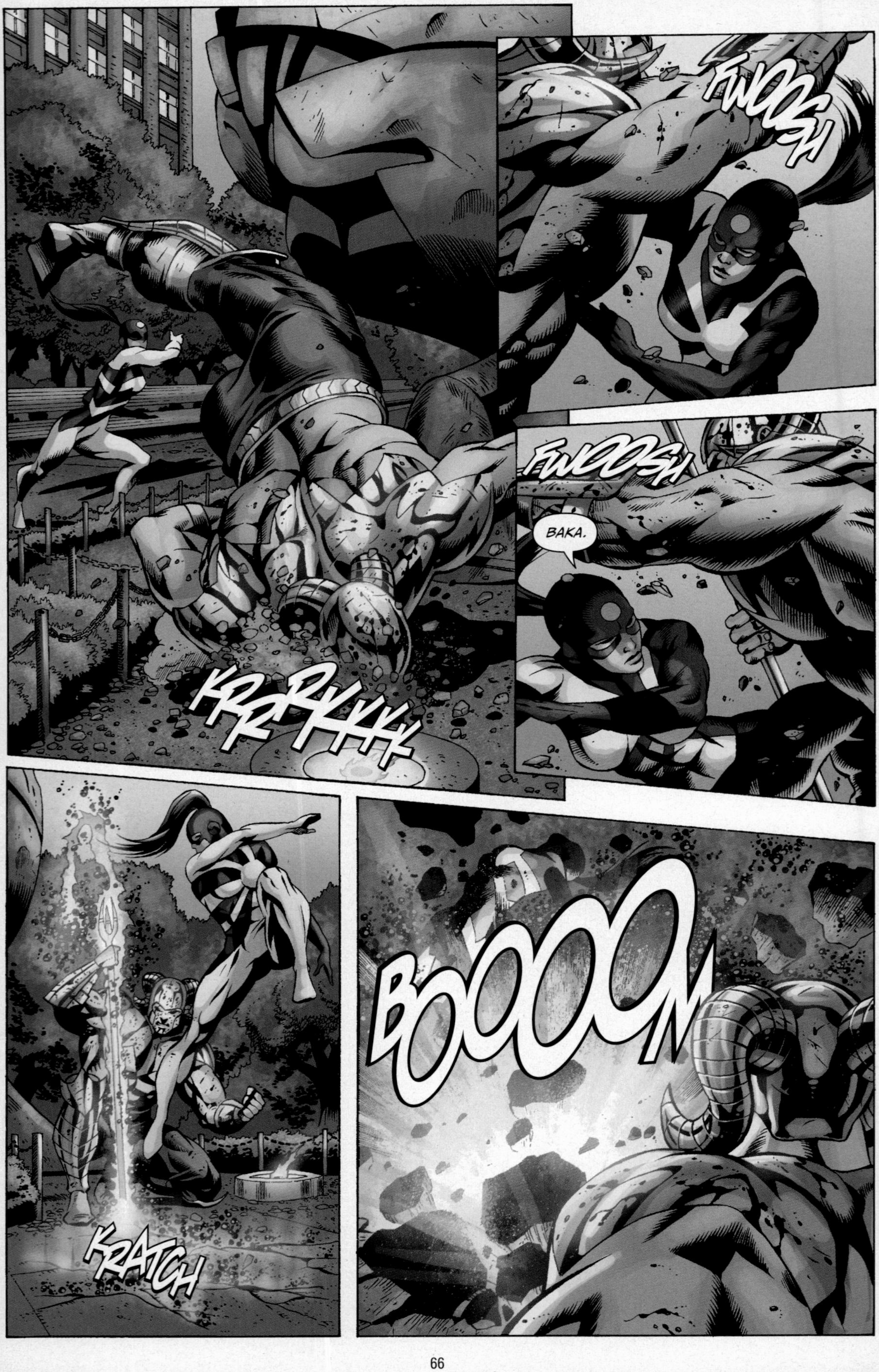
FWOOSH
KRRRKKKK
FWOOSH
BAKA.
KRATCH
BOOOOM

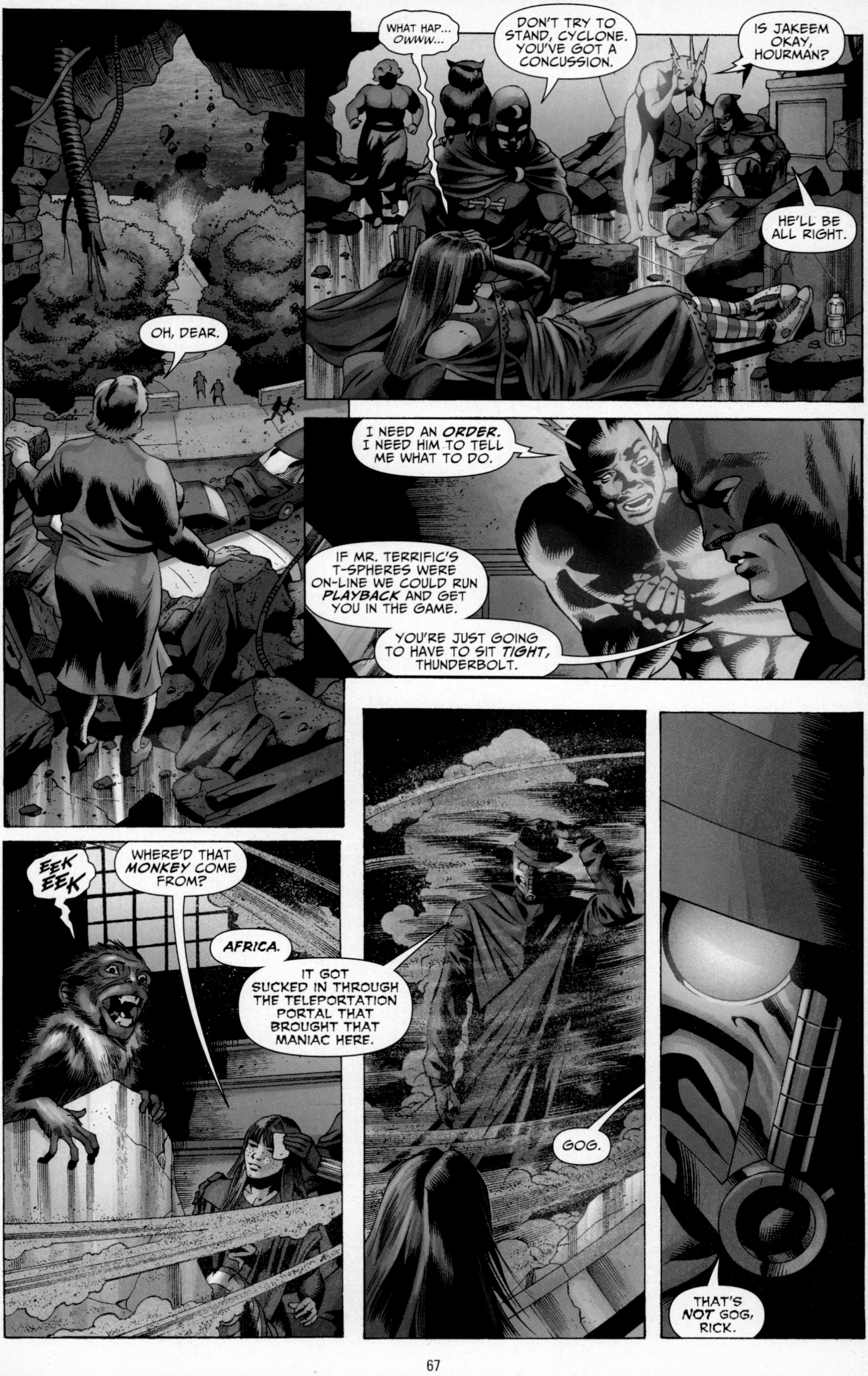

OH, DEAR.
WHAT HAP... OWWW...
DON'T TRY TO STAND, CYCLONE. YOU'VE GOT A CONCUSSION.
IS JAKEEM OKAY, HOURMAN?
HE'LL BE ALL RIGHT.
I NEED AN ORDER. I NEED HIM TO TELL ME WHAT TO DO.
IF MR. TERRIFIC'S T-SPHERES WERE ON-LINE WE COULD RUN PLAYBACK AND GET YOU IN THE GAME.
YOU'RE JUST GOING TO HAVE TO SIT TIGHT, THUNDERBOLT.
EEK EEK
WHERE'D THAT MONKEY COME FROM?
AFRICA.
IT GOT SUCKED IN THROUGH THE TELEPORTATION PORTAL THAT BROUGHT THAT MANIAC HERE.
GOG.
THAT'S NOT GOG, RICK.

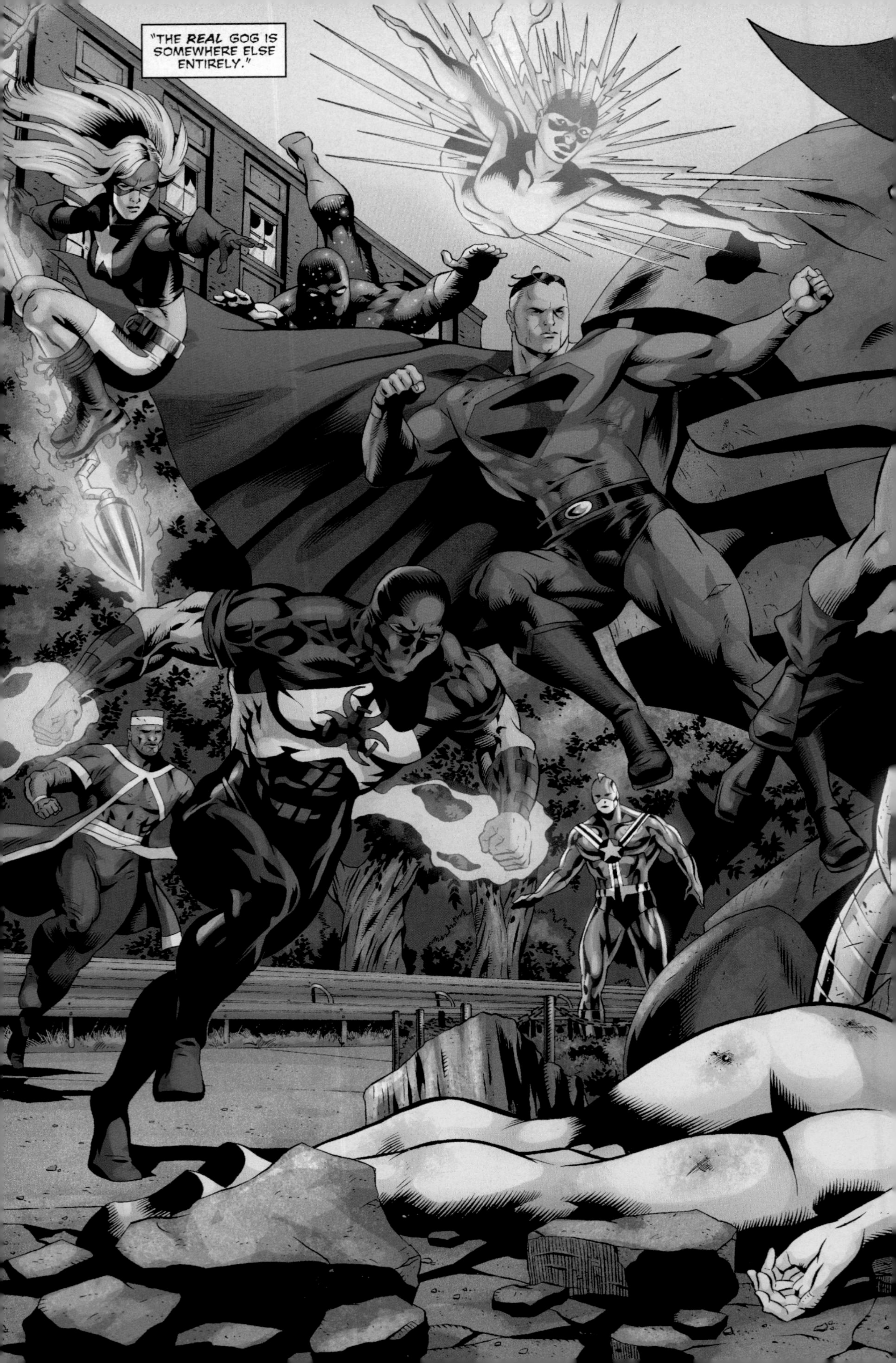
"THE REAL GOG IS SOMEWHERE ELSE ENTIRELY."

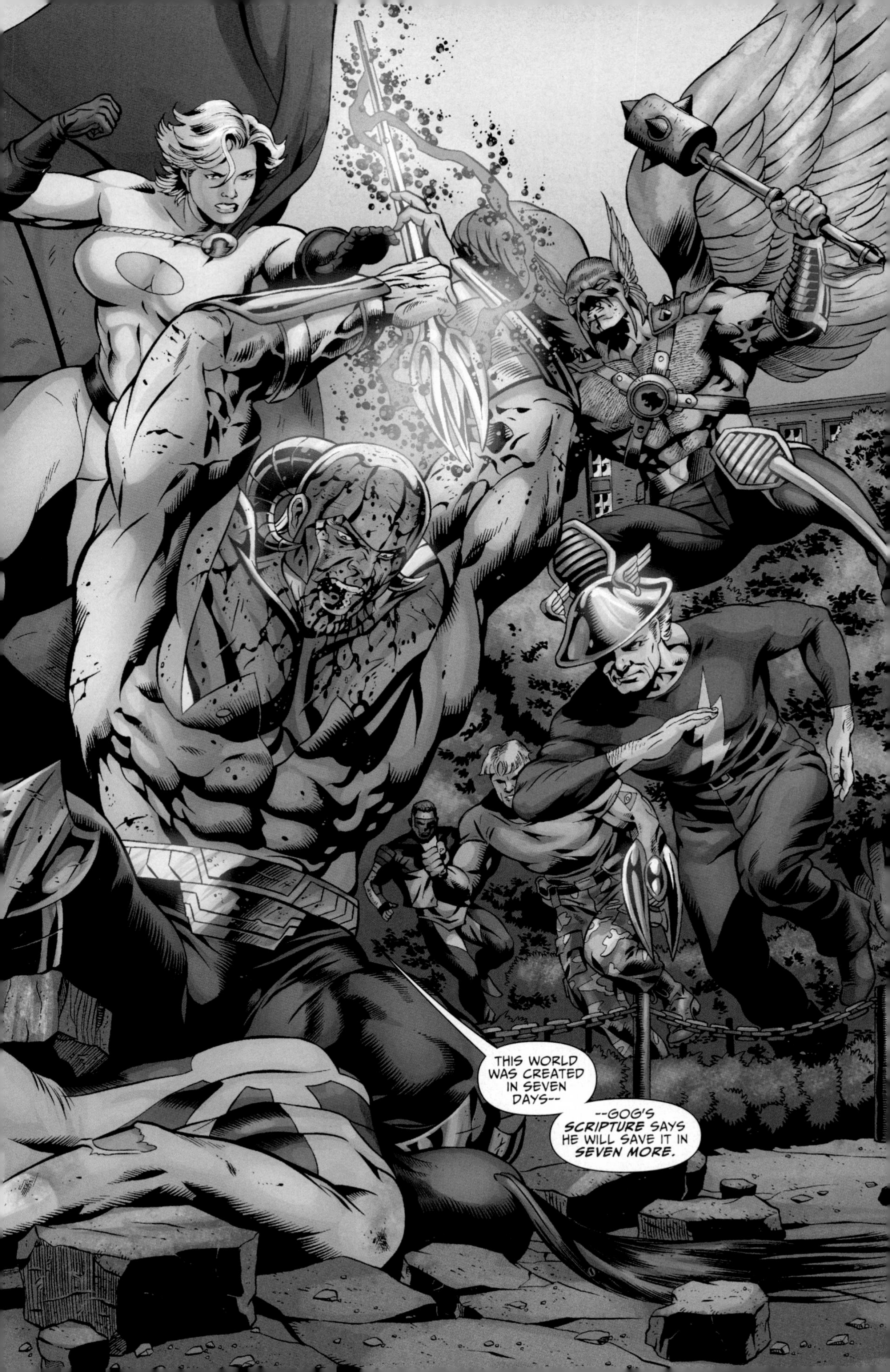
THIS WORLD WAS CREATED IN SEVEN DAYS--
--GOG'S **SCRIPTURE** SAYS HE WILL SAVE IT IN **SEVEN MORE.**

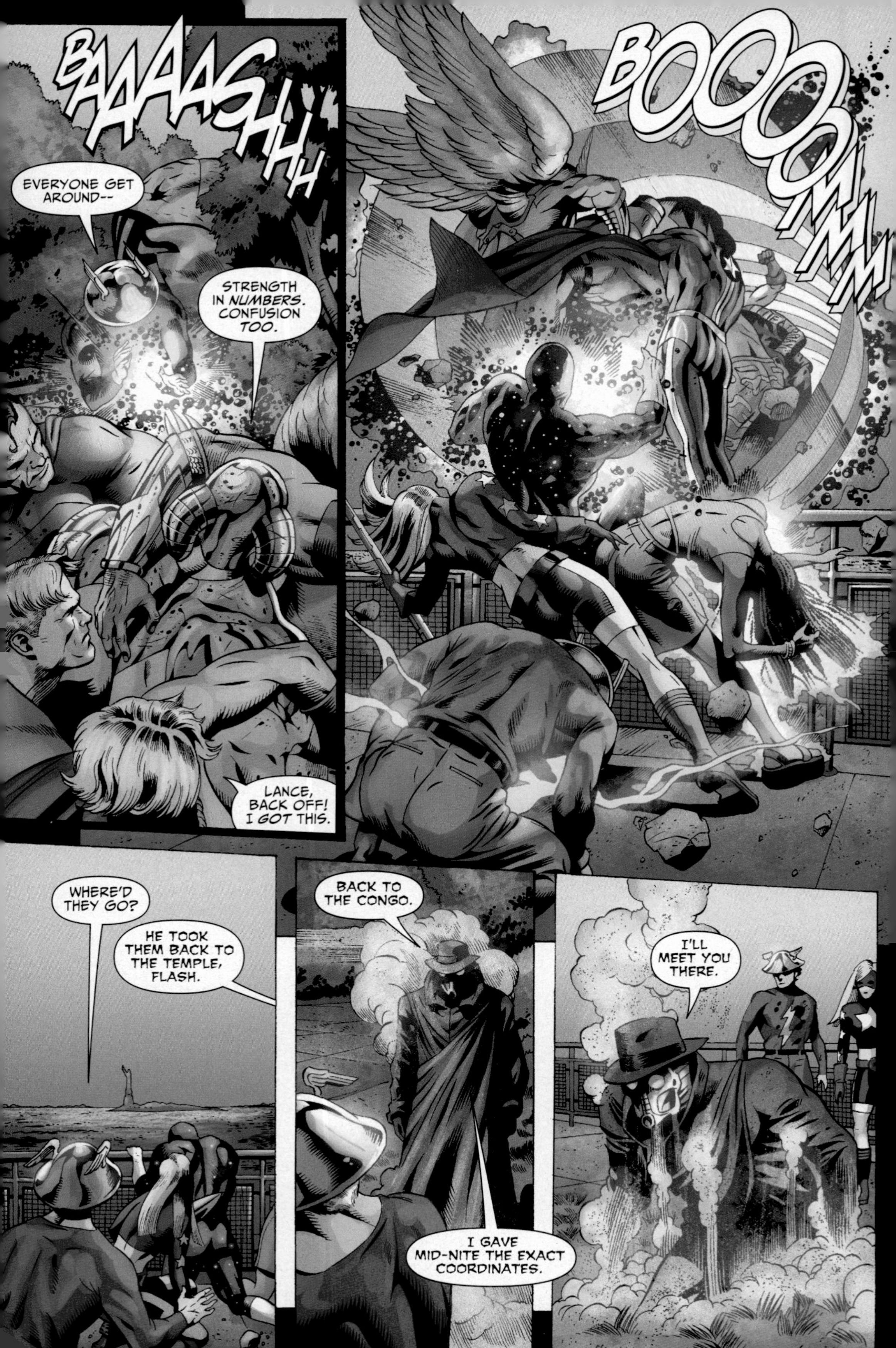
BAAAASHHH
EVERYONE GET AROUND--
STRENGTH IN NUMBERS. CONFUSION TOO.
LANCE, BACK OFF! I GOT THIS.
BOOOOMMM
WHERE'D THEY GO?
HE TOOK THEM BACK TO THE TEMPLE, FLASH.
BACK TO THE CONGO.
I GAVE MID-NITE THE EXACT COORDINATES.
I'LL MEET YOU THERE.

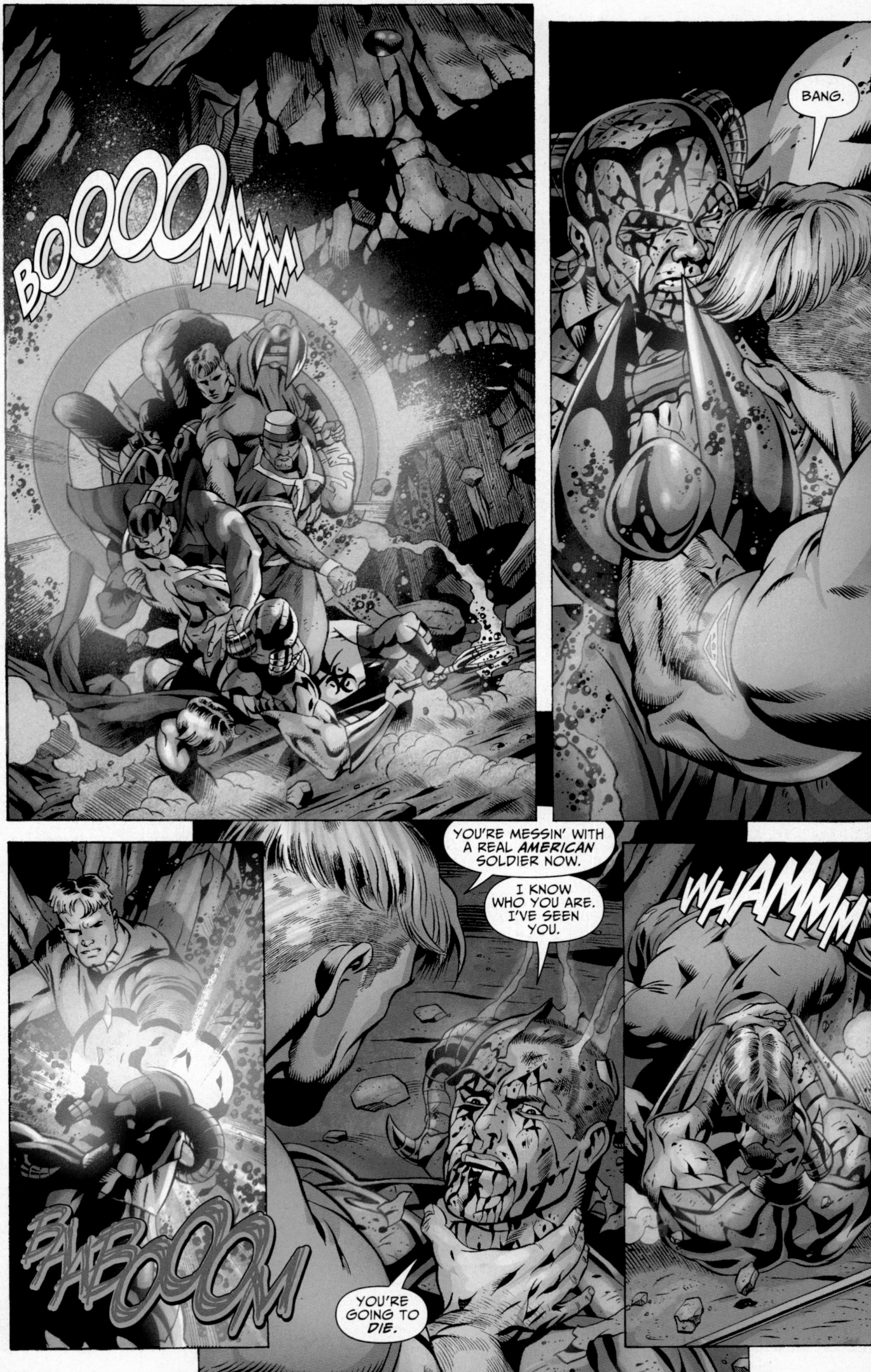
BOOOOMMMM
BANG.
BABOOOM
YOU'RE MESSIN' WITH A REAL AMERICAN SOLDIER NOW.
I KNOW WHO YOU ARE. I'VE SEEN YOU.
YOU'RE GOING TO DIE.
WHAMMM

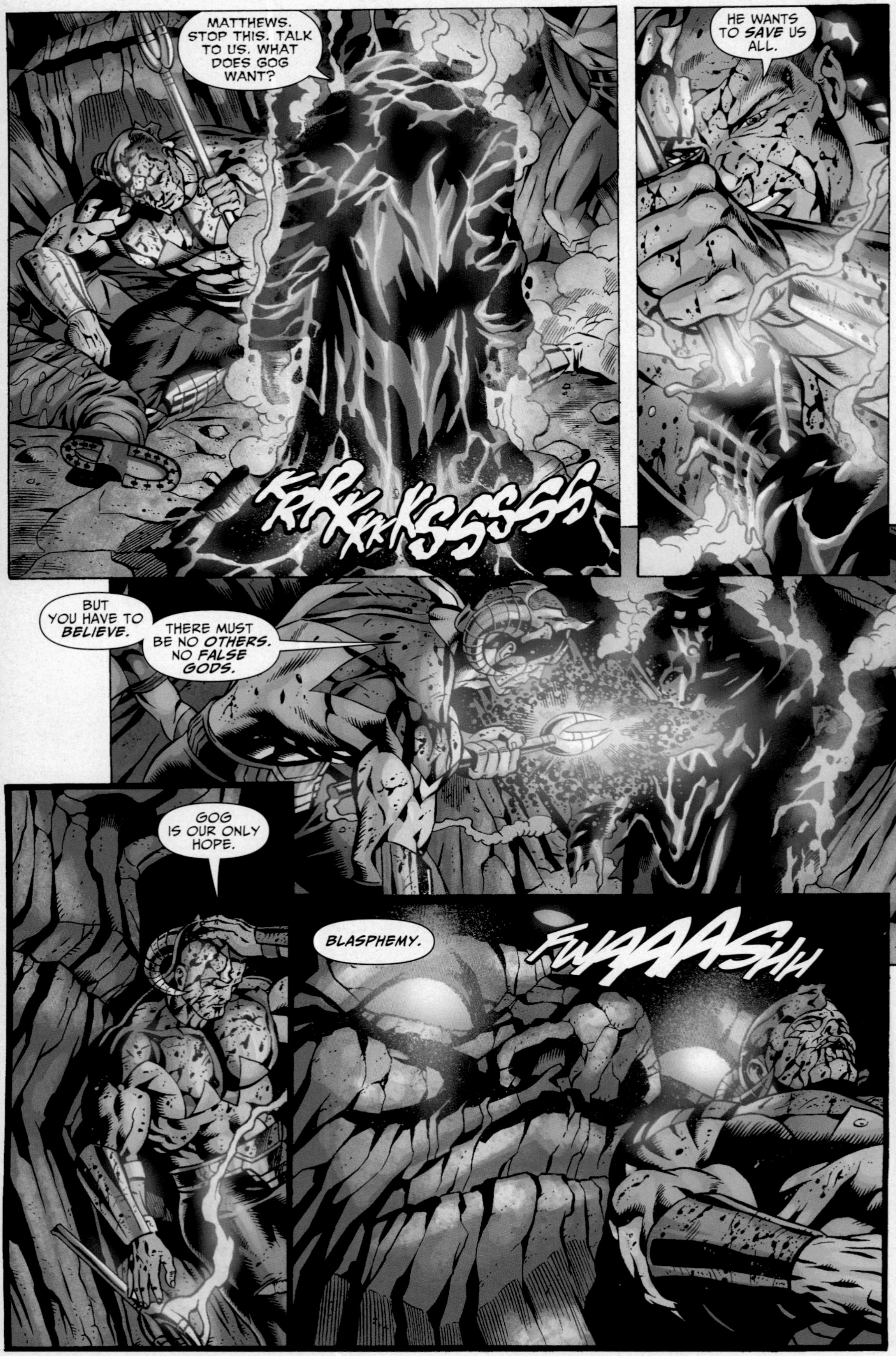
MATTHEWS. STOP THIS. TALK TO US. WHAT DOES GOG WANT?
KRRKKKSSSSSS
HE WANTS TO SAVE US ALL.
BUT YOU HAVE TO BELIEVE.
THERE MUST BE NO OTHERS. NO FALSE GODS.
GOG IS OUR ONLY HOPE.
BLASPHEMY.
FWAAASHH

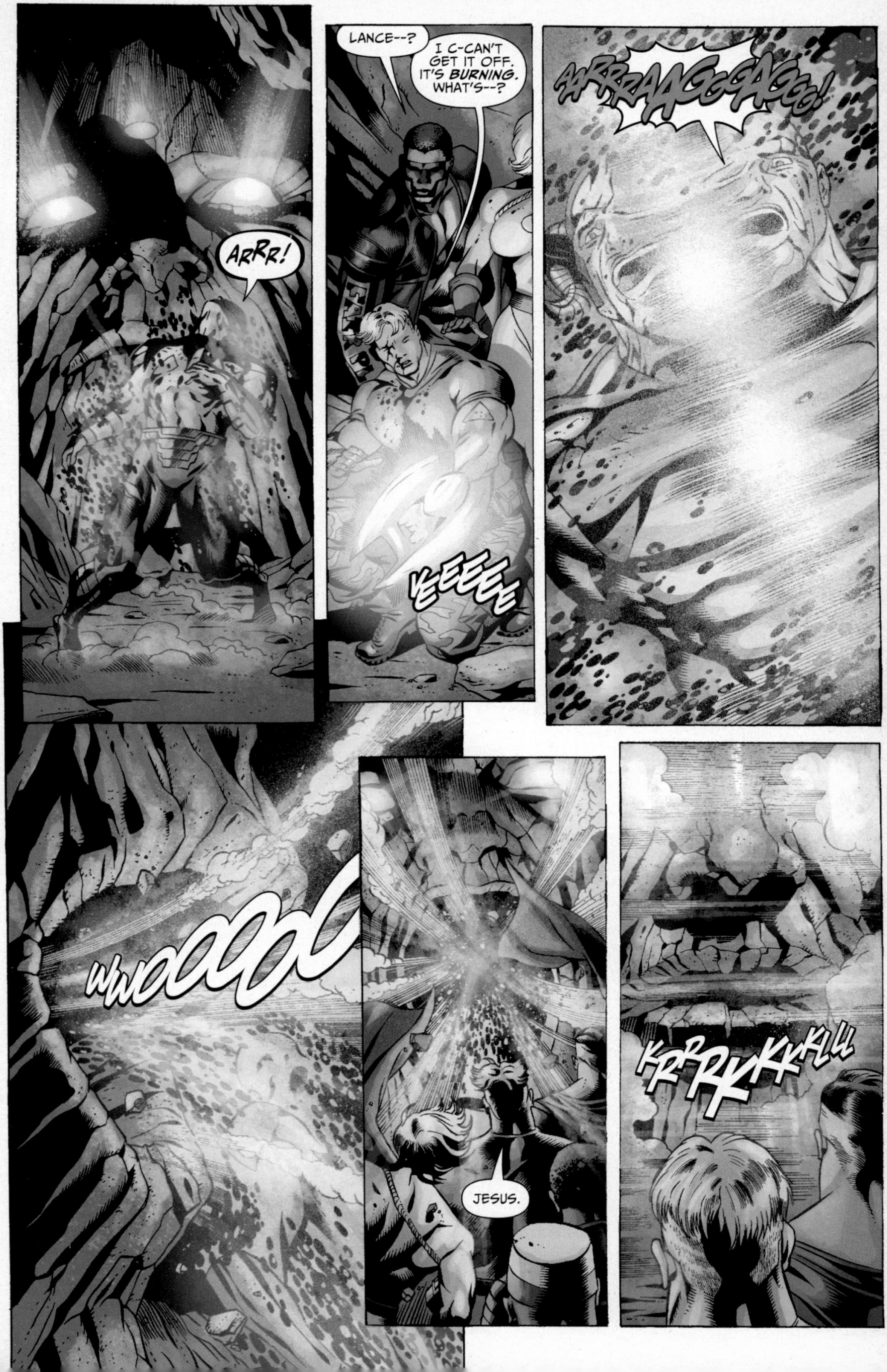
ARRR!
LANCE--?
I C-CAN'T GET IT OFF. IT'S BURNING. WHAT'S--?
VEEEEE
AARRRAAAGGGAGGG!
WWOOOOO
JESUS.
KRRRKKKKLU

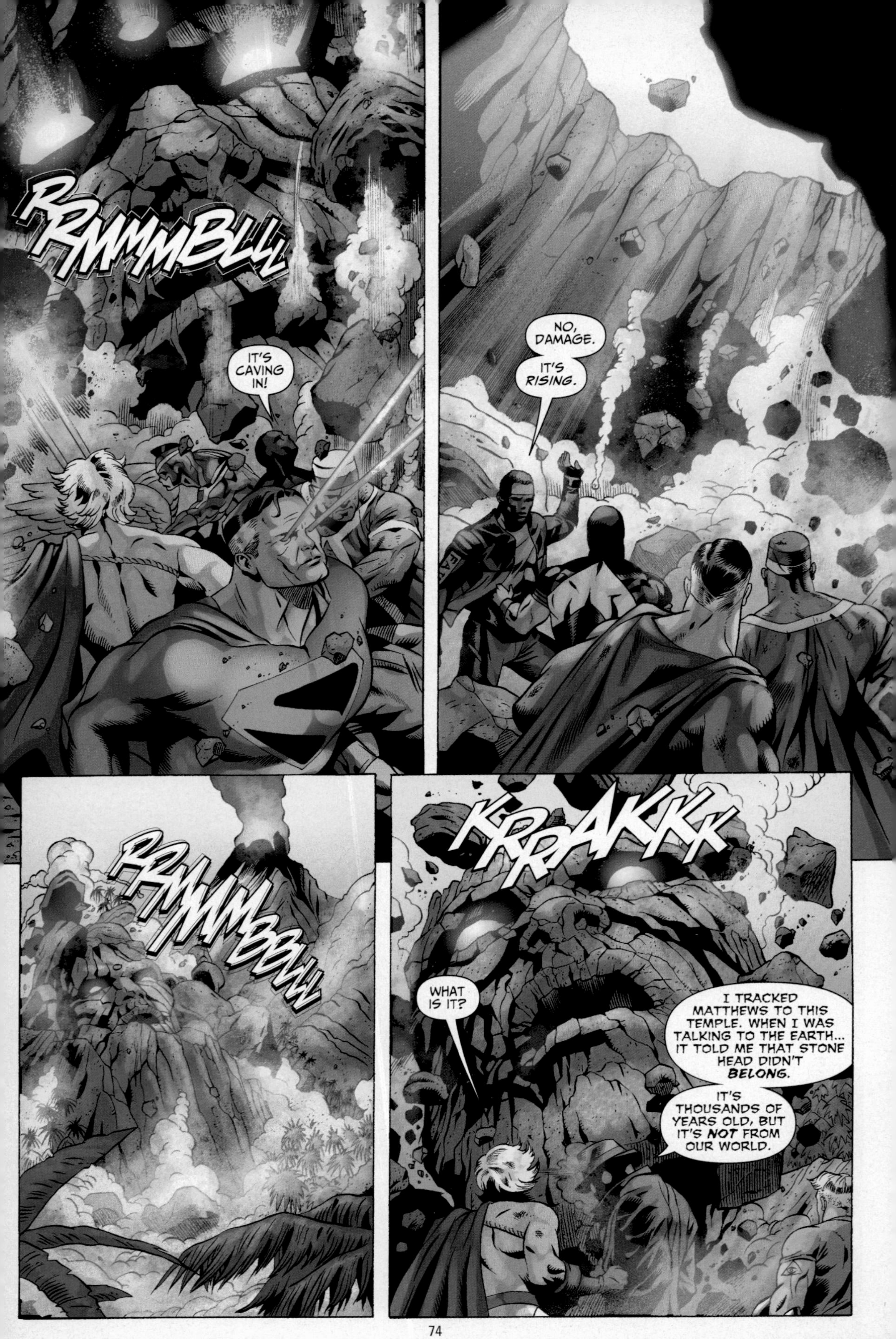
RRMMMBLLL
IT'S CAVING IN!
NO, DAMAGE.
IT'S RISING.
RRMMMBBLL
KRRAKKK
WHAT IS IT?
I TRACKED MATTHEWS TO THIS TEMPLE. WHEN I WAS TALKING TO THE EARTH... IT TOLD ME THAT STONE HEAD DIDN'T BELONG.
IT'S THOUSANDS OF YEARS OLD, BUT IT'S NOT FROM OUR WORLD.

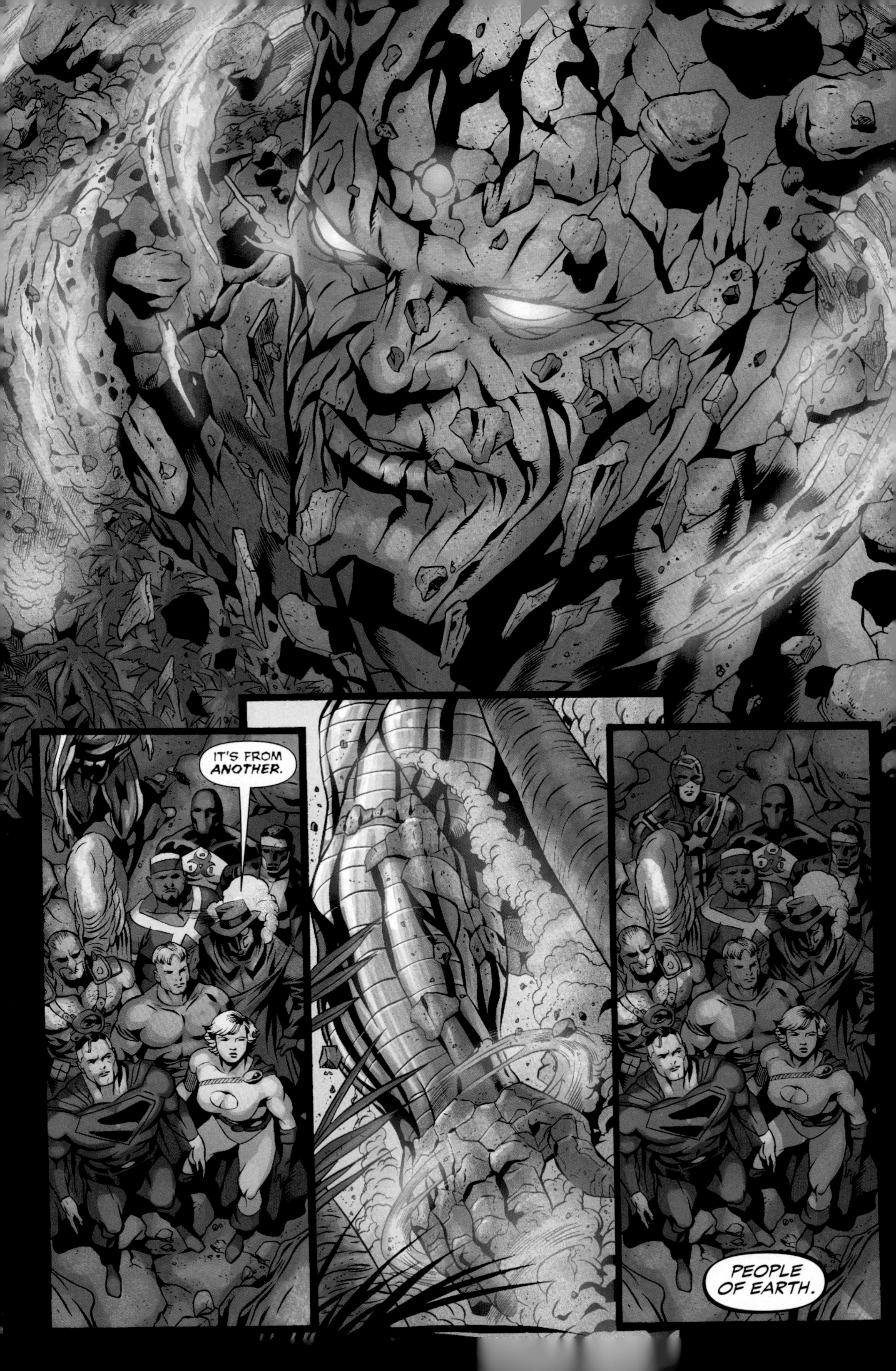
IT'S FROM ANOTHER.
PEOPLE OF EARTH.

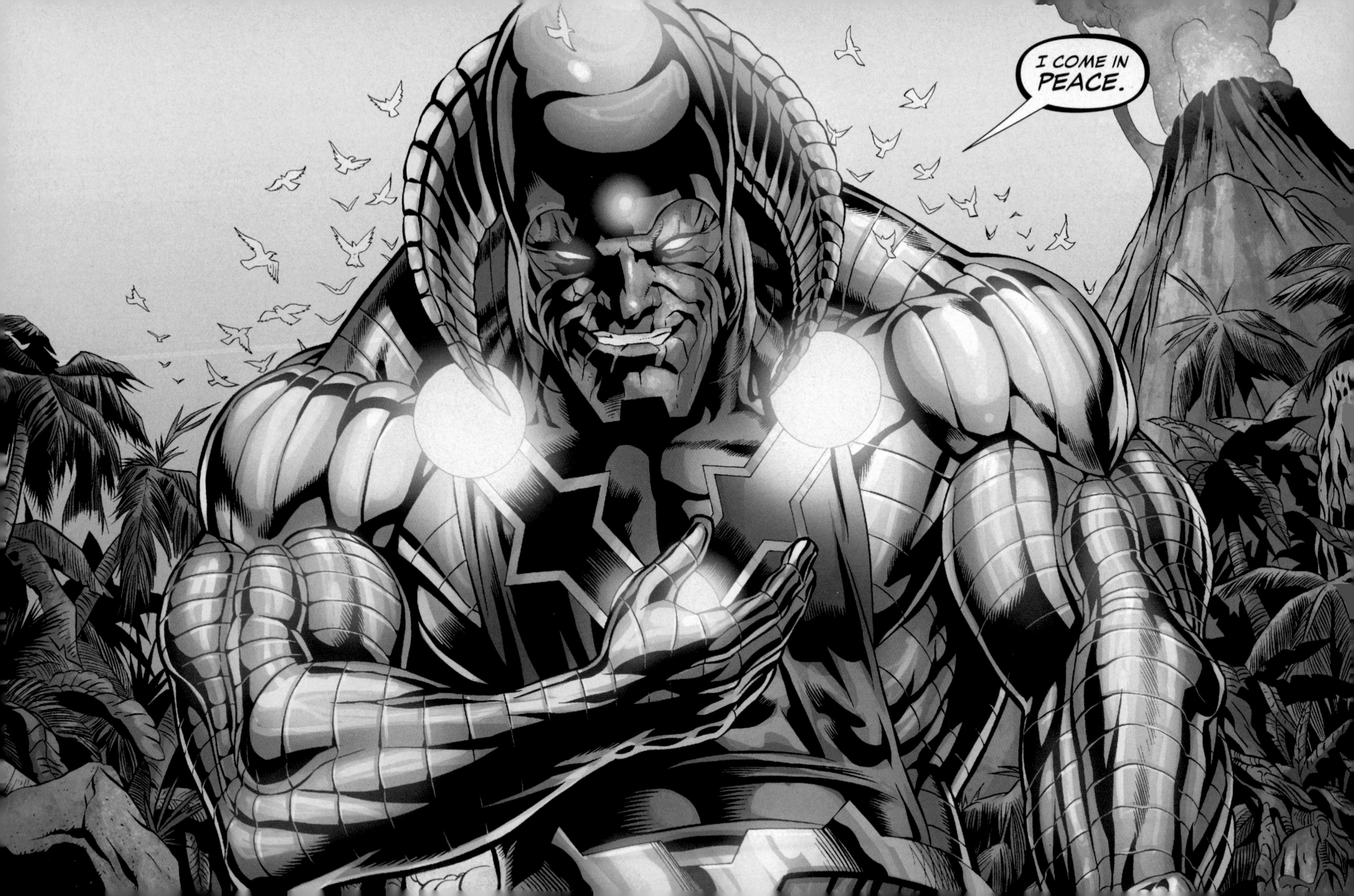
I COME IN PEACE.

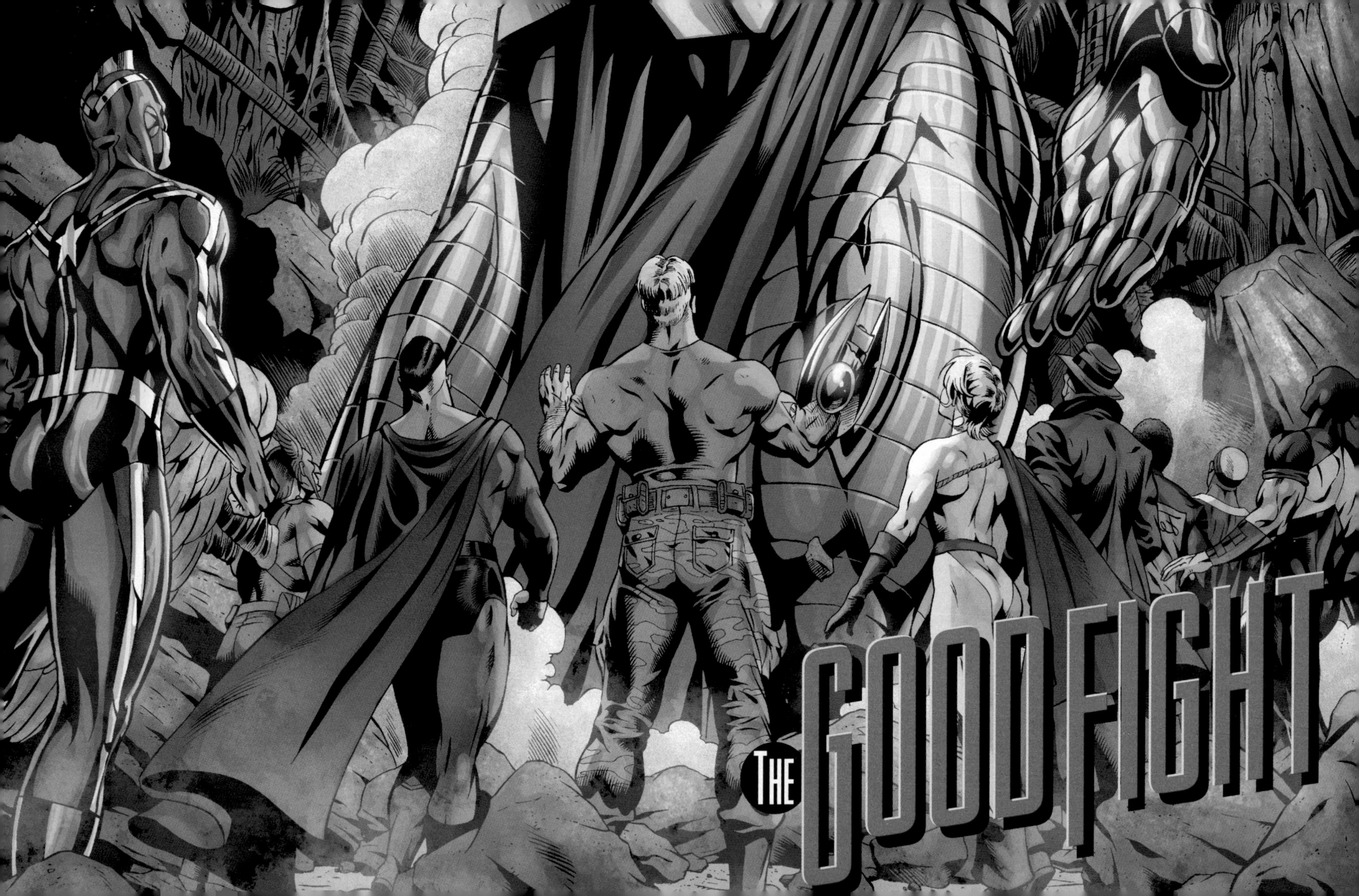
THE GOOD FIGHT

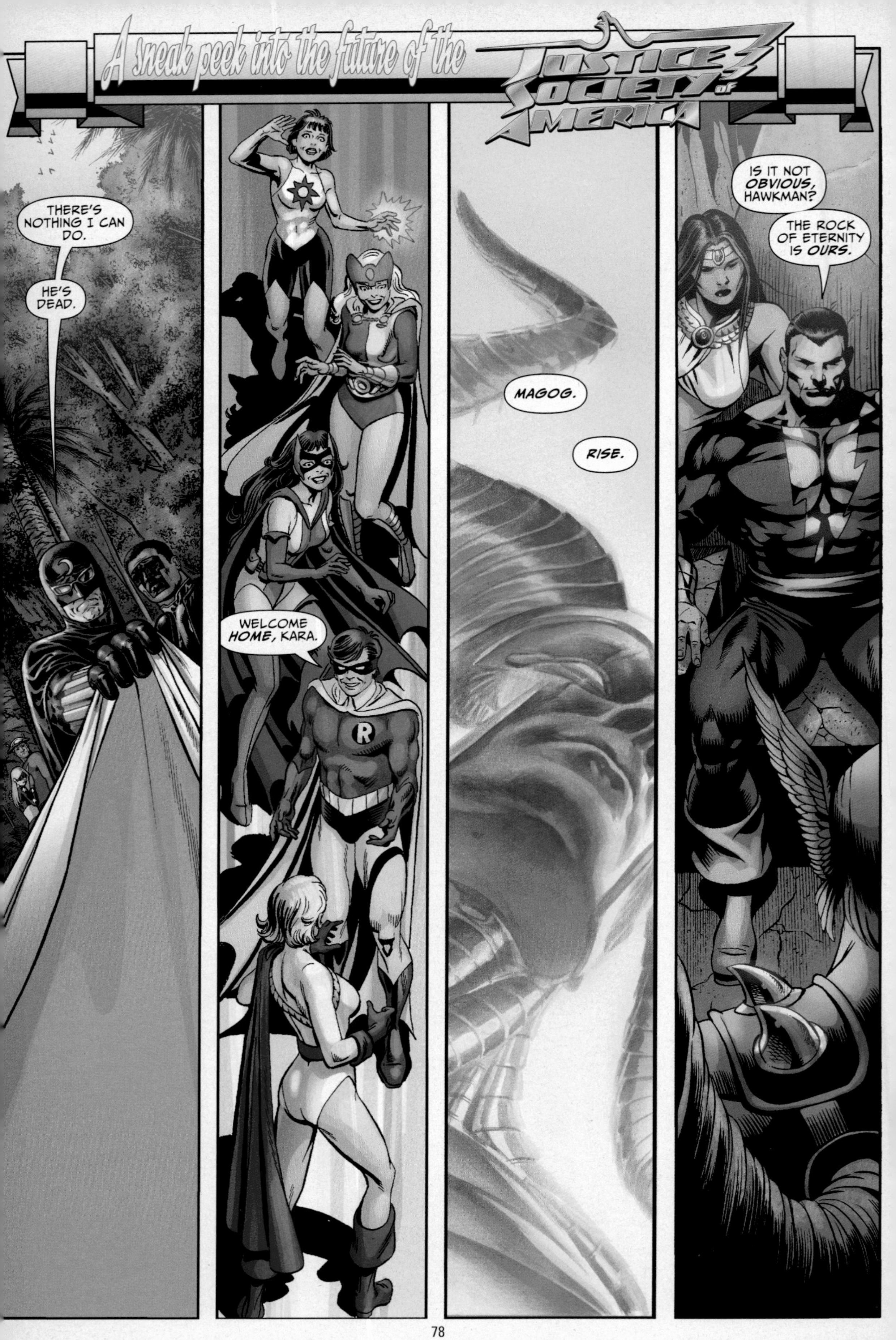
A sneak peek into the future of the
JUSTICE SOCIETY of AMERICA
THERE'S NOTHING I CAN DO.
HE'S DEAD.
WELCOME HOME, KARA.
MAGOG.
RISE.
IS IT NOT OBVIOUS, HAWKMAN?
THE ROCK OF ETERNITY IS OURS.

JUSTICE SOCIETY OF AMERICA #16 cover A by Alex Ross

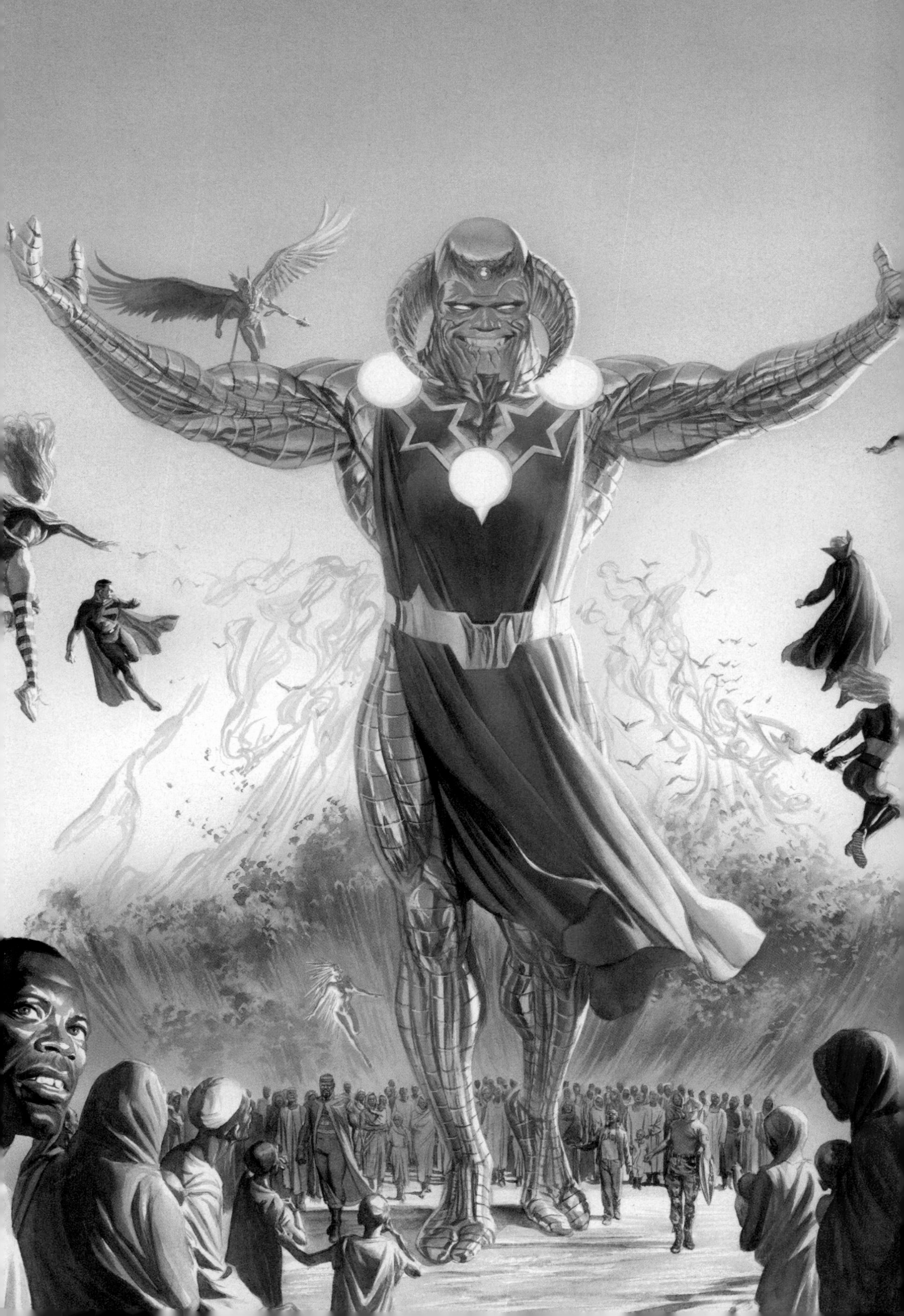

JUSTICE SOCIETY OF AMERICA #16 cover B by **Dale Eaglesham & Prentis Rollins** Interior art by **Fernando Pasarin & Rebecca Buchman**

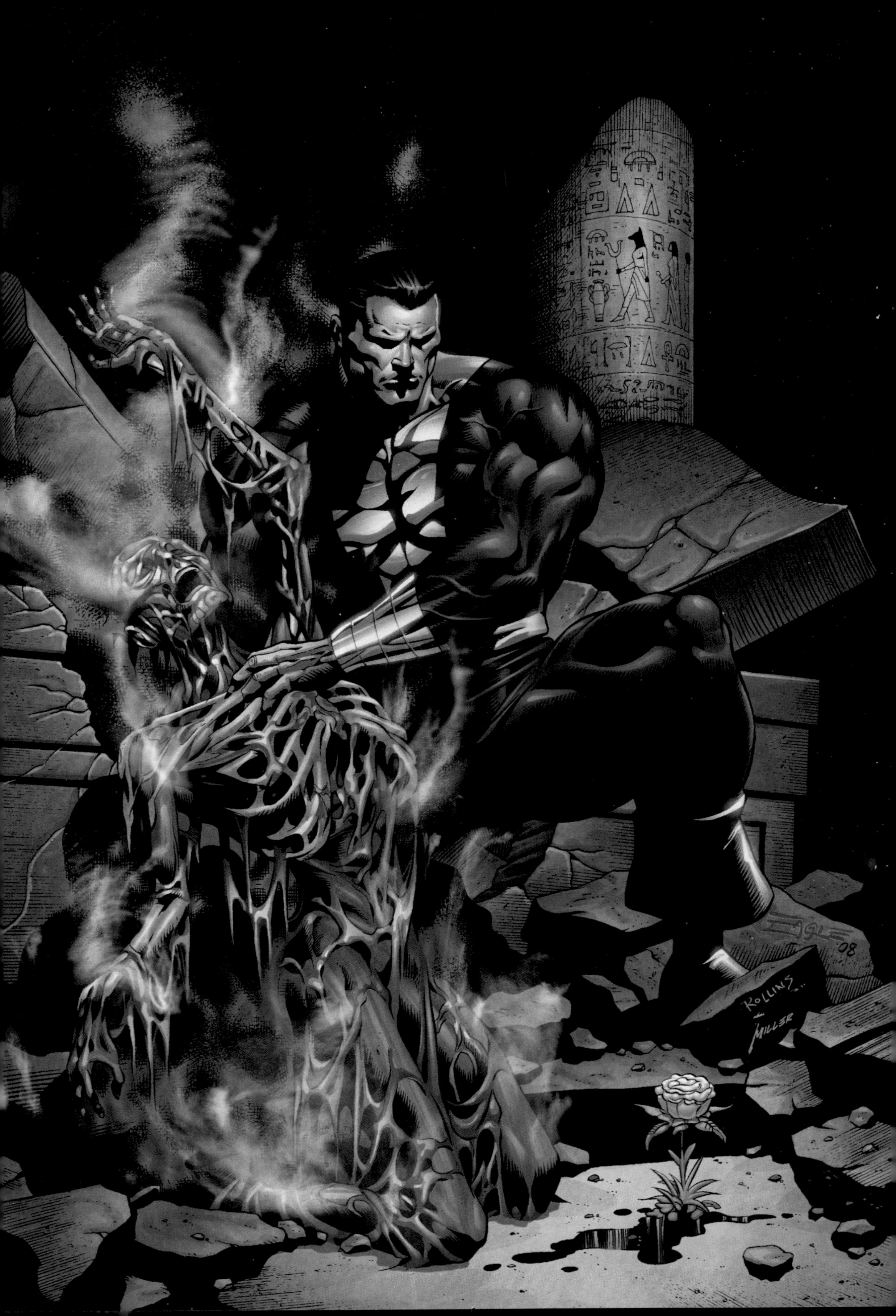

AL PRATT WAS SHORT. REALLY SHORT.

THAT'S THE FIRST THING I THOUGHT WHEN I FOUND OUT HE WAS MY DAD.

HE PUT ON A BLUE WRESTLING MASK AND A CAPE AND CALLED HIMSELF THE ATOM. I CAN'T BELIEVE THEY DIDN'T BURST OUT LAUGHING.

WILDCAT SAID PRATT USED TO BE THE FIRST ONE TO JUMP INTO THE FIGHT--

YOU *JUST* BOUGHT YOURSELF A WHOLE *HEAP* OF *GRIEF*, FRIEND.

--AND THE FIRST ONE TO BE KNOCKED ON HIS ASS--

--UNTIL THE DAY HE WAS TRANSFORMED FROM "THE MIGHTY MITE" INTO "THE HUMAN ATOMIC BOMB."

THAT *DETONATION* POWER IS THE *ONLY* THING PRATT EVER GAVE ME.

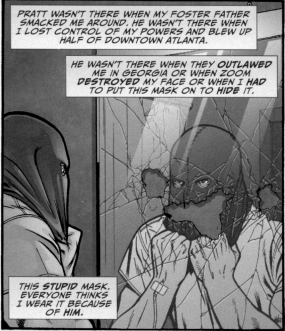

PRATT WASN'T THERE WHEN MY FOSTER FATHER SMACKED ME AROUND. HE WASN'T THERE WHEN I LOST CONTROL OF MY POWERS AND BLEW UP HALF OF DOWNTOWN ATLANTA.

HE WASN'T THERE WHEN THEY *OUTLAWED* ME IN GEORGIA OR WHEN ZOOM *DESTROYED* MY FACE OR WHEN I HAD TO PUT THIS MASK ON TO *HIDE* IT.

THIS *STUPID* MASK. EVERYONE THINKS I WEAR IT BECAUSE OF HIM.

THEY THINK I JOINED THE JUSTICE SOCIETY BECAUSE OF HIM.

BUT I *NEVER* EVEN MET AL PRATT.

HEY!

WHO'S GONNA PAY FOR OUR CAR?!

I ONLY TAGGED ALONG BECAUSE I WANTED TO GET OUT OF TROUBLE.

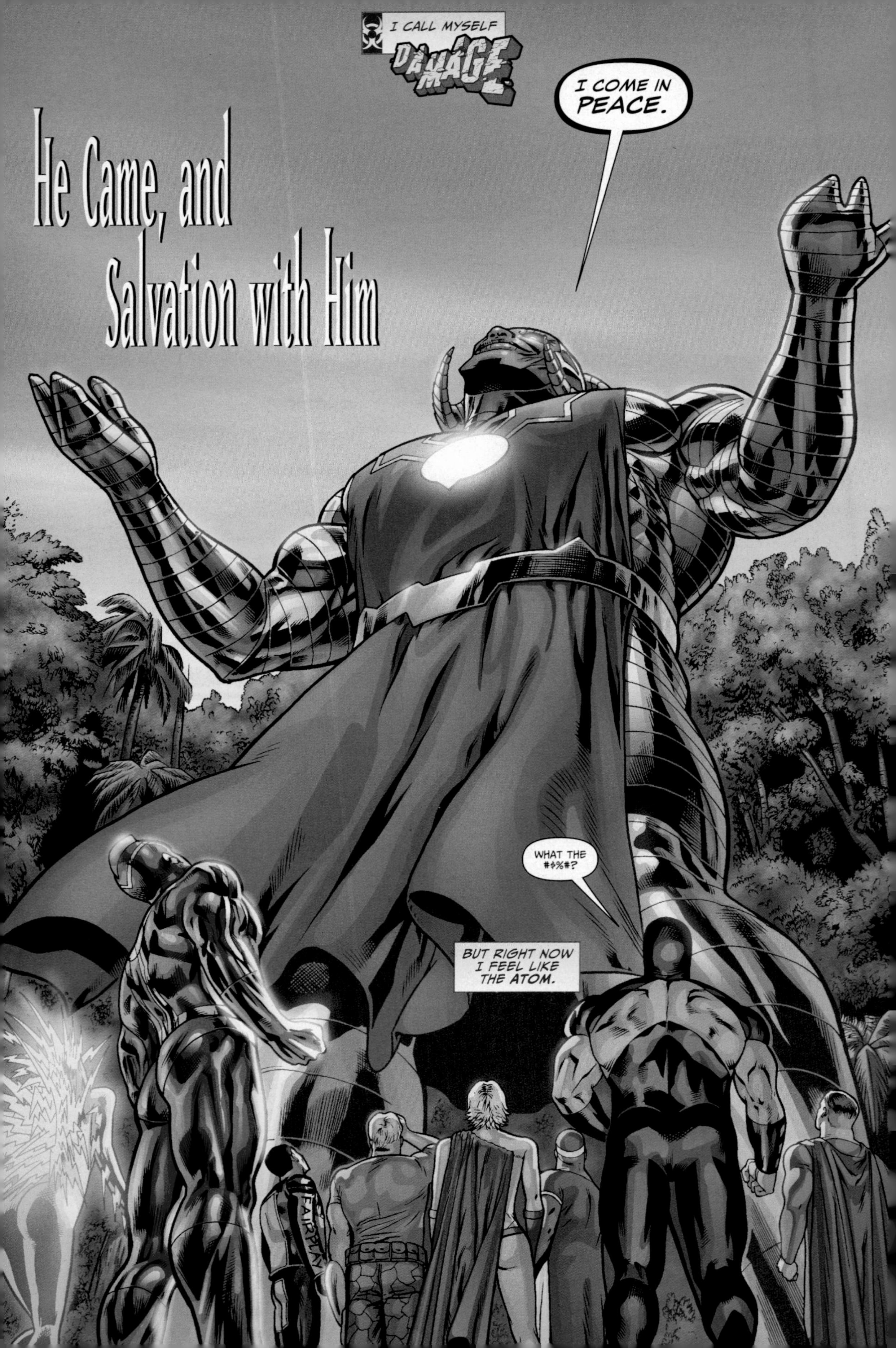
I CALL MYSELF
DAMAGE
He Came, and Salvation with Him
I COME IN PEACE.
WHAT THE #$%#?
BUT RIGHT NOW I FEEL LIKE THE ATOM.
FAIRPLAY

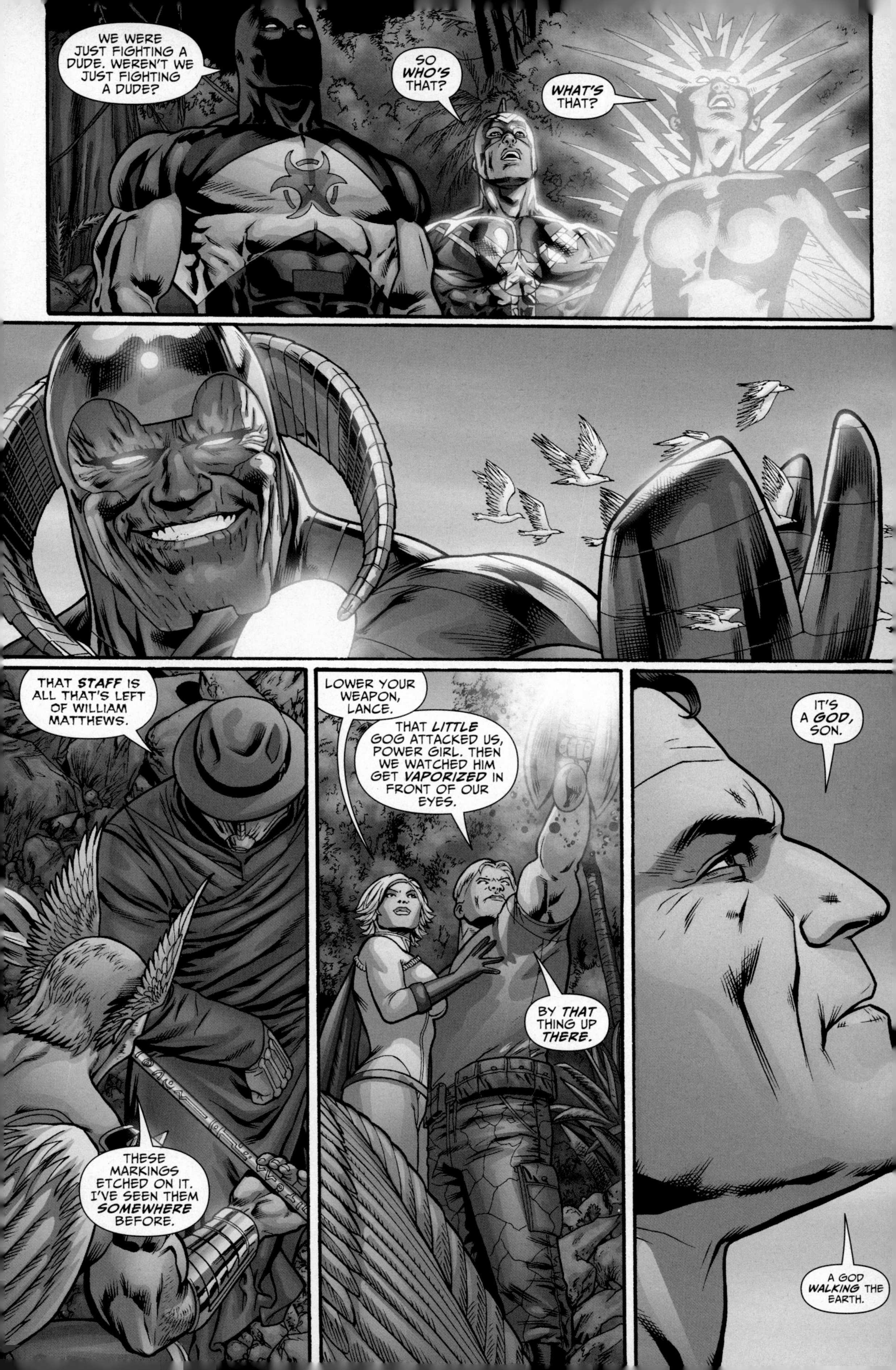
WE WERE JUST FIGHTING A DUDE. WEREN'T WE JUST FIGHTING A DUDE?
SO WHO'S THAT?
WHAT'S THAT?
THAT STAFF IS ALL THAT'S LEFT OF WILLIAM MATTHEWS.
THESE MARKINGS ETCHED ON IT. I'VE SEEN THEM SOMEWHERE BEFORE.
LOWER YOUR WEAPON, LANCE.
THAT LITTLE GOG ATTACKED US, POWER GIRL. THEN WE WATCHED HIM GET VAPORIZED IN FRONT OF OUR EYES.
BY THAT THING UP THERE.
IT'S A GOD, SON.
A GOD WALKING THE EARTH.

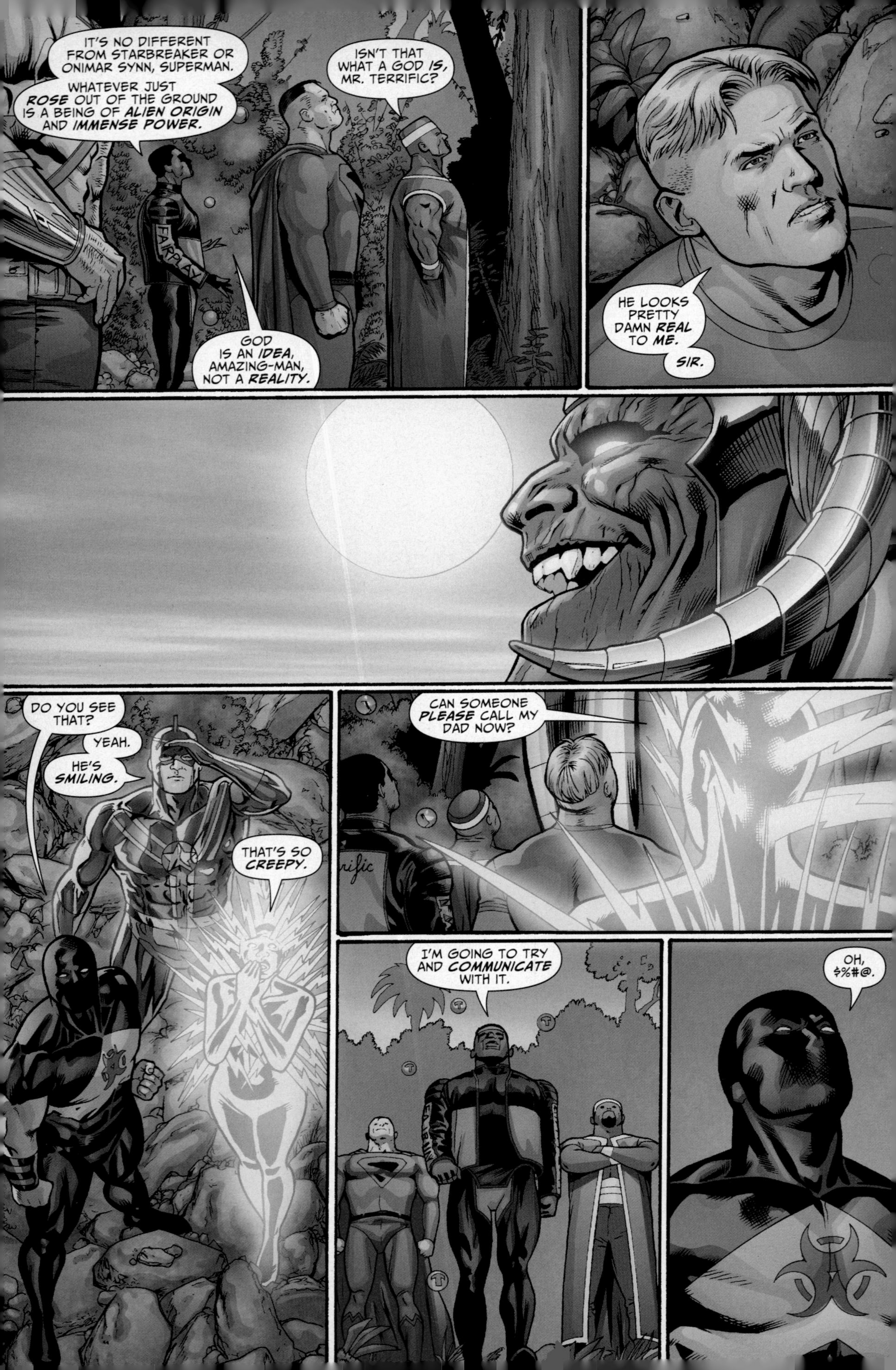
IT'S NO DIFFERENT FROM STARBREAKER OR ONIMAR SYNN, SUPERMAN.
WHATEVER JUST ROSE OUT OF THE GROUND IS A BEING OF ALIEN ORIGIN AND IMMENSE POWER.
ISN'T THAT WHAT A GOD IS, MR. TERRIFIC?
GOD IS AN IDEA, AMAZING-MAN, NOT A REALITY.
HE LOOKS PRETTY DAMN REAL TO ME.
SIR.
DO YOU SEE THAT?
YEAH.
HE'S SMILING.
THAT'S SO CREEPY.
CAN SOMEONE PLEASE CALL MY DAD NOW?
I'M GOING TO TRY AND COMMUNICATE WITH IT.
OH, $%#@.

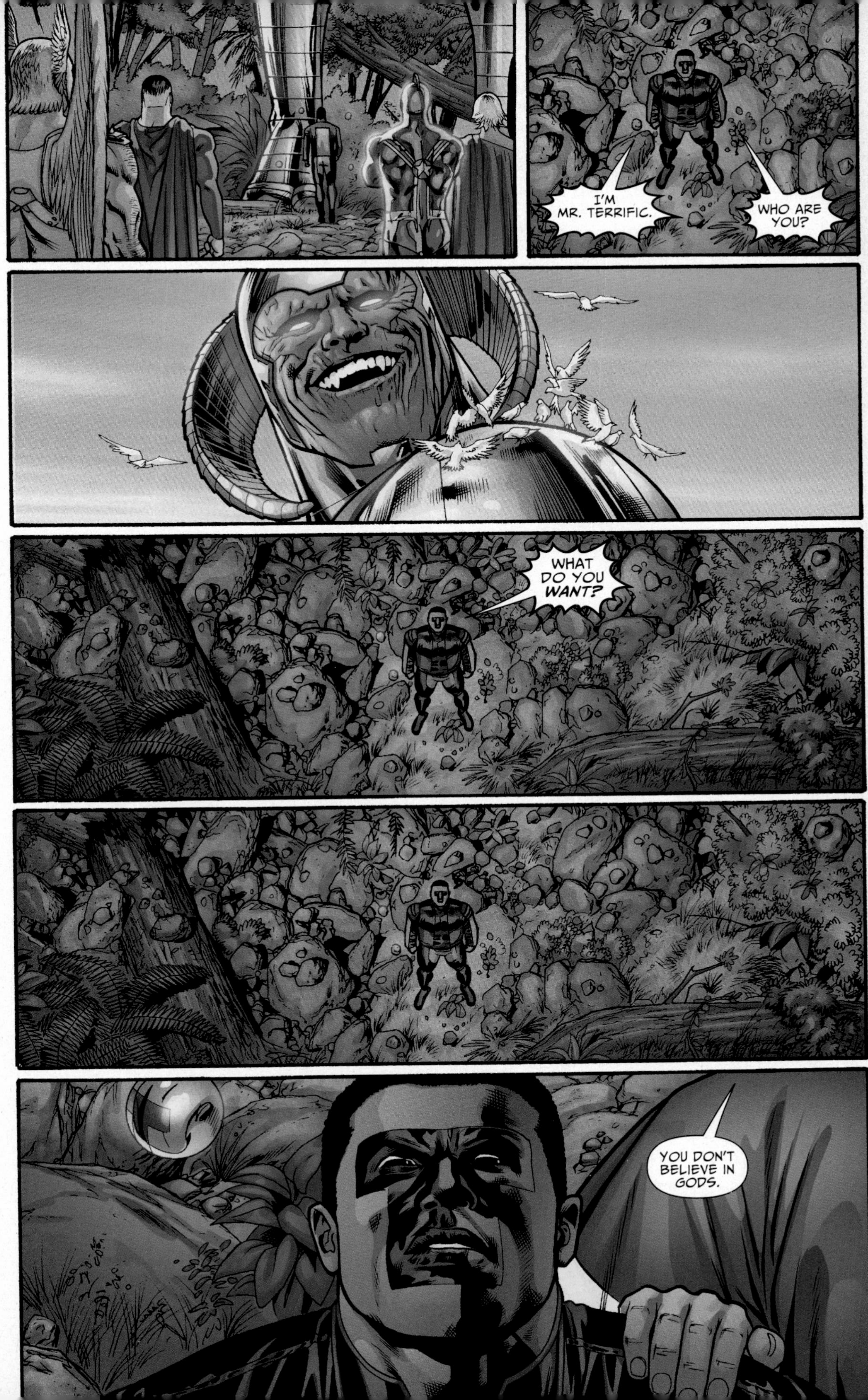
I'M MR. TERRIFIC.
WHO ARE YOU?
WHAT DO YOU WANT?
YOU DON'T BELIEVE IN GODS.

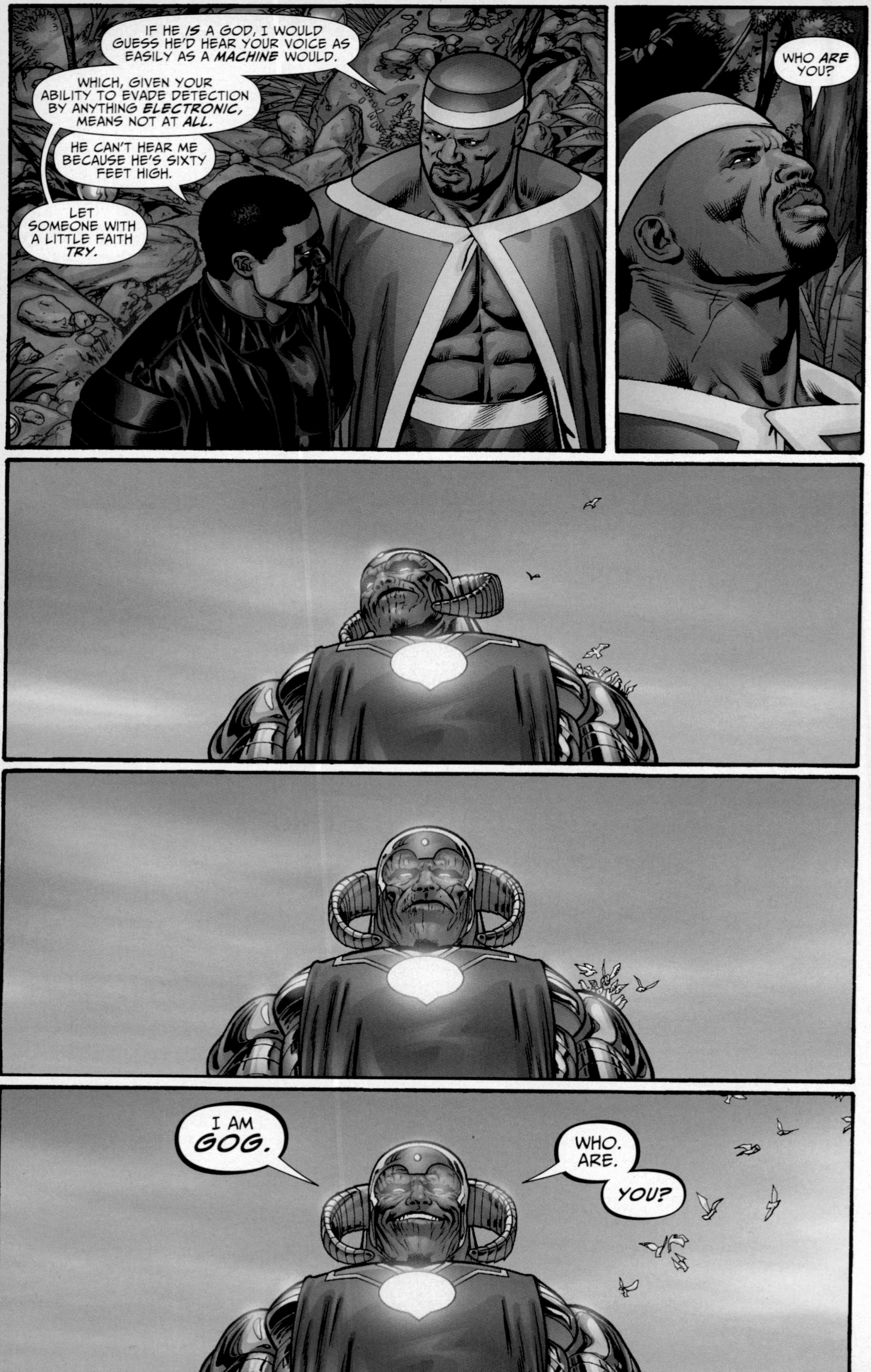
IF HE IS A GOD, I WOULD GUESS HE'D HEAR YOUR VOICE AS EASILY AS A MACHINE WOULD.
WHICH, GIVEN YOUR ABILITY TO EVADE DETECTION BY ANYTHING ELECTRONIC, MEANS NOT AT ALL.
HE CAN'T HEAR ME BECAUSE HE'S SIXTY FEET HIGH.
LET SOMEONE WITH A LITTLE FAITH TRY.
WHO ARE YOU?
I AM GOG.
WHO. ARE. YOU?

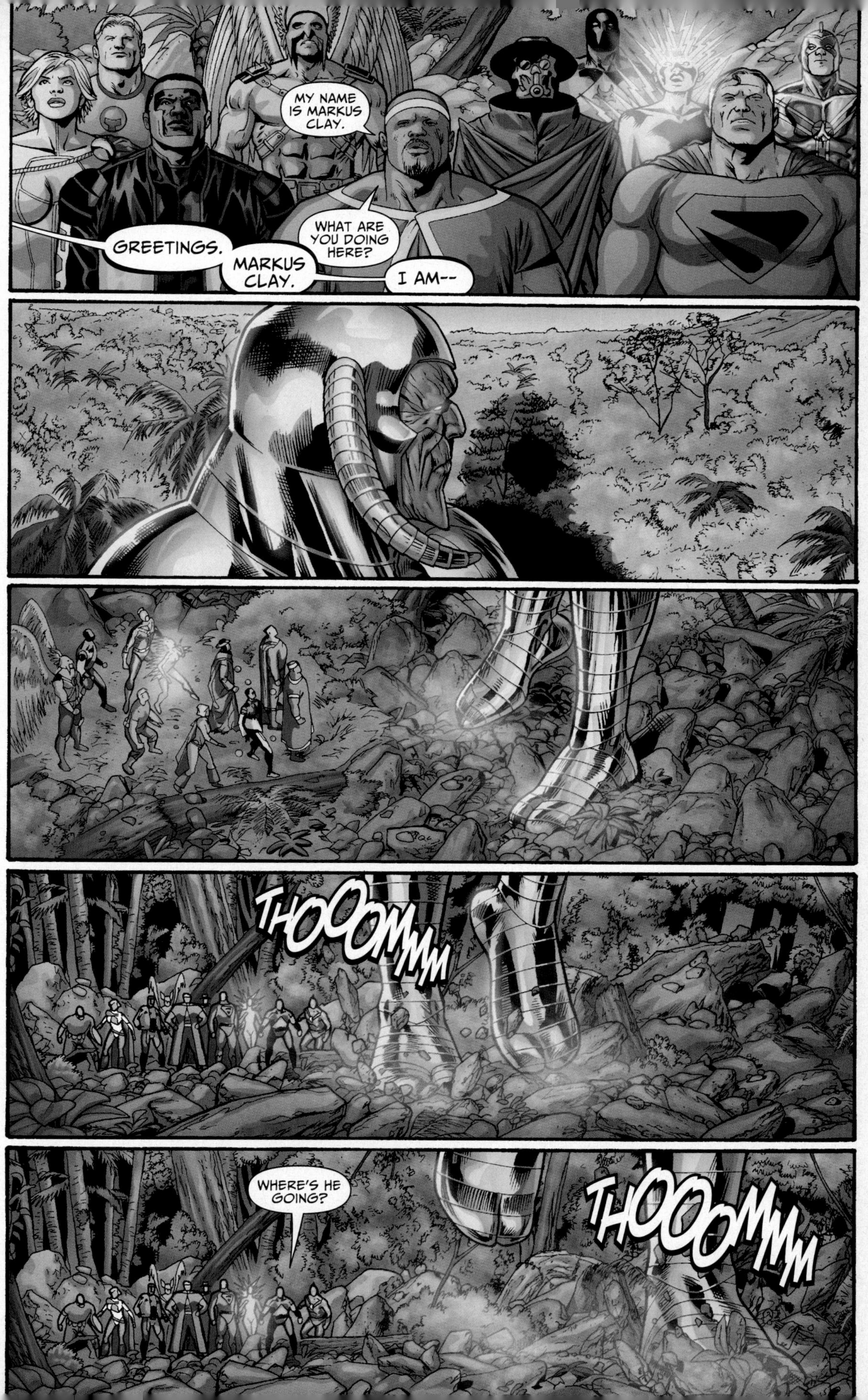
MY NAME IS MARKUS CLAY.
GREETINGS.
MARKUS CLAY.
WHAT ARE YOU DOING HERE?
I AM--
THOOOMMM
WHERE'S HE GOING?
THOOOMMMM

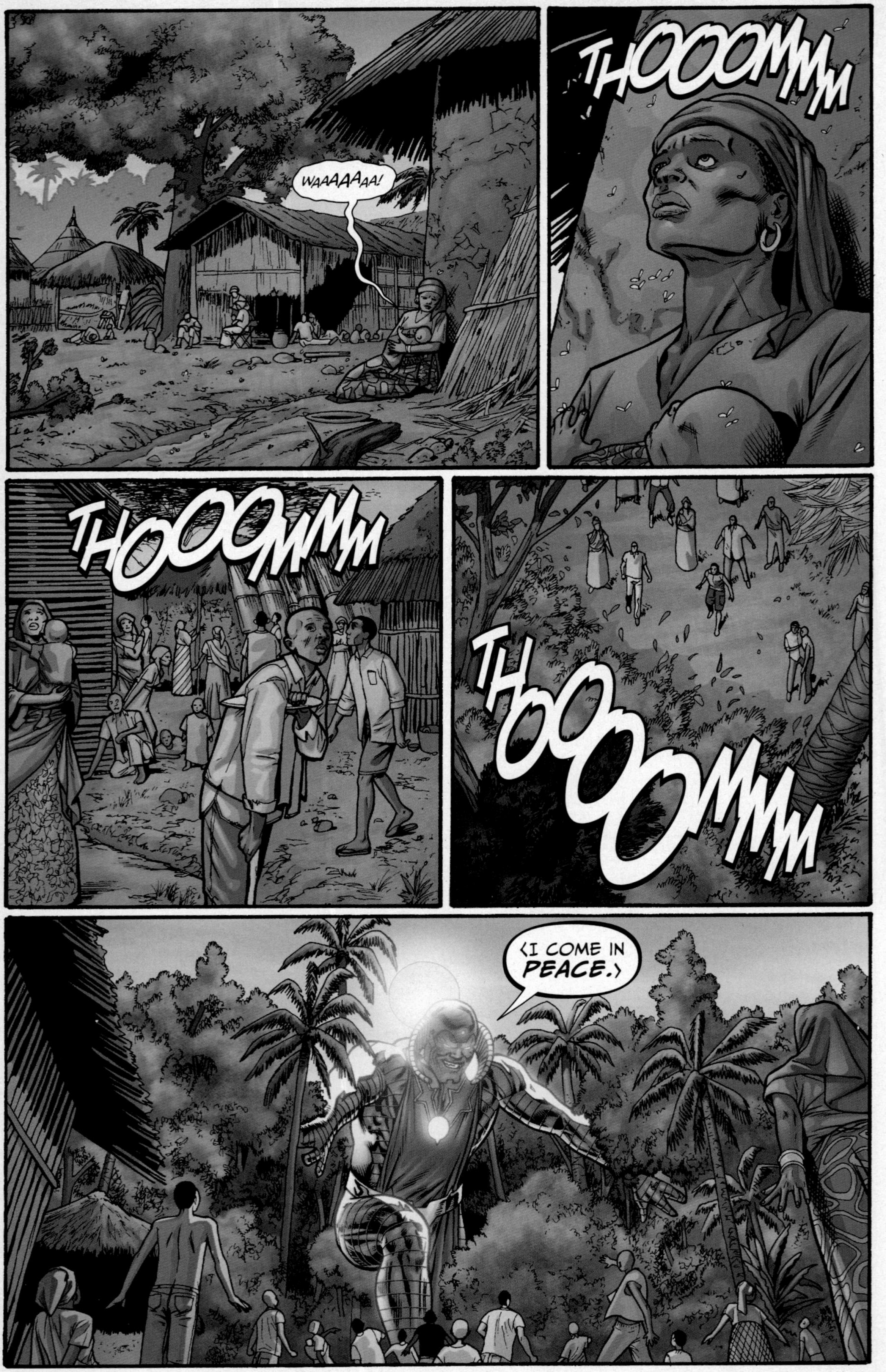
WAAAAAA!
THOOOOMMM
THOOOMMMM
THOOOOMMMM
⟨I COME IN PEACE.⟩

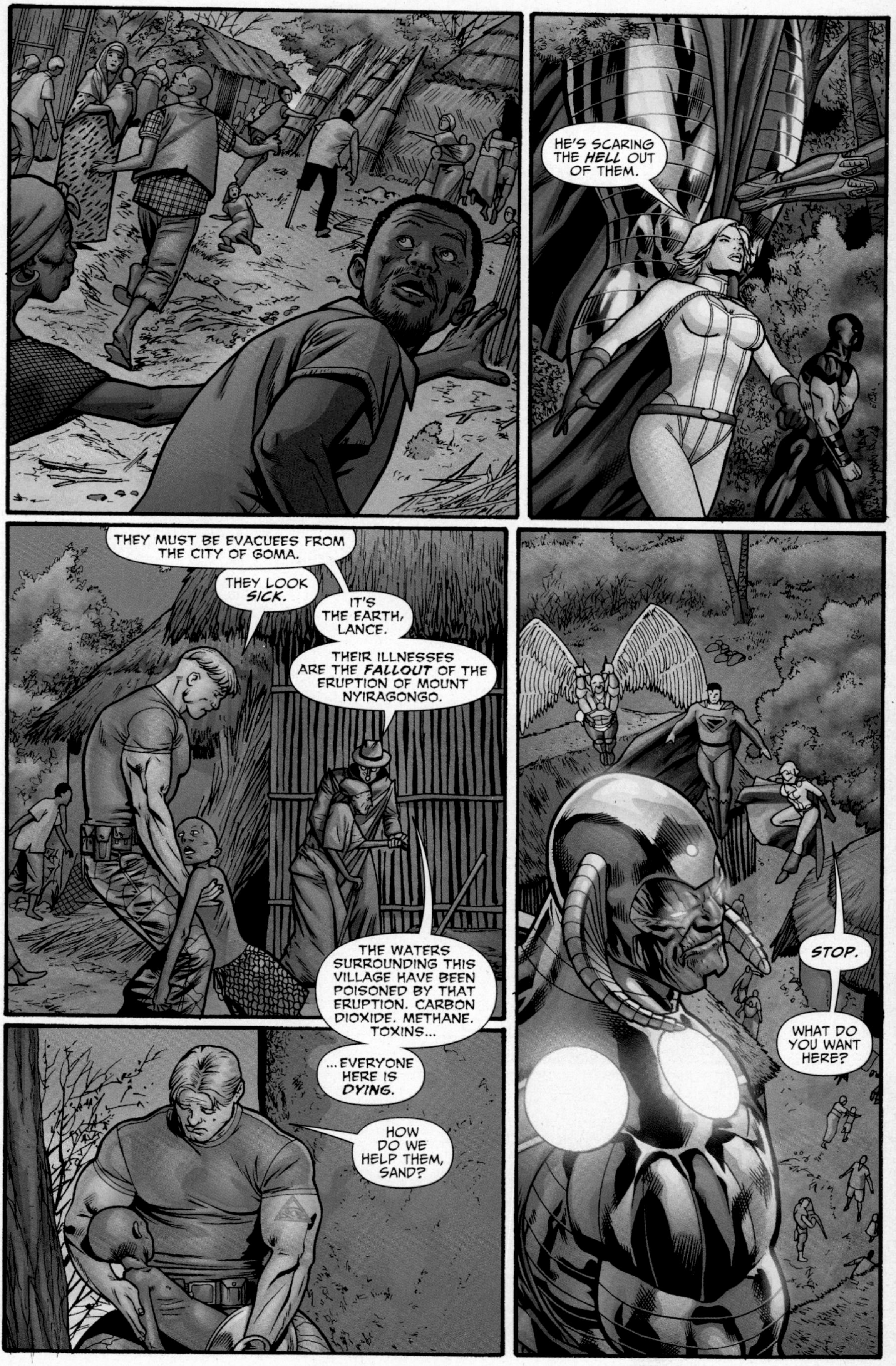
HE'S SCARING THE HELL OUT OF THEM.
THEY MUST BE EVACUEES FROM THE CITY OF GOMA.
THEY LOOK SICK.
IT'S THE EARTH, LANCE.
THEIR ILLNESSES ARE THE FALLOUT OF THE ERUPTION OF MOUNT NYIRAGONGO.
THE WATERS SURROUNDING THIS VILLAGE HAVE BEEN POISONED BY THAT ERUPTION. CARBON DIOXIDE. METHANE. TOXINS...
...EVERYONE HERE IS DYING.
HOW DO WE HELP THEM, SAND?
STOP.
WHAT DO YOU WANT HERE?

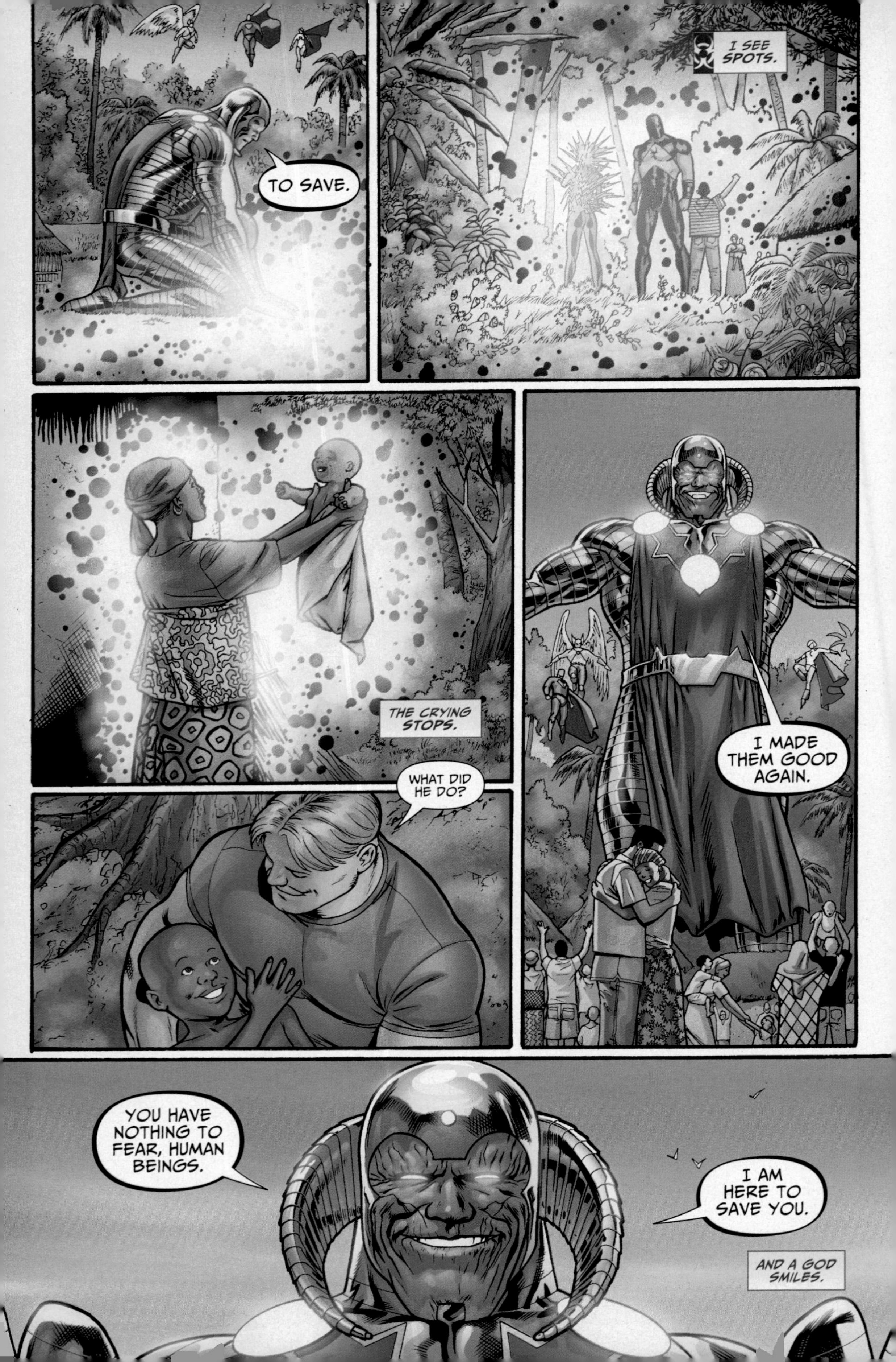
TO SAVE.
I SEE SPOTS.
THE CRYING STOPS.
WHAT DID HE DO?
I MADE THEM GOOD AGAIN.
YOU HAVE NOTHING TO FEAR, HUMAN BEINGS.
I AM HERE TO SAVE YOU.
AND A GOD SMILES.

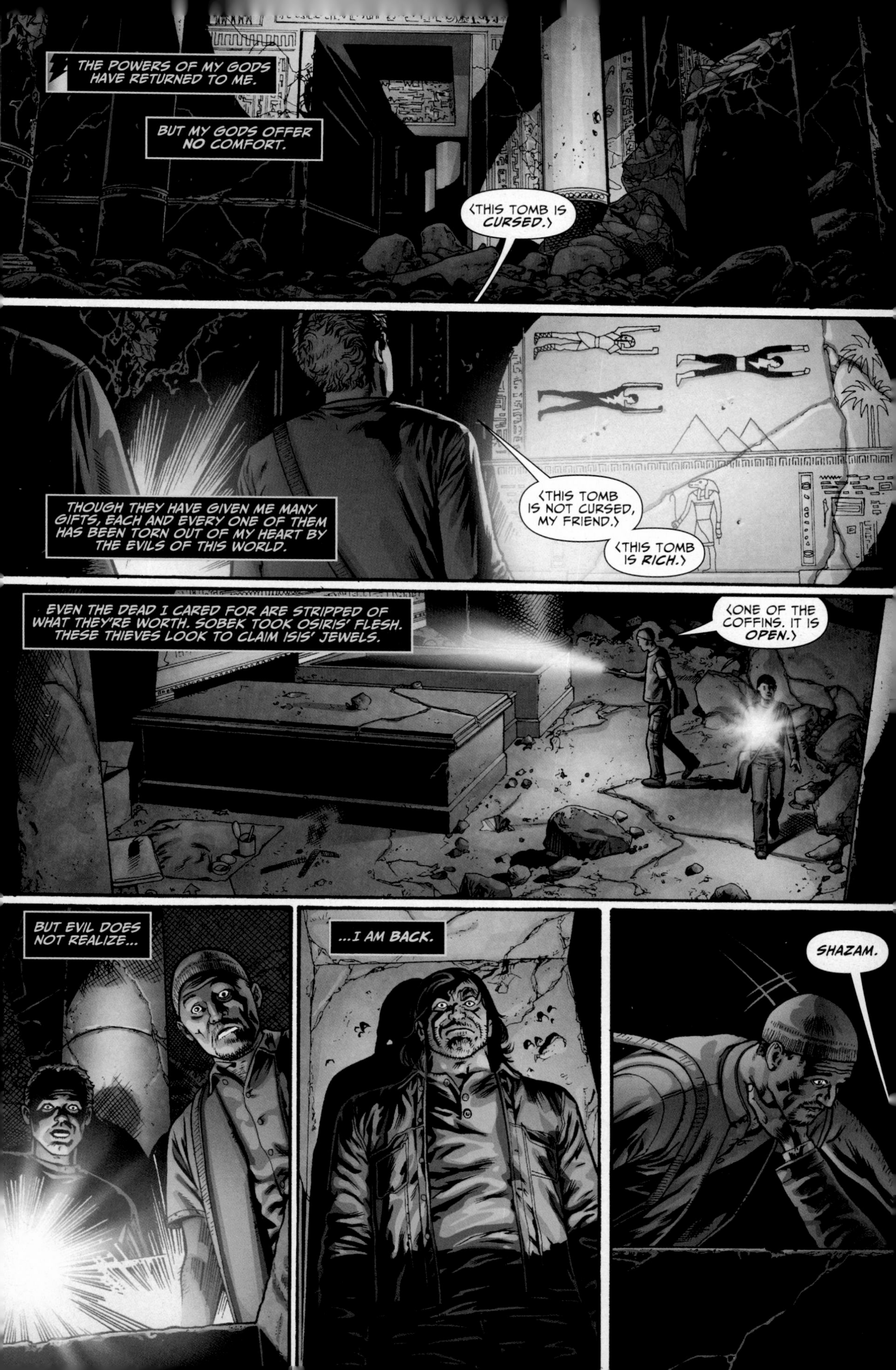

THE POWERS OF MY GODS HAVE RETURNED TO ME.
BUT MY GODS OFFER NO COMFORT.
<THIS TOMB IS CURSED.>
THOUGH THEY HAVE GIVEN ME MANY GIFTS, EACH AND EVERY ONE OF THEM HAS BEEN TORN OUT OF MY HEART BY THE EVILS OF THIS WORLD.
<THIS TOMB IS NOT CURSED, MY FRIEND.>
<THIS TOMB IS RICH.>
EVEN THE DEAD I CARED FOR ARE STRIPPED OF WHAT THEY'RE WORTH. SOBEK TOOK OSIRIS' FLESH. THESE THIEVES LOOK TO CLAIM ISIS' JEWELS.
<ONE OF THE COFFINS. IT IS OPEN.>
BUT EVIL DOES NOT REALIZE...
...I AM BACK.
SHAZAM.

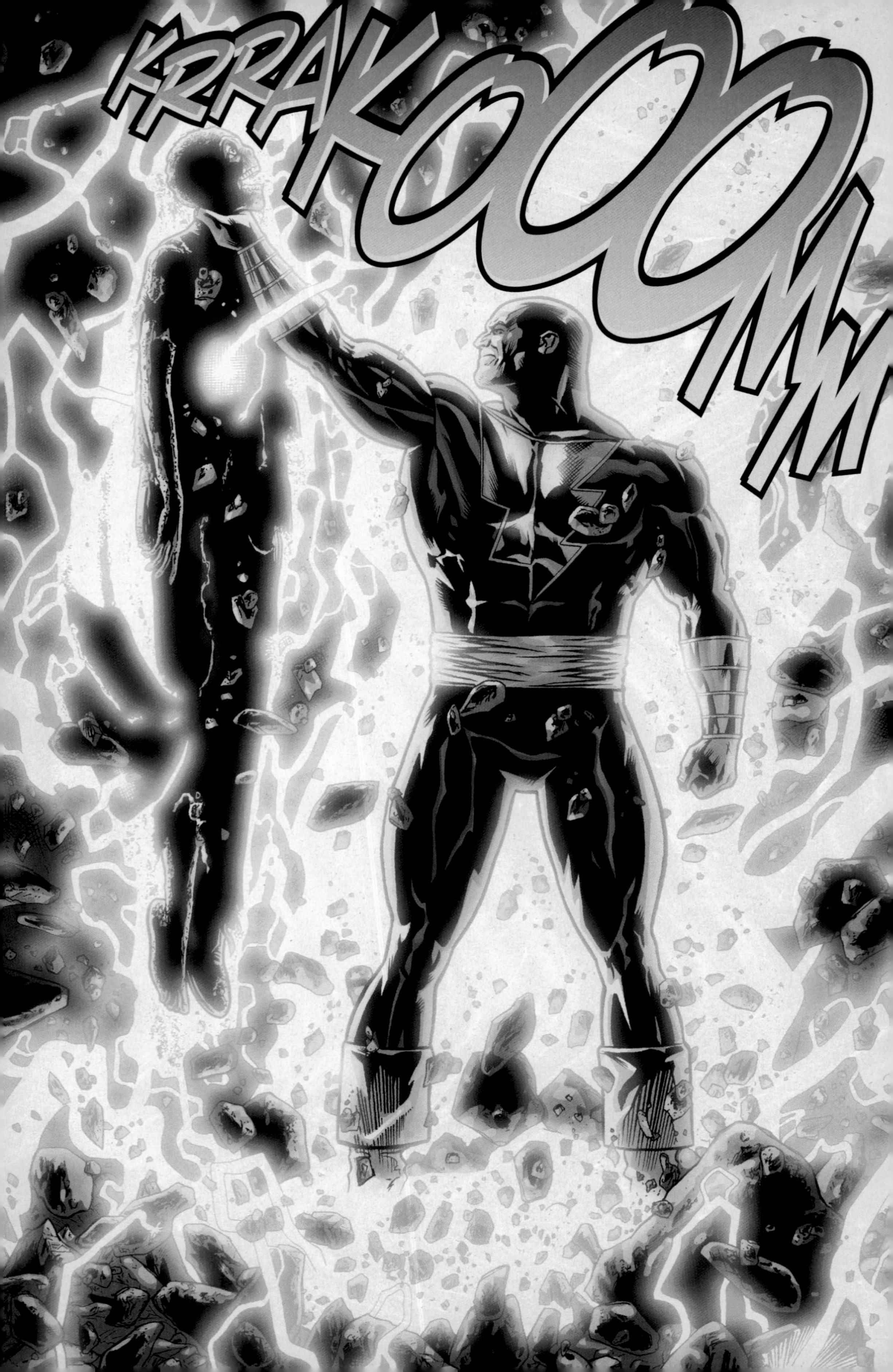
KRRAKOOOMM

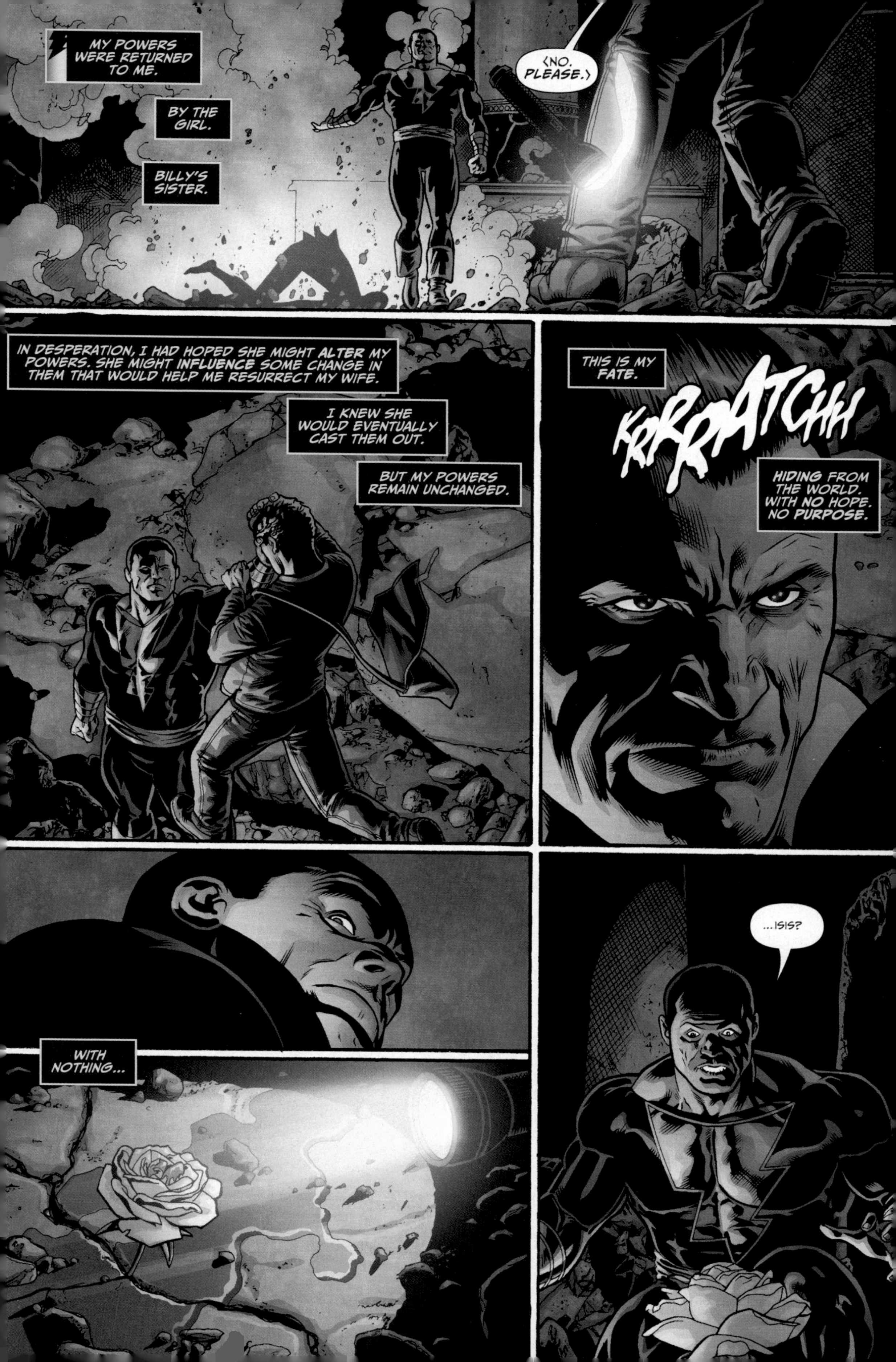
MY POWERS WERE RETURNED TO ME.
BY THE GIRL.
BILLY'S SISTER.
<NO. PLEASE.>
IN DESPERATION, I HAD HOPED SHE MIGHT ALTER MY POWERS. SHE MIGHT INFLUENCE SOME CHANGE IN THEM THAT WOULD HELP ME RESURRECT MY WIFE.
I KNEW SHE WOULD EVENTUALLY CAST THEM OUT.
BUT MY POWERS REMAIN UNCHANGED.
THIS IS MY FATE.
KRRRATCHH
HIDING FROM THE WORLD. WITH NO HOPE. NO PURPOSE.
WITH NOTHING...
...ISIS?

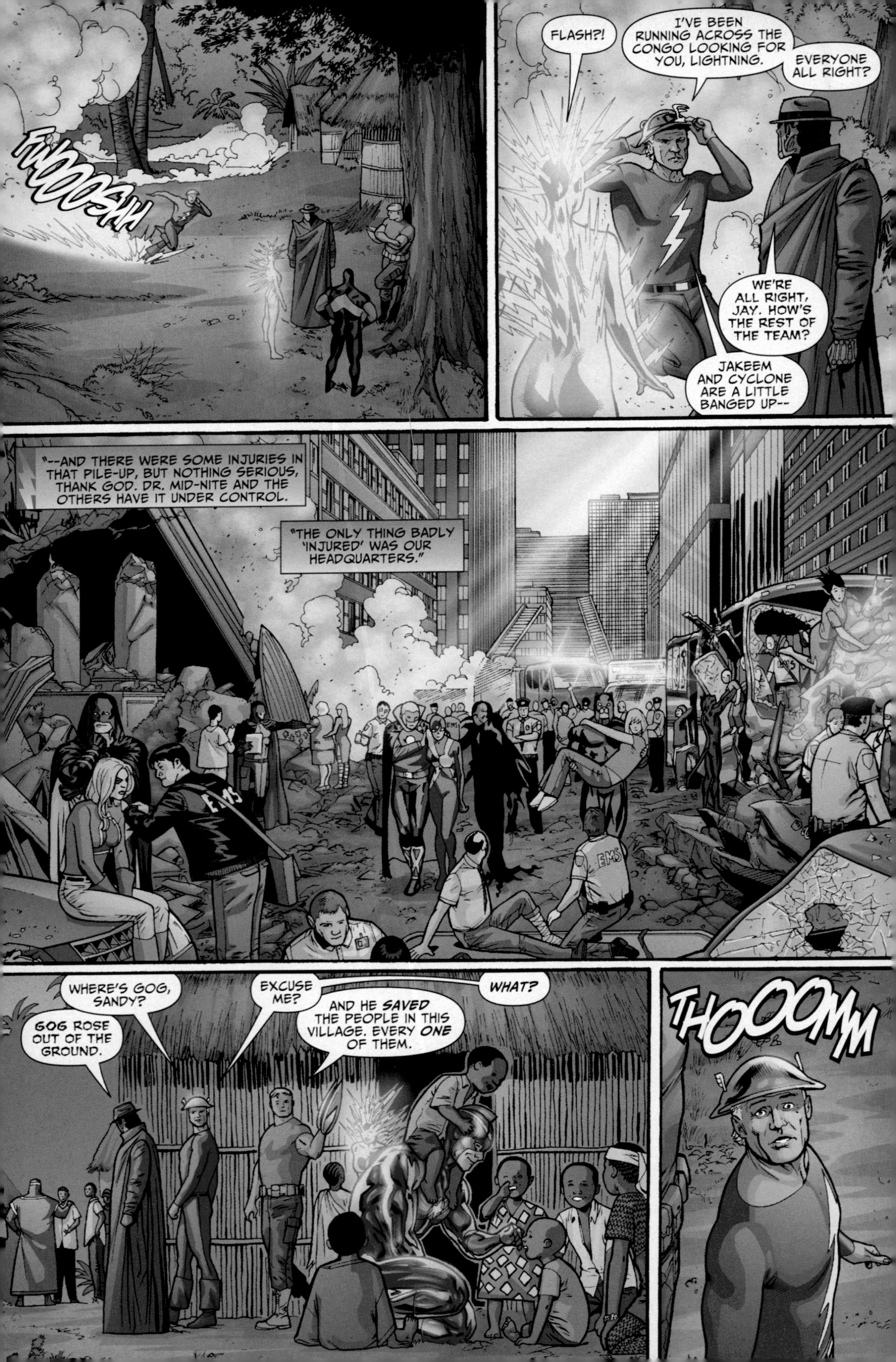
FWOOOSHH
FLASH?!
I'VE BEEN RUNNING ACROSS THE CONGO LOOKING FOR YOU, LIGHTNING.
EVERYONE ALL RIGHT?
WE'RE ALL RIGHT, JAY. HOW'S THE REST OF THE TEAM?
JAKEEM AND CYCLONE ARE A LITTLE BANGED UP--
"--AND THERE WERE SOME INJURIES IN THAT PILE-UP, BUT NOTHING SERIOUS, THANK GOD. DR. MID-NITE AND THE OTHERS HAVE IT UNDER CONTROL.
"THE ONLY THING BADLY 'INJURED' WAS OUR HEADQUARTERS."
WHERE'S GOG, SANDY?
GOG ROSE OUT OF THE GROUND.
EXCUSE ME?
AND HE *SAVED* THE PEOPLE IN THIS VILLAGE. EVERY *ONE* OF THEM.
WHAT?
THOOOMM

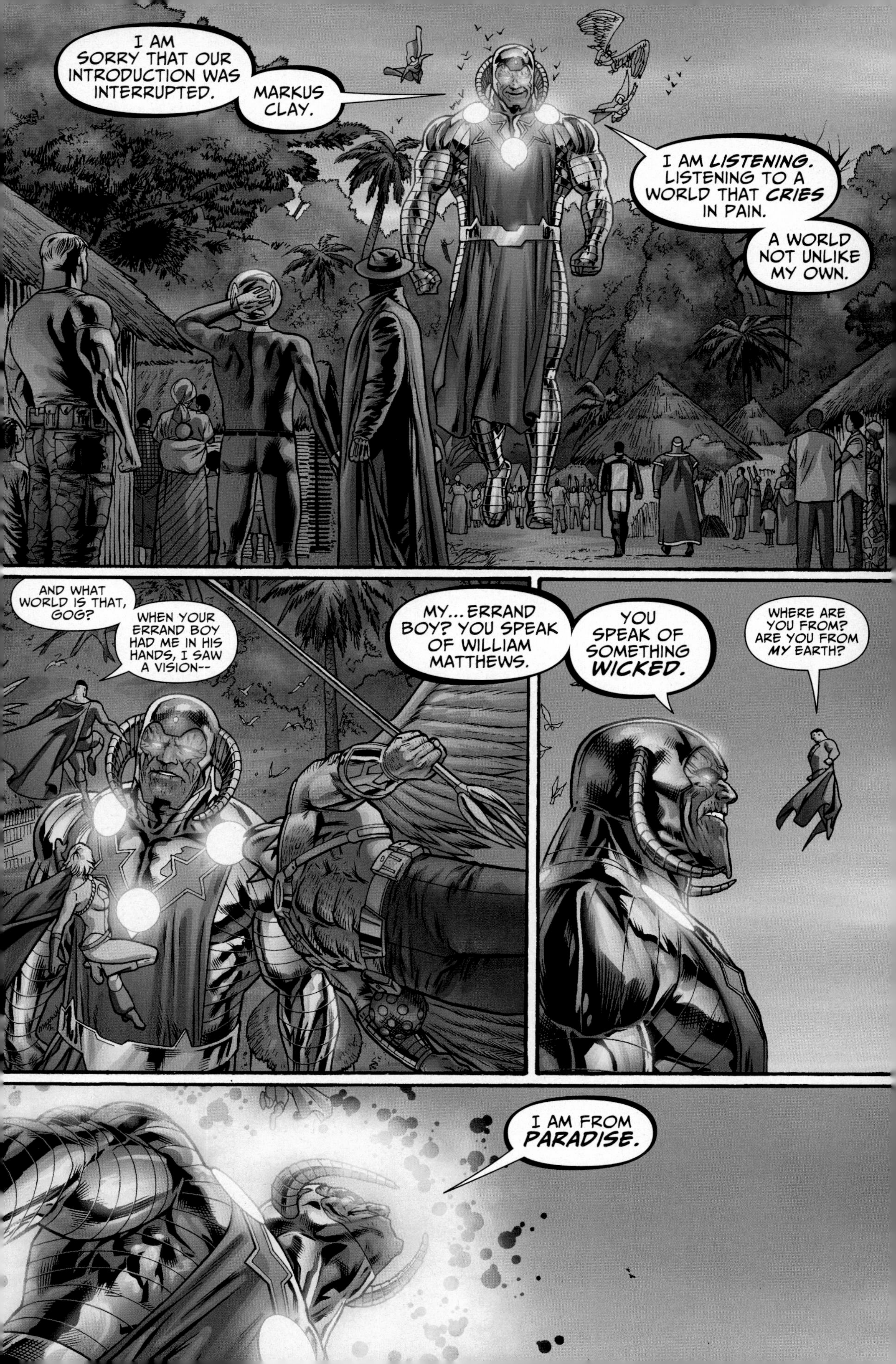
I AM SORRY THAT OUR INTRODUCTION WAS INTERRUPTED.
MARKUS CLAY.
I AM LISTENING. LISTENING TO A WORLD THAT CRIES IN PAIN.
A WORLD NOT UNLIKE MY OWN.
AND WHAT WORLD IS THAT, GOG?
WHEN YOUR ERRAND BOY HAD ME IN HIS HANDS, I SAW A VISION--
MY...ERRAND BOY? YOU SPEAK OF WILLIAM MATTHEWS.
YOU SPEAK OF SOMETHING WICKED.
WHERE ARE YOU FROM? ARE YOU FROM MY EARTH?
I AM FROM PARADISE.

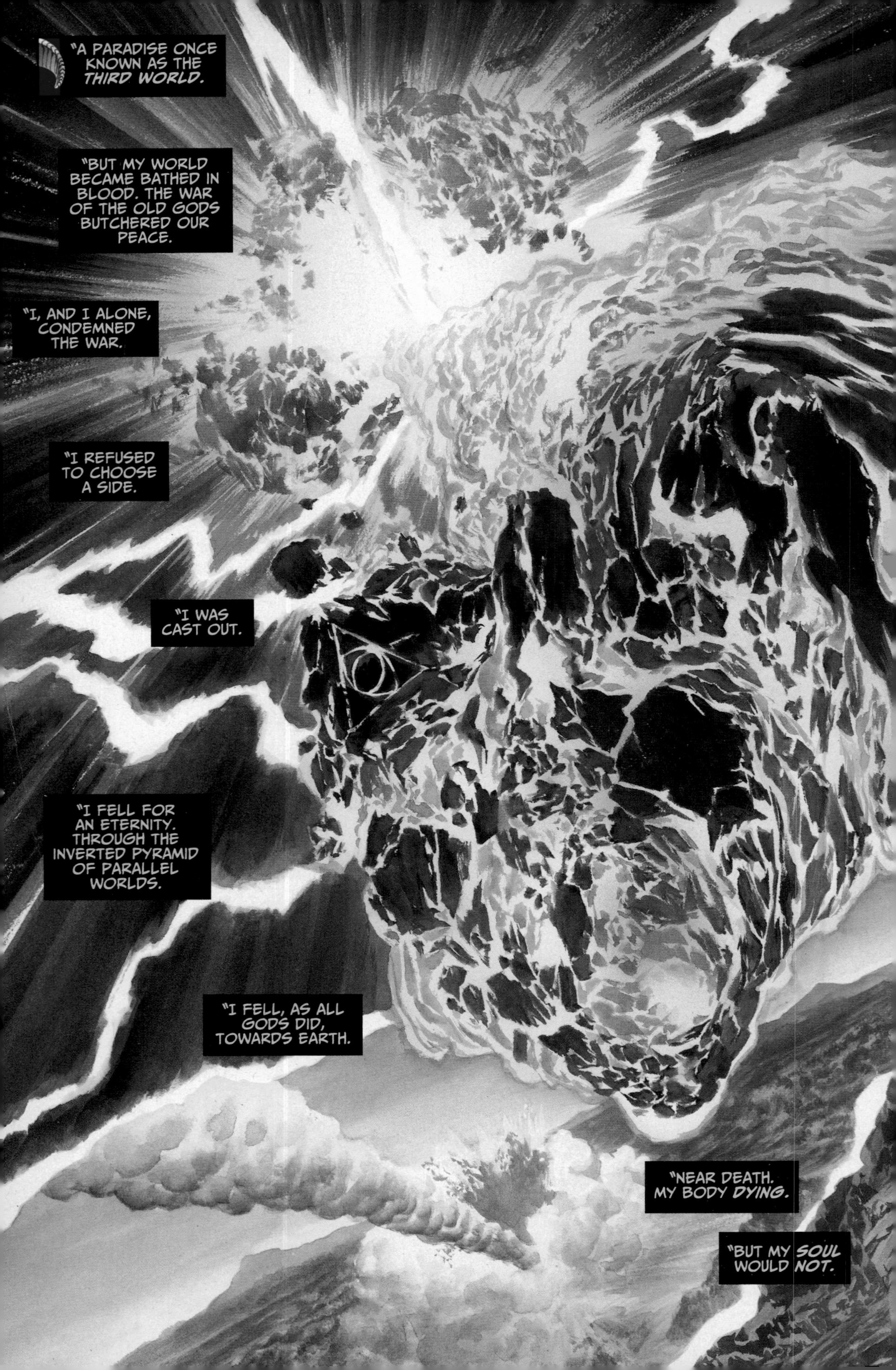
"A PARADISE ONCE KNOWN AS THE *THIRD WORLD*.
"BUT MY WORLD BECAME BATHED IN BLOOD. THE WAR OF THE OLD GODS BUTCHERED OUR PEACE.
"I, AND I ALONE, CONDEMNED THE WAR.
"I REFUSED TO CHOOSE A SIDE.
"I WAS CAST OUT.
"I FELL FOR AN ETERNITY. THROUGH THE INVERTED PYRAMID OF PARALLEL WORLDS.
"I FELL, AS ALL GODS DID, TOWARDS EARTH.
"NEAR DEATH. MY BODY *DYING*.
"BUT MY *SOUL* WOULD *NOT*.

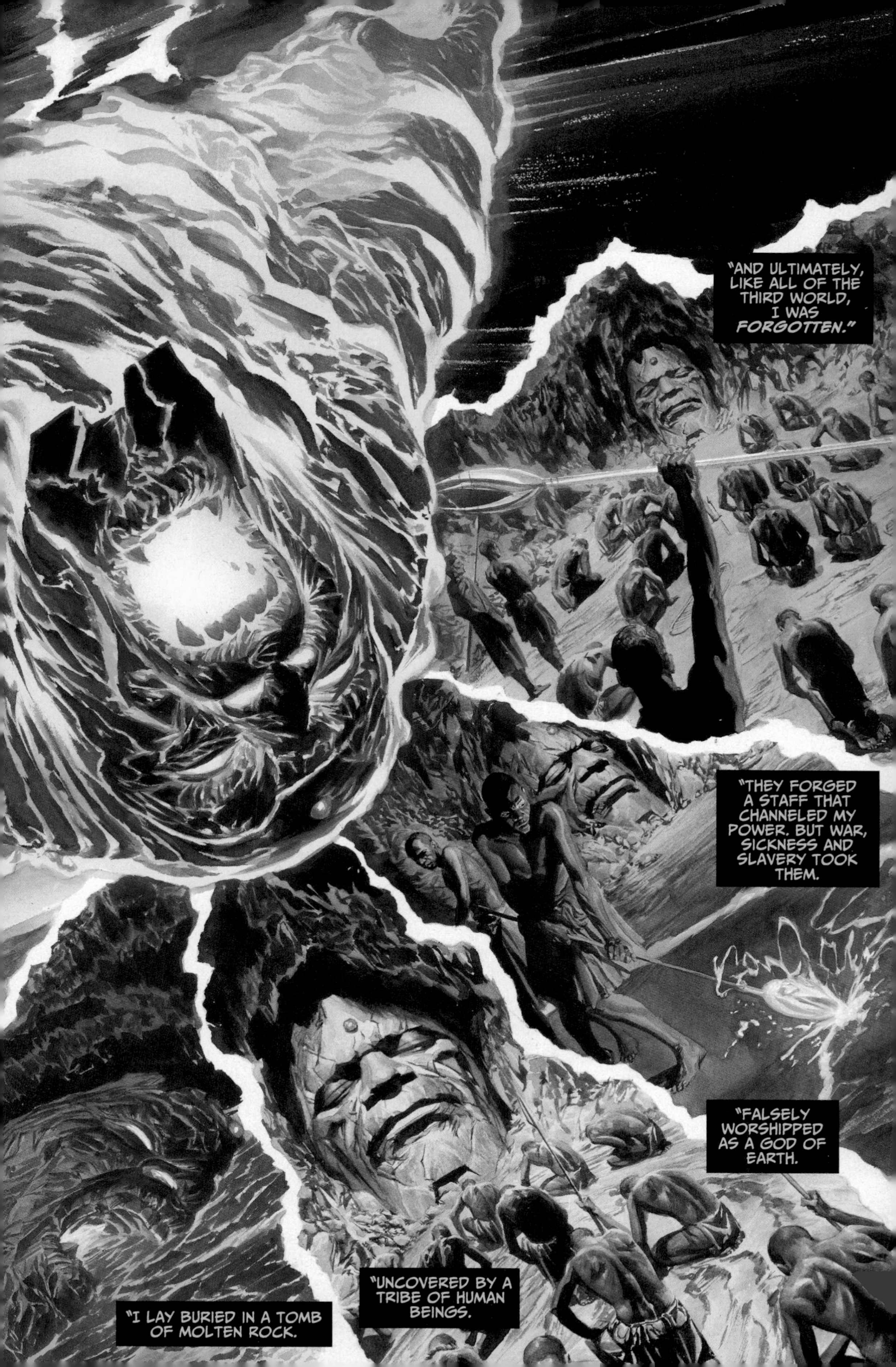
"I LAY BURIED IN A TOMB OF MOLTEN ROCK.
"UNCOVERED BY A TRIBE OF HUMAN BEINGS.
"FALSELY WORSHIPPED AS A GOD OF EARTH.
"THEY FORGED A STAFF THAT CHANNELED MY POWER. BUT WAR, SICKNESS AND SLAVERY TOOK THEM.
"AND ULTIMATELY, LIKE ALL OF THE THIRD WORLD, I WAS *FORGOTTEN.*"

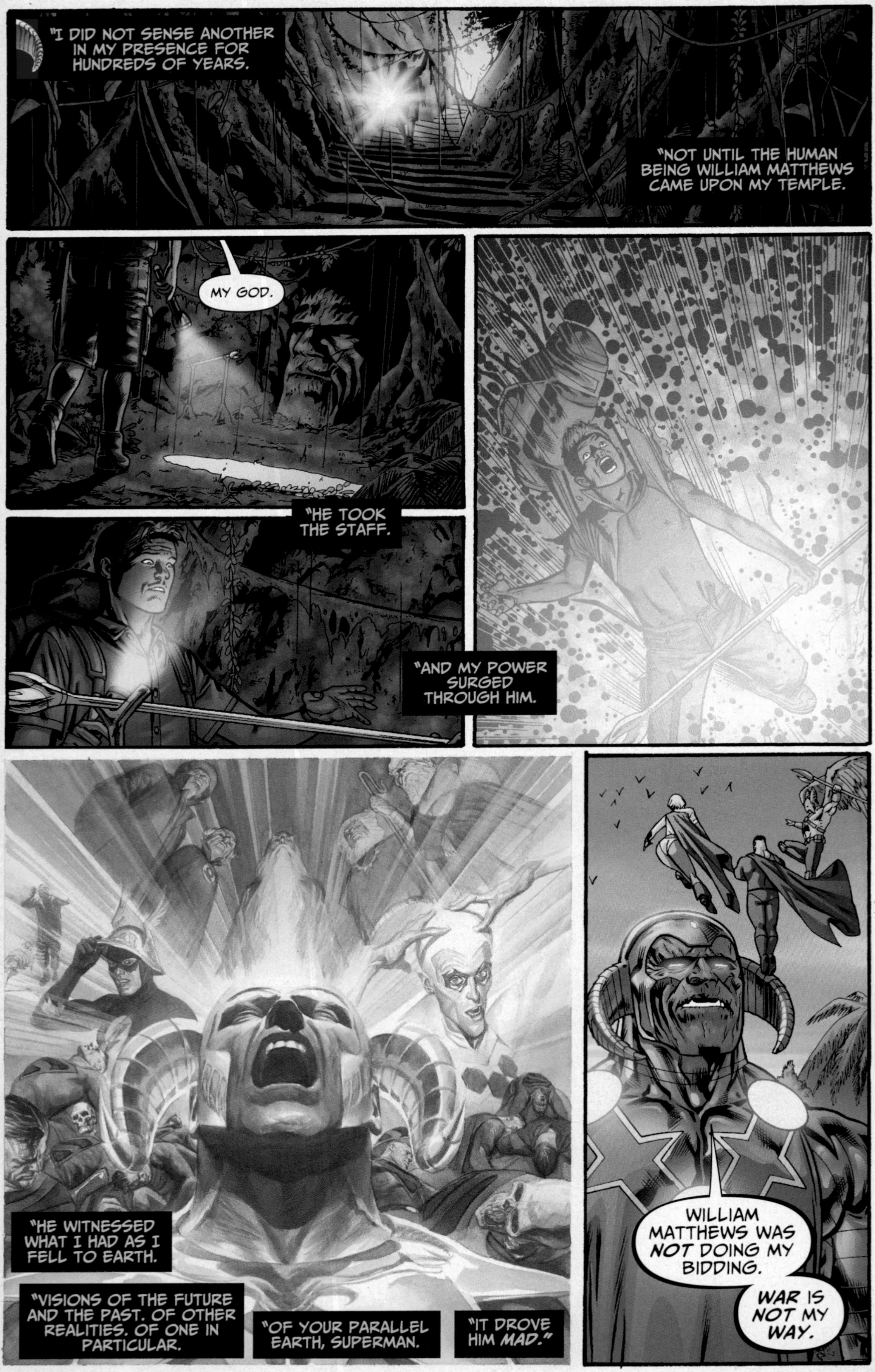
"I DID NOT SENSE ANOTHER IN MY PRESENCE FOR HUNDREDS OF YEARS.
"NOT UNTIL THE HUMAN BEING WILLIAM MATTHEWS CAME UPON MY TEMPLE.
MY GOD.
"HE TOOK THE STAFF.
"AND MY POWER SURGED THROUGH HIM.
"HE WITNESSED WHAT I HAD AS I FELL TO EARTH.
"VISIONS OF THE FUTURE AND THE PAST. OF OTHER REALITIES. OF ONE IN PARTICULAR.
"OF YOUR PARALLEL EARTH, SUPERMAN.
"IT DROVE HIM *MAD*."
WILLIAM MATTHEWS WAS *NOT* DOING MY BIDDING.
WAR IS *NOT* MY *WAY*.

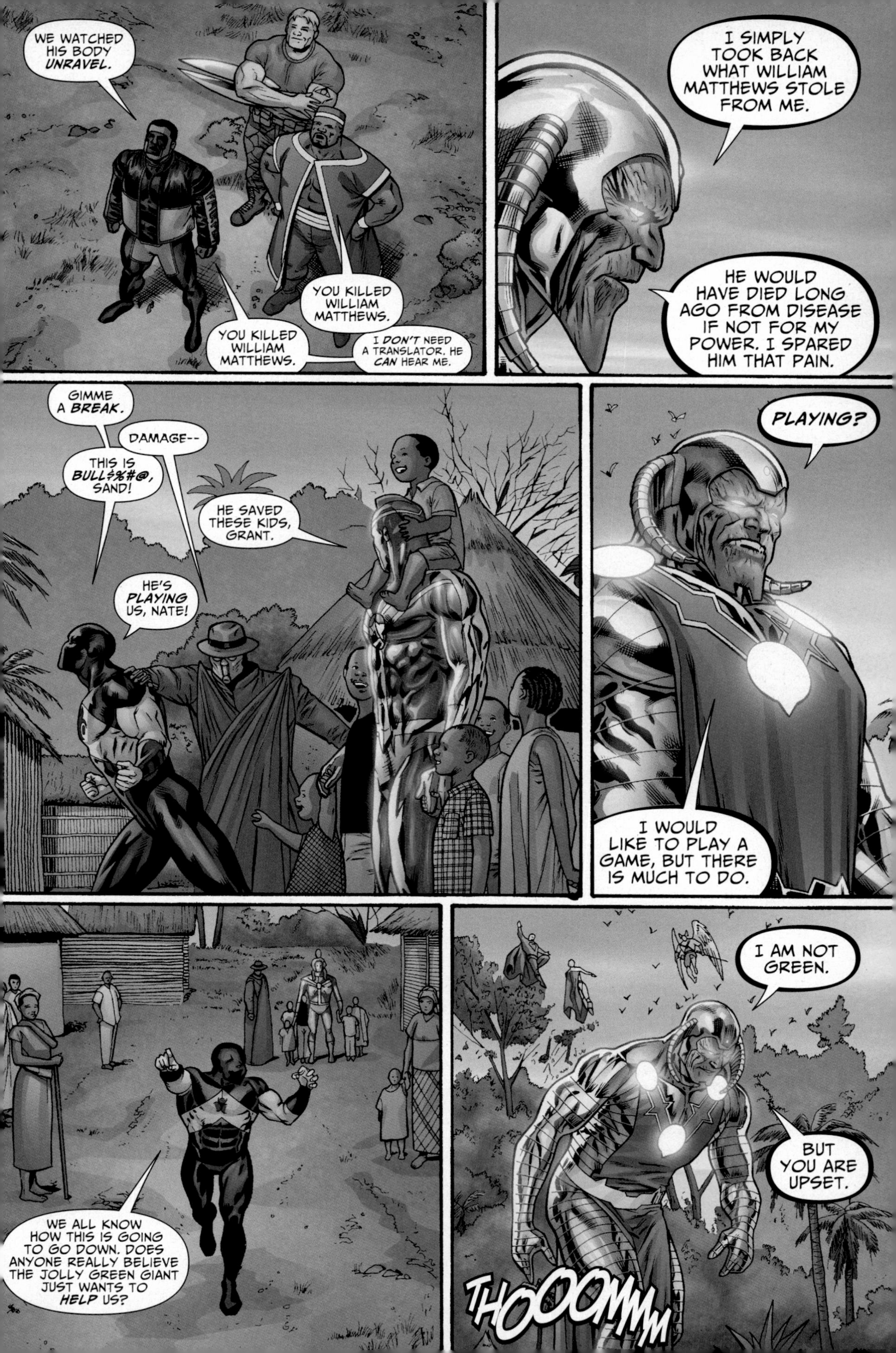

WE WATCHED HIS BODY UNRAVEL.
YOU KILLED WILLIAM MATTHEWS.
YOU KILLED WILLIAM MATTHEWS.
I DON'T NEED A TRANSLATOR. HE CAN HEAR ME.
I SIMPLY TOOK BACK WHAT WILLIAM MATTHEWS STOLE FROM ME.
HE WOULD HAVE DIED LONG AGO FROM DISEASE IF NOT FOR MY POWER. I SPARED HIM THAT PAIN.
GIMME A BREAK.
DAMAGE--
THIS IS BULL$%#@, SAND!
HE SAVED THESE KIDS, GRANT.
HE'S PLAYING US, NATE!
PLAYING?
I WOULD LIKE TO PLAY A GAME, BUT THERE IS MUCH TO DO.
WE ALL KNOW HOW THIS IS GOING TO GO DOWN. DOES ANYONE REALLY BELIEVE THE JOLLY GREEN GIANT JUST WANTS TO HELP US?
I AM NOT GREEN.
BUT YOU ARE UPSET.
THOOOMMM

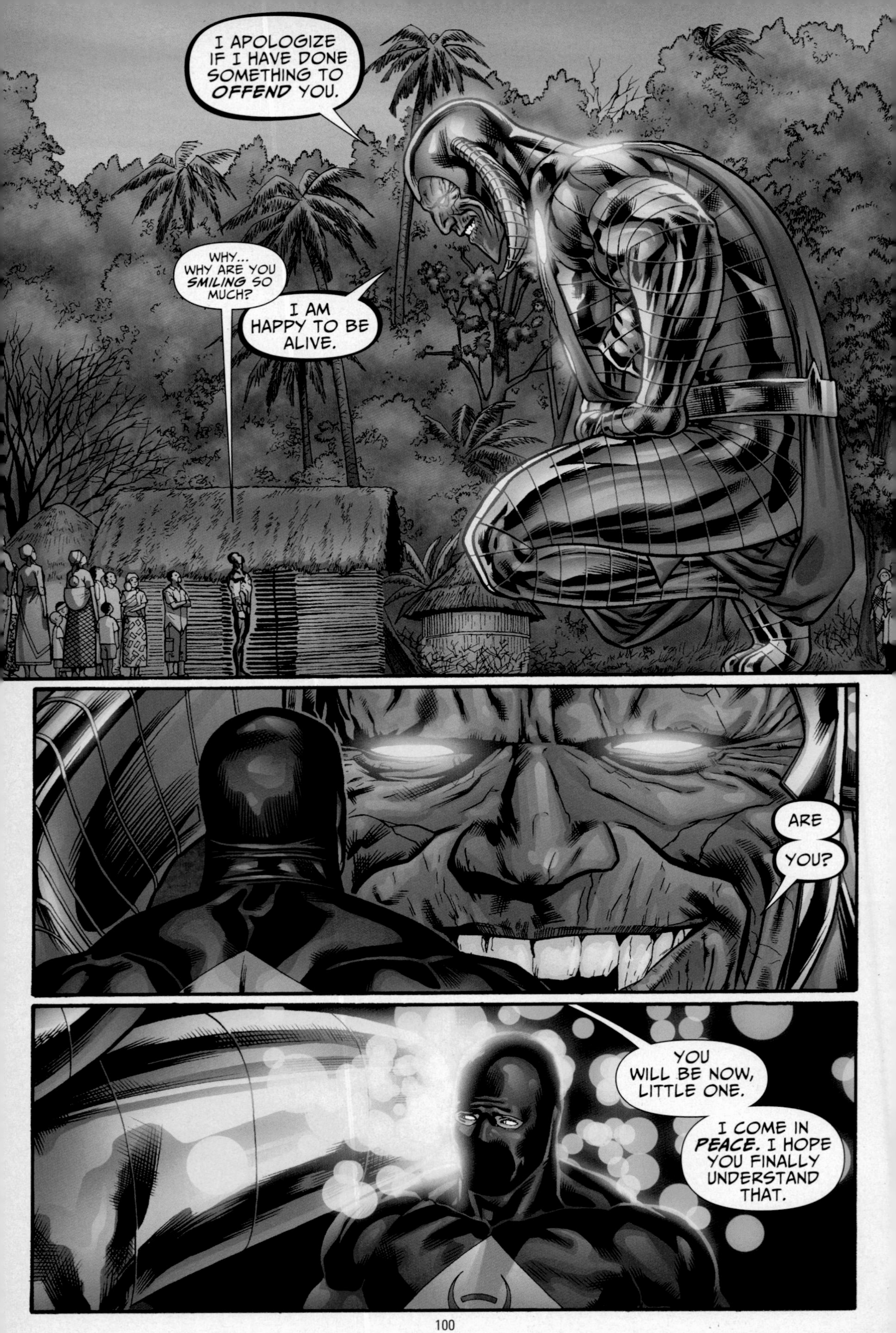
I APOLOGIZE IF I HAVE DONE SOMETHING TO OFFEND YOU.
WHY... WHY ARE YOU SMILING SO MUCH?
I AM HAPPY TO BE ALIVE.
ARE
YOU?
YOU WILL BE NOW, LITTLE ONE.
I COME IN PEACE. I HOPE YOU FINALLY UNDERSTAND THAT.

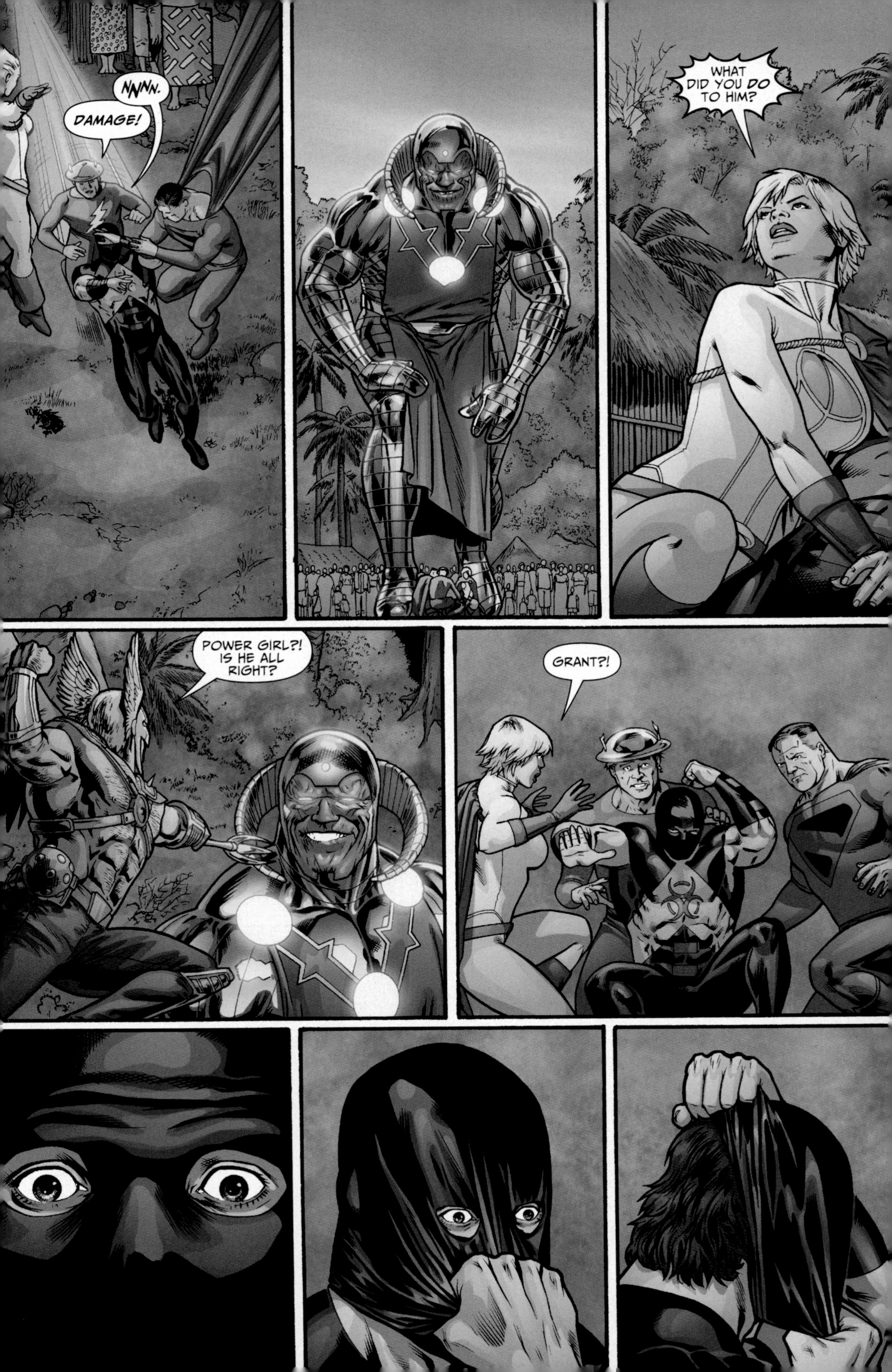
NNNN.
DAMAGE!
WHAT DID YOU DO TO HIM?
POWER GIRL?! IS HE ALL RIGHT?
GRANT?!

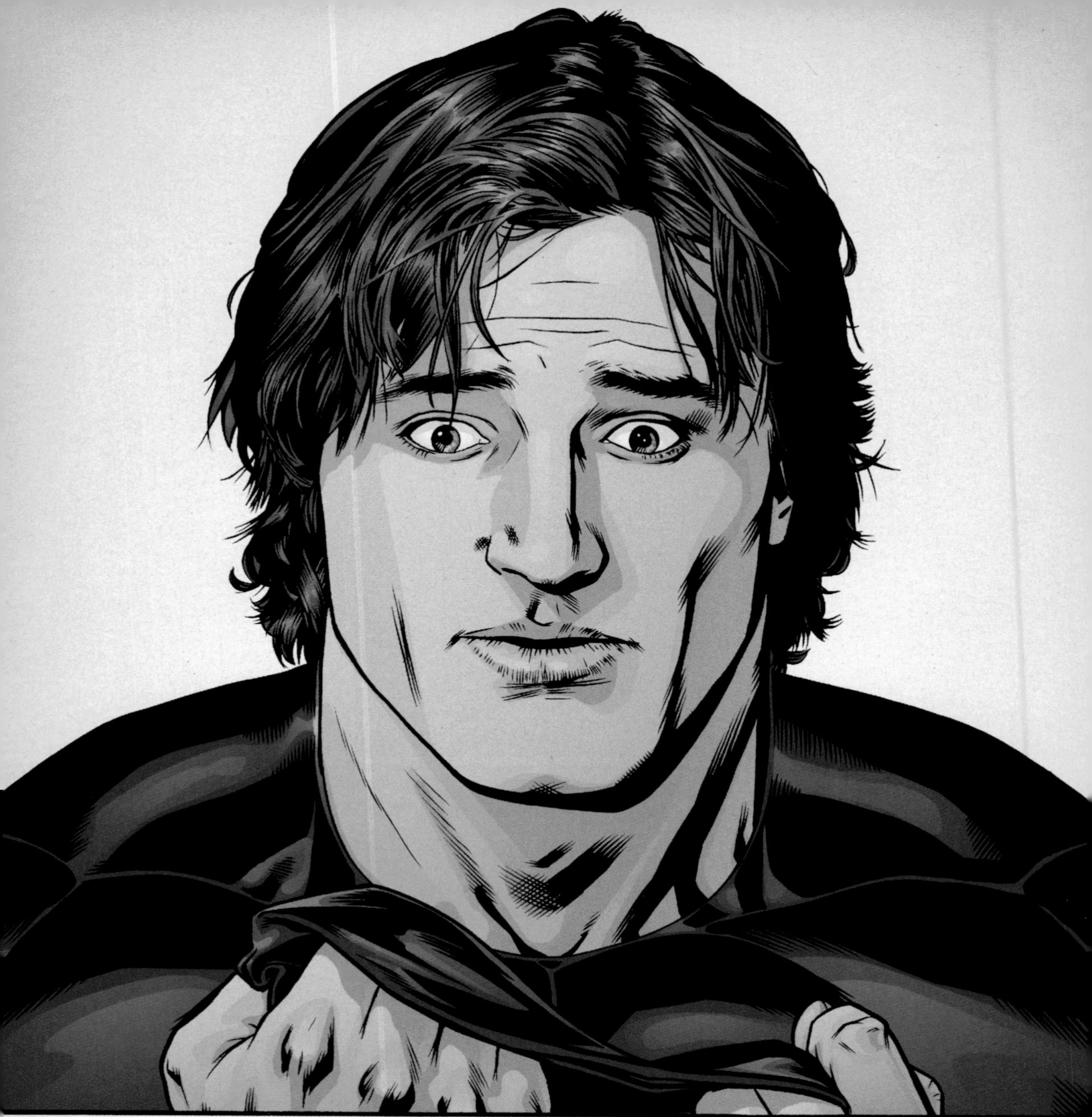

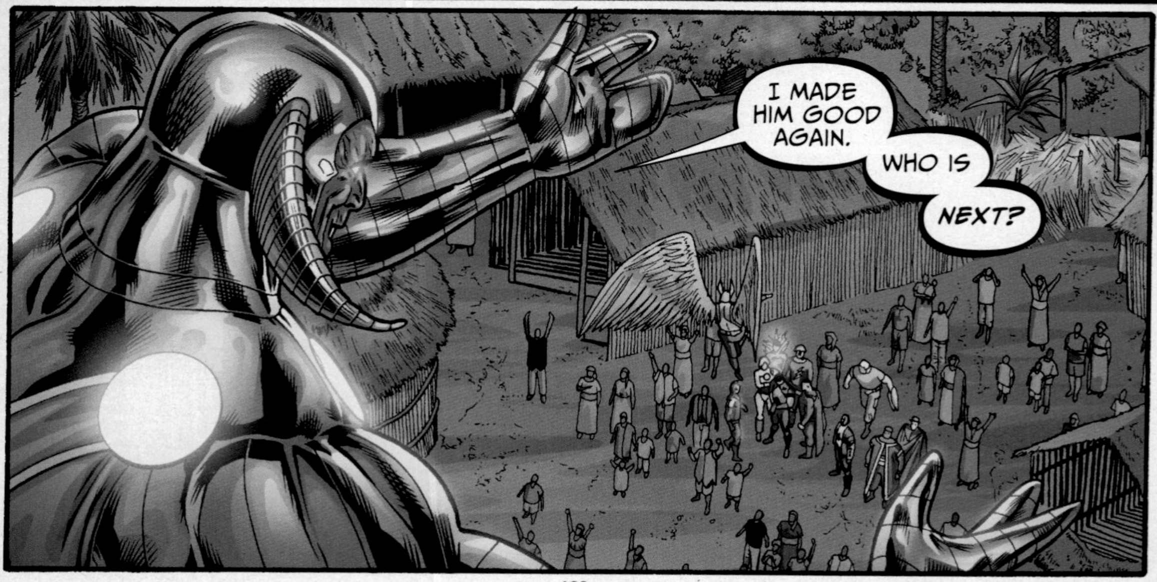
I MADE HIM GOOD AGAIN.
WHO IS
NEXT?

JUSTICE SOCIETY OF AMERICA #17 cover A by Alex Ross

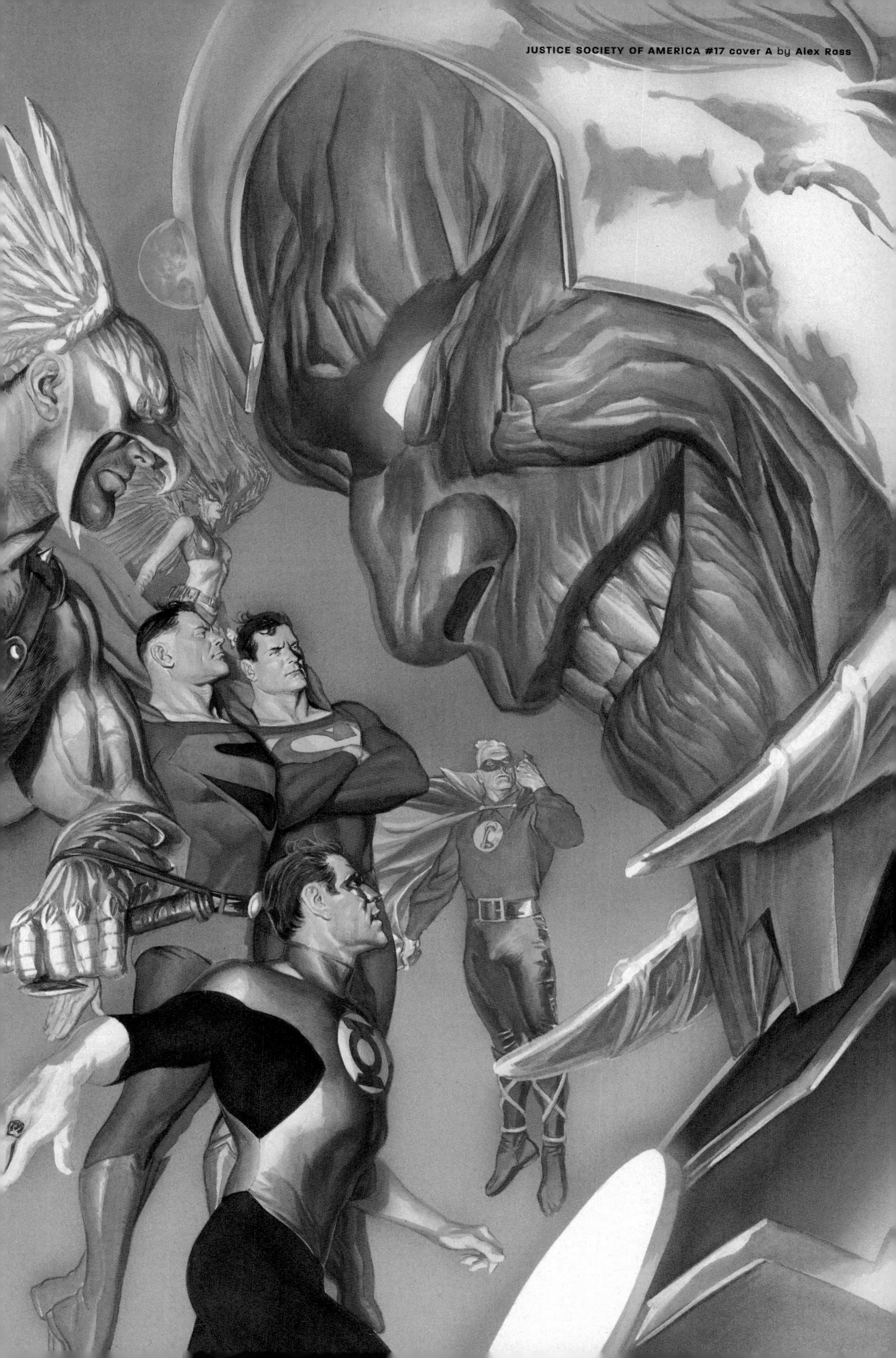

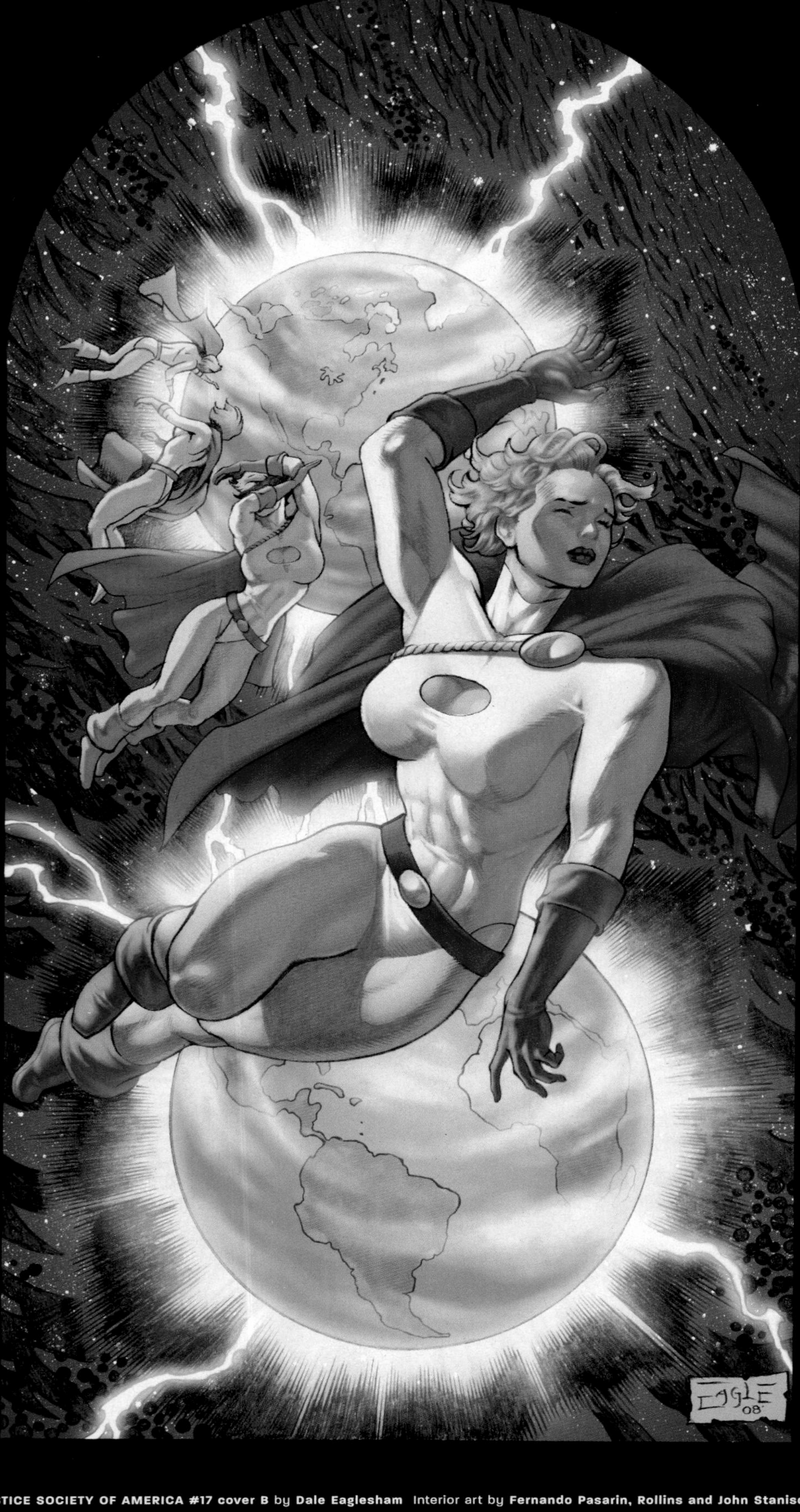
EAGLE
08

JUSTICE SOCIETY OF AMERICA #17 cover B by **Dale Eaglesham** Interior art by **Fernando Pasarin, Rollins and John Stanisci**

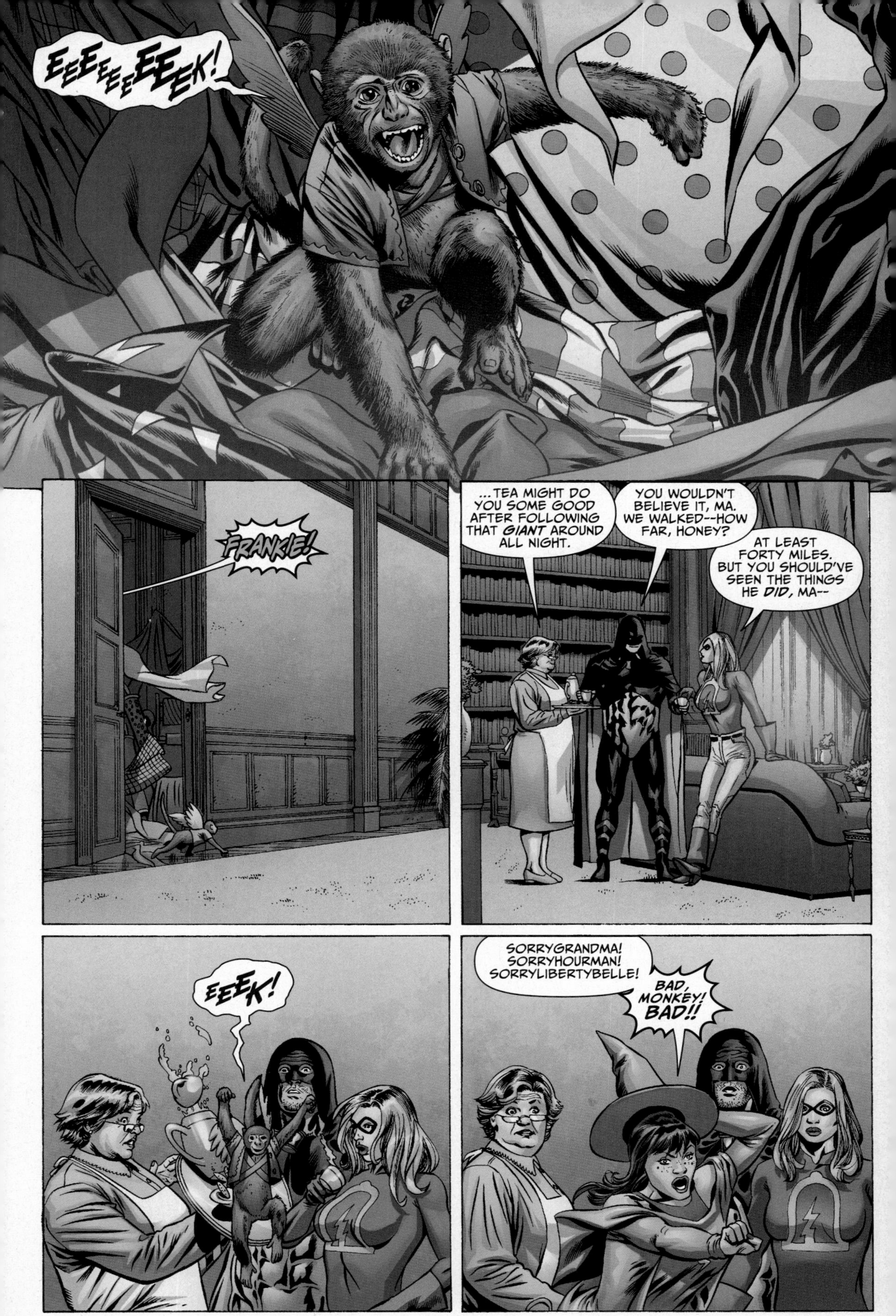
EEEEEEEEEK!
FRANKIE!
...TEA MIGHT DO YOU SOME GOOD AFTER FOLLOWING THAT GIANT AROUND ALL NIGHT.
YOU WOULDN'T BELIEVE IT, MA. WE WALKED--HOW FAR, HONEY?
AT LEAST FORTY MILES. BUT YOU SHOULD'VE SEEN THE THINGS HE DID, MA--
EEEK!
SORRYGRANDMA! SORRYHOURMAN! SORRYLIBERTYBELLE!
BAD, MONKEY! BAD!!

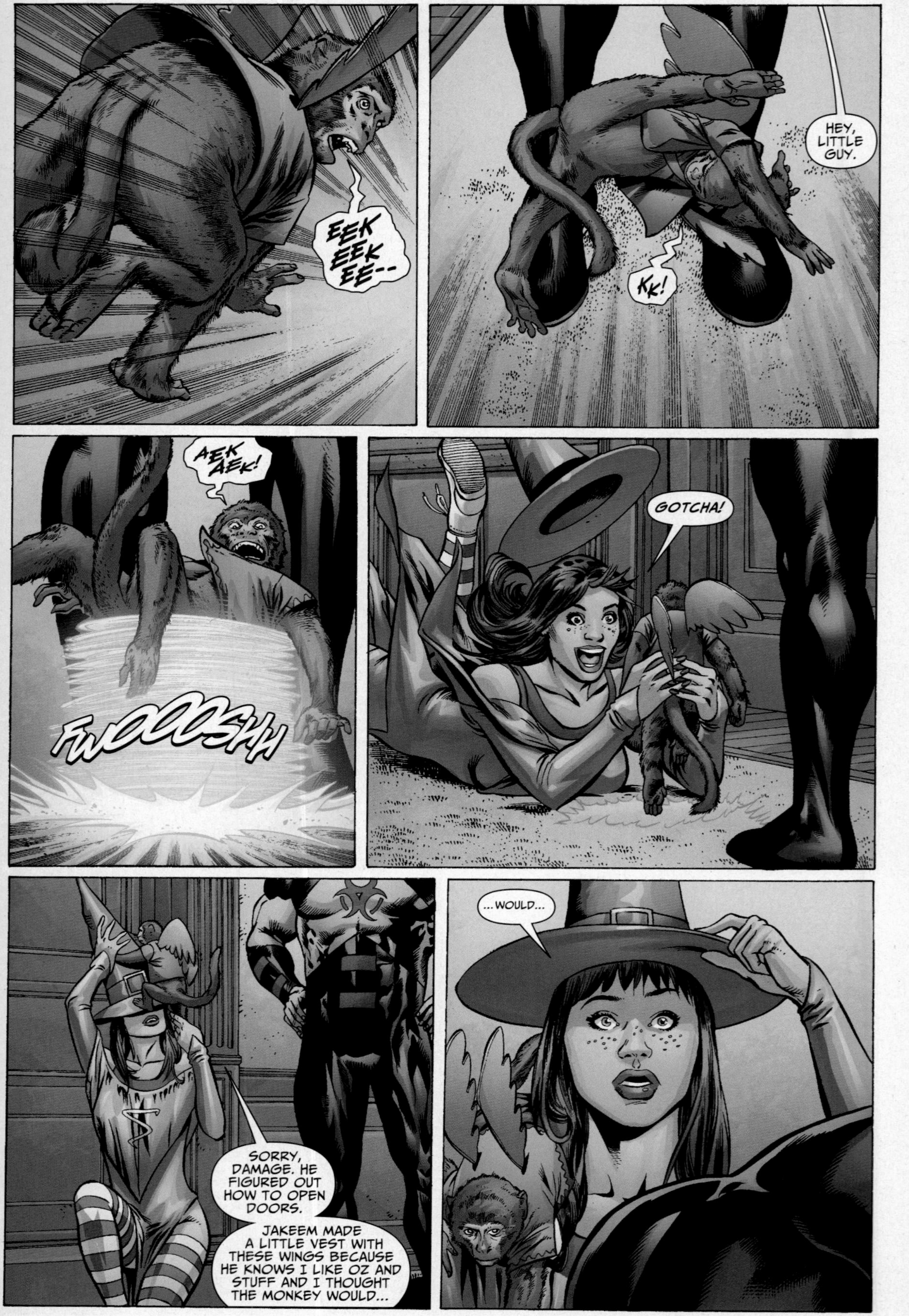
EEK EEK EE--
HEY, LITTLE GUY.
KK!
AEK AEK!
FWOOOSHH
GOTCHA!
SORRY, DAMAGE. HE FIGURED OUT HOW TO OPEN DOORS.
JAKEEM MADE A LITTLE VEST WITH THESE WINGS BECAUSE HE KNOWS I LIKE OZ AND STUFF AND I THOUGHT THE MONKEY WOULD...
...WOULD...

Wish Fulfillment

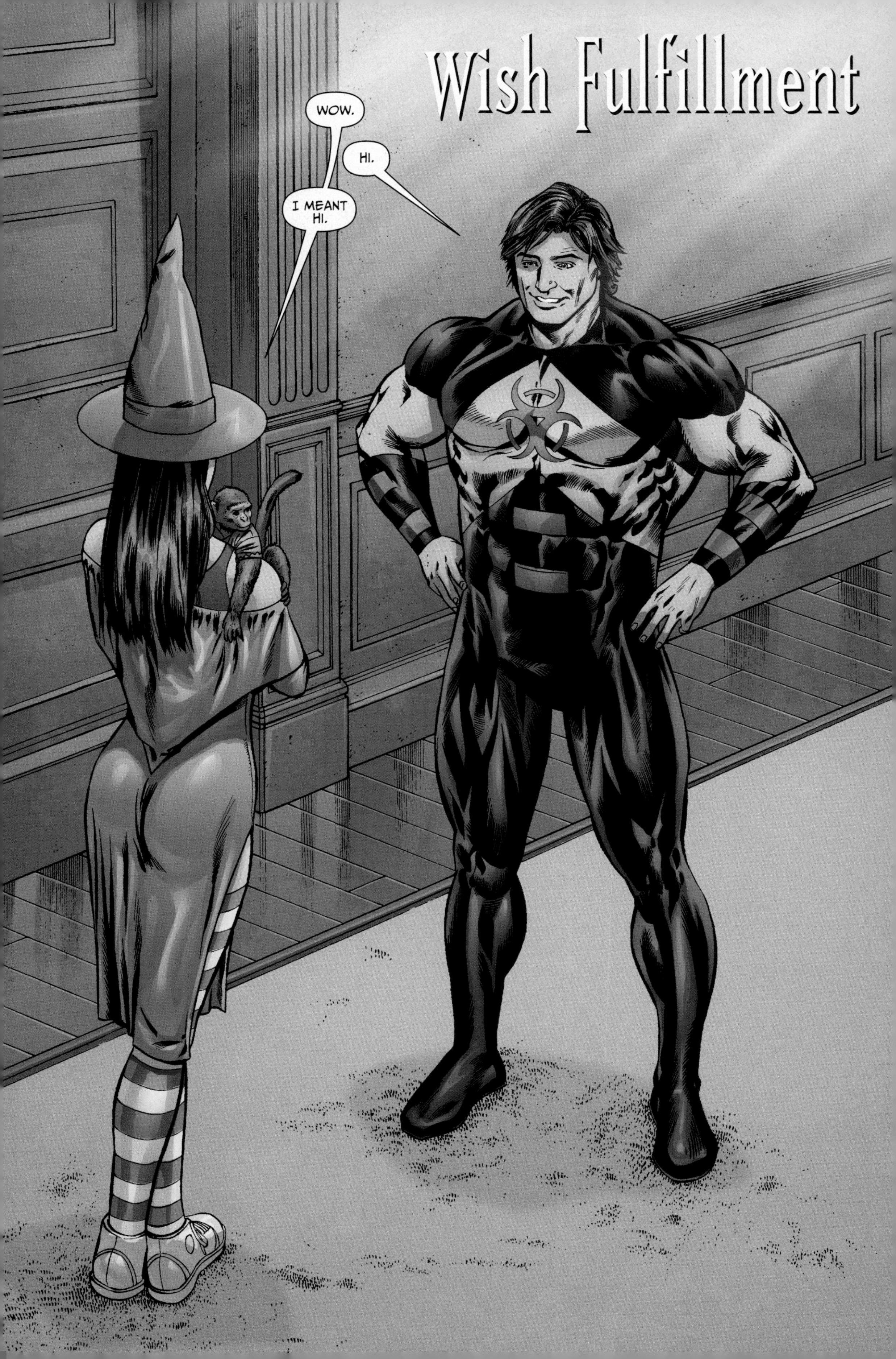
WOW.
I MEANT HI.
HI.

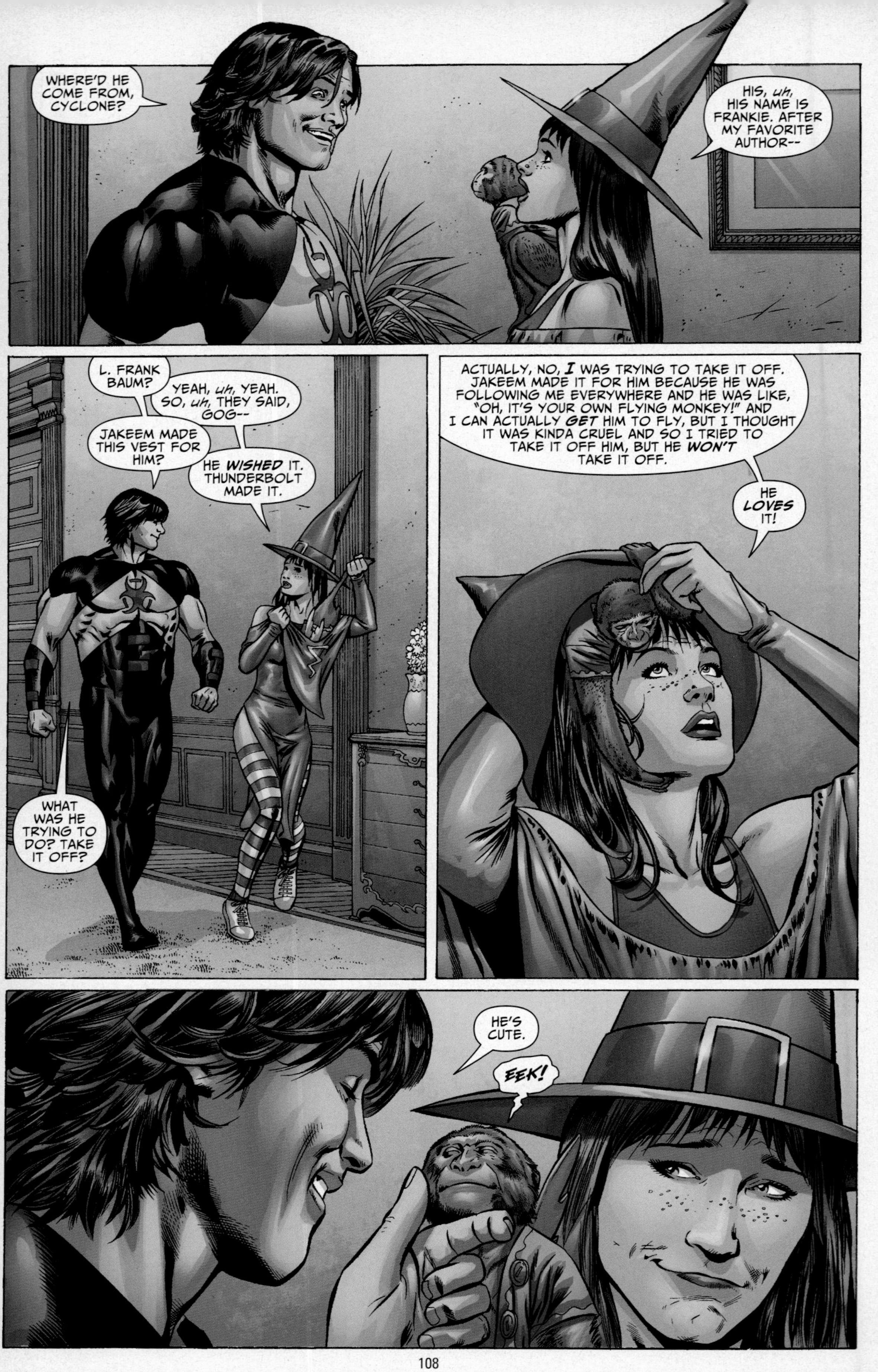
WHERE'D HE COME FROM, CYCLONE?
HIS, *uh*, HIS NAME IS FRANKIE. AFTER MY FAVORITE AUTHOR--
L. FRANK BAUM?
YEAH, *uh*, YEAH. SO, *uh*, THEY SAID, GOG--
JAKEEM MADE THIS VEST FOR HIM?
HE **WISHED** IT. THUNDERBOLT MADE IT.
WHAT WAS HE TRYING TO DO? TAKE IT OFF?
ACTUALLY, NO, **I** WAS TRYING TO TAKE IT OFF. JAKEEM MADE IT FOR HIM BECAUSE HE WAS FOLLOWING ME EVERYWHERE AND HE WAS LIKE, "OH, IT'S YOUR OWN FLYING MONKEY!" AND I CAN ACTUALLY **GET** HIM TO FLY, BUT I THOUGHT IT WAS KINDA CRUEL AND SO I TRIED TO TAKE IT OFF HIM, BUT HE **WON'T** TAKE IT OFF.
HE **LOVES** IT!
HE'S CUTE.
EEK!

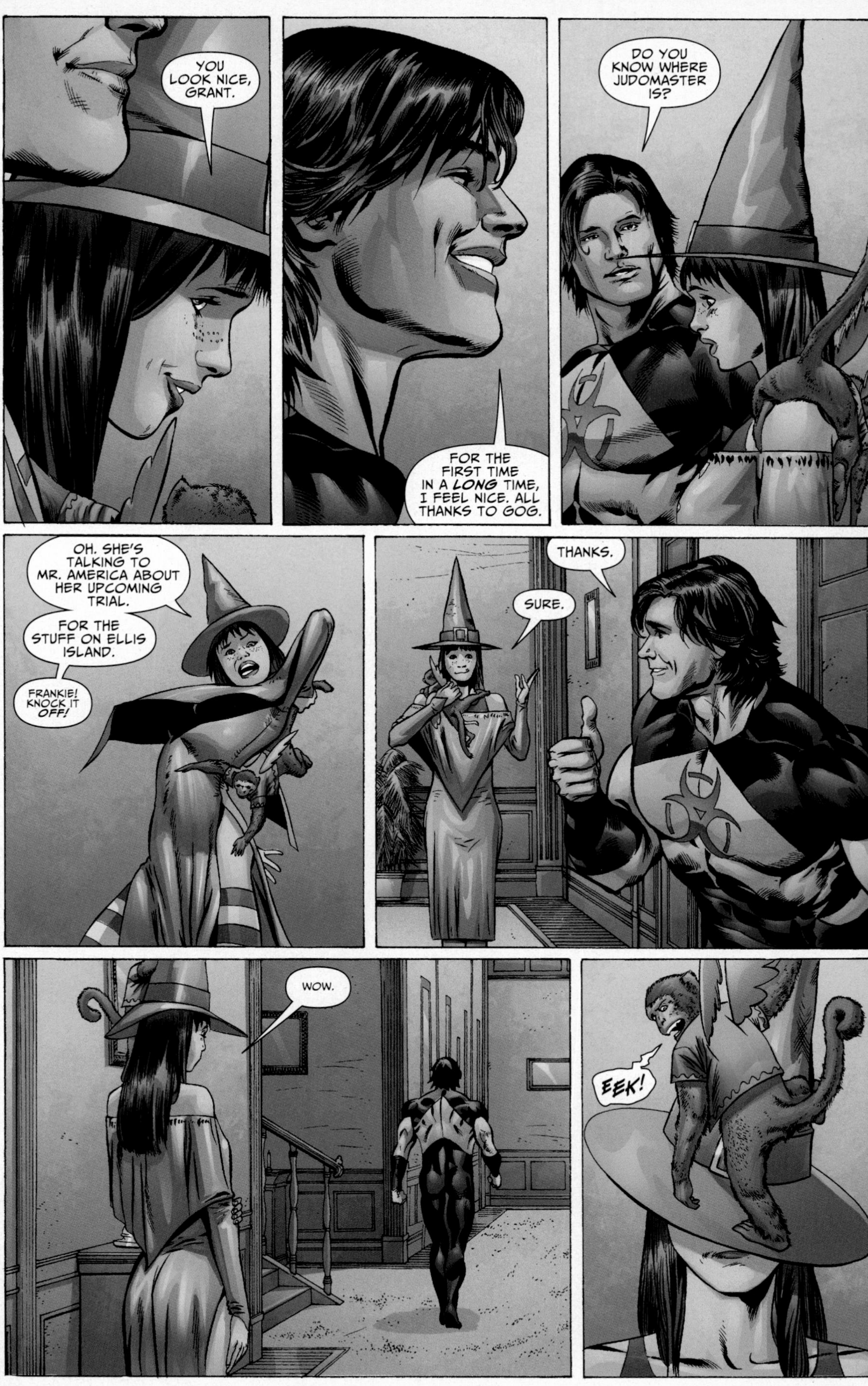
YOU LOOK NICE, GRANT.
FOR THE FIRST TIME IN A LONG TIME, I FEEL NICE. ALL THANKS TO GOG.
DO YOU KNOW WHERE JUDOMASTER IS?
OH. SHE'S TALKING TO MR. AMERICA ABOUT HER UPCOMING TRIAL.
FOR THE STUFF ON ELLIS ISLAND.
FRANKIE! KNOCK IT OFF!
THANKS.
SURE.
WOW.
EEK!

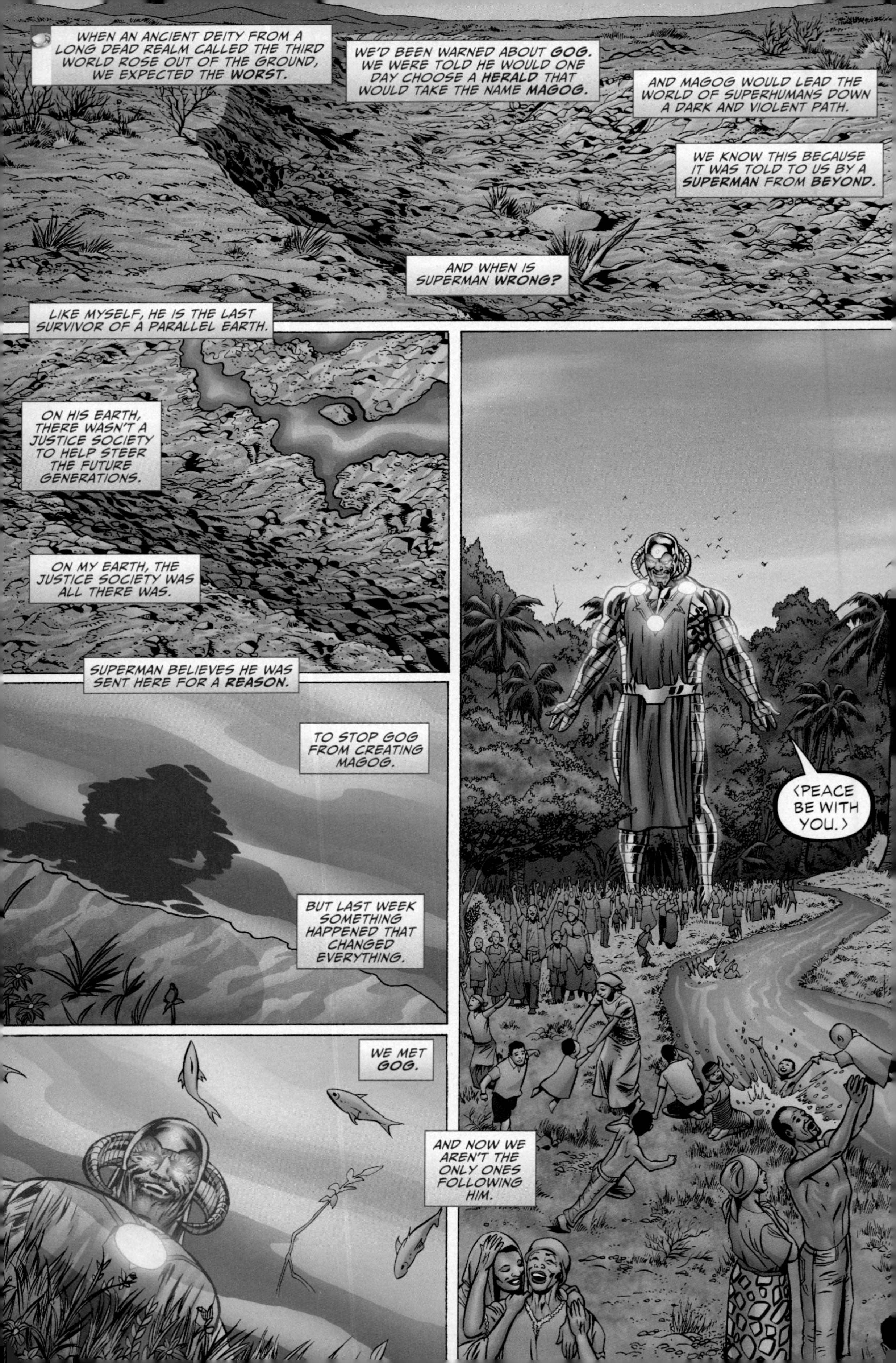

WHEN AN ANCIENT DEITY FROM A LONG DEAD REALM CALLED THE THIRD WORLD ROSE OUT OF THE GROUND, WE EXPECTED THE WORST.
WE'D BEEN WARNED ABOUT GOG. WE WERE TOLD HE WOULD ONE DAY CHOOSE A HERALD THAT WOULD TAKE THE NAME MAGOG.
AND MAGOG WOULD LEAD THE WORLD OF SUPERHUMANS DOWN A DARK AND VIOLENT PATH.
WE KNOW THIS BECAUSE IT WAS TOLD TO US BY A SUPERMAN FROM BEYOND.
AND WHEN IS SUPERMAN WRONG?
LIKE MYSELF, HE IS THE LAST SURVIVOR OF A PARALLEL EARTH.
ON HIS EARTH, THERE WASN'T A JUSTICE SOCIETY TO HELP STEER THE FUTURE GENERATIONS.
ON MY EARTH, THE JUSTICE SOCIETY WAS ALL THERE WAS.
SUPERMAN BELIEVES HE WAS SENT HERE FOR A REASON.
TO STOP GOG FROM CREATING MAGOG.
BUT LAST WEEK SOMETHING HAPPENED THAT CHANGED EVERYTHING.
WE MET GOG.
⟨PEACE BE WITH YOU.⟩
AND NOW WE AREN'T THE ONLY ONES FOLLOWING HIM.

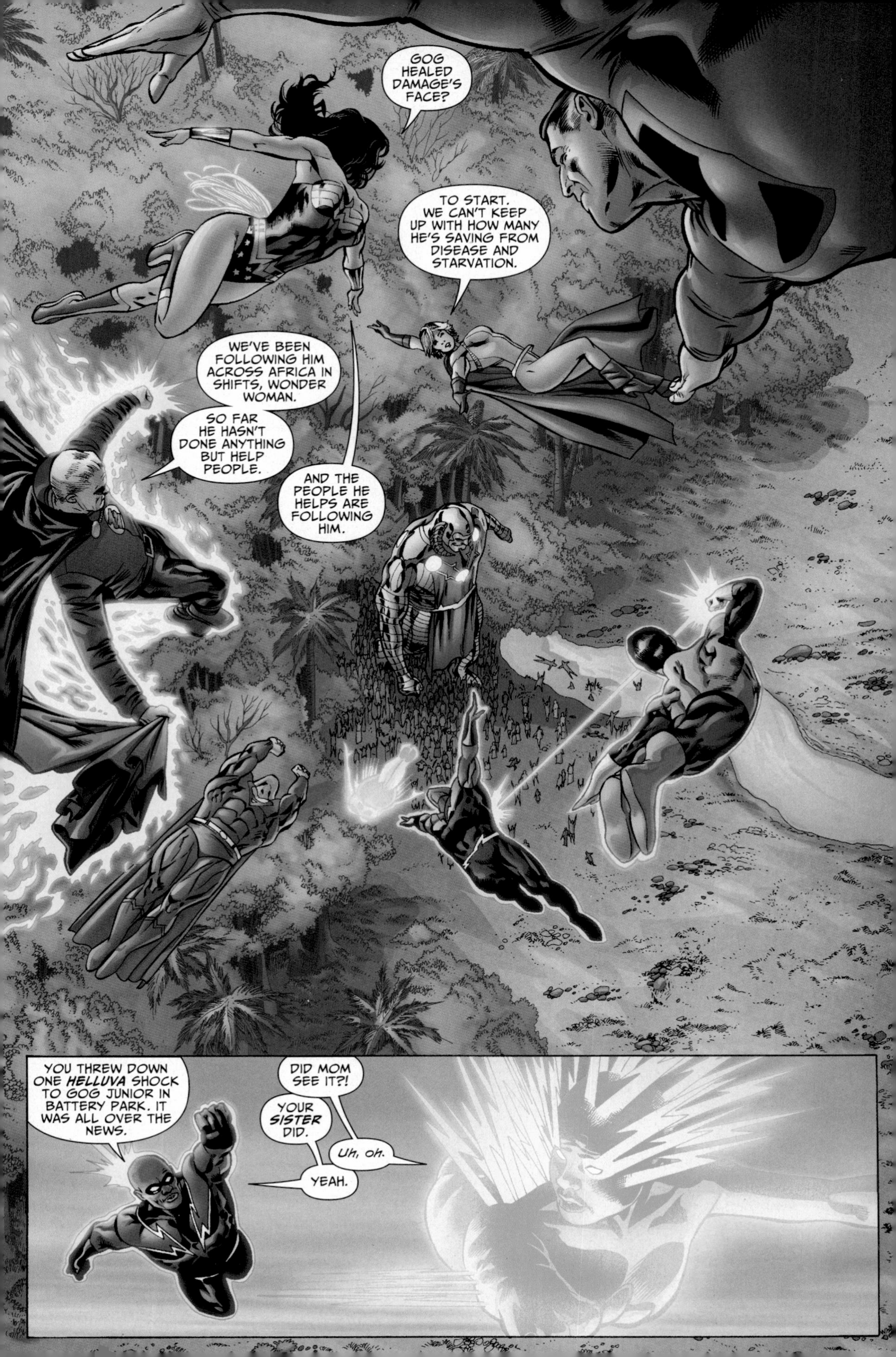
GOG HEALED DAMAGE'S FACE?
TO START. WE CAN'T KEEP UP WITH HOW MANY HE'S SAVING FROM DISEASE AND STARVATION.
WE'VE BEEN FOLLOWING HIM ACROSS AFRICA IN SHIFTS, WONDER WOMAN.
SO FAR HE HASN'T DONE ANYTHING BUT HELP PEOPLE.
AND THE PEOPLE HE HELPS ARE FOLLOWING HIM.
YOU THREW DOWN ONE HELLUVA SHOCK TO GOG JUNIOR IN BATTERY PARK. IT WAS ALL OVER THE NEWS.
DID MOM SEE IT?!
YOUR SISTER DID.
Uh, oh.
YEAH.

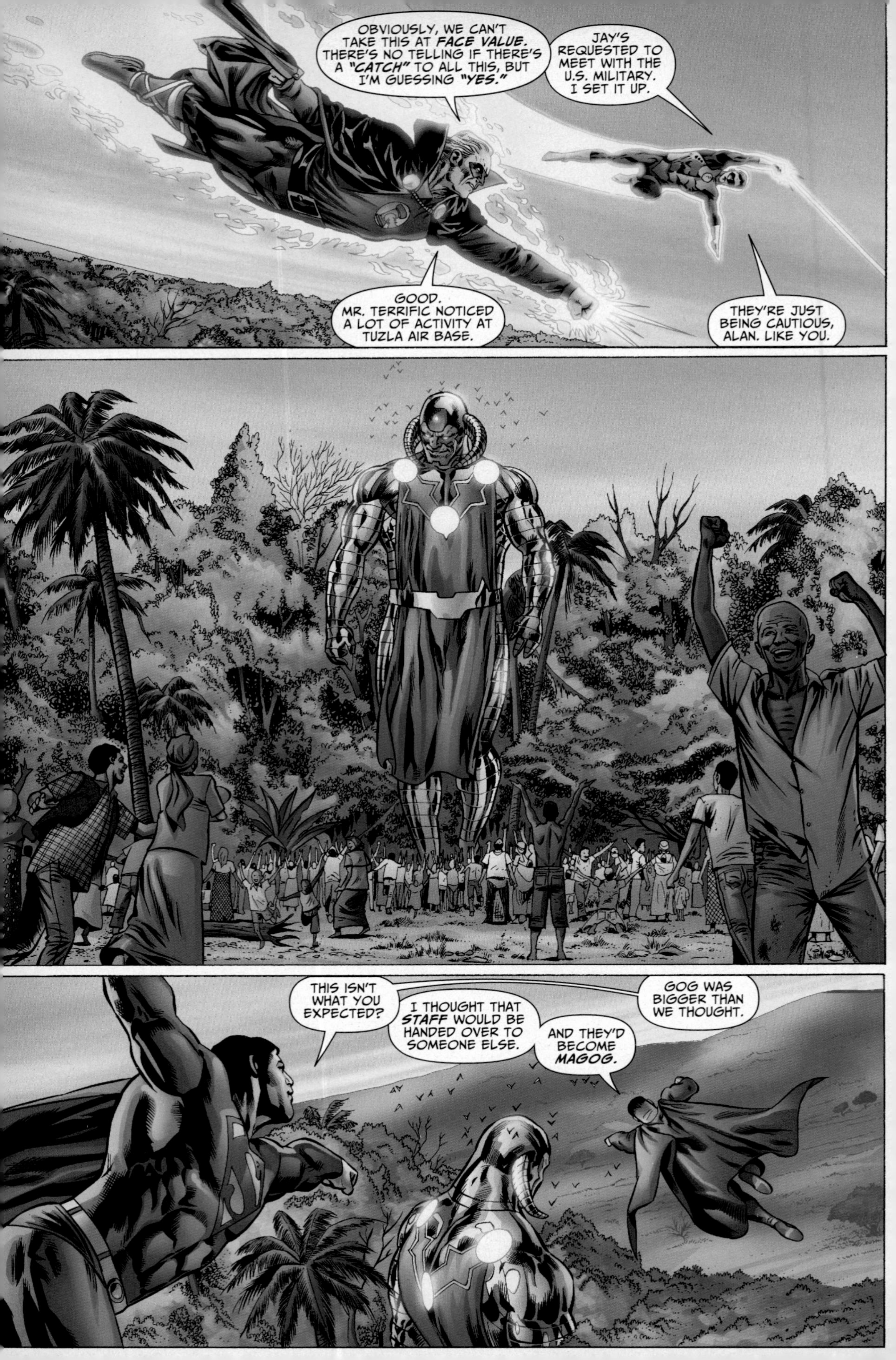
OBVIOUSLY, WE CAN'T TAKE THIS AT FACE VALUE. THERE'S NO TELLING IF THERE'S A "CATCH" TO ALL THIS, BUT I'M GUESSING "YES."
JAY'S REQUESTED TO MEET WITH THE U.S. MILITARY. I SET IT UP.
GOOD. MR. TERRIFIC NOTICED A LOT OF ACTIVITY AT TUZLA AIR BASE.
THEY'RE JUST BEING CAUTIOUS, ALAN. LIKE YOU.
THIS ISN'T WHAT YOU EXPECTED?
GOG WAS BIGGER THAN WE THOUGHT.
I THOUGHT THAT STAFF WOULD BE HANDED OVER TO SOMEONE ELSE.
AND THEY'D BECOME MAGOG.

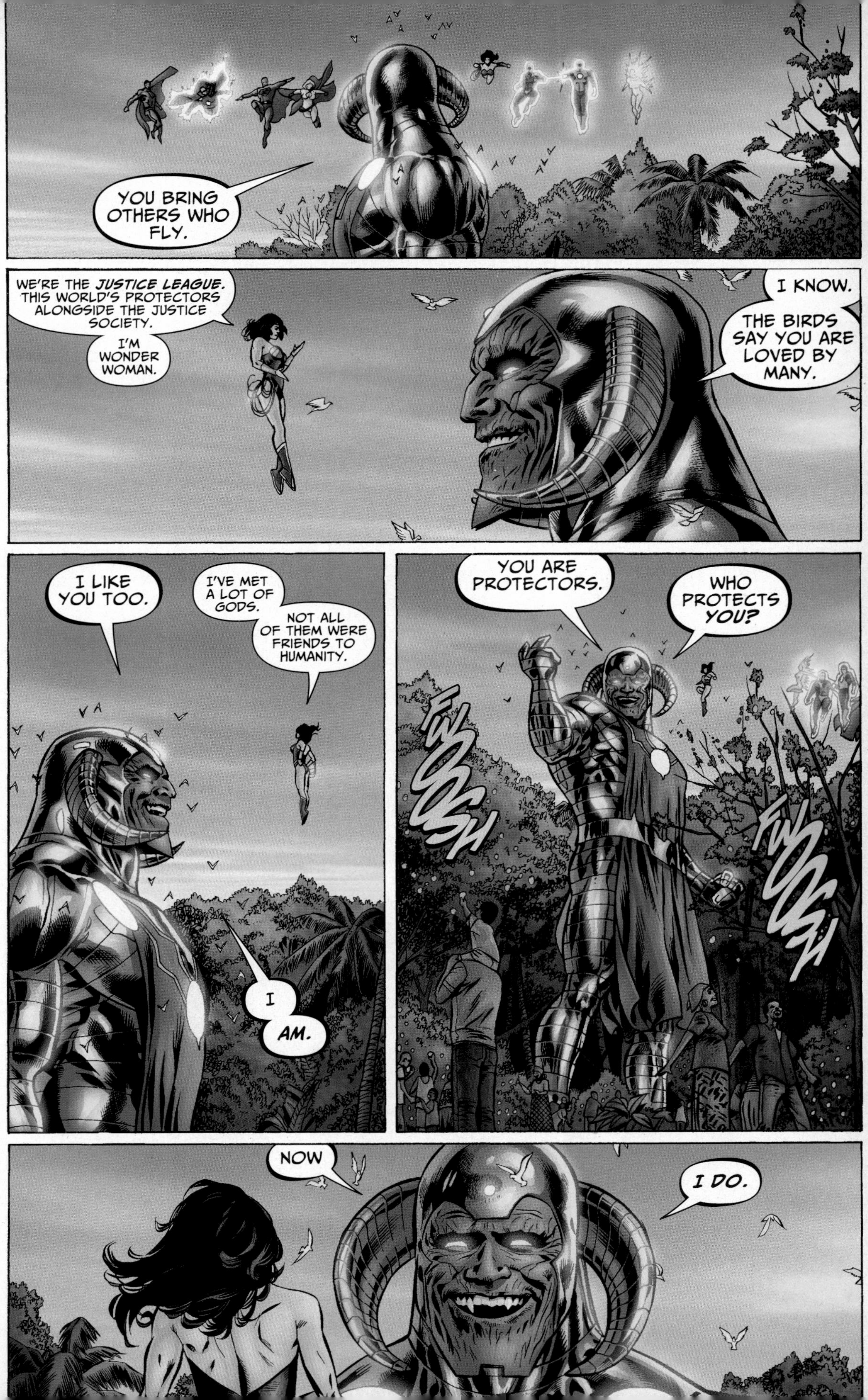
YOU BRING OTHERS WHO FLY.
WE'RE THE *JUSTICE LEAGUE*. THIS WORLD'S PROTECTORS ALONGSIDE THE JUSTICE SOCIETY.
I'M WONDER WOMAN.
I KNOW.
THE BIRDS SAY YOU ARE LOVED BY MANY.
I LIKE YOU TOO.
I'VE MET A LOT OF GODS.
NOT ALL OF THEM WERE FRIENDS TO HUMANITY.
I
AM.
YOU ARE PROTECTORS.
WHO PROTECTS *YOU?*
FWOOOSH
FWOOOSH
NOW
I DO.

PORTSMOUTH.

DONG

...I ASK YOU TO GIVE THANKS TO THIS BEING, THIS *GOG*, BUT REMEMBER. HE IS AS MUCH *OUR GOD* AS *SUPERMAN*.

THIS *GIANT* WHO WALKS THE EARTH, WHO HAS SAVED *HUNDREDS* AND TRANSFORMED *DISEASED* AND *BARREN* LANDS INTO PLACES OF *WONDER*, HE IS A *WELCOME* PRESENCE, BUT HE IS NOT OUR *CREATOR*.

WE RESERVE OUR *FAITH* FOR HIM, OUR *LORD*.

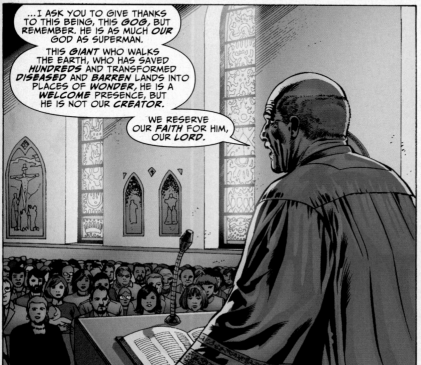

AMEN.

PIETER.

MICHAEL? OUR SHIFT DOESN'T START UNTIL TONIGHT. WHAT ARE YOU DOING HERE?

DO YOU BELIEVE IT?

DO YOU REALLY BELIEVE WE HAVE A *GOD* WALKING THE EARTH?

I DO.

BUT AS FATHER JACOBS SAYS, HE'S NOT *MY* GOD.

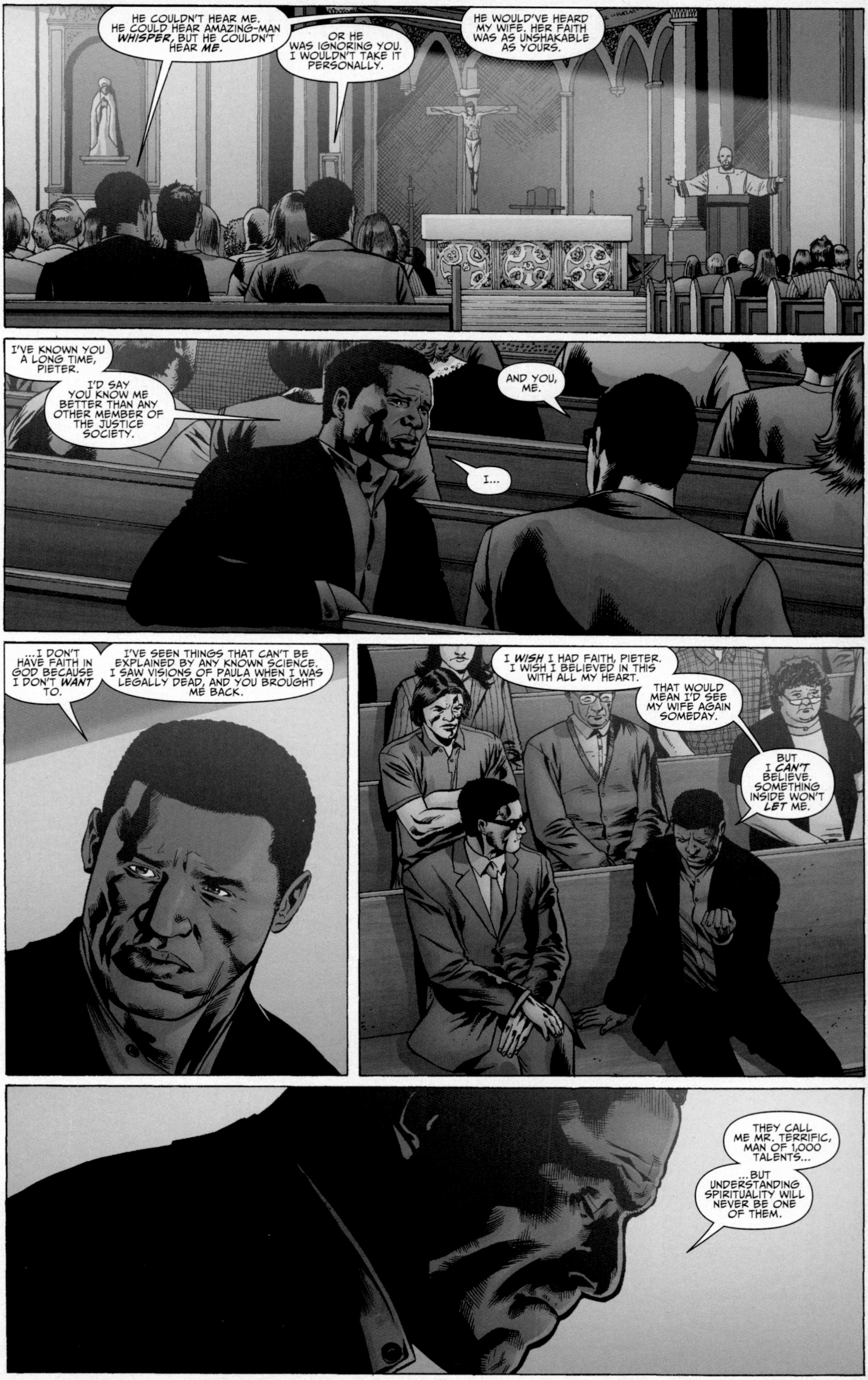
HE COULDN'T HEAR ME. HE COULD HEAR AMAZING-MAN *WHISPER*, BUT HE COULDN'T HEAR *ME*.
OR HE WAS IGNORING YOU. I WOULDN'T TAKE IT PERSONALLY.
HE WOULD'VE HEARD MY WIFE. HER FAITH WAS AS UNSHAKABLE AS YOURS.
I'VE KNOWN YOU A LONG TIME, PIETER.
I'D SAY YOU KNOW ME BETTER THAN ANY OTHER MEMBER OF THE JUSTICE SOCIETY.
AND YOU, ME.
I...
...I DON'T HAVE FAITH IN GOD BECAUSE I DON'T *WANT* TO.
I'VE SEEN THINGS THAT CAN'T BE EXPLAINED BY ANY KNOWN SCIENCE. I SAW VISIONS OF PAULA WHEN I WAS LEGALLY DEAD, AND YOU BROUGHT ME BACK.
I *WISH* I HAD FAITH, PIETER. I WISH I BELIEVED IN THIS WITH ALL MY HEART.
THAT WOULD MEAN I'D SEE MY WIFE AGAIN SOMEDAY.
BUT I *CAN'T* BELIEVE. SOMETHING INSIDE WON'T *LET* ME.
THEY CALL ME MR. TERRIFIC, MAN OF 1,000 TALENTS...
...BUT UNDERSTANDING SPIRITUALITY WILL NEVER BE ONE OF THEM.

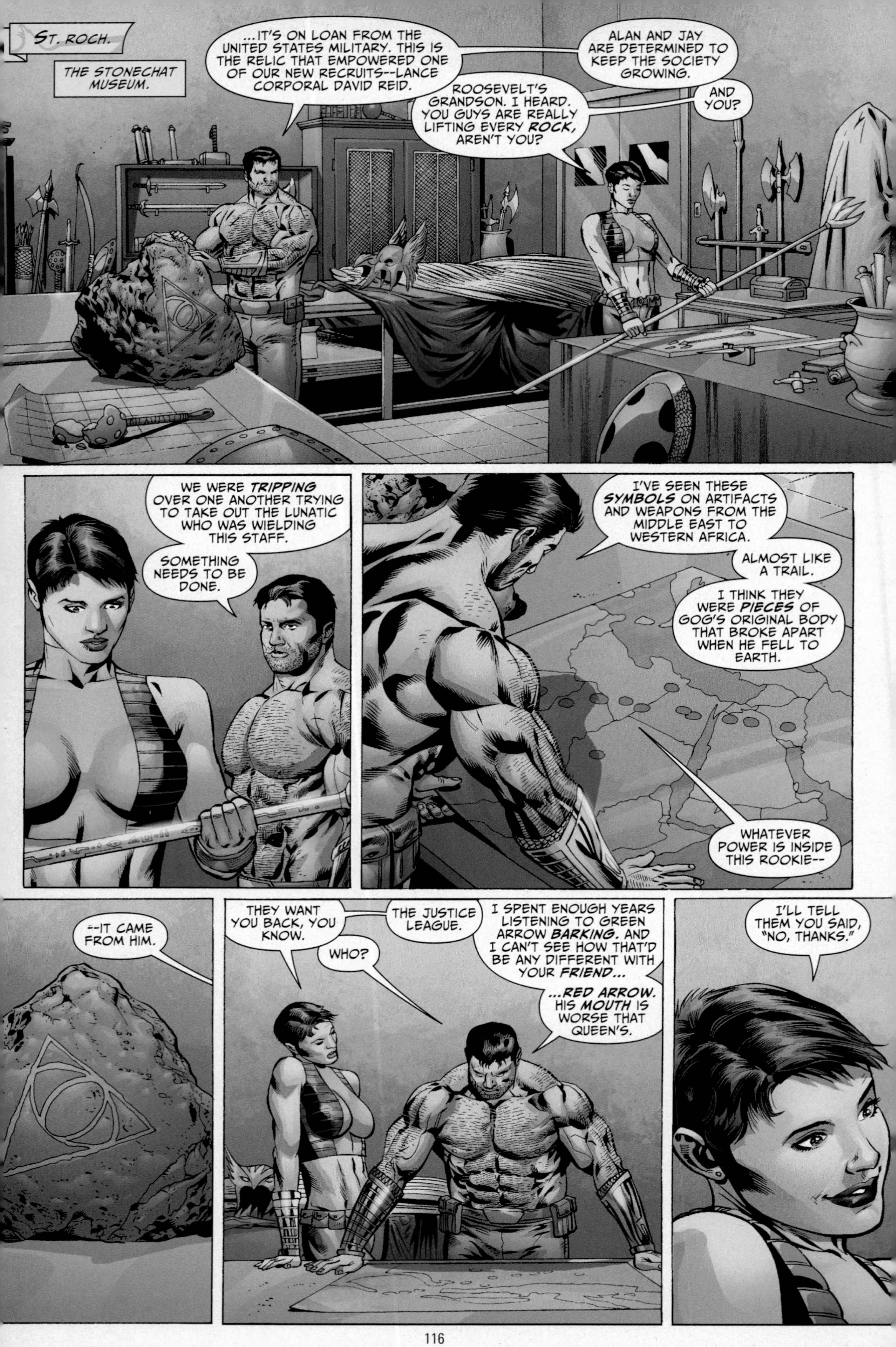

ST. ROCH.
THE STONECHAT MUSEUM.
...IT'S ON LOAN FROM THE UNITED STATES MILITARY. THIS IS THE RELIC THAT EMPOWERED ONE OF OUR NEW RECRUITS--LANCE CORPORAL DAVID REID.
ALAN AND JAY ARE DETERMINED TO KEEP THE SOCIETY GROWING.
ROOSEVELT'S GRANDSON. I HEARD. YOU GUYS ARE REALLY LIFTING EVERY ROCK, AREN'T YOU?
AND YOU?
WE WERE TRIPPING OVER ONE ANOTHER TRYING TO TAKE OUT THE LUNATIC WHO WAS WIELDING THIS STAFF.
SOMETHING NEEDS TO BE DONE.
I'VE SEEN THESE SYMBOLS ON ARTIFACTS AND WEAPONS FROM THE MIDDLE EAST TO WESTERN AFRICA.
ALMOST LIKE A TRAIL.
I THINK THEY WERE PIECES OF GOG'S ORIGINAL BODY THAT BROKE APART WHEN HE FELL TO EARTH.
WHATEVER POWER IS INSIDE THIS ROOKIE--
--IT CAME FROM HIM.
THEY WANT YOU BACK, YOU KNOW.
WHO?
THE JUSTICE LEAGUE.
I SPENT ENOUGH YEARS LISTENING TO GREEN ARROW BARKING. AND I CAN'T SEE HOW THAT'D BE ANY DIFFERENT WITH YOUR FRIEND...
...RED ARROW. HIS MOUTH IS WORSE THAT QUEEN'S.
I'LL TELL THEM YOU SAID, "NO, THANKS."

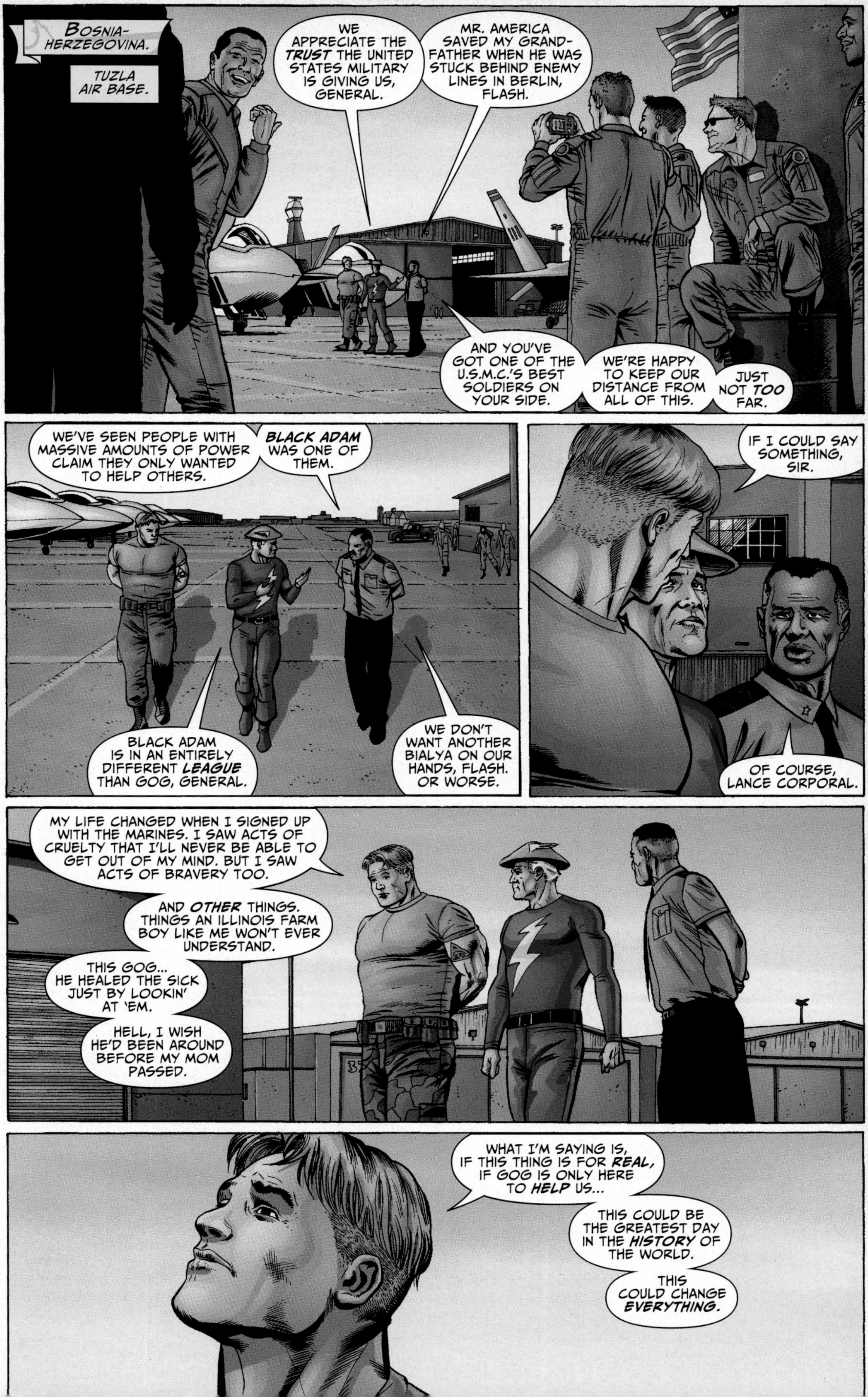
BOSNIA-HERZEGOVINA.
TUZLA AIR BASE.
WE APPRECIATE THE TRUST THE UNITED STATES MILITARY IS GIVING US, GENERAL.
MR. AMERICA SAVED MY GRAND-FATHER WHEN HE WAS STUCK BEHIND ENEMY LINES IN BERLIN, FLASH.
AND YOU'VE GOT ONE OF THE U.S.M.C.'S BEST SOLDIERS ON YOUR SIDE.
WE'RE HAPPY TO KEEP OUR DISTANCE FROM ALL OF THIS.
JUST NOT TOO FAR.
WE'VE SEEN PEOPLE WITH MASSIVE AMOUNTS OF POWER CLAIM THEY ONLY WANTED TO HELP OTHERS.
BLACK ADAM WAS ONE OF THEM.
BLACK ADAM IS IN AN ENTIRELY DIFFERENT LEAGUE THAN GOG, GENERAL.
WE DON'T WANT ANOTHER BIALYA ON OUR HANDS, FLASH. OR WORSE.
IF I COULD SAY SOMETHING, SIR.
OF COURSE, LANCE CORPORAL.
MY LIFE CHANGED WHEN I SIGNED UP WITH THE MARINES. I SAW ACTS OF CRUELTY THAT I'LL NEVER BE ABLE TO GET OUT OF MY MIND. BUT I SAW ACTS OF BRAVERY TOO.
AND OTHER THINGS. THINGS AN ILLINOIS FARM BOY LIKE ME WON'T EVER UNDERSTAND.
THIS GOG... HE HEALED THE SICK JUST BY LOOKIN' AT 'EM.
HELL, I WISH HE'D BEEN AROUND BEFORE MY MOM PASSED.
WHAT I'M SAYING IS, IF THIS THING IS FOR REAL, IF GOG IS ONLY HERE TO HELP US...
THIS COULD BE THE GREATEST DAY IN THE HISTORY OF THE WORLD.
THIS COULD CHANGE EVERYTHING.

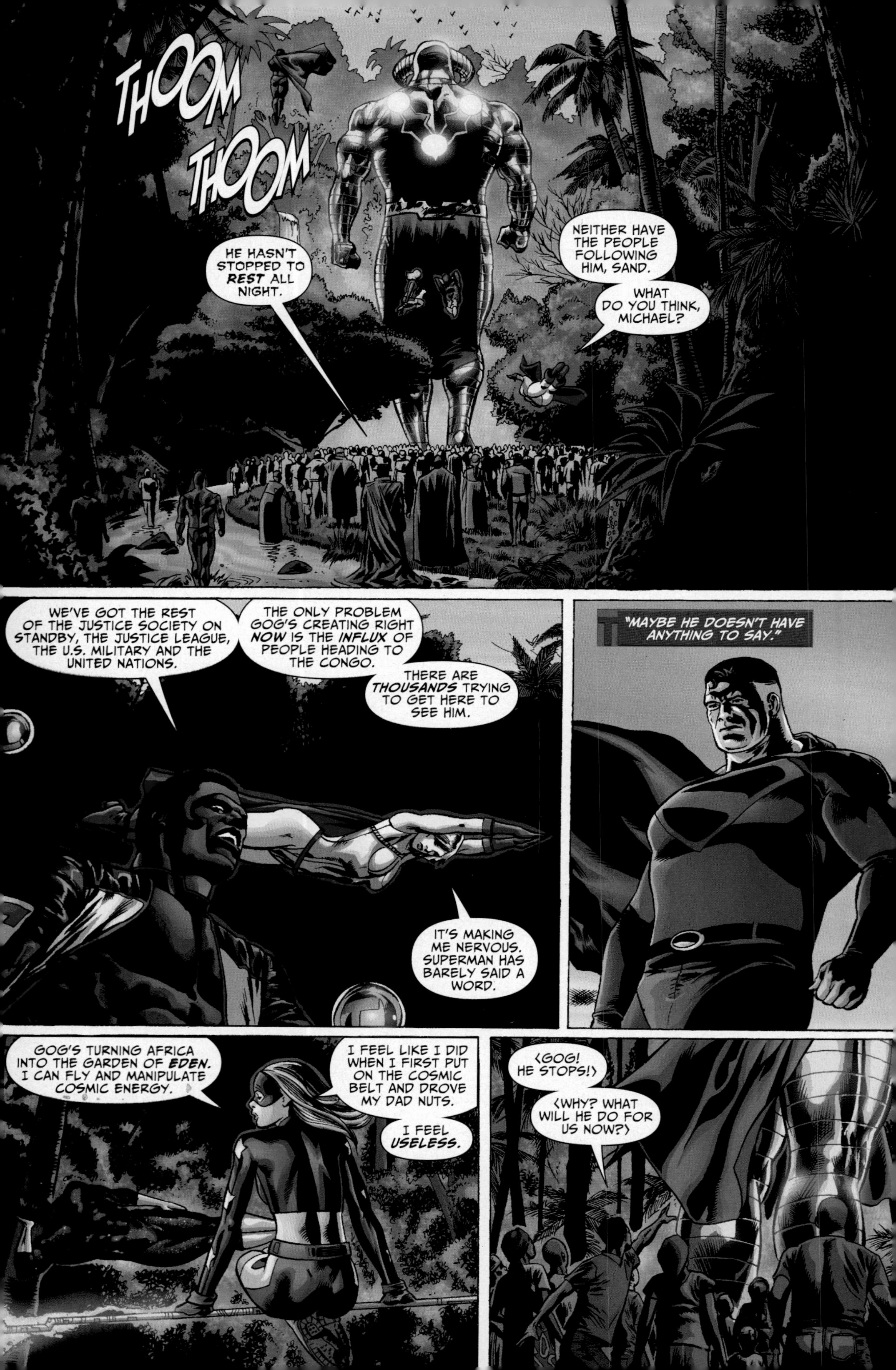
THOOM
THOOM
HE HASN'T STOPPED TO REST ALL NIGHT.
NEITHER HAVE THE PEOPLE FOLLOWING HIM, SAND.
WHAT DO YOU THINK, MICHAEL?
WE'VE GOT THE REST OF THE JUSTICE SOCIETY ON STANDBY, THE JUSTICE LEAGUE, THE U.S. MILITARY AND THE UNITED NATIONS.
THE ONLY PROBLEM GOG'S CREATING RIGHT NOW IS THE INFLUX OF PEOPLE HEADING TO THE CONGO.
THERE ARE THOUSANDS TRYING TO GET HERE TO SEE HIM.
IT'S MAKING ME NERVOUS. SUPERMAN HAS BARELY SAID A WORD.
"MAYBE HE DOESN'T HAVE ANYTHING TO SAY."
GOG'S TURNING AFRICA INTO THE GARDEN OF EDEN. I CAN FLY AND MANIPULATE COSMIC ENERGY.
I FEEL LIKE I DID WHEN I FIRST PUT ON THE COSMIC BELT AND DROVE MY DAD NUTS.
I FEEL USELESS.
‹GOG! HE STOPS!›
‹WHY? WHAT WILL HE DO FOR US NOW?›

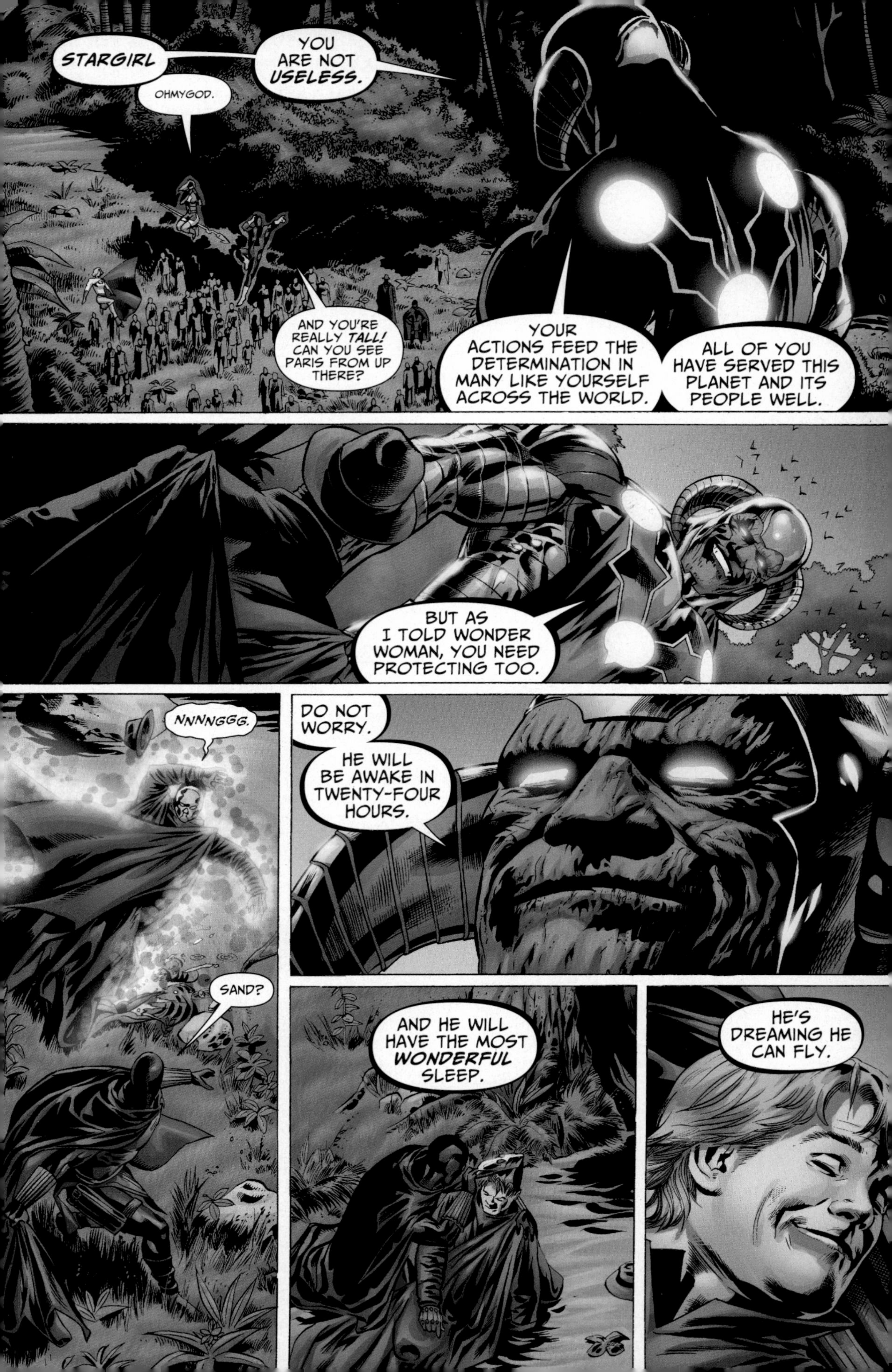
STARGIRL
YOU ARE NOT USELESS.
OHMYGOD.
AND YOU'RE REALLY TALL! CAN YOU SEE PARIS FROM UP THERE?
YOUR ACTIONS FEED THE DETERMINATION IN MANY LIKE YOURSELF ACROSS THE WORLD.
ALL OF YOU HAVE SERVED THIS PLANET AND ITS PEOPLE WELL.
BUT AS I TOLD WONDER WOMAN, YOU NEED PROTECTING TOO.
NNNNGGG.
SAND?
DO NOT WORRY.
HE WILL BE AWAKE IN TWENTY-FOUR HOURS.
AND HE WILL HAVE THE MOST WONDERFUL SLEEP.
HE'S DREAMING HE CAN FLY.

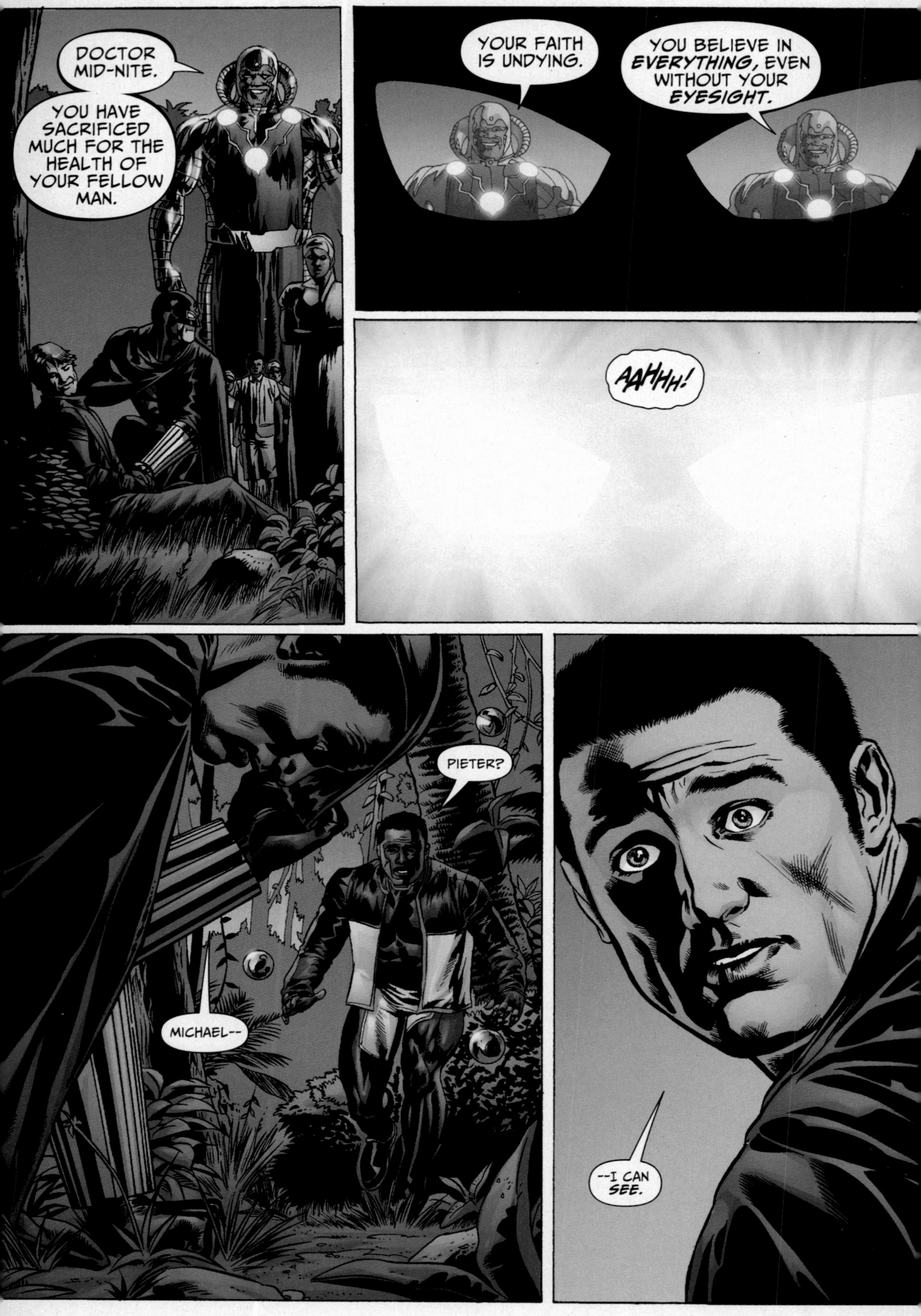
DOCTOR MID-NITE.
YOU HAVE SACRIFICED MUCH FOR THE HEALTH OF YOUR FELLOW MAN.
YOUR FAITH IS UNDYING.
YOU BELIEVE IN EVERYTHING, EVEN WITHOUT YOUR EYESIGHT.
AAHHH!
PIETER?
MICHAEL--
--I CAN SEE.

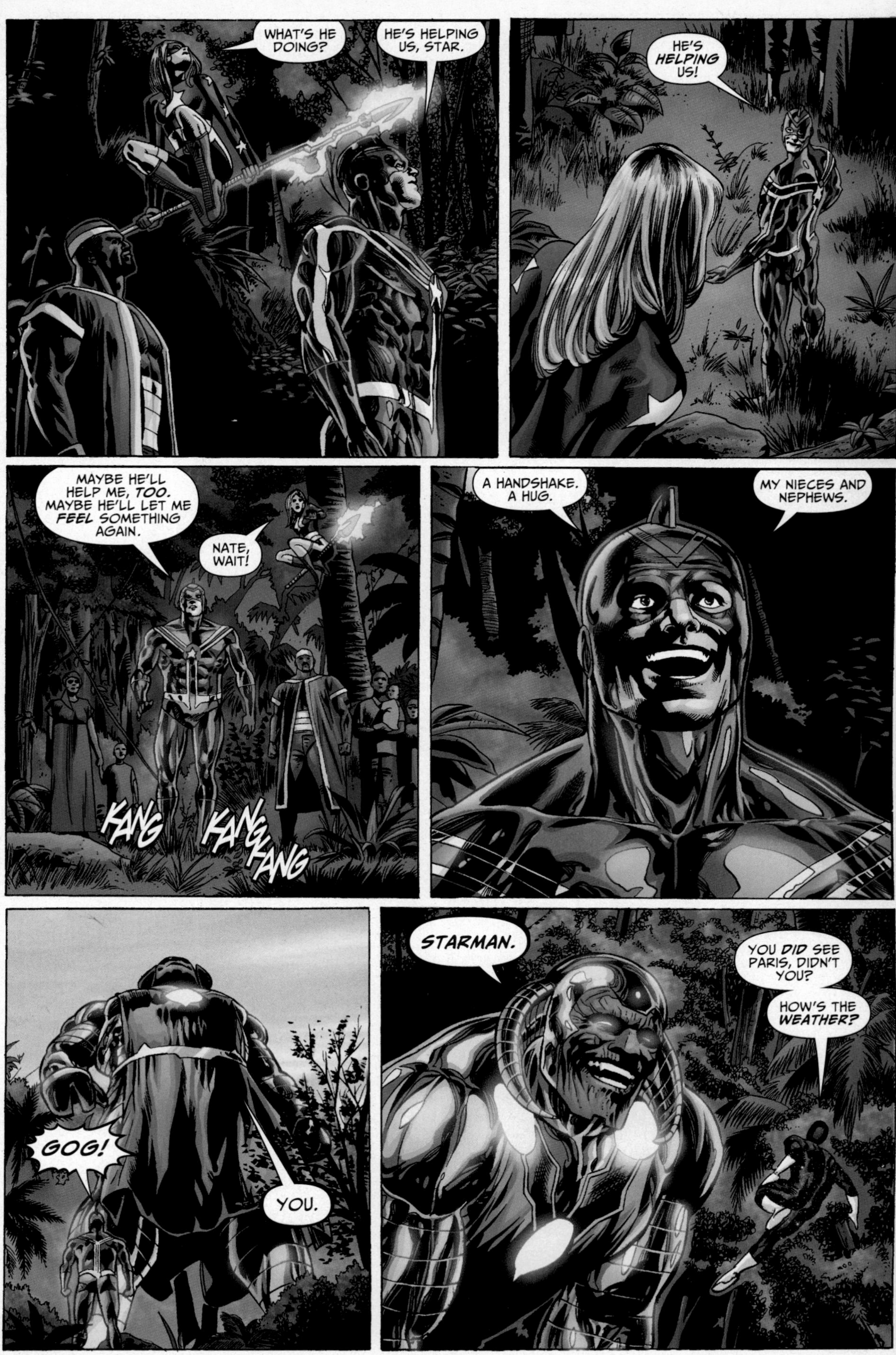
WHAT'S HE DOING?
HE'S HELPING US, STAR.
HE'S HELPING US!
MAYBE HE'LL HELP ME, TOO. MAYBE HE'LL LET ME FEEL SOMETHING AGAIN.
NATE, WAIT!
KANG
KANGKANG
A HANDSHAKE. A HUG.
MY NIECES AND NEPHEWS.
GOG!
YOU.
STARMAN.
YOU DID SEE PARIS, DIDN'T YOU?
HOW'S THE WEATHER?

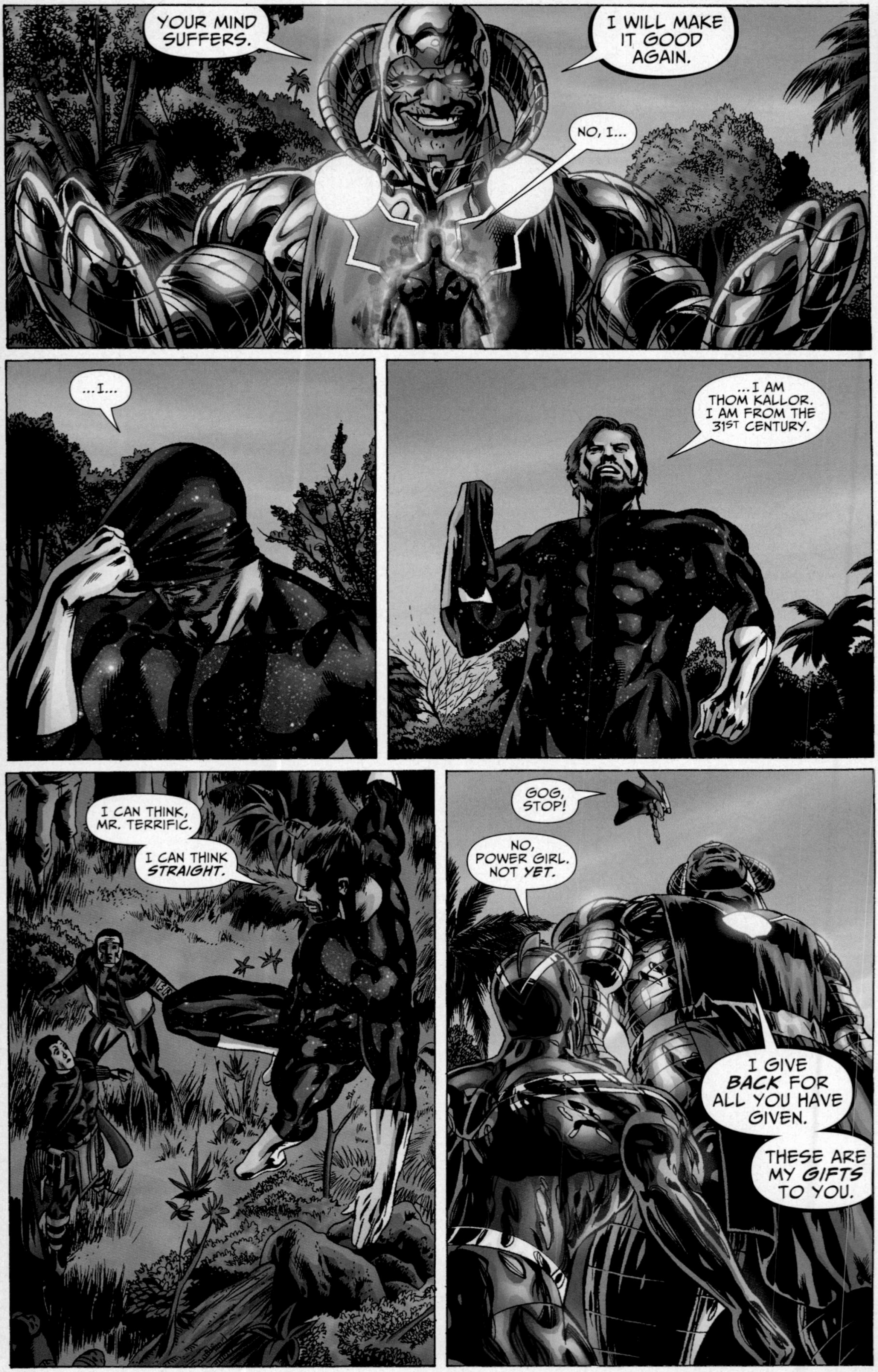
YOUR MIND SUFFERS.
I WILL MAKE IT GOOD AGAIN.
NO, I...
...I...
...I AM THOM KALLOR. I AM FROM THE 31ST CENTURY.
I CAN THINK, MR. TERRIFIC.
I CAN THINK STRAIGHT.
GOG, STOP!
NO, POWER GIRL. NOT YET.
I GIVE BACK FOR ALL YOU HAVE GIVEN.
THESE ARE MY GIFTS TO YOU.

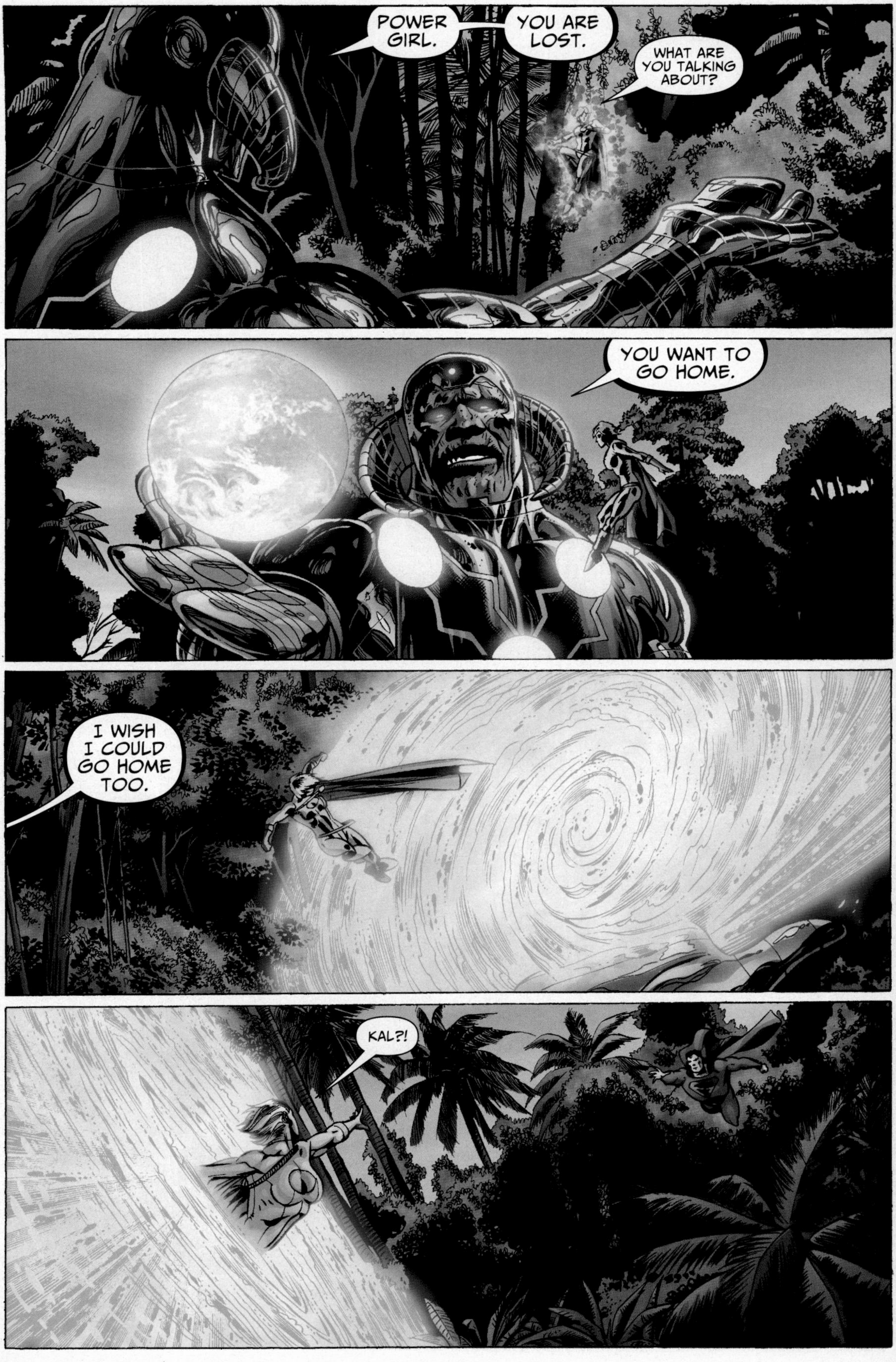
POWER GIRL.
YOU ARE LOST.
WHAT ARE YOU TALKING ABOUT?
YOU WANT TO GO HOME.
I WISH I COULD GO HOME TOO.
KAL?!

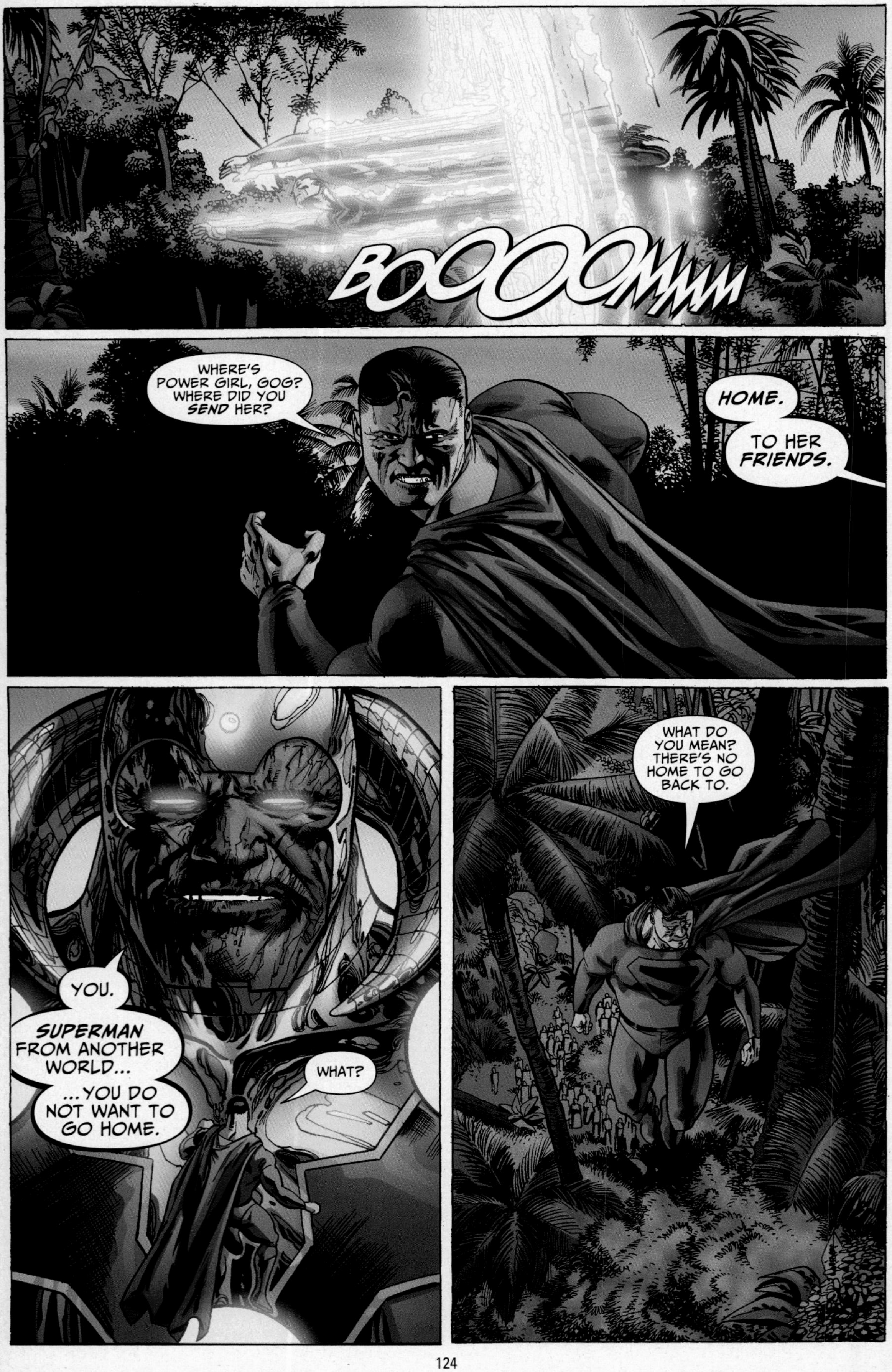
BOOOOOMMMM
WHERE'S POWER GIRL, GOG? WHERE DID YOU SEND HER?
HOME.
TO HER FRIENDS.
YOU.
SUPERMAN FROM ANOTHER WORLD...
...YOU DO NOT WANT TO GO HOME.
WHAT?
WHAT DO YOU MEAN? THERE'S NO HOME TO GO BACK TO.

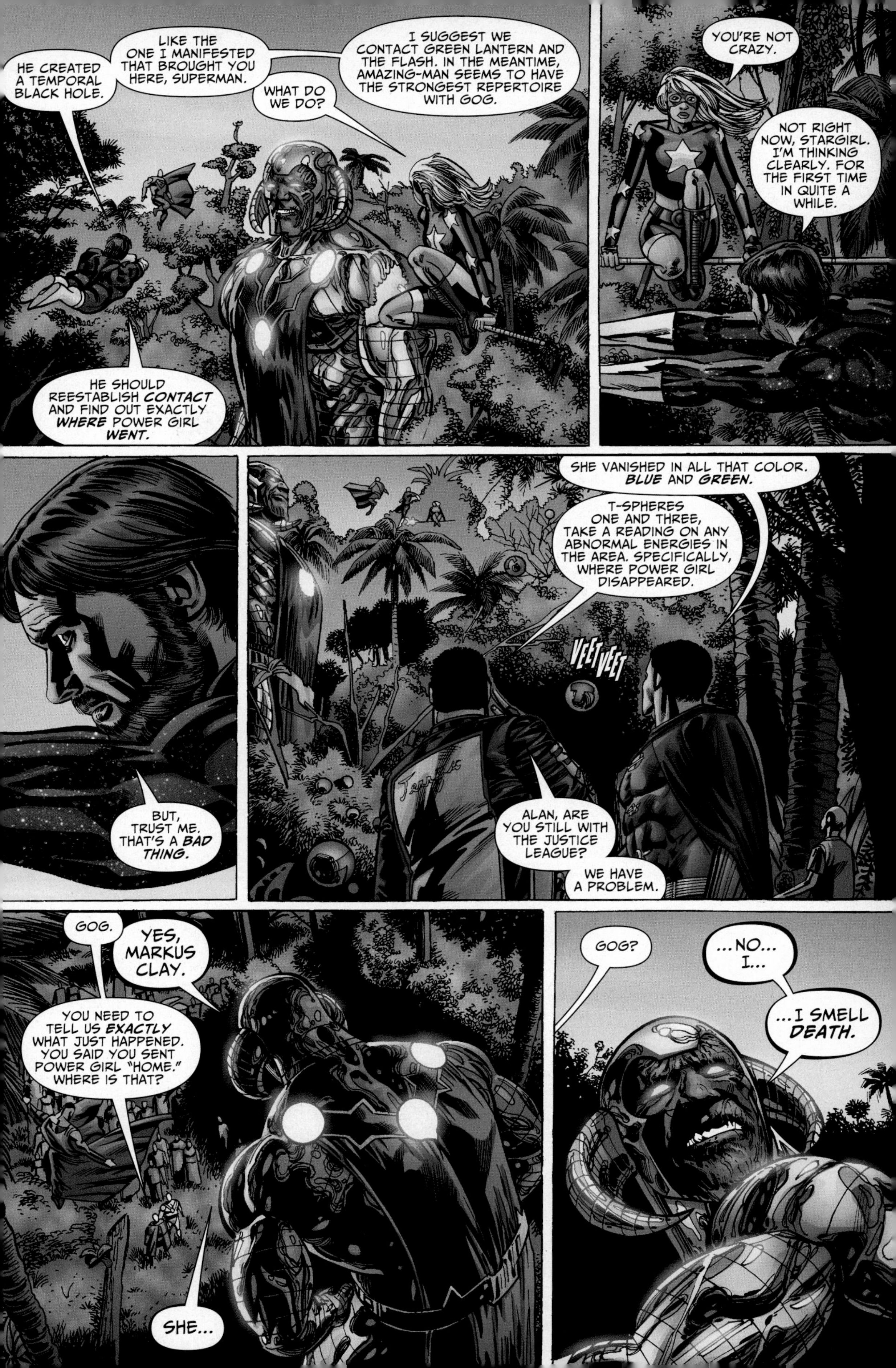
HE CREATED A TEMPORAL BLACK HOLE.
LIKE THE ONE I MANIFESTED THAT BROUGHT YOU HERE, SUPERMAN.
WHAT DO WE DO?
I SUGGEST WE CONTACT GREEN LANTERN AND THE FLASH. IN THE MEANTIME, AMAZING-MAN SEEMS TO HAVE THE STRONGEST REPERTOIRE WITH GOG.
HE SHOULD REESTABLISH CONTACT AND FIND OUT EXACTLY WHERE POWER GIRL WENT.
YOU'RE NOT CRAZY.
NOT RIGHT NOW, STARGIRL. I'M THINKING CLEARLY. FOR THE FIRST TIME IN QUITE A WHILE.
BUT, TRUST ME. THAT'S A BAD THING.
SHE VANISHED IN ALL THAT COLOR. BLUE AND GREEN.
T-SPHERES ONE AND THREE, TAKE A READING ON ANY ABNORMAL ENERGIES IN THE AREA. SPECIFICALLY, WHERE POWER GIRL DISAPPEARED.
VEET VEET
ALAN, ARE YOU STILL WITH THE JUSTICE LEAGUE?
WE HAVE A PROBLEM.
GOG.
YES, MARKUS CLAY.
YOU NEED TO TELL US EXACTLY WHAT JUST HAPPENED. YOU SAID YOU SENT POWER GIRL "HOME." WHERE IS THAT?
SHE...
GOG?
...NO... I...
...I SMELL DEATH.

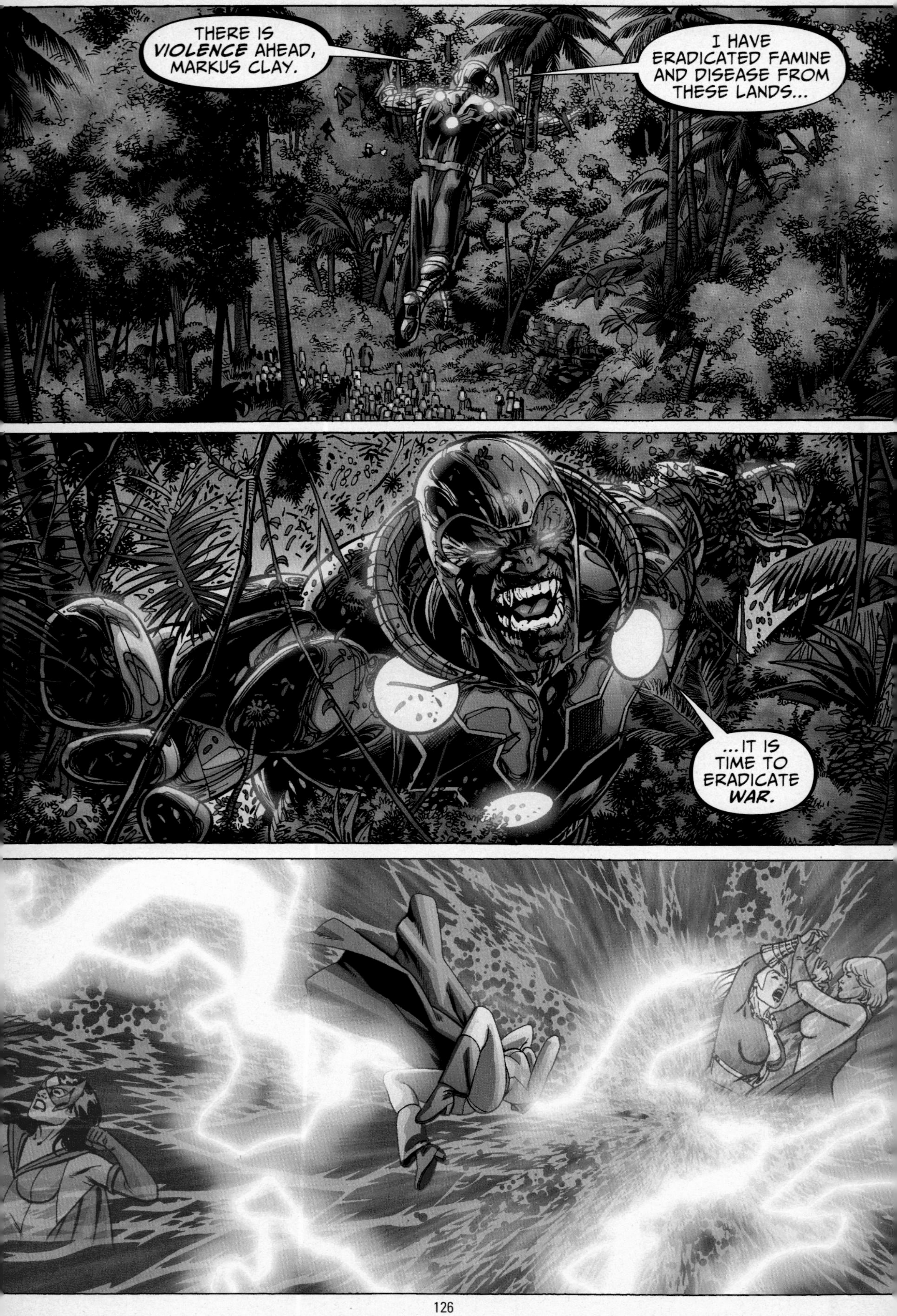
THERE IS VIOLENCE AHEAD, MARKUS CLAY.
I HAVE ERADICATED FAMINE AND DISEASE FROM THESE LANDS...
...IT IS TIME TO ERADICATE WAR.

JUSTICE SOCIETY OF AMERICA ANNUAL #1 cover by Alex Ross Interior art by Jerry Ordway & Bob Wiacek

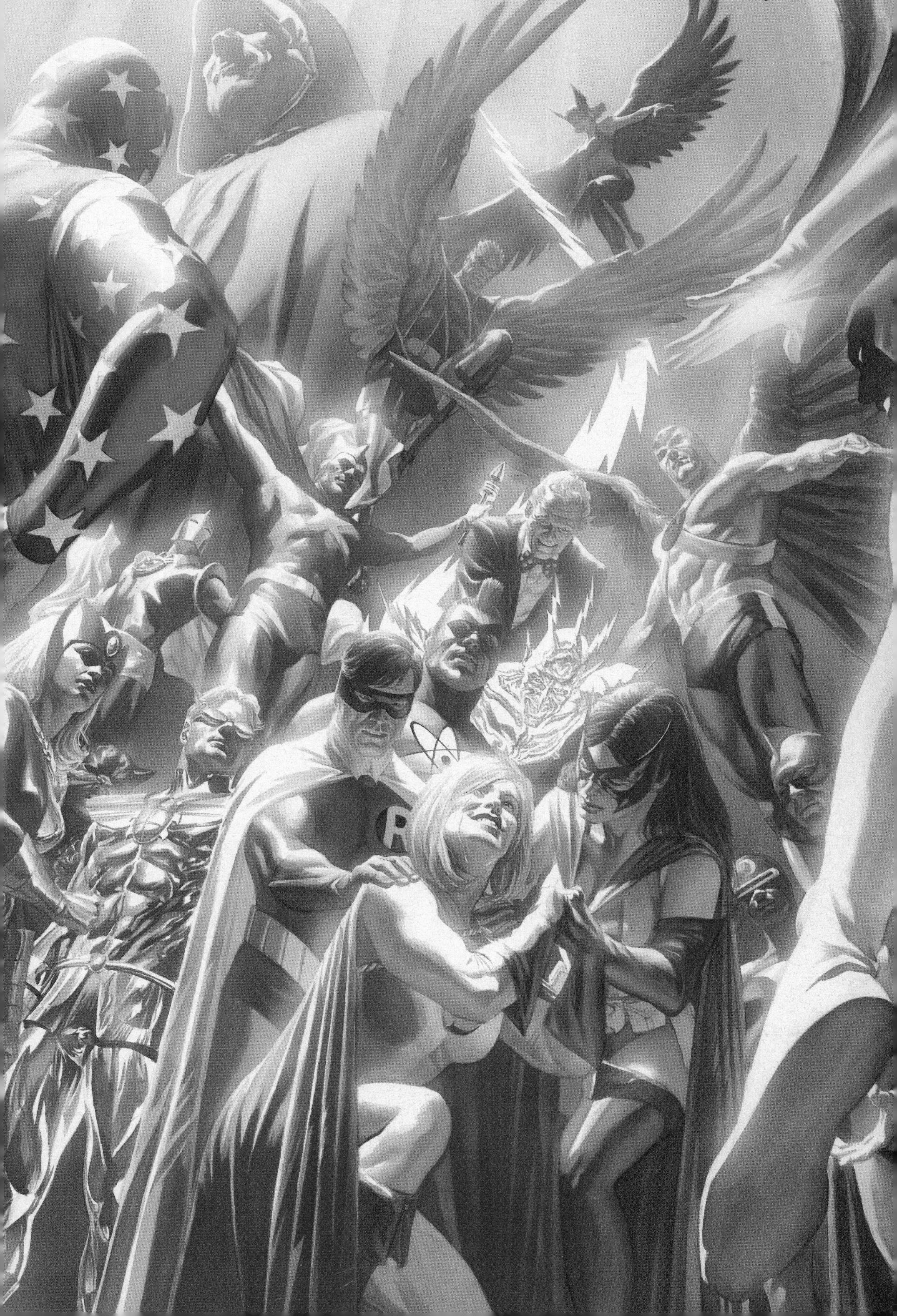

Helena Wayne created by **Paul Levitz** and **Joe Staton**

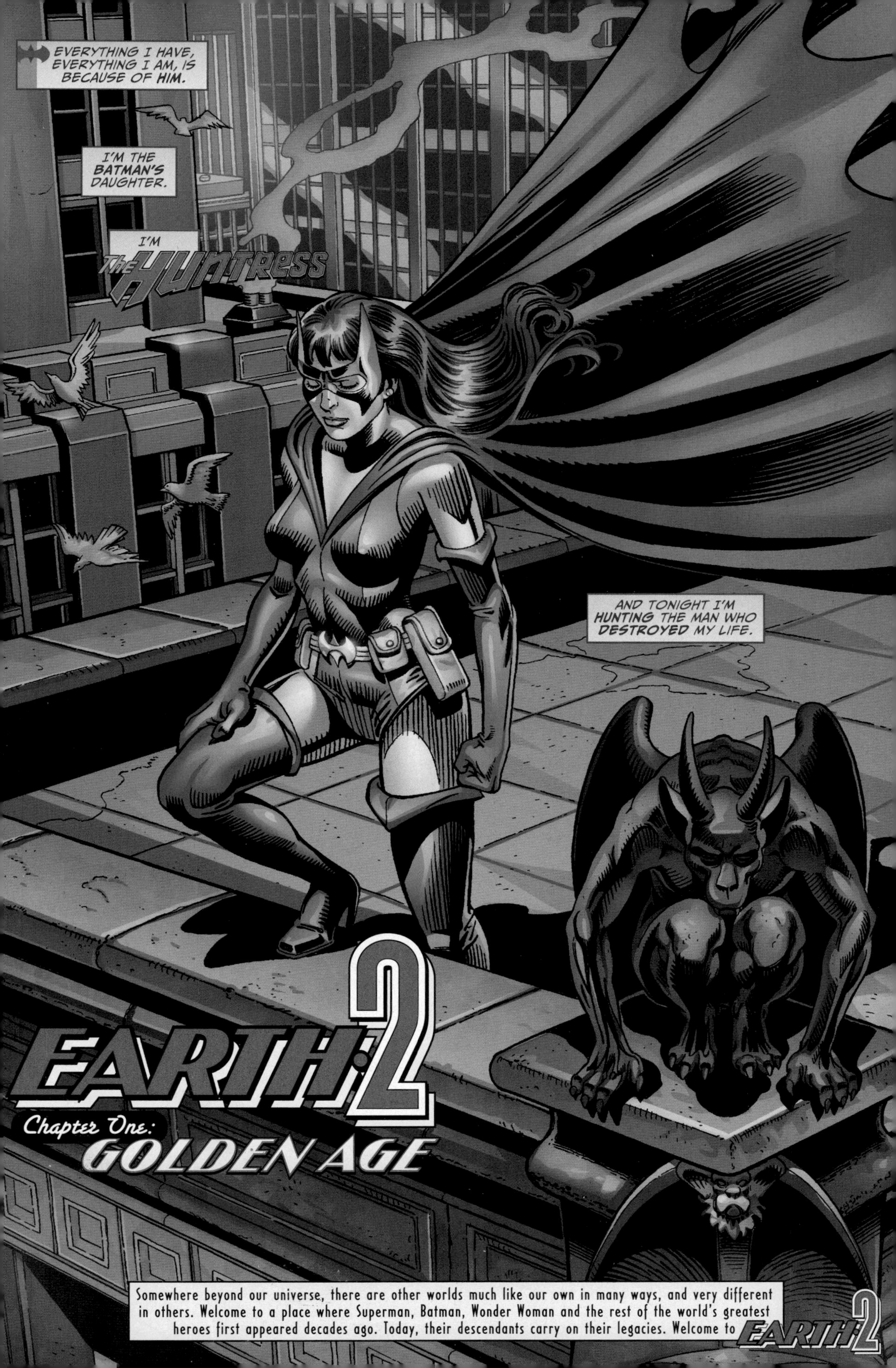
EVERYTHING I HAVE, EVERYTHING I AM, IS BECAUSE OF HIM.
I'M THE BATMAN'S DAUGHTER.
I'M The HUNTRESS
AND TONIGHT I'M HUNTING THE MAN WHO DESTROYED MY LIFE.
EARTH 2
Chapter One: GOLDEN AGE
Somewhere beyond our universe, there are other worlds much like our own in many ways, and very different in others. Welcome to a place where Superman, Batman, Wonder Woman and the rest of the world's greatest heroes first appeared decades ago. Today, their descendants carry on their legacies. Welcome to EARTH 2

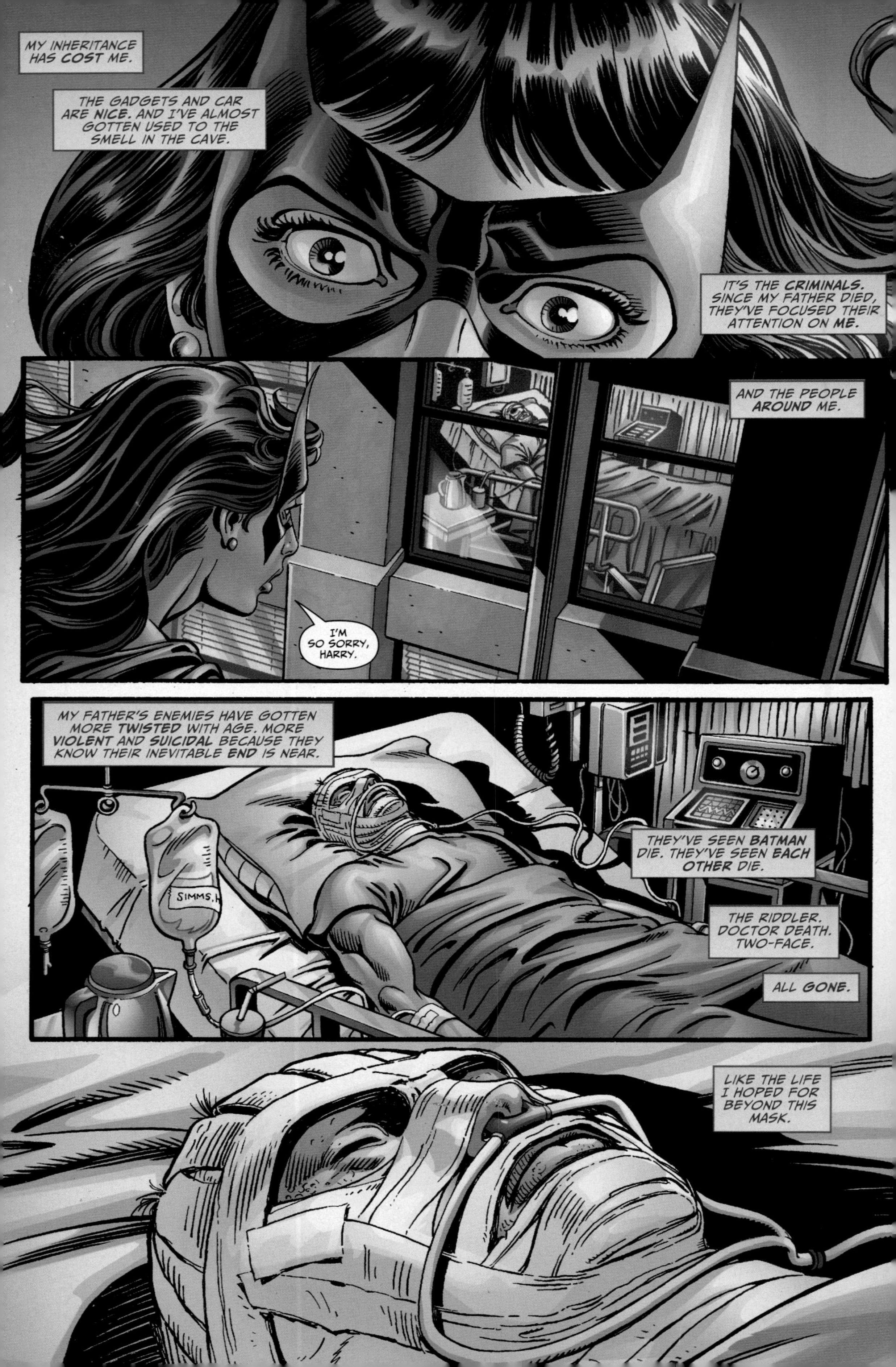
MY INHERITANCE HAS COST ME.
THE GADGETS AND CAR ARE NICE. AND I'VE ALMOST GOTTEN USED TO THE SMELL IN THE CAVE.
IT'S THE CRIMINALS. SINCE MY FATHER DIED, THEY'VE FOCUSED THEIR ATTENTION ON ME.
AND THE PEOPLE AROUND ME.
I'M SO SORRY, HARRY.
MY FATHER'S ENEMIES HAVE GOTTEN MORE TWISTED WITH AGE. MORE VIOLENT AND SUICIDAL BECAUSE THEY KNOW THEIR INEVITABLE END IS NEAR.
SIMMS, H
THEY'VE SEEN BATMAN DIE. THEY'VE SEEN EACH OTHER DIE.
THE RIDDLER. DOCTOR DEATH. TWO-FACE.
ALL GONE.
LIKE THE LIFE I HOPED FOR BEYOND THIS MASK.

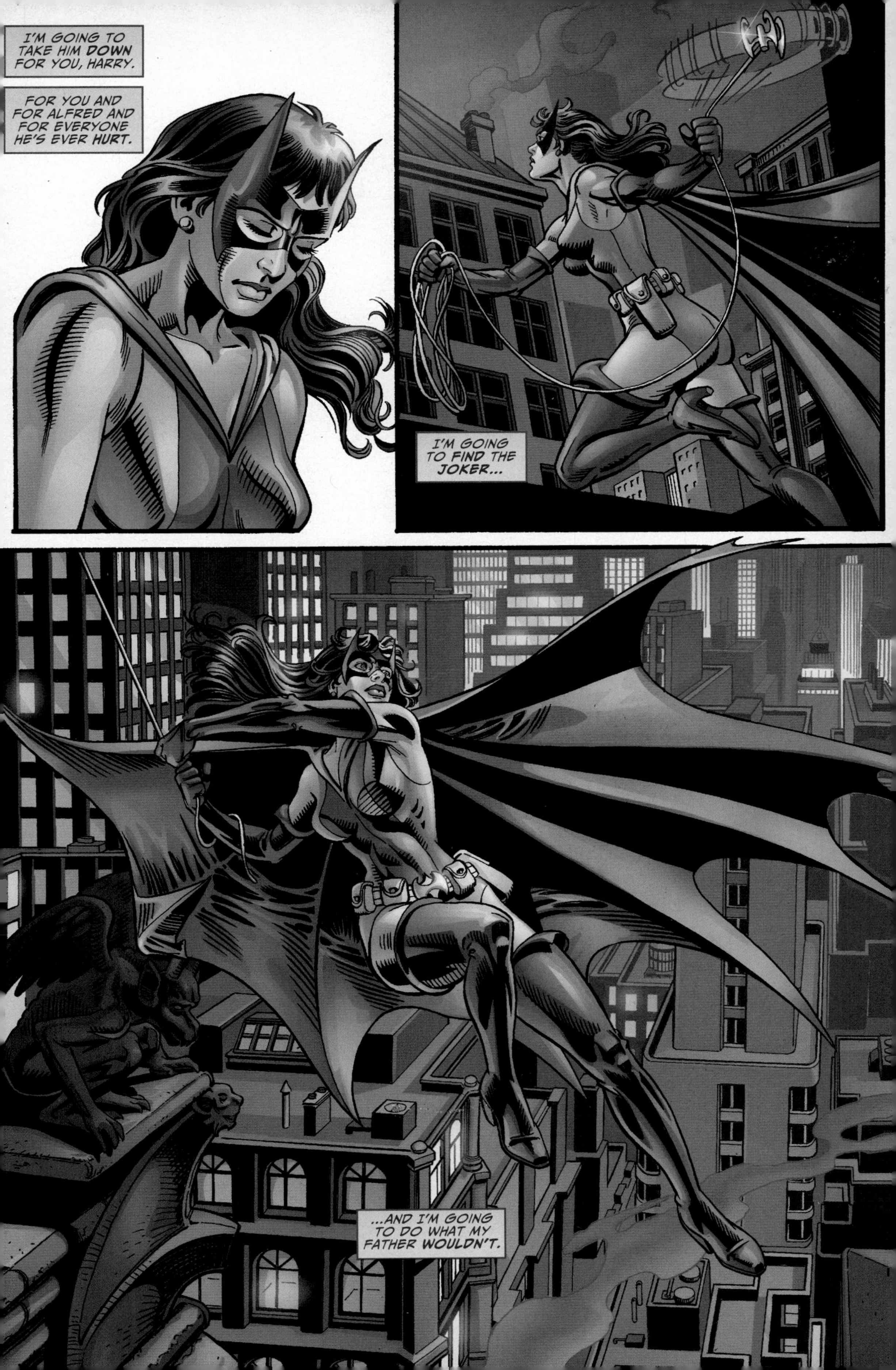

I'M GOING TO TAKE HIM DOWN FOR YOU, HARRY.
FOR YOU AND FOR ALFRED AND FOR EVERYONE HE'S EVER HURT.
I'M GOING TO FIND THE JOKER...
...AND I'M GOING TO DO WHAT MY FATHER WOULDN'T.

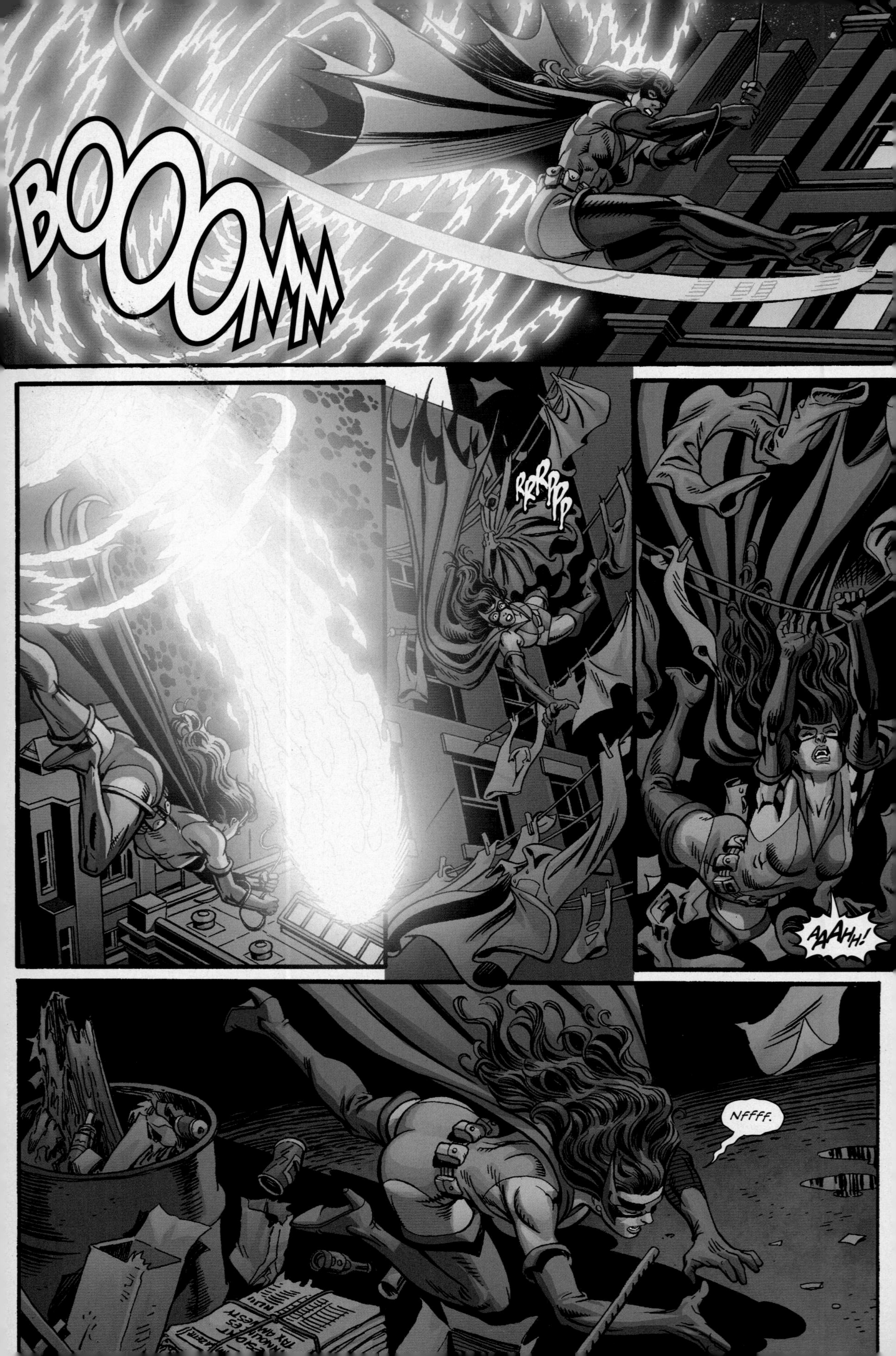
BOOOMM
RRRPPP
AAAHH!
NFFFF.

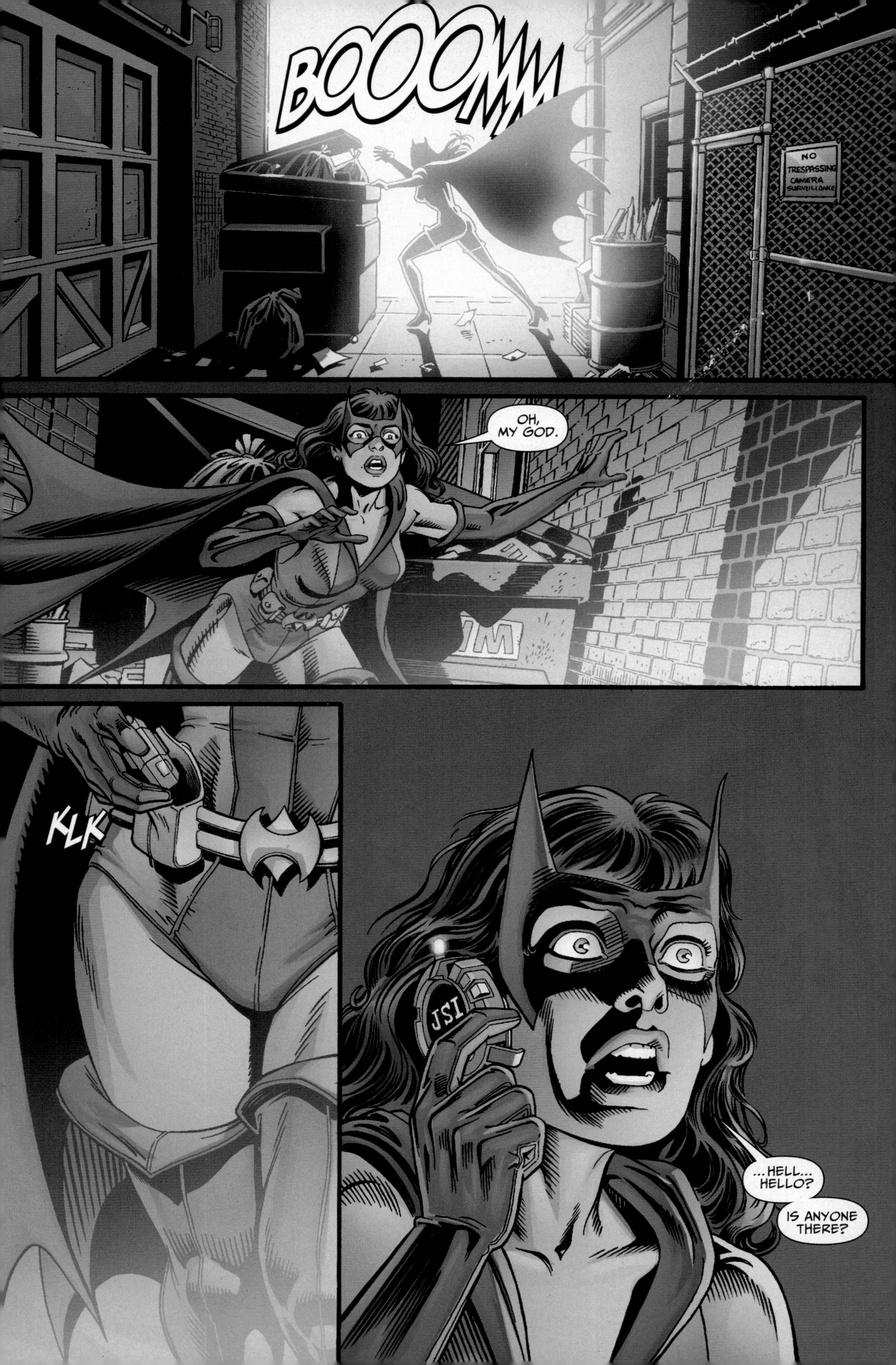
BOOOMM
NO TRESPASSING CAMERA SURVEILLANCE
OH, MY GOD.
KLK
JSI
...HELL... HELLO?
IS ANYONE THERE?

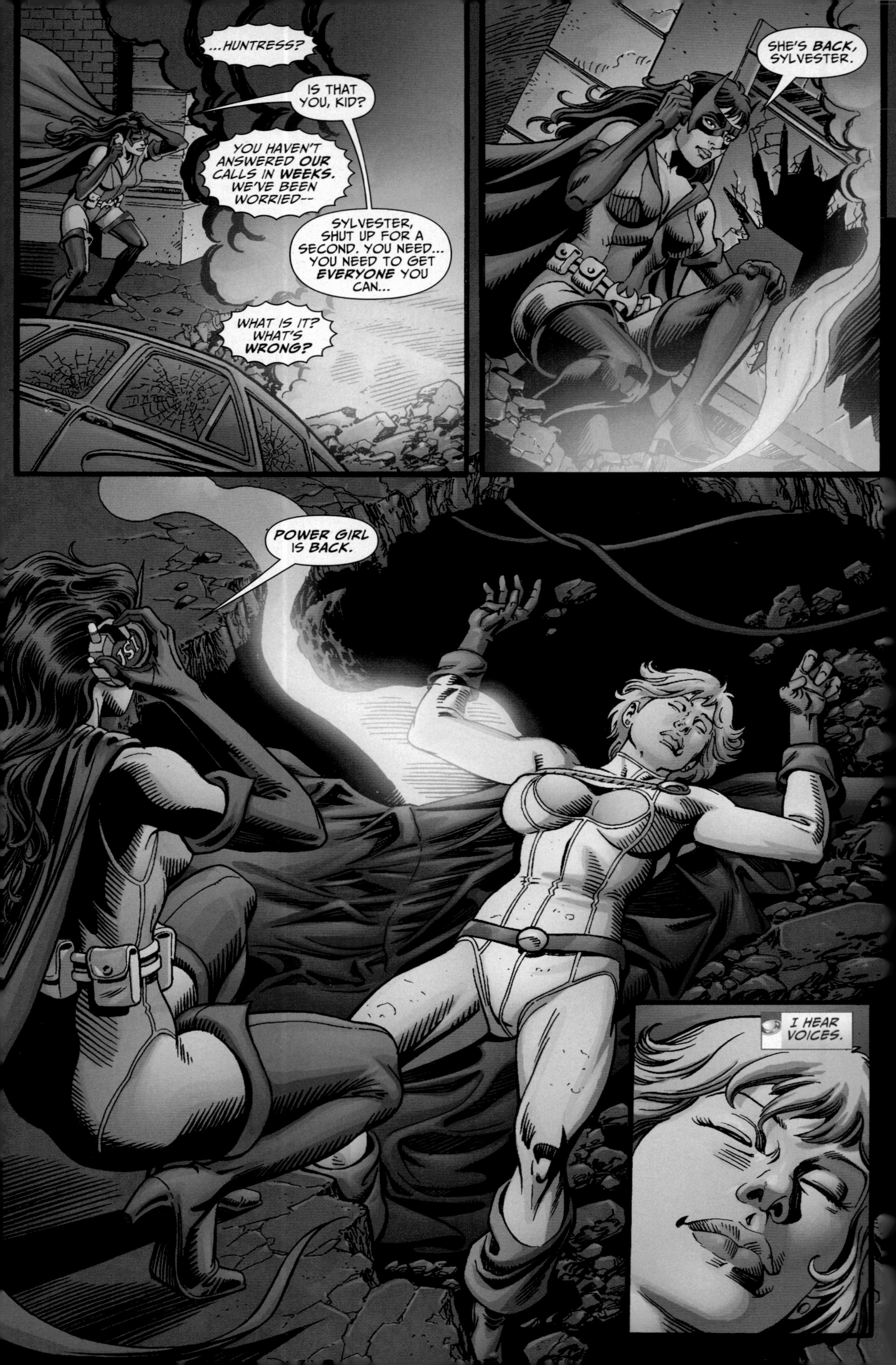
...HUNTRESS?
IS THAT YOU, KID?
YOU HAVEN'T ANSWERED OUR CALLS IN WEEKS. WE'VE BEEN WORRIED--
SYLVESTER, SHUT UP FOR A SECOND. YOU NEED... YOU NEED TO GET EVERYONE YOU CAN...
WHAT IS IT? WHAT'S WRONG?
SHE'S BACK, SYLVESTER.
POWER GIRL IS BACK.
JSA
I HEAR VOICES.

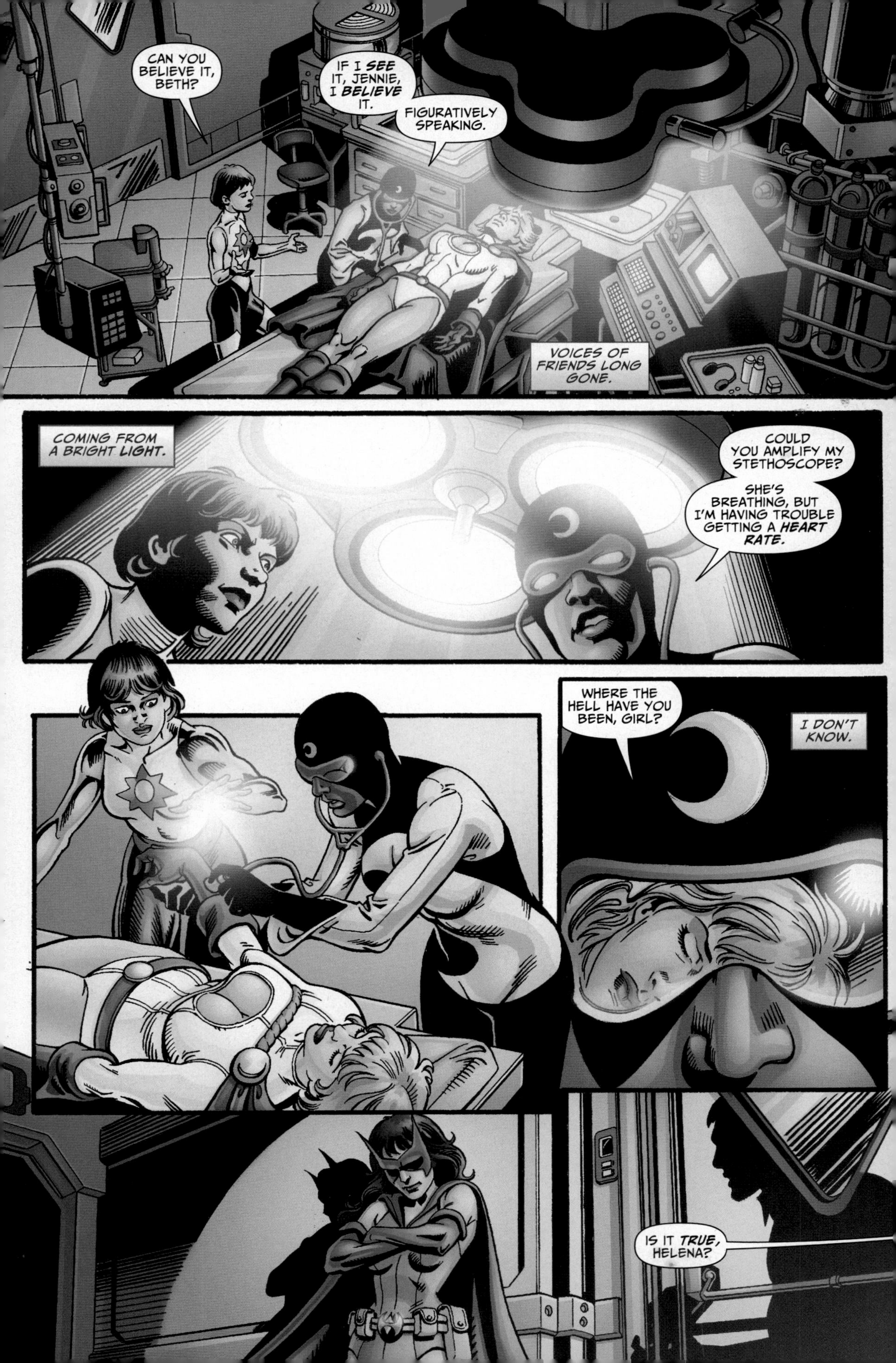
CAN YOU BELIEVE IT, BETH?
IF I SEE IT, JENNIE, I BELIEVE IT.
FIGURATIVELY SPEAKING.
VOICES OF FRIENDS LONG GONE.
COMING FROM A BRIGHT LIGHT.
COULD YOU AMPLIFY MY STETHOSCOPE?
SHE'S BREATHING, BUT I'M HAVING TROUBLE GETTING A HEART RATE.
WHERE THE HELL HAVE YOU BEEN, GIRL?
I DON'T KNOW.
IS IT TRUE, HELENA?

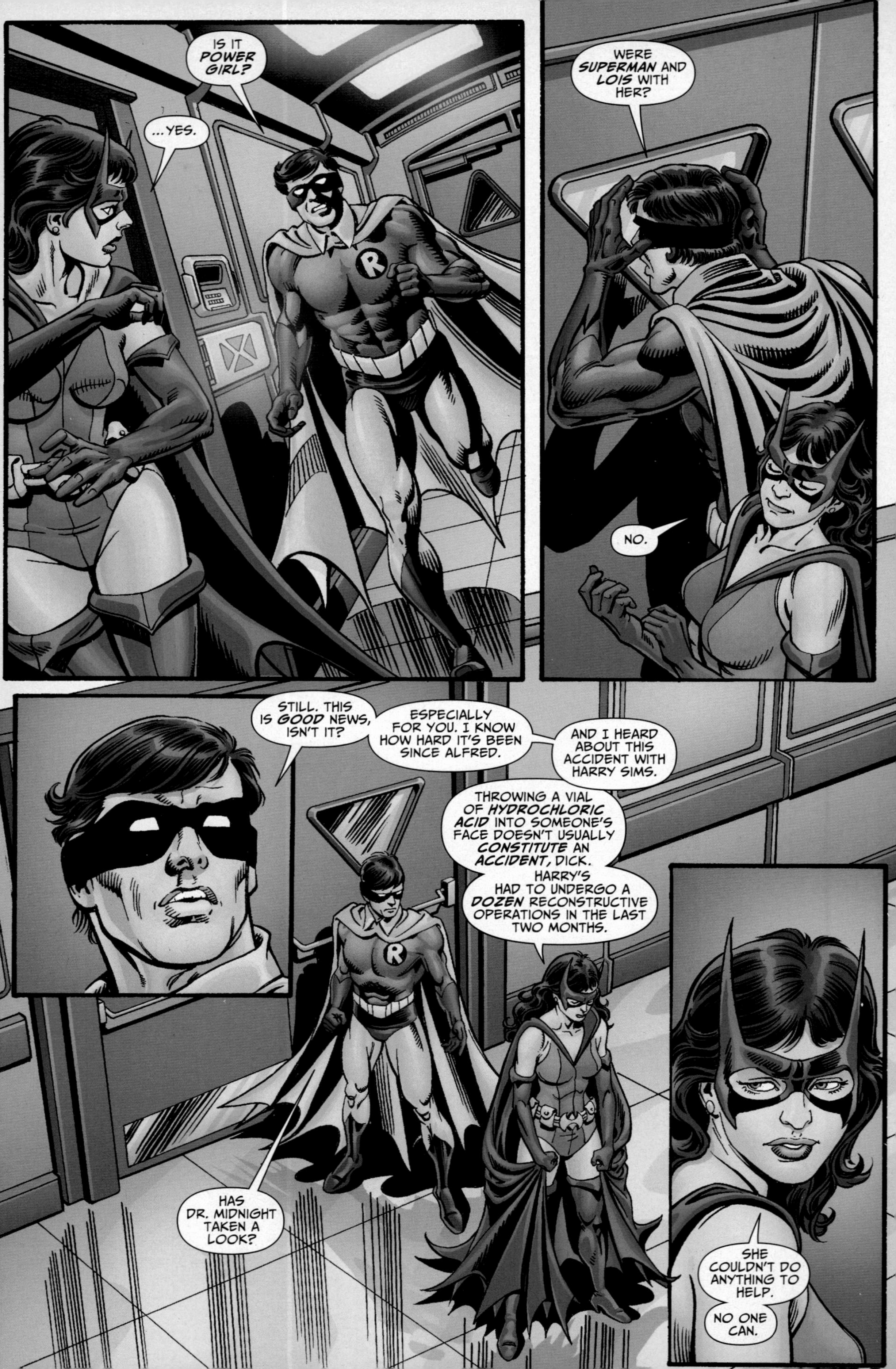
IS IT POWER GIRL?
...YES.
WERE SUPERMAN AND LOIS WITH HER?
NO.
STILL. THIS IS GOOD NEWS, ISN'T IT?
ESPECIALLY FOR YOU. I KNOW HOW HARD IT'S BEEN SINCE ALFRED.
AND I HEARD ABOUT THIS ACCIDENT WITH HARRY SIMS.
THROWING A VIAL OF HYDROCHLORIC ACID INTO SOMEONE'S FACE DOESN'T USUALLY CONSTITUTE AN ACCIDENT, DICK.
HARRY'S HAD TO UNDERGO A DOZEN RECONSTRUCTIVE OPERATIONS IN THE LAST TWO MONTHS.
HAS DR. MIDNIGHT TAKEN A LOOK?
SHE COULDN'T DO ANYTHING TO HELP.
NO ONE CAN.

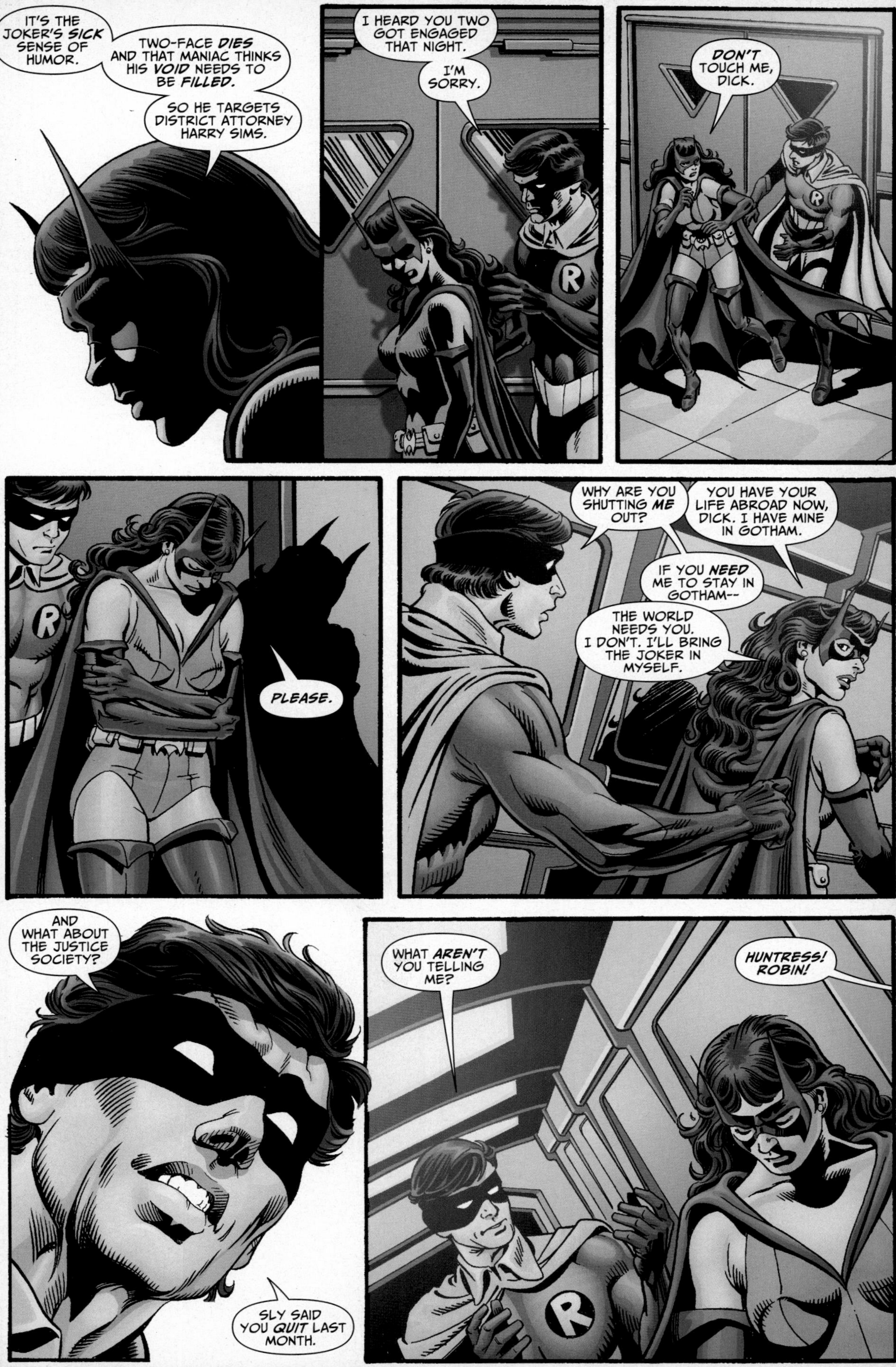
IT'S THE JOKER'S SICK SENSE OF HUMOR.
TWO-FACE DIES AND THAT MANIAC THINKS HIS VOID NEEDS TO BE FILLED.
SO HE TARGETS DISTRICT ATTORNEY HARRY SIMS.
I HEARD YOU TWO GOT ENGAGED THAT NIGHT.
I'M SORRY.
DON'T TOUCH ME, DICK.
PLEASE.
WHY ARE YOU SHUTTING ME OUT?
YOU HAVE YOUR LIFE ABROAD NOW, DICK. I HAVE MINE IN GOTHAM.
IF YOU NEED ME TO STAY IN GOTHAM--
THE WORLD NEEDS YOU. I DON'T. I'LL BRING THE JOKER IN MYSELF.
AND WHAT ABOUT THE JUSTICE SOCIETY?
SLY SAID YOU QUIT LAST MONTH.
WHAT AREN'T YOU TELLING ME?
HUNTRESS! ROBIN!

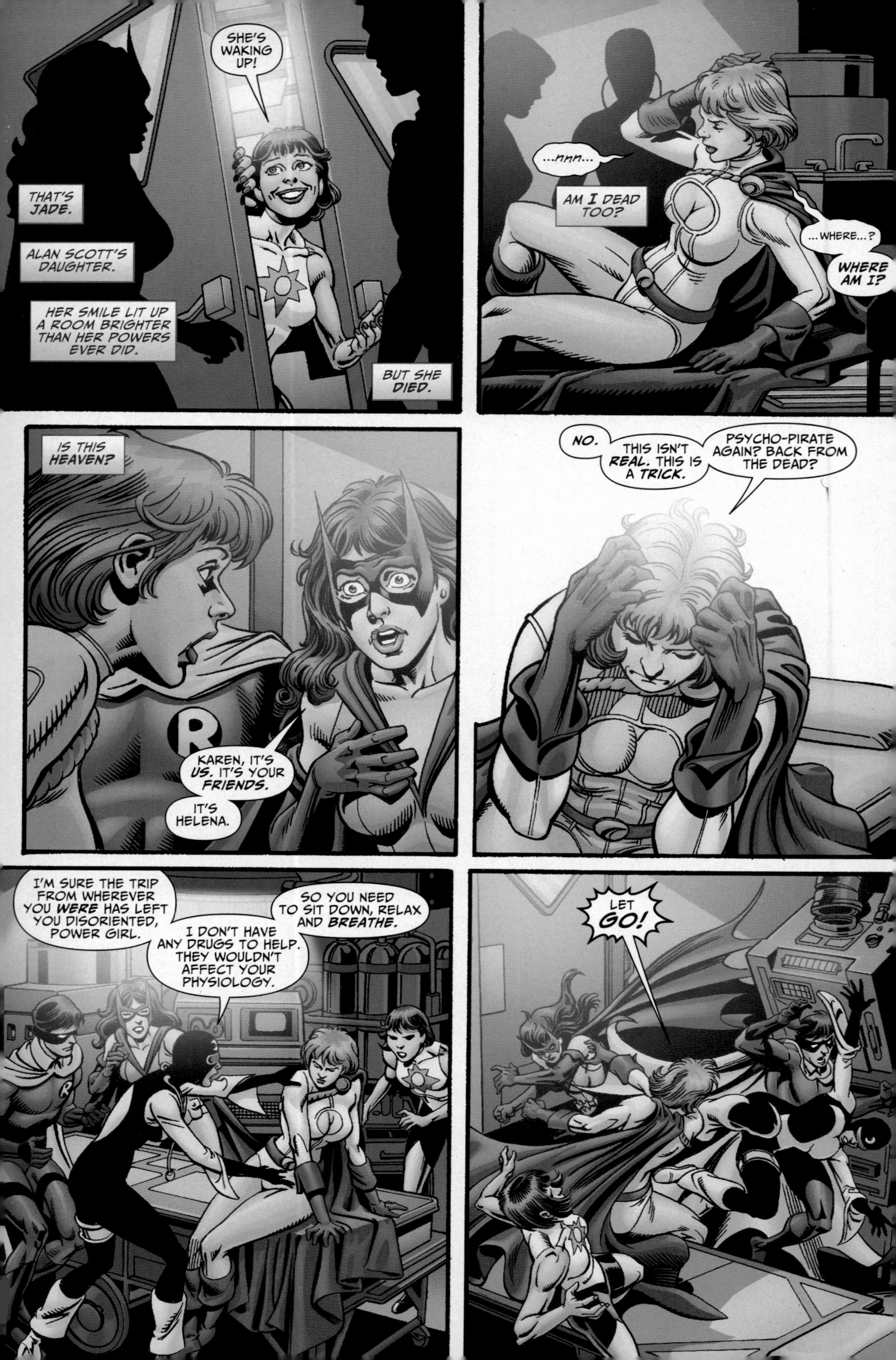
SHE'S WAKING UP!
THAT'S JADE.
ALAN SCOTT'S DAUGHTER.
HER SMILE LIT UP A ROOM BRIGHTER THAN HER POWERS EVER DID.
BUT SHE DIED.
...nnn...
AM I DEAD TOO?
...WHERE...?
WHERE AM I?
IS THIS HEAVEN?
KAREN, IT'S US. IT'S YOUR FRIENDS.
IT'S HELENA.
NO.
THIS ISN'T REAL. THIS IS A TRICK.
PSYCHO-PIRATE AGAIN? BACK FROM THE DEAD?
I'M SURE THE TRIP FROM WHEREVER YOU WERE HAS LEFT YOU DISORIENTED, POWER GIRL.
I DON'T HAVE ANY DRUGS TO HELP. THEY WOULDN'T AFFECT YOUR PHYSIOLOGY.
SO YOU NEED TO SIT DOWN, RELAX AND BREATHE.
LET GO!

BOOOOMM

THINK, KARA, THINK.

WHAT'S THE LAST THING YOU REMEMBER?

YOU WERE WITH... YOU WERE WITH THE JUSTICE SOCIETY OF AMERICA.

YOU WERE STANDING AT THE FEET OF A GOD.

HE GAVE DR. MID-NITE HIS **SIGHT** BACK. HE CURED STARMAN'S SCHIZOPHRENIA.

THEN HE LOOKED AT YOU...

YOU ARE LOST.

KRRASSSHHH

...AND THEN...

JUSTI **SOCIET** **FINITY**

THIS ISN'T POSSIBLE.

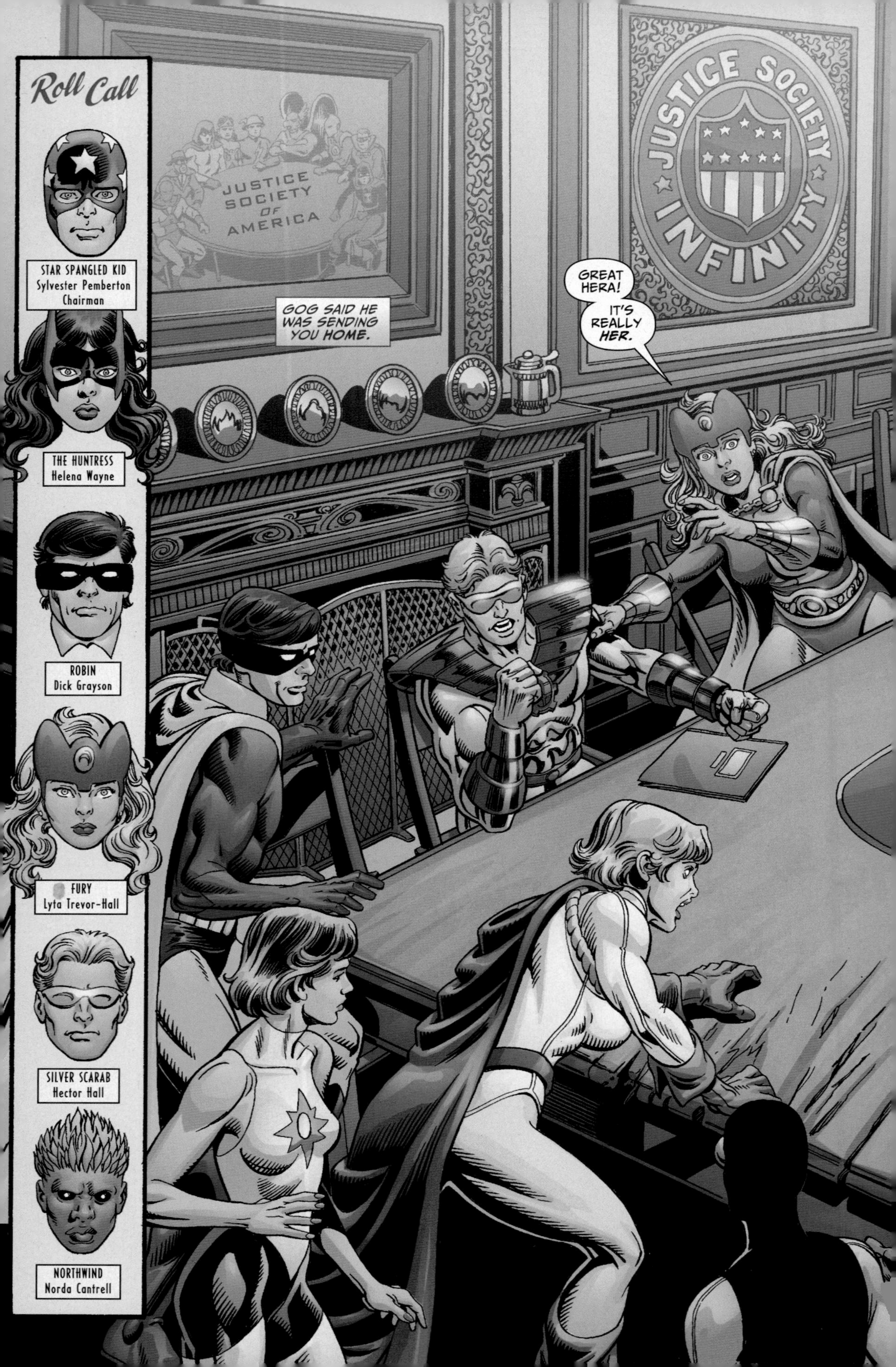

Roll Call
STAR SPANGLED KID
Sylvester Pemberton
Chairman
THE HUNTRESS
Helena Wayne
ROBIN
Dick Grayson
FURY
Lyta Trevor-Hall
SILVER SCARAB
Hector Hall
NORTHWIND
Norda Cantrell
JUSTICE SOCIETY OF AMERICA
JUSTICE SOCIETY INFINITY
GOG SAID HE WAS SENDING YOU HOME.
GREAT HERA!
IT'S REALLY HER.

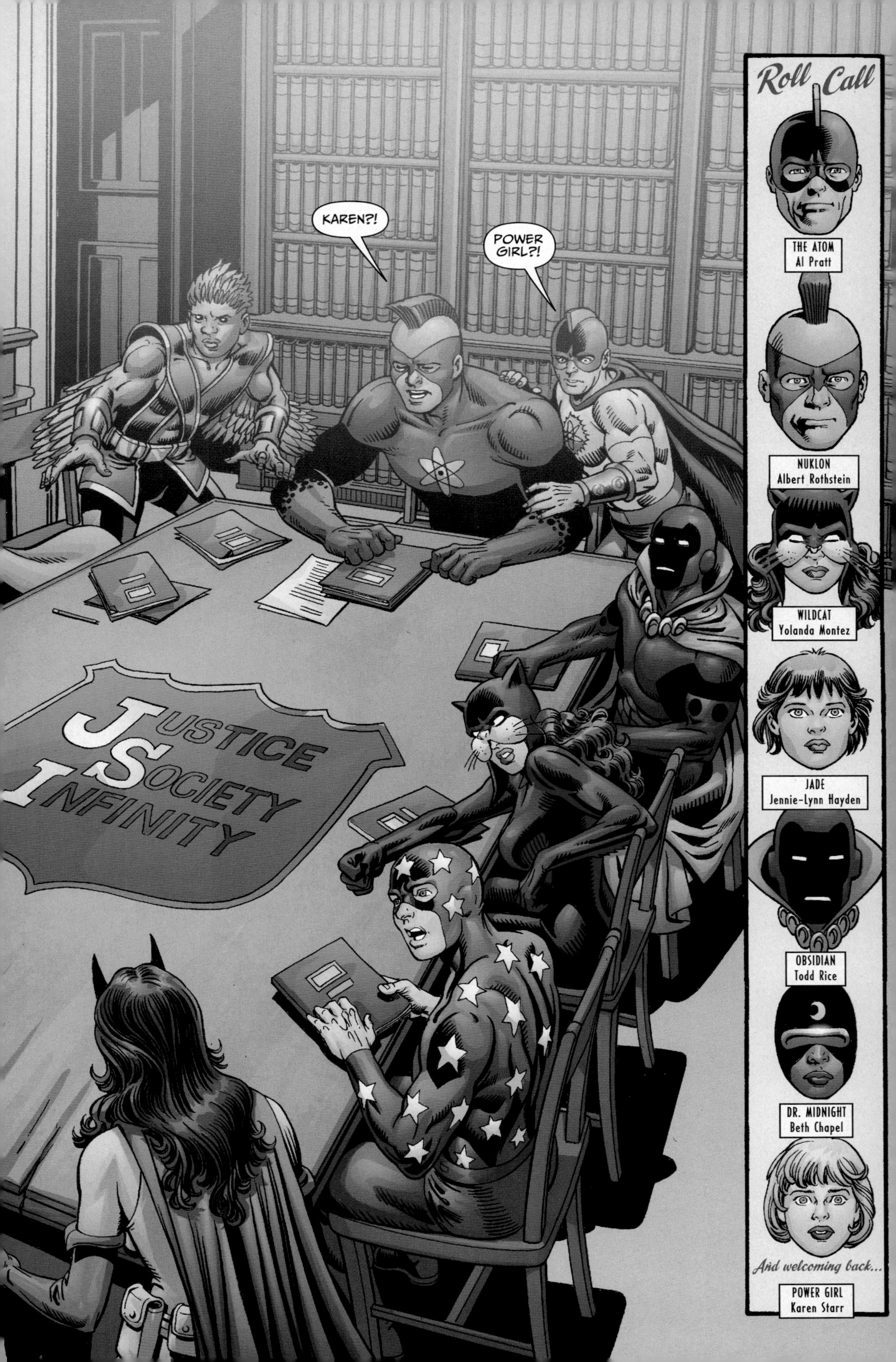

KAREN?!
POWER GIRL?!
JUSTICE SOCIETY INFINITY
Roll Call
THE ATOM
Al Pratt
NUKLON
Albert Rothstein
WILDCAT
Yolanda Montez
JADE
Jennie-Lynn Hayden
OBSIDIAN
Todd Rice
DR. MIDNIGHT
Beth Chapel
And welcoming back...
POWER GIRL
Karen Starr

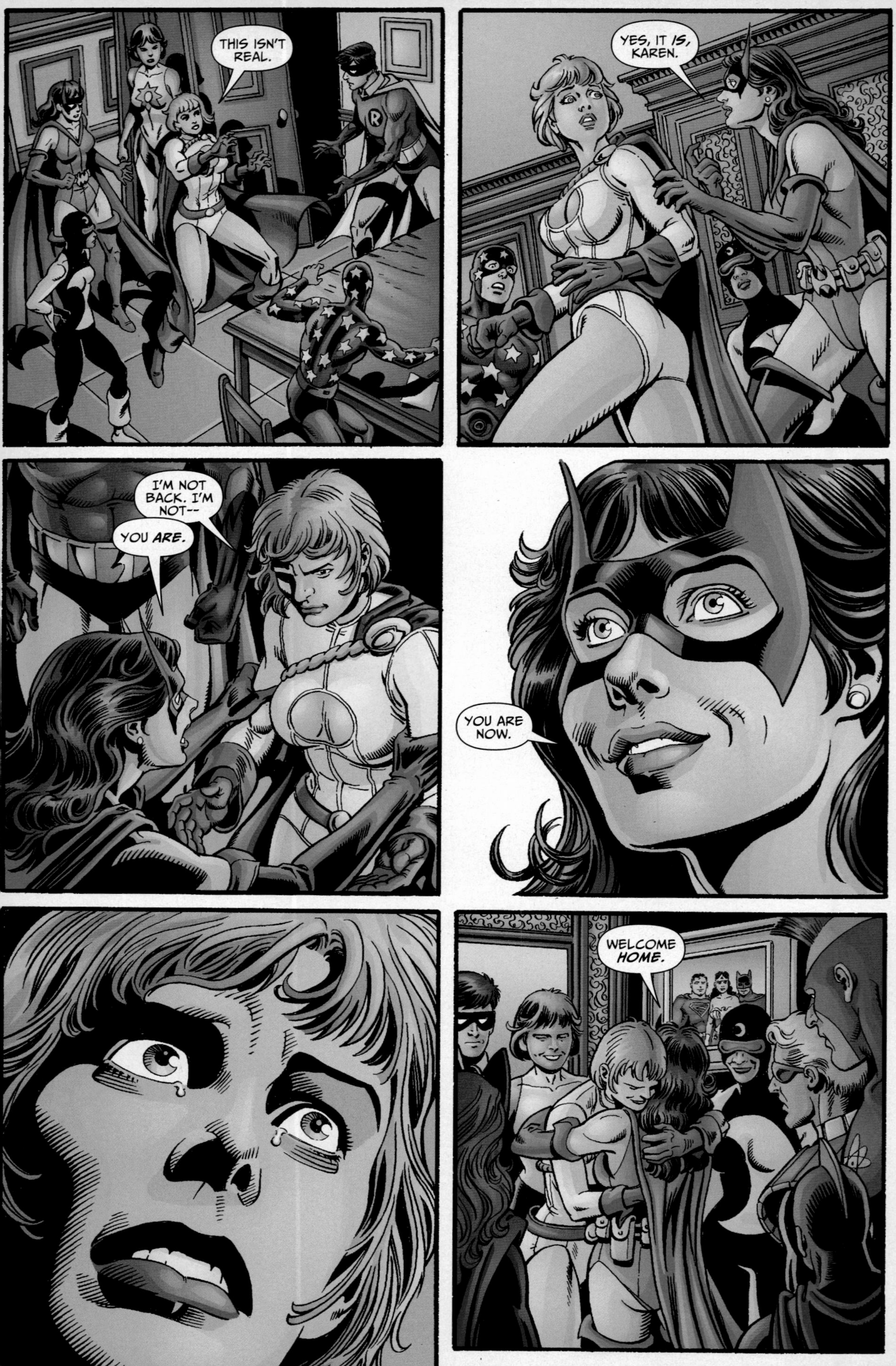
THIS ISN'T REAL.
YES, IT *IS*, KAREN.
I'M NOT BACK. I'M NOT--
YOU *ARE*.
YOU ARE NOW.
WELCOME *HOME*.

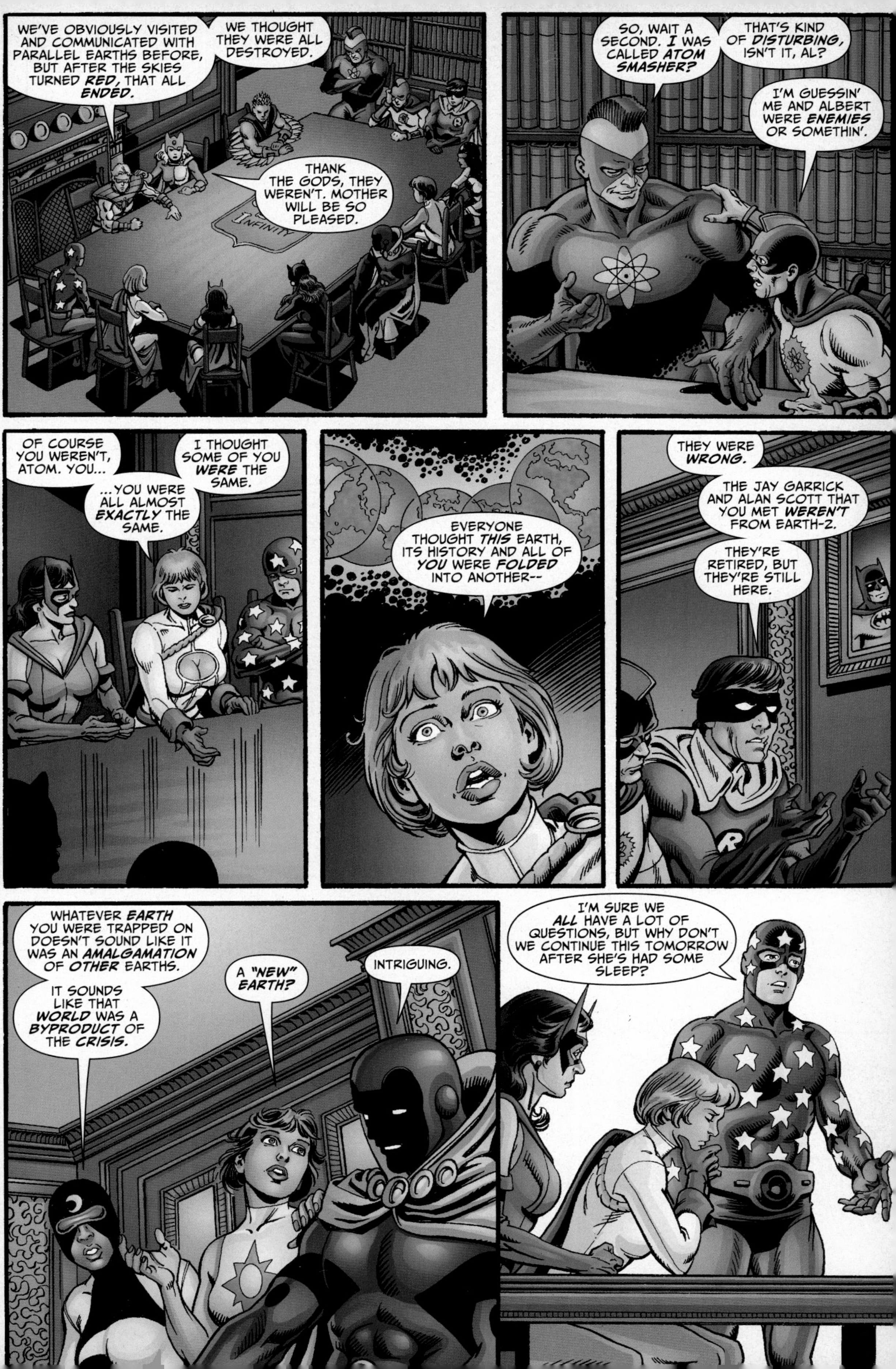
WE'VE OBVIOUSLY VISITED AND COMMUNICATED WITH PARALLEL EARTHS BEFORE, BUT AFTER THE SKIES TURNED RED, THAT ALL ENDED.
WE THOUGHT THEY WERE ALL DESTROYED.
THANK THE GODS, THEY WEREN'T. MOTHER WILL BE SO PLEASED.
INFINITY
SO, WAIT A SECOND. I WAS CALLED ATOM SMASHER?
THAT'S KIND OF DISTURBING, ISN'T IT, AL?
I'M GUESSIN' ME AND ALBERT WERE ENEMIES OR SOMETHIN'.
OF COURSE YOU WEREN'T, ATOM. YOU...
I THOUGHT SOME OF YOU WERE THE SAME.
...YOU WERE ALL ALMOST EXACTLY THE SAME.
EVERYONE THOUGHT THIS EARTH, ITS HISTORY AND ALL OF YOU WERE FOLDED INTO ANOTHER--
THEY WERE WRONG.
THE JAY GARRICK AND ALAN SCOTT THAT YOU MET WEREN'T FROM EARTH-2.
THEY'RE RETIRED, BUT THEY'RE STILL HERE.
WHATEVER EARTH YOU WERE TRAPPED ON DOESN'T SOUND LIKE IT WAS AN AMALGAMATION OF OTHER EARTHS.
IT SOUNDS LIKE THAT WORLD WAS A BYPRODUCT OF THE CRISIS.
A "NEW" EARTH?
INTRIGUING.
I'M SURE WE ALL HAVE A LOT OF QUESTIONS, BUT WHY DON'T WE CONTINUE THIS TOMORROW AFTER SHE'S HAD SOME SLEEP?

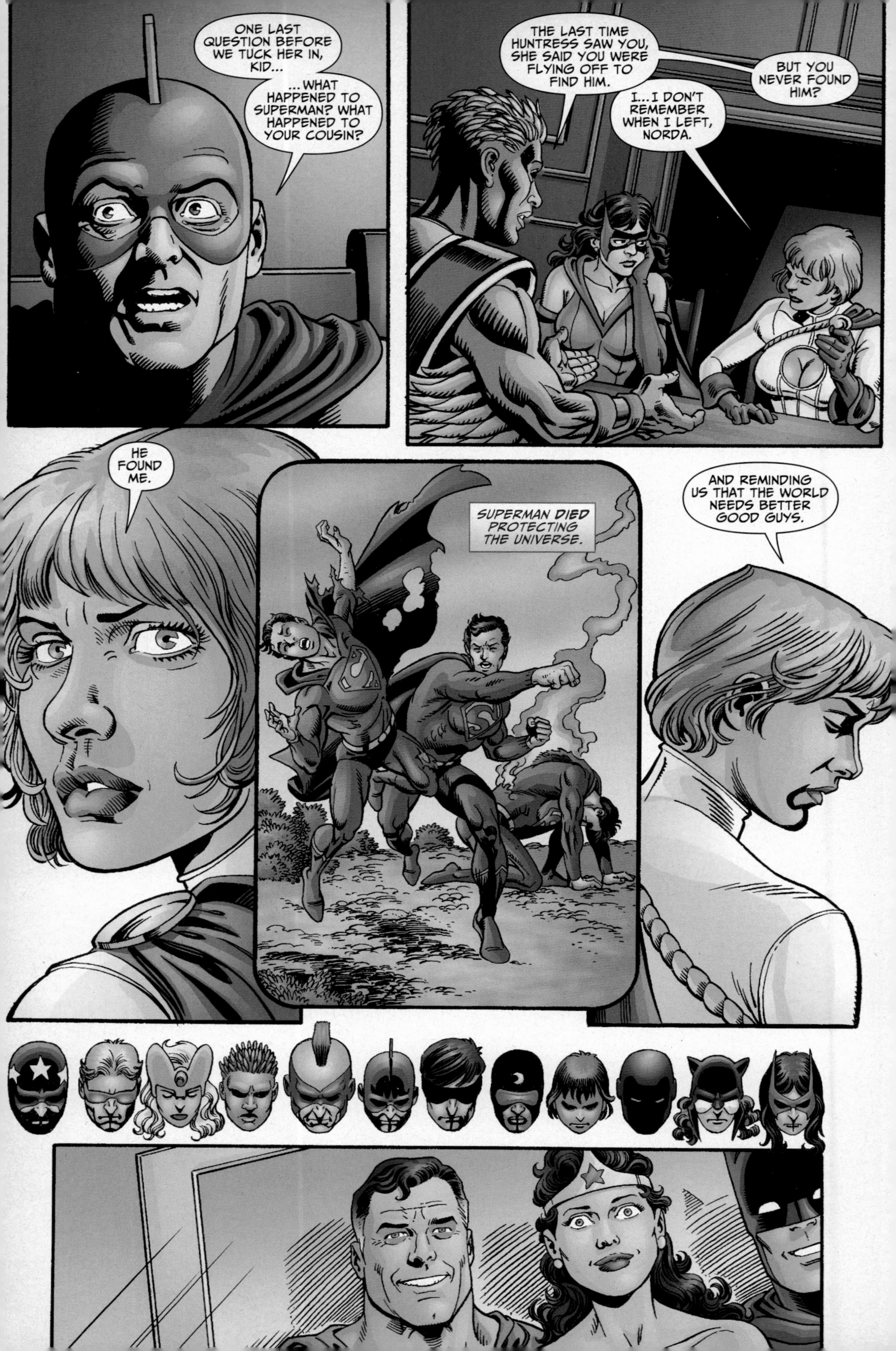
ONE LAST QUESTION BEFORE WE TUCK HER IN, KID...
...WHAT HAPPENED TO SUPERMAN? WHAT HAPPENED TO YOUR COUSIN?
THE LAST TIME HUNTRESS SAW YOU, SHE SAID YOU WERE FLYING OFF TO FIND HIM.
BUT YOU NEVER FOUND HIM?
I...I DON'T REMEMBER WHEN I LEFT, NORDA.
HE FOUND ME.
SUPERMAN DIED PROTECTING THE UNIVERSE.
AND REMINDING US THAT THE WORLD NEEDS BETTER GOOD GUYS.

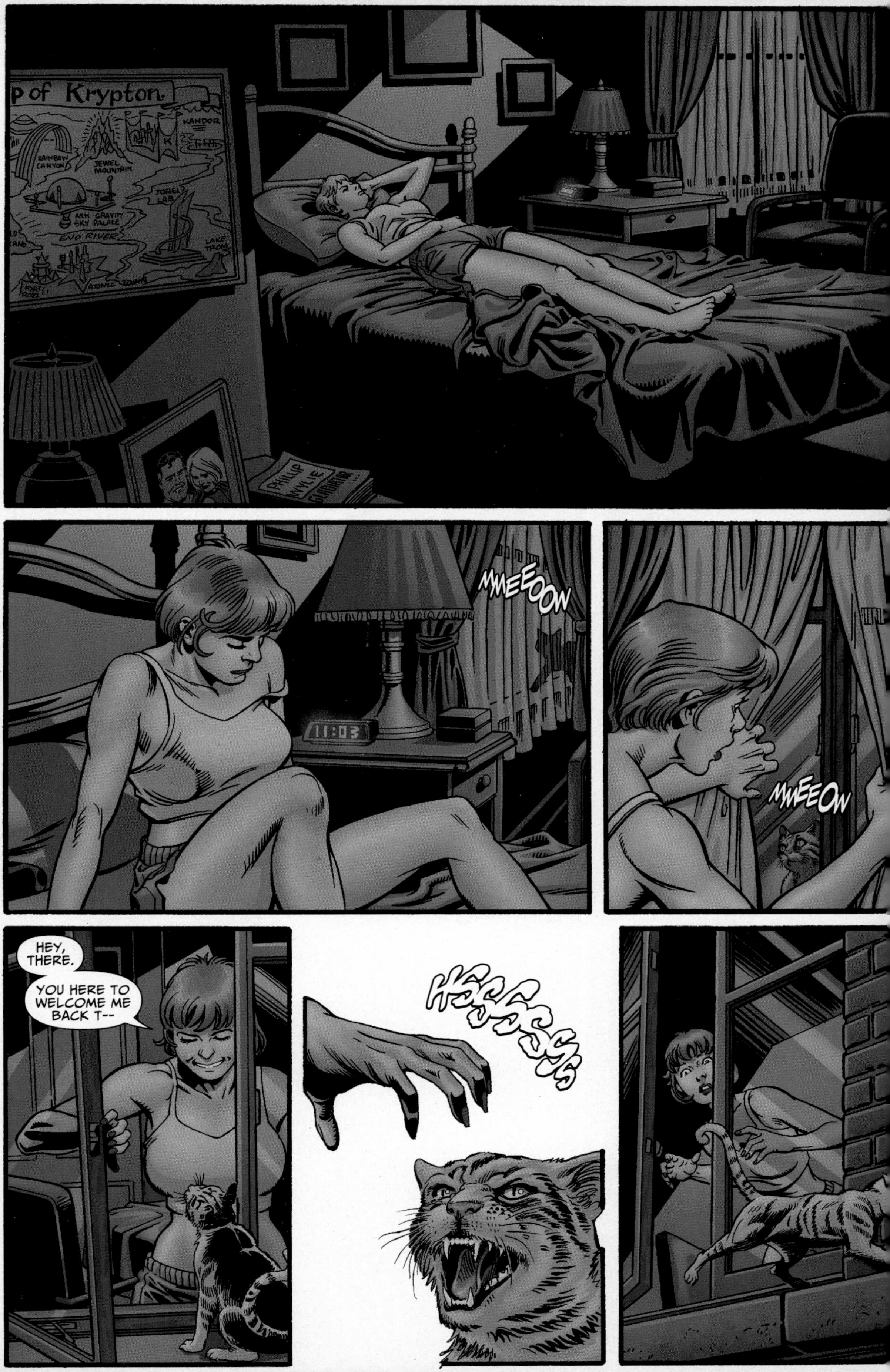

p of Krypton
KANDOR
RAINBOW CANYON
JEWEL MOUNTAIN
JOREL LAB
ANTI GRAVITY SKY PALACE
ENO RIVER
LAKE TRON
ATOMIC TOWN
PHILLIP WYLIE GLADIATOR
11:03
MMEEOOW
MMEEOW
HEY, THERE.
YOU HERE TO WELCOME ME BACK T--
HSSSSSS

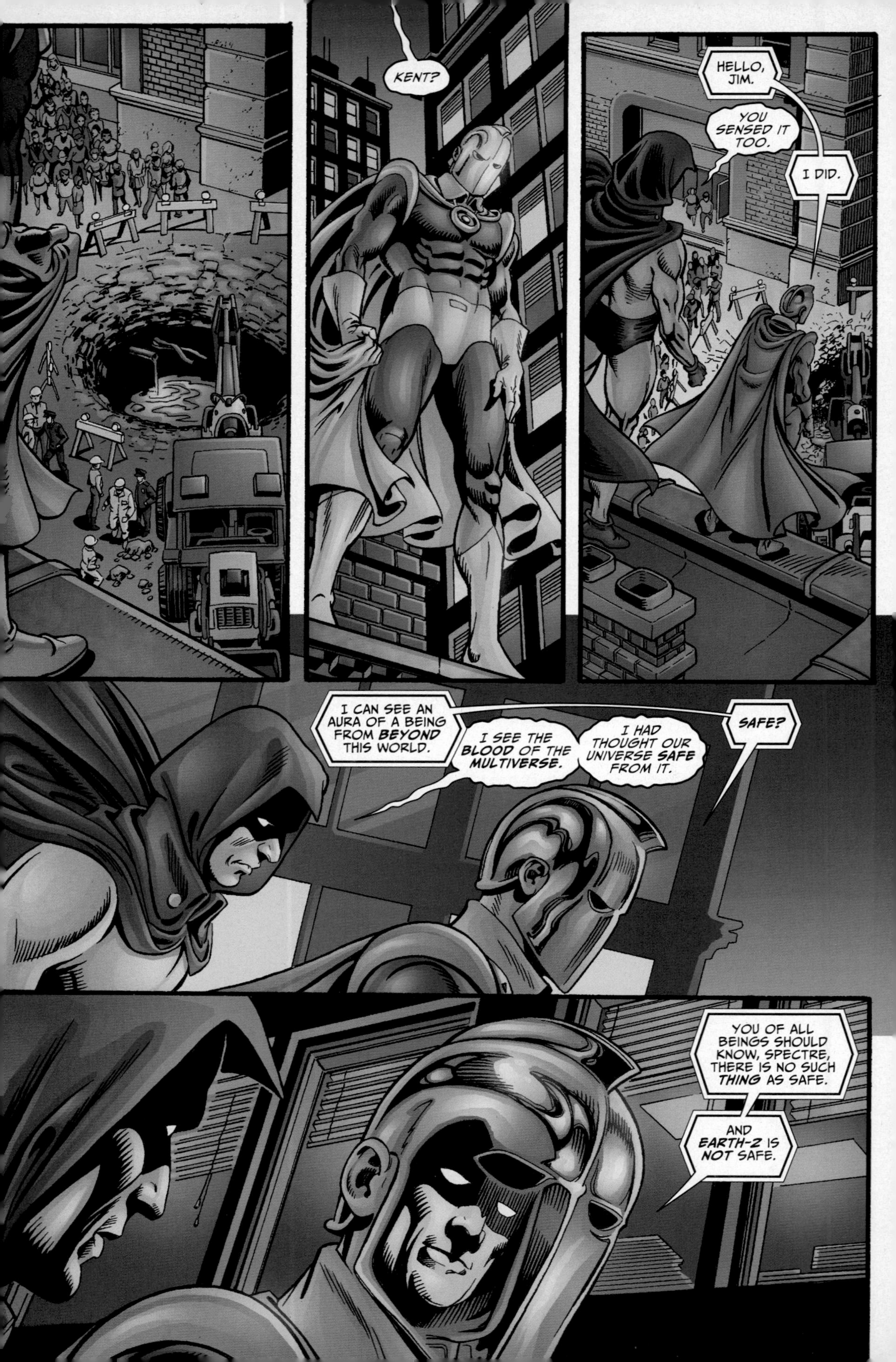

KENT?
HELLO, JIM.
YOU SENSED IT TOO.
I DID.
I CAN SEE AN AURA OF A BEING FROM BEYOND THIS WORLD.
I SEE THE BLOOD OF THE MULTIVERSE.
I HAD THOUGHT OUR UNIVERSE SAFE FROM IT.
SAFE?
YOU OF ALL BEINGS SHOULD KNOW, SPECTRE, THERE IS NO SUCH THING AS SAFE.
AND EARTH-2 IS NOT SAFE.

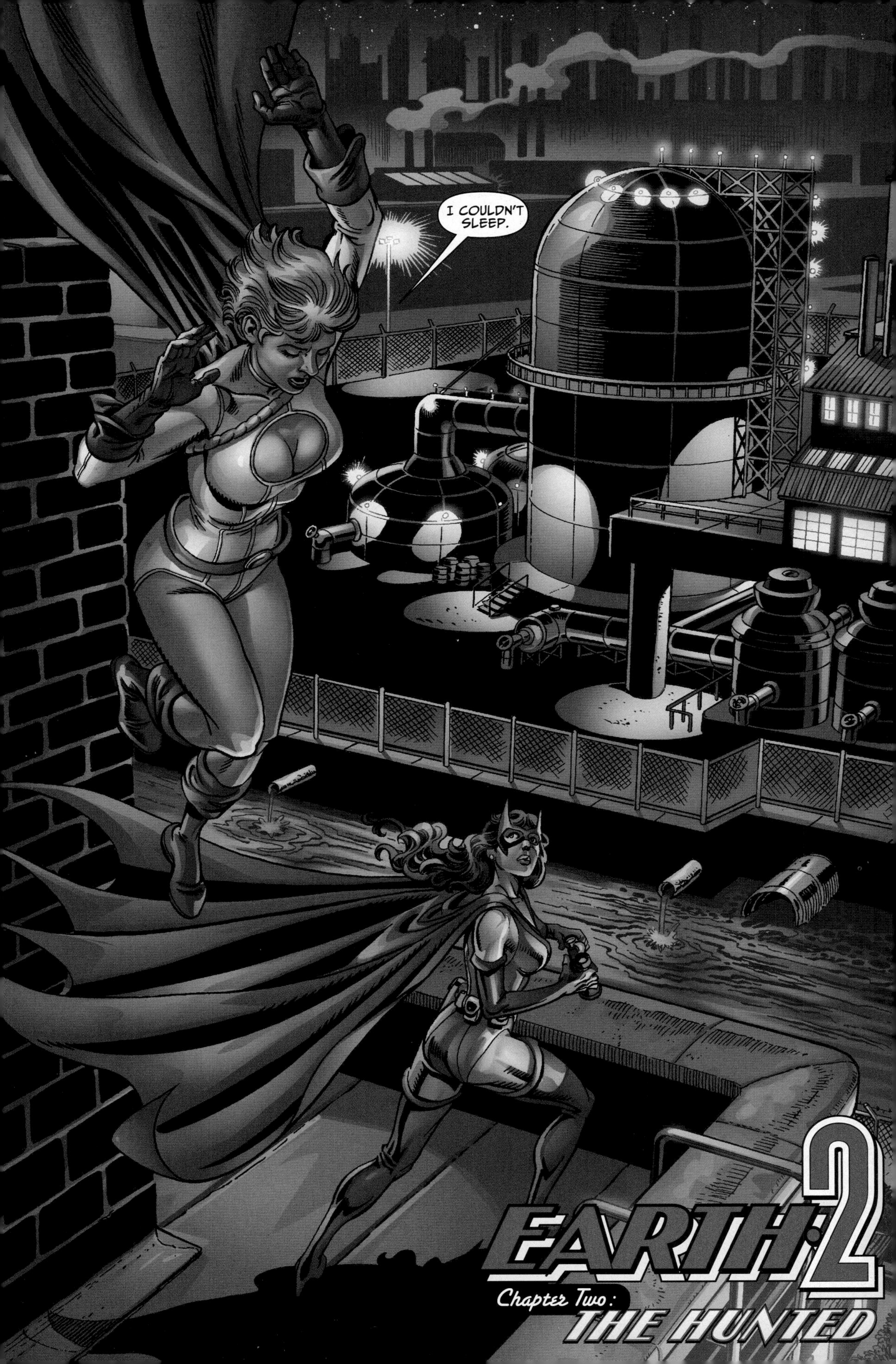
I COULDN'T SLEEP.
EARTH 2
Chapter Two:
THE HUNTED

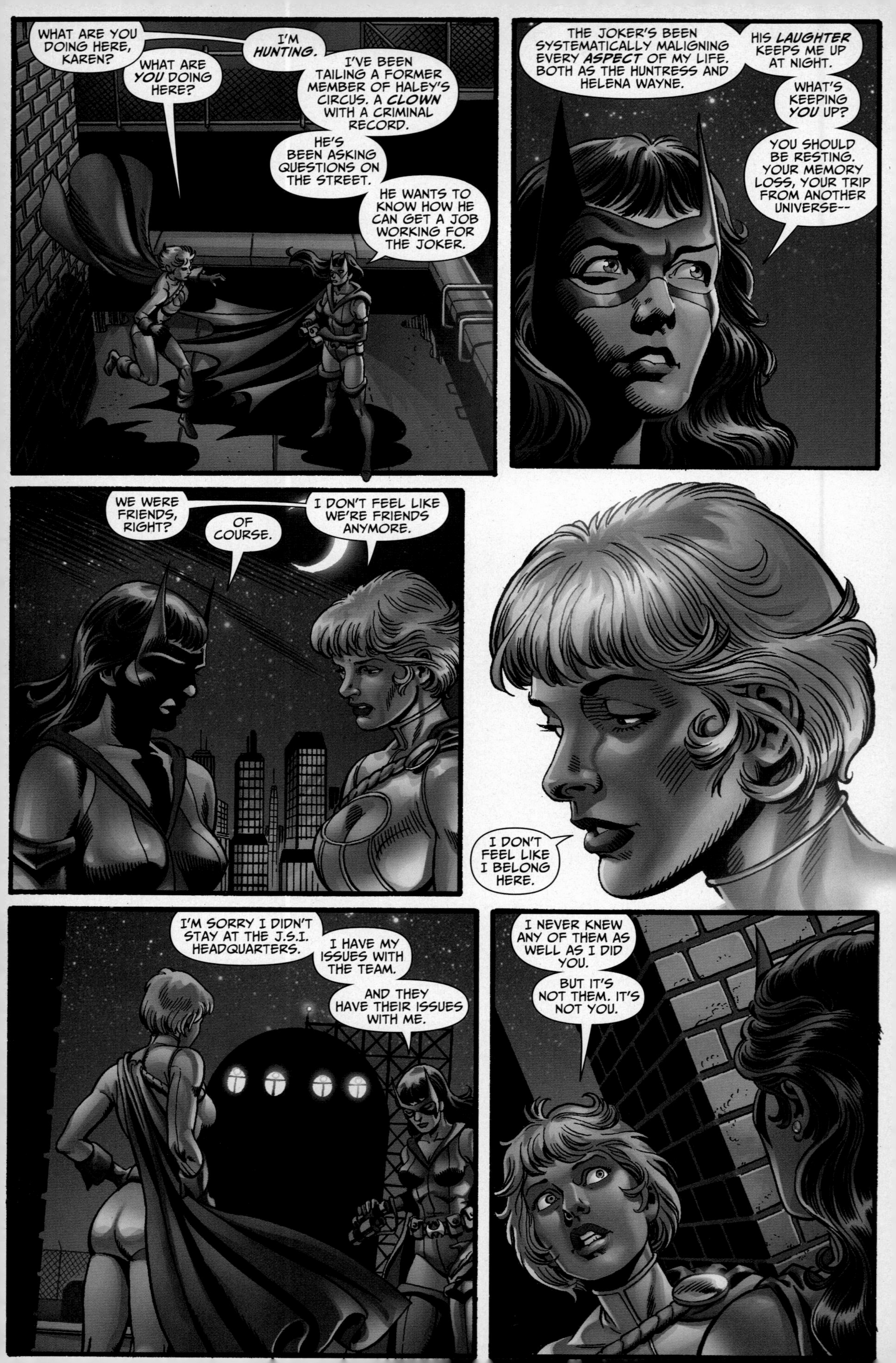
WHAT ARE YOU DOING HERE, KAREN?
I'M HUNTING.
WHAT ARE YOU DOING HERE?
I'VE BEEN TAILING A FORMER MEMBER OF HALEY'S CIRCUS. A CLOWN WITH A CRIMINAL RECORD.
HE'S BEEN ASKING QUESTIONS ON THE STREET.
HE WANTS TO KNOW HOW HE CAN GET A JOB WORKING FOR THE JOKER.
THE JOKER'S BEEN SYSTEMATICALLY MALIGNING EVERY ASPECT OF MY LIFE. BOTH AS THE HUNTRESS AND HELENA WAYNE.
HIS LAUGHTER KEEPS ME UP AT NIGHT.
WHAT'S KEEPING YOU UP?
YOU SHOULD BE RESTING. YOUR MEMORY LOSS, YOUR TRIP FROM ANOTHER UNIVERSE--
WE WERE FRIENDS, RIGHT?
OF COURSE.
I DON'T FEEL LIKE WE'RE FRIENDS ANYMORE.
I DON'T FEEL LIKE I BELONG HERE.
I'M SORRY I DIDN'T STAY AT THE J.S.I. HEADQUARTERS.
I HAVE MY ISSUES WITH THE TEAM.
AND THEY HAVE THEIR ISSUES WITH ME.
I NEVER KNEW ANY OF THEM AS WELL AS I DID YOU.
BUT IT'S NOT THEM. IT'S NOT YOU.

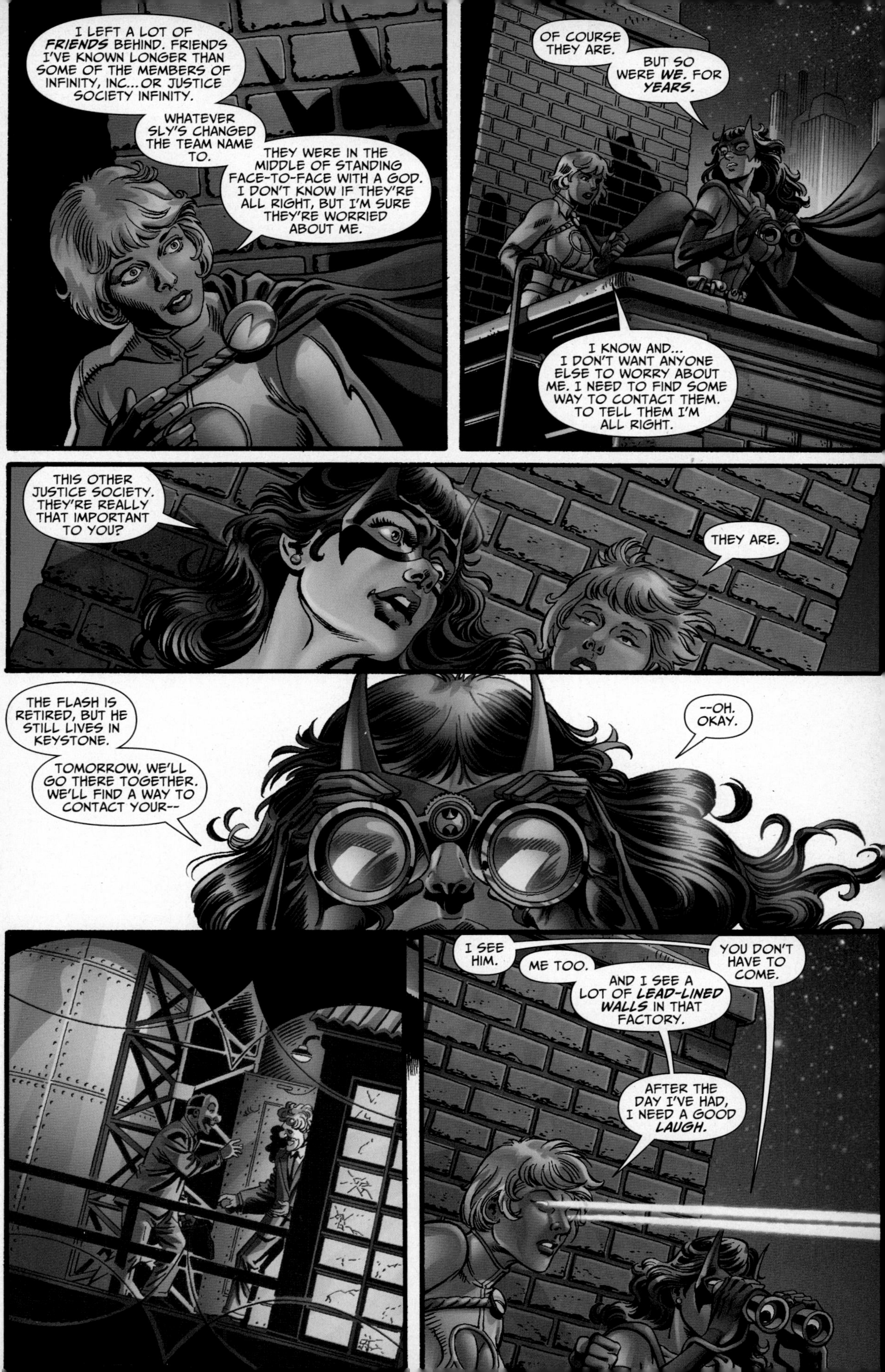

I LEFT A LOT OF FRIENDS BEHIND. FRIENDS I'VE KNOWN LONGER THAN SOME OF THE MEMBERS OF INFINITY, INC... OR JUSTICE SOCIETY INFINITY.
WHATEVER SLY'S CHANGED THE TEAM NAME TO.
THEY WERE IN THE MIDDLE OF STANDING FACE-TO-FACE WITH A GOD. I DON'T KNOW IF THEY'RE ALL RIGHT, BUT I'M SURE THEY'RE WORRIED ABOUT ME.
OF COURSE THEY ARE.
BUT SO WERE WE. FOR YEARS.
I KNOW AND... I DON'T WANT ANYONE ELSE TO WORRY ABOUT ME. I NEED TO FIND SOME WAY TO CONTACT THEM. TO TELL THEM I'M ALL RIGHT.
THIS OTHER JUSTICE SOCIETY. THEY'RE REALLY THAT IMPORTANT TO YOU?
THEY ARE.
THE FLASH IS RETIRED, BUT HE STILL LIVES IN KEYSTONE.
TOMORROW, WE'LL GO THERE TOGETHER. WE'LL FIND A WAY TO CONTACT YOUR--
--OH. OKAY.
I SEE HIM.
ME TOO.
AND I SEE A LOT OF LEAD-LINED WALLS IN THAT FACTORY.
YOU DON'T HAVE TO COME.
AFTER THE DAY I'VE HAD, I NEED A GOOD LAUGH.

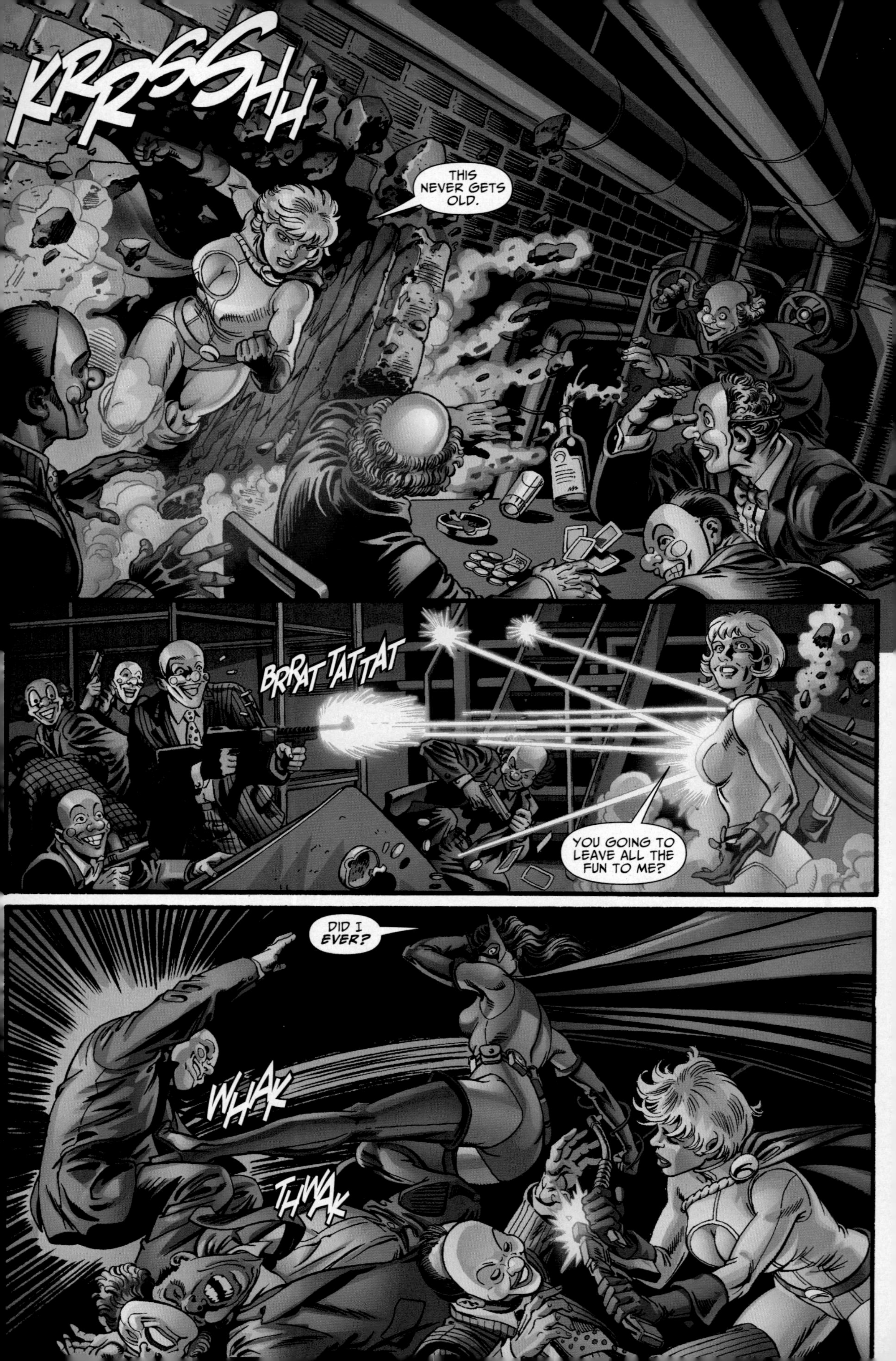
KRRSSHH
THIS NEVER GETS OLD.
BRRAT TAT TAT
YOU GOING TO LEAVE ALL THE FUN TO ME?
DID I EVER?
WHAK
THWAK

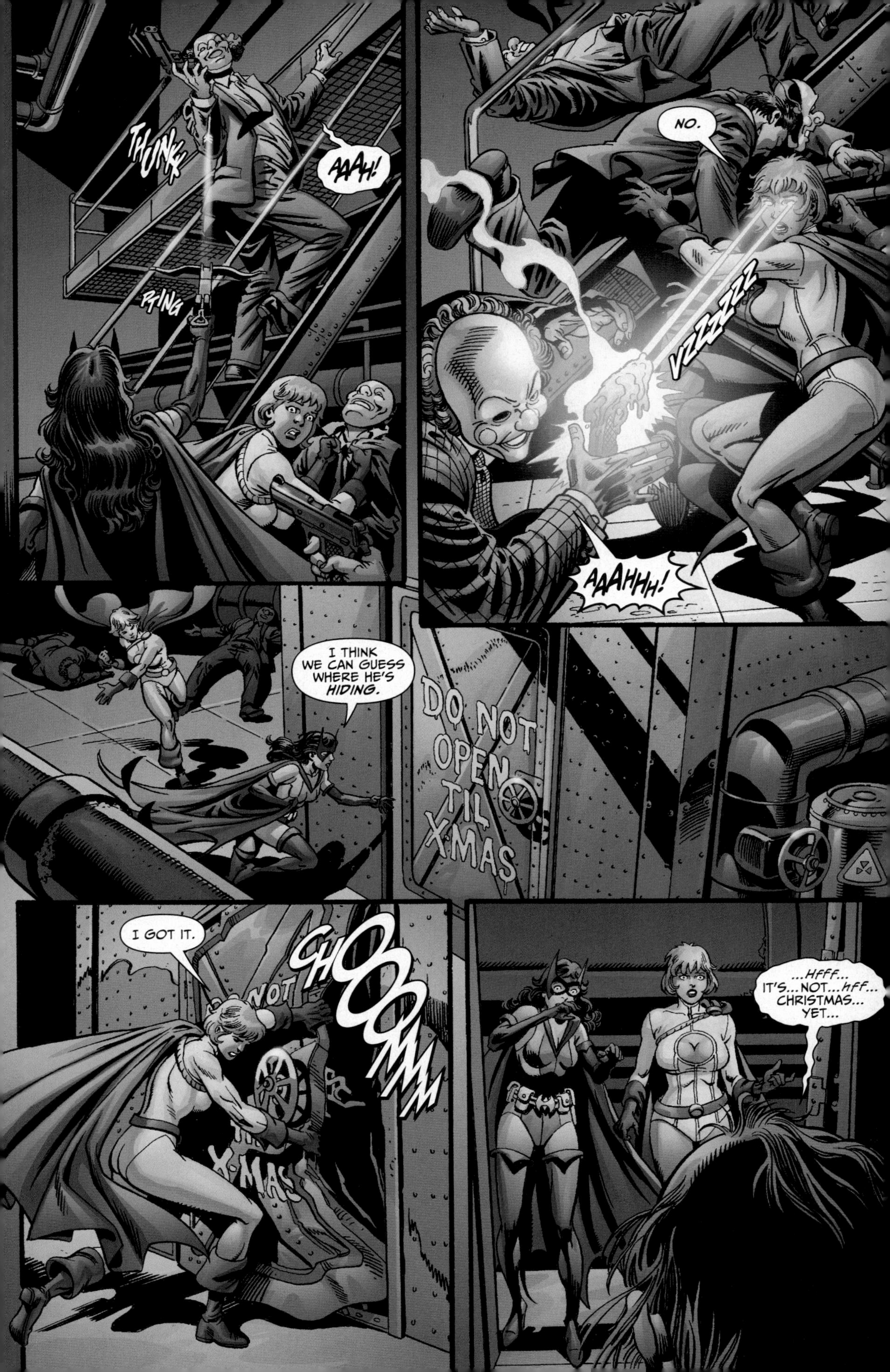
THUNK
AAAH!
PING
NO.
VZZZZZZZ
AAAHHH!
I THINK WE CAN GUESS WHERE HE'S HIDING.
DO NOT OPEN TIL X-MAS
I GOT IT.
CHOOOMMM
...HFFF... IT'S...NOT...HFF... CHRISTMAS... YET...

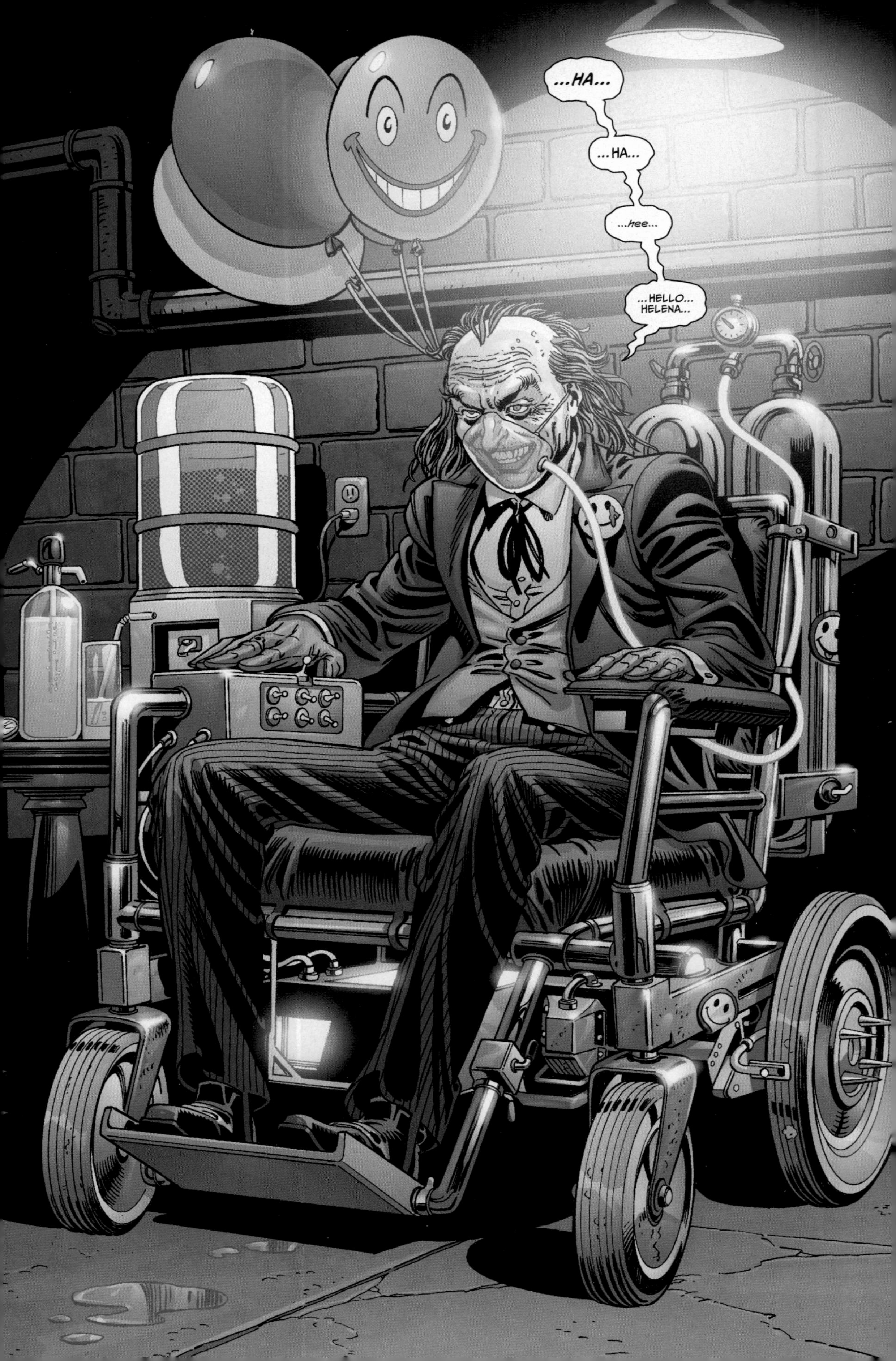
...HA...
...HA...
...hee...
...HELLO...
HELENA...

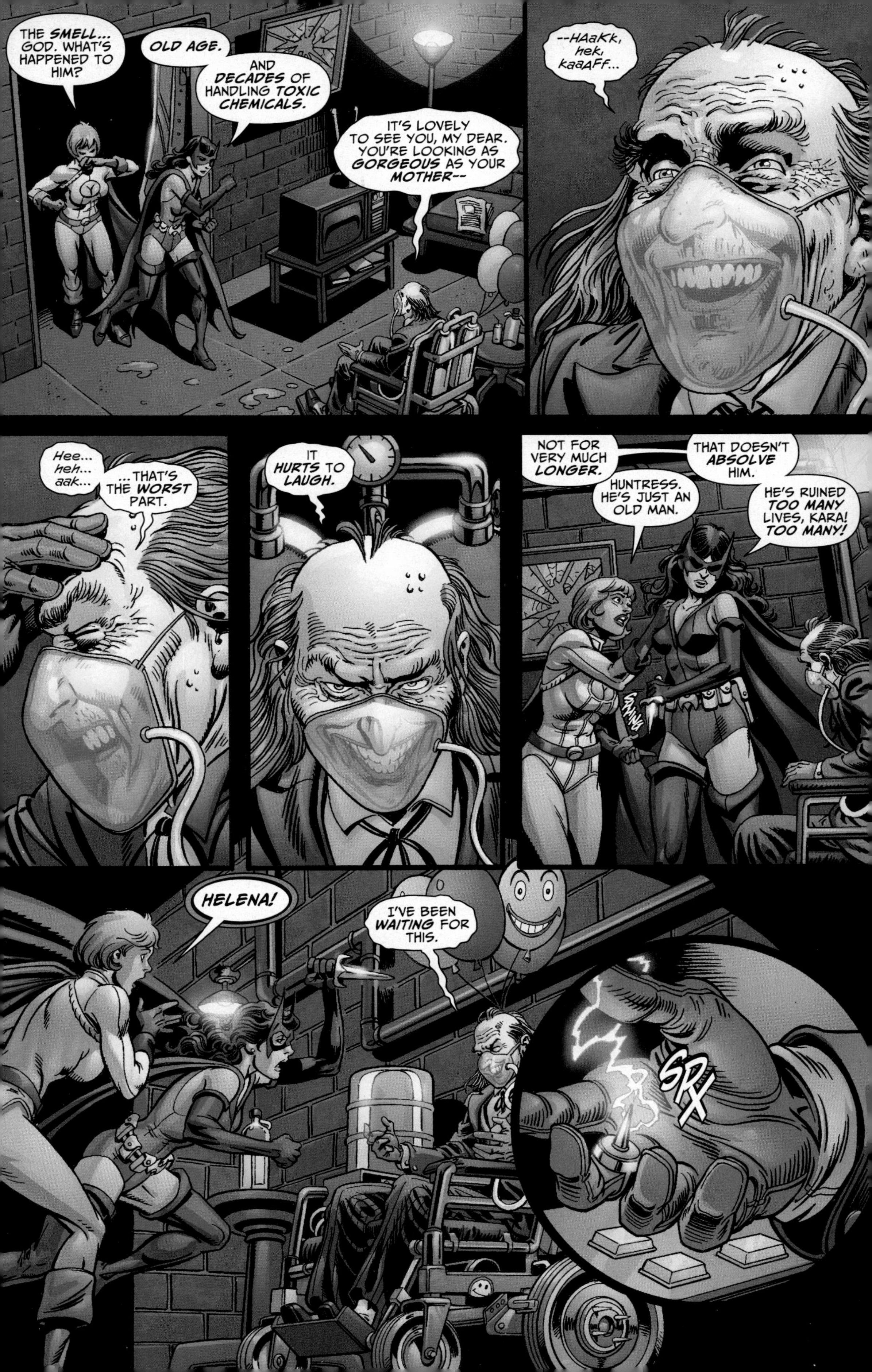
THE SMELL... GOD. WHAT'S HAPPENED TO HIM?
OLD AGE.
AND DECADES OF HANDLING TOXIC CHEMICALS.
IT'S LOVELY TO SEE YOU, MY DEAR. YOU'RE LOOKING AS GORGEOUS AS YOUR MOTHER--
--HAaKk, hek, kaaAFF...
Hee... heh... aak...
...THAT'S THE WORST PART.
IT HURTS TO LAUGH.
HUNTRESS. HE'S JUST AN OLD MAN.
NOT FOR VERY MUCH LONGER.
THAT DOESN'T ABSOLVE HIM.
HE'S RUINED TOO MANY LIVES, KARA! TOO MANY!
HELENA!
I'VE BEEN WAITING FOR THIS.
SPX

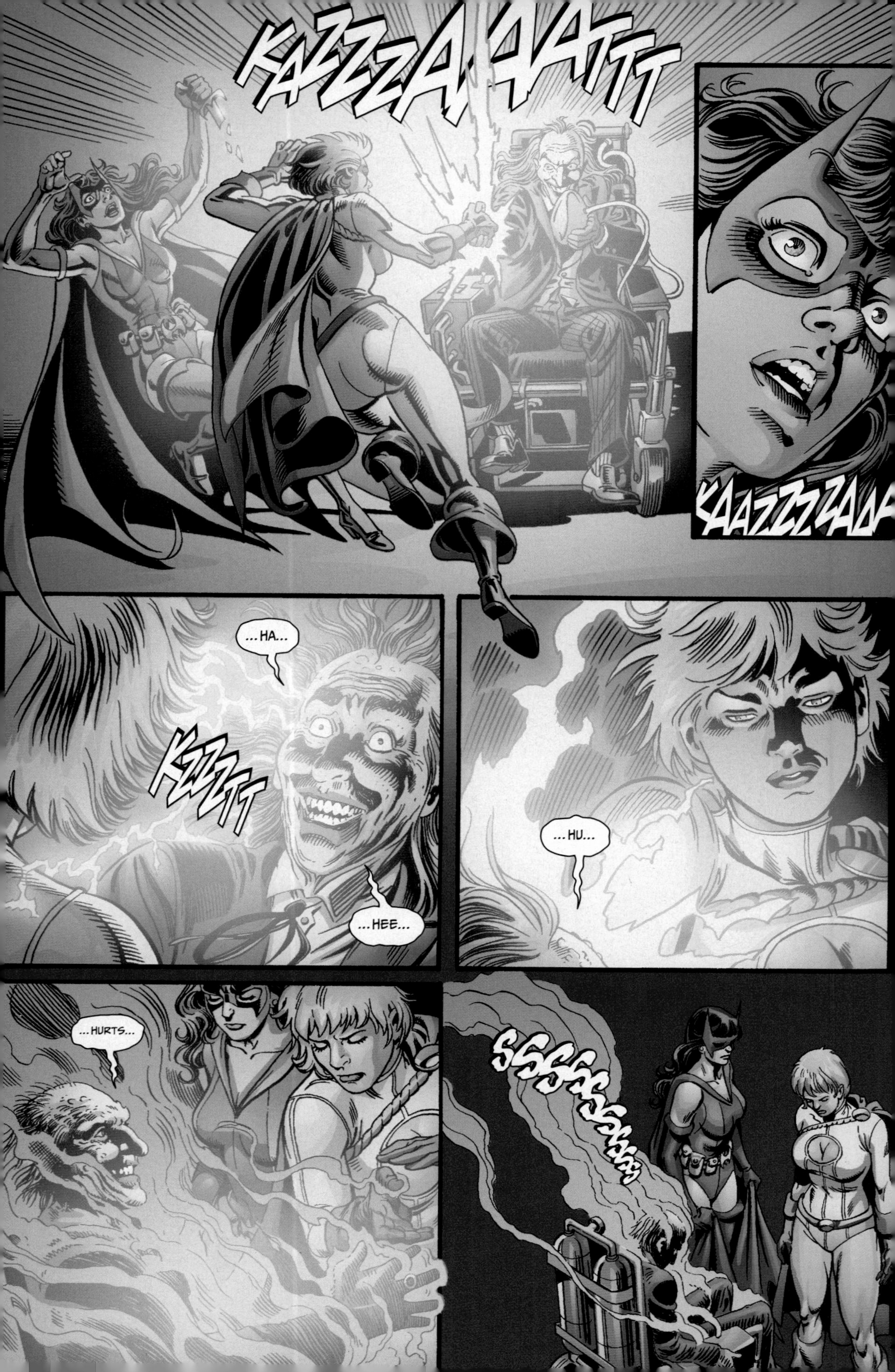
KAZZZAAAATTT
KAAZZZZAA
...HA...
KZZZTTT
...HEE...
...HU...
...HURTS...
SSSSSSSSSS

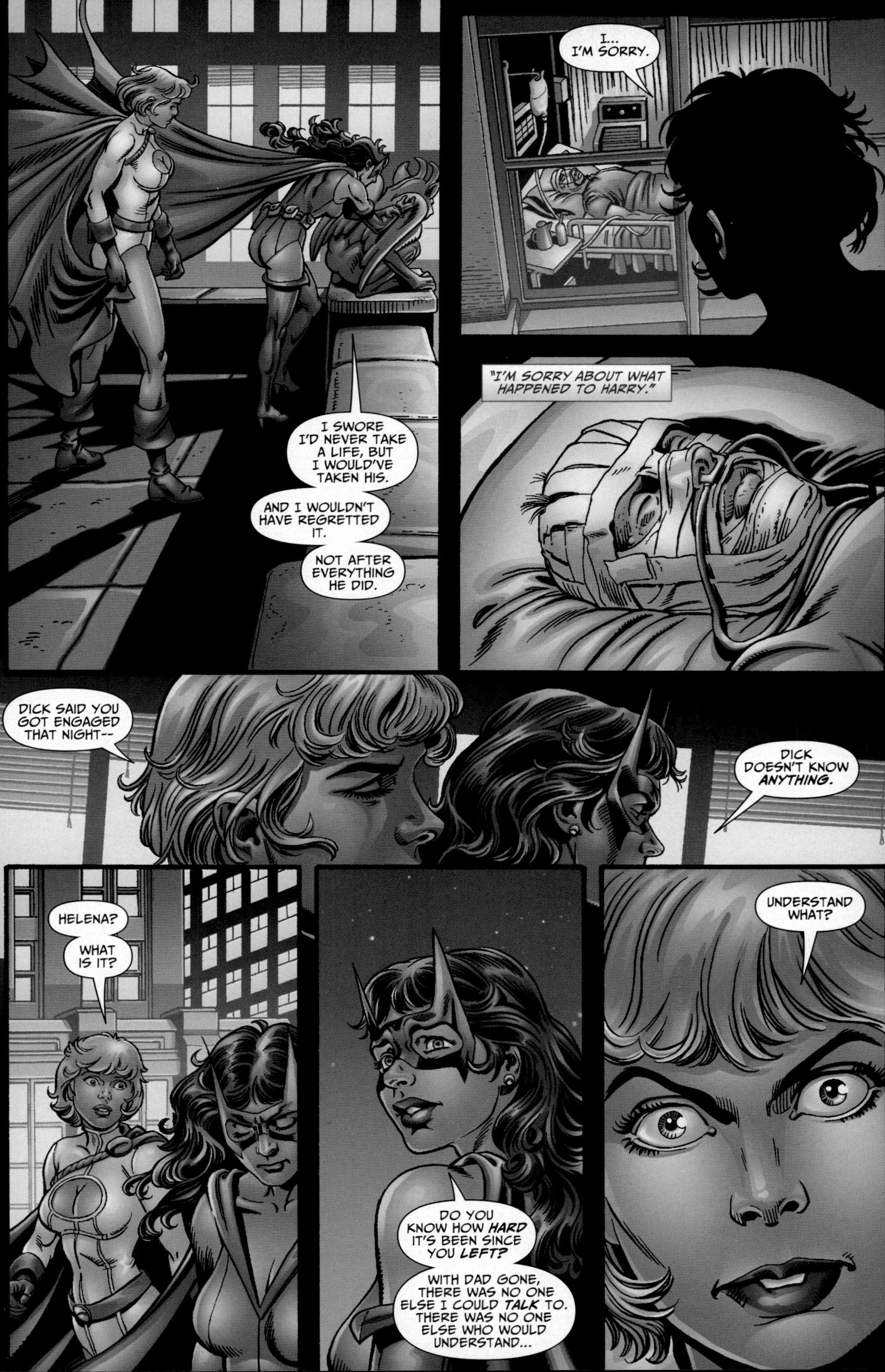
I SWORE I'D NEVER TAKE A LIFE, BUT I WOULD'VE TAKEN HIS.
AND I WOULDN'T HAVE REGRETTED IT.
NOT AFTER EVERYTHING HE DID.
I... I'M SORRY.
"I'M SORRY ABOUT WHAT HAPPENED TO HARRY."
DICK SAID YOU GOT ENGAGED THAT NIGHT--
DICK DOESN'T KNOW ANYTHING.
HELENA?
WHAT IS IT?
DO YOU KNOW HOW HARD IT'S BEEN SINCE YOU LEFT?
WITH DAD GONE, THERE WAS NO ONE ELSE I COULD TALK TO. THERE WAS NO ONE ELSE WHO WOULD UNDERSTAND...
UNDERSTAND WHAT?

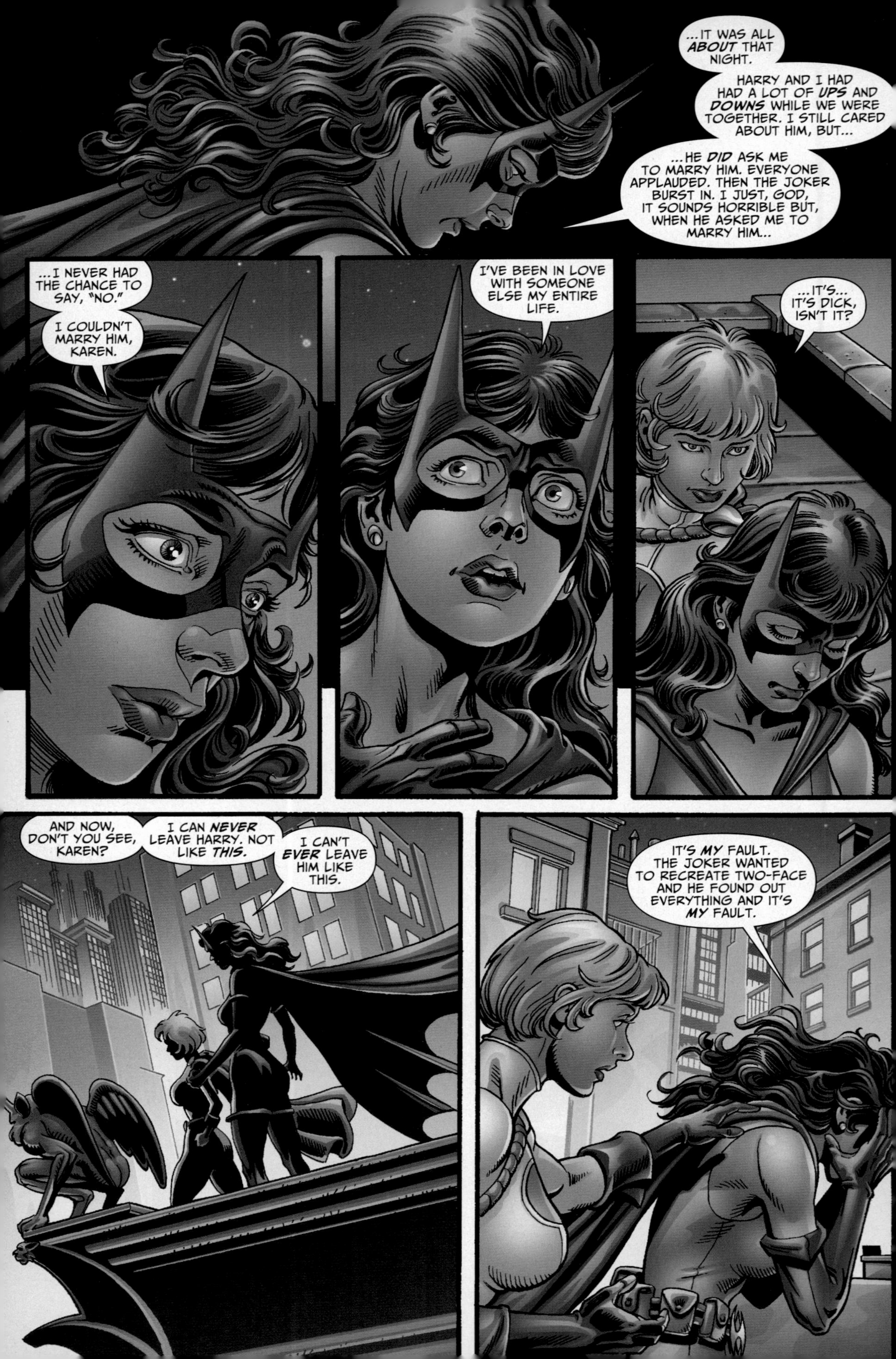
...IT WAS ALL ABOUT THAT NIGHT.
HARRY AND I HAD HAD A LOT OF UPS AND DOWNS WHILE WE WERE TOGETHER. I STILL CARED ABOUT HIM, BUT...
...HE DID ASK ME TO MARRY HIM. EVERYONE APPLAUDED. THEN THE JOKER BURST IN. I JUST, GOD, IT SOUNDS HORRIBLE BUT, WHEN HE ASKED ME TO MARRY HIM...
...I NEVER HAD THE CHANCE TO SAY, "NO."
I COULDN'T MARRY HIM, KAREN.
I'VE BEEN IN LOVE WITH SOMEONE ELSE MY ENTIRE LIFE.
...IT'S... IT'S DICK, ISN'T IT?
AND NOW, DON'T YOU SEE, KAREN?
I CAN NEVER LEAVE HARRY. NOT LIKE THIS.
I CAN'T EVER LEAVE HIM LIKE THIS.
IT'S MY FAULT. THE JOKER WANTED TO RECREATE TWO-FACE AND HE FOUND OUT EVERYTHING AND IT'S MY FAULT.

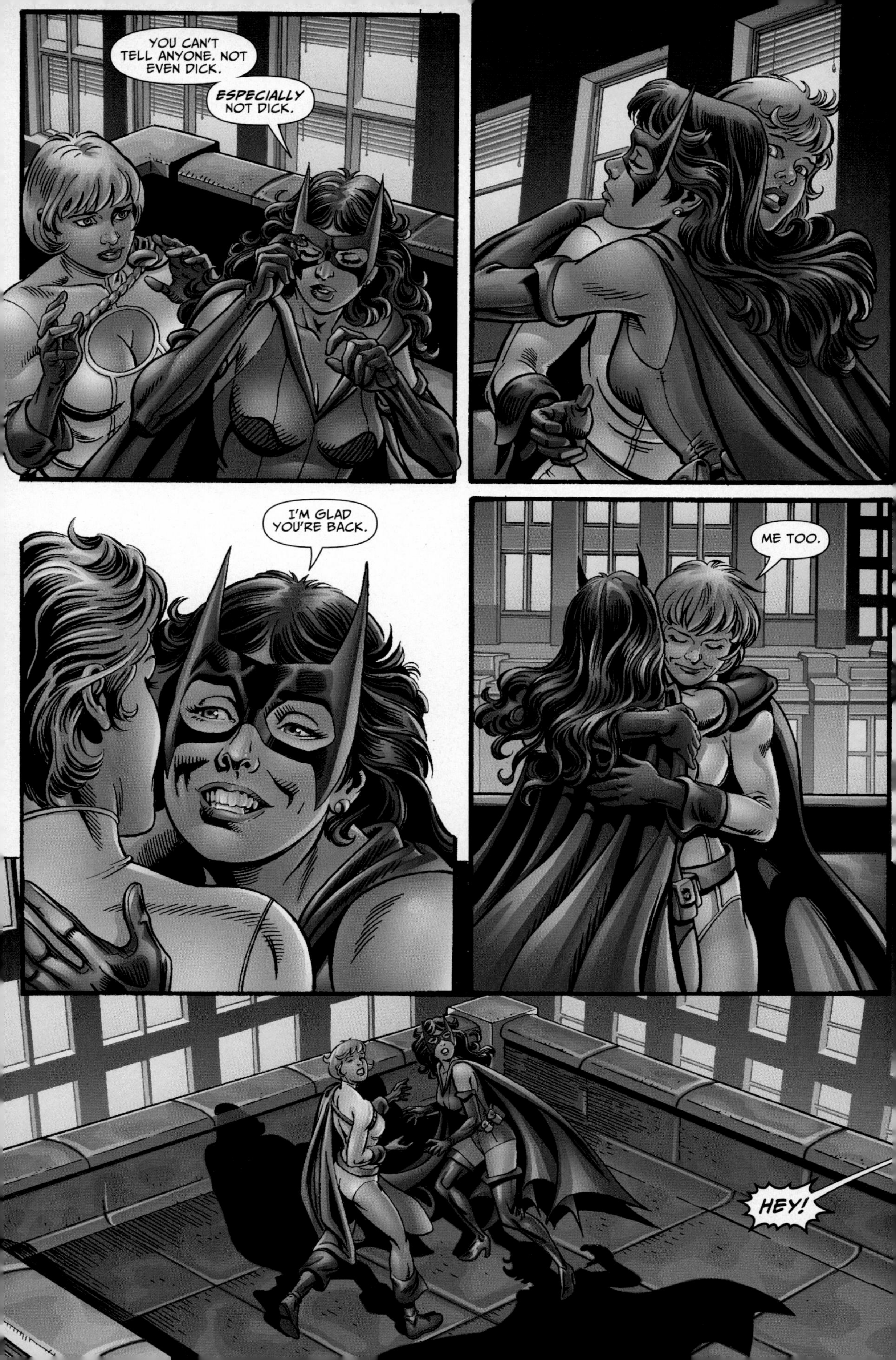
YOU CAN'T TELL ANYONE. NOT EVEN DICK.
ESPECIALLY NOT DICK.
I'M GLAD YOU'RE BACK.
ME TOO.
HEY!

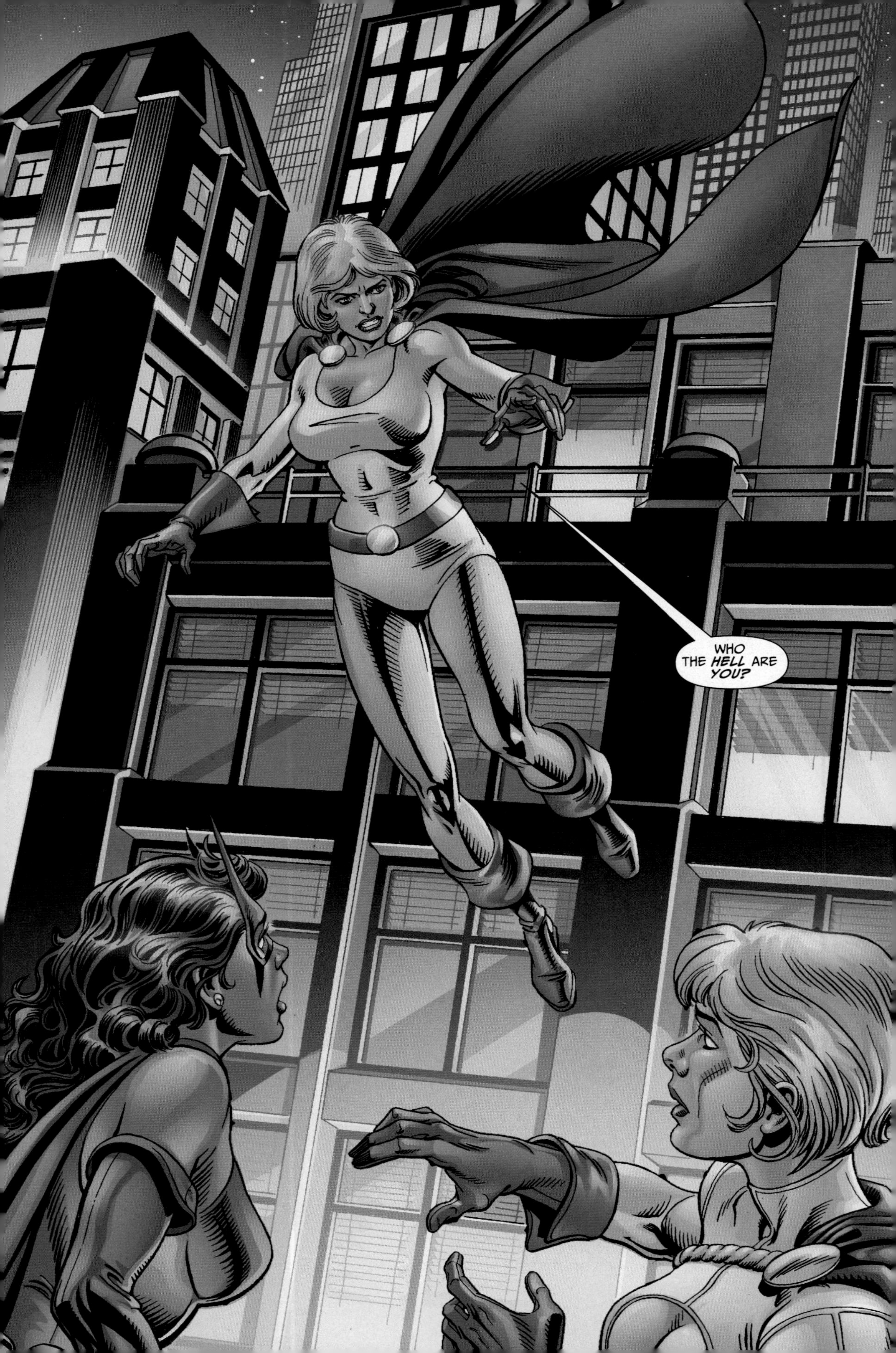
WHO THE HELL ARE YOU?

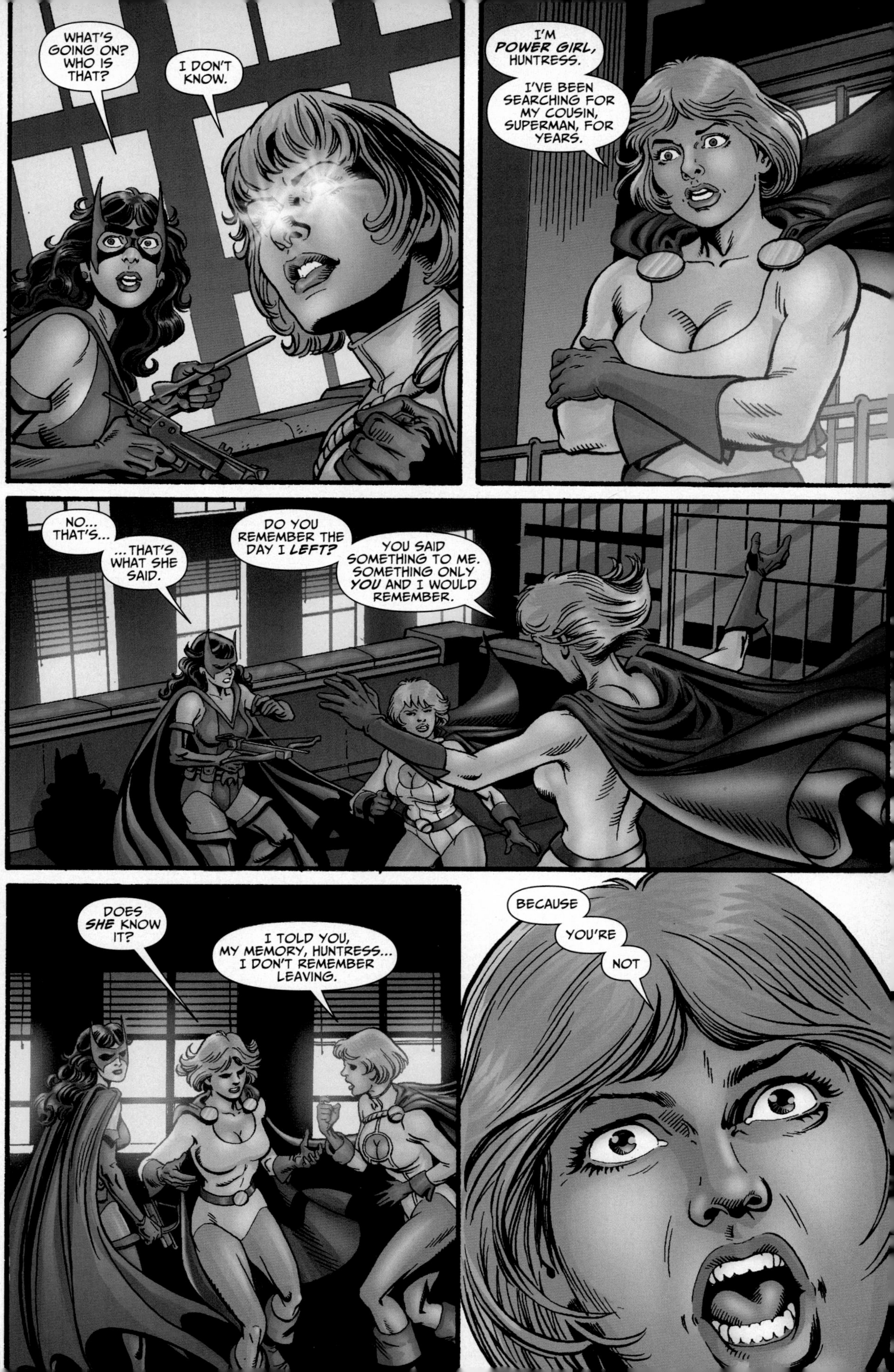
WHAT'S GOING ON? WHO IS THAT?
I DON'T KNOW.
I'M POWER GIRL, HUNTRESS.
I'VE BEEN SEARCHING FOR MY COUSIN, SUPERMAN, FOR YEARS.
NO... THAT'S...
...THAT'S WHAT SHE SAID.
DO YOU REMEMBER THE DAY I LEFT?
YOU SAID SOMETHING TO ME. SOMETHING ONLY YOU AND I WOULD REMEMBER.
DOES SHE KNOW IT?
I TOLD YOU, MY MEMORY, HUNTRESS... I DON'T REMEMBER LEAVING.
BECAUSE
YOU'RE
NOT

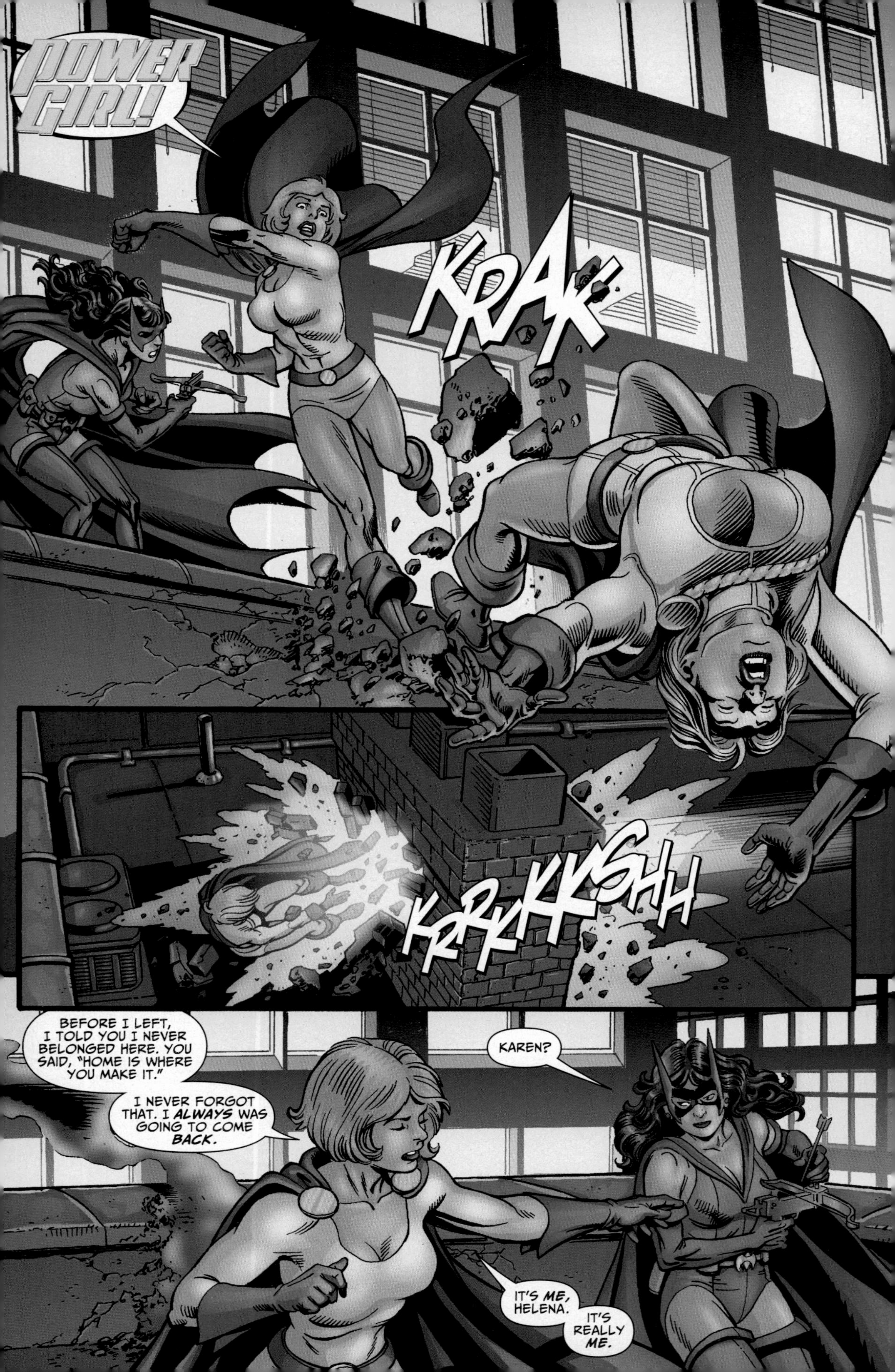
POWER GIRL!
KRAK!
KRRKKKSHH
BEFORE I LEFT, I TOLD YOU I NEVER BELONGED HERE. YOU SAID, "HOME IS WHERE YOU MAKE IT."
I NEVER FORGOT THAT. I ALWAYS WAS GOING TO COME BACK.
KAREN?
IT'S ME, HELENA.
IT'S REALLY ME.

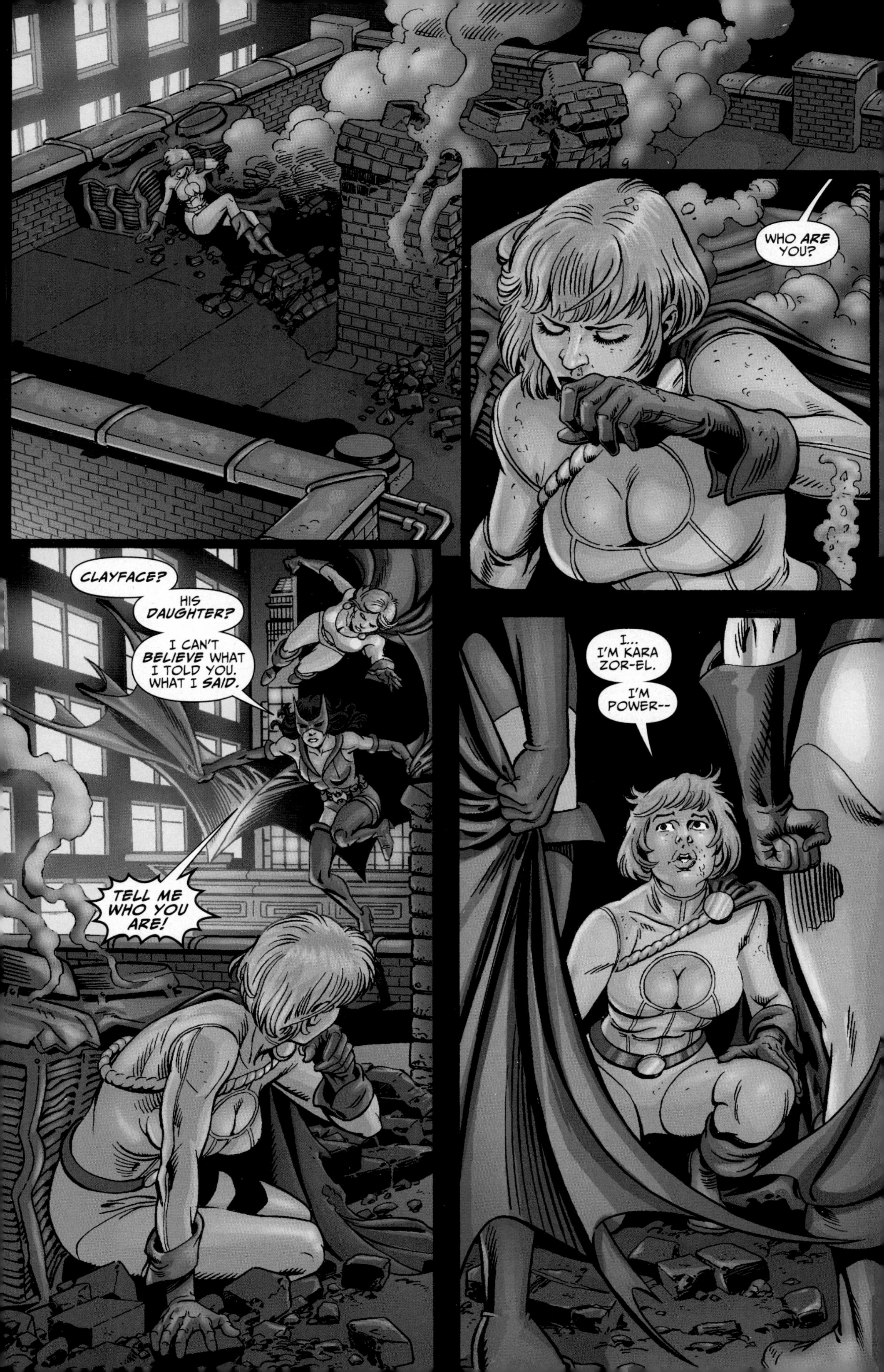
WHO ARE YOU?
CLAYFACE?
HIS DAUGHTER?
I CAN'T BELIEVE WHAT I TOLD YOU. WHAT I SAID.
TELL ME WHO YOU ARE!
I... I'M KARA ZOR-EL.
I'M POWER--

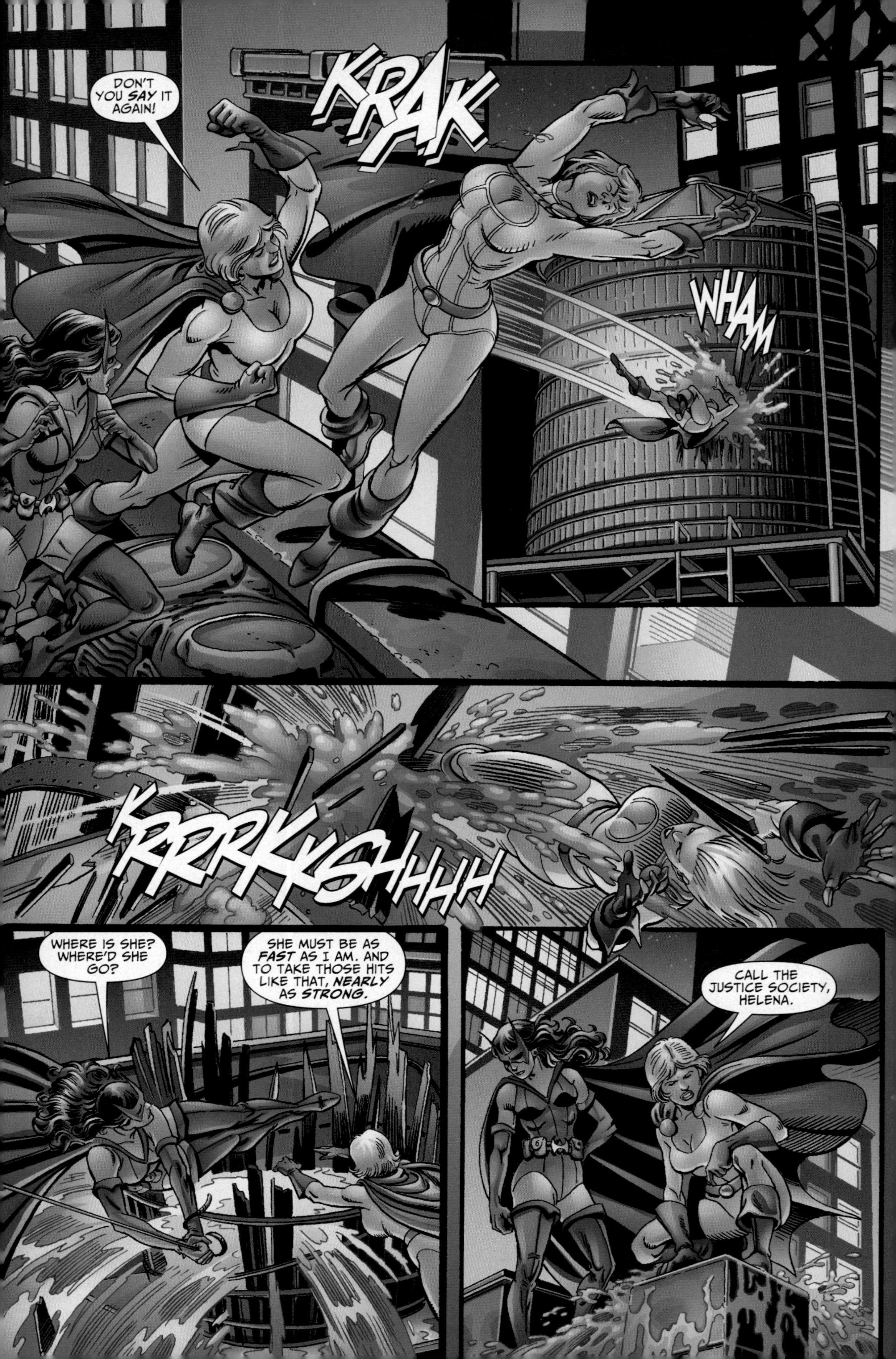
DON'T YOU SAY IT AGAIN!
KRAK
WHAM
KRRRKSHHHH
WHERE IS SHE? WHERE'D SHE GO?
SHE MUST BE AS FAST AS I AM. AND TO TAKE THOSE HITS LIKE THAT, NEARLY AS STRONG.
CALL THE JUSTICE SOCIETY, HELENA.

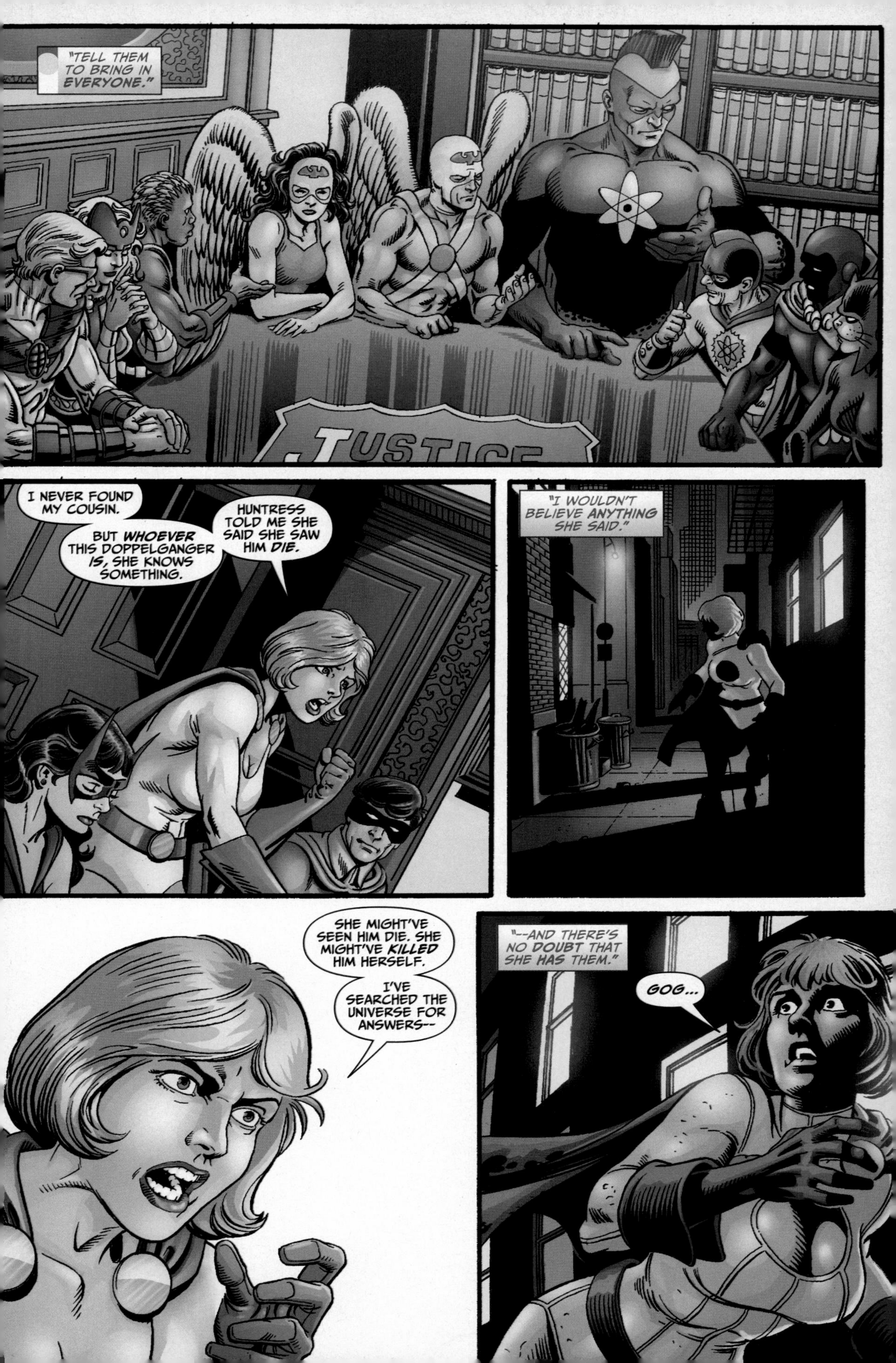
"TELL THEM TO BRING IN EVERYONE."
JUSTICE
I NEVER FOUND MY COUSIN.
BUT WHOEVER THIS DOPPELGANGER IS, SHE KNOWS SOMETHING.
HUNTRESS TOLD ME SHE SAID SHE SAW HIM DIE.
"I WOULDN'T BELIEVE ANYTHING SHE SAID."
SHE MIGHT'VE SEEN HIM DIE. SHE MIGHT'VE KILLED HIM HERSELF.
I'VE SEARCHED THE UNIVERSE FOR ANSWERS--
"--AND THERE'S NO DOUBT THAT SHE HAS THEM."
GOG...

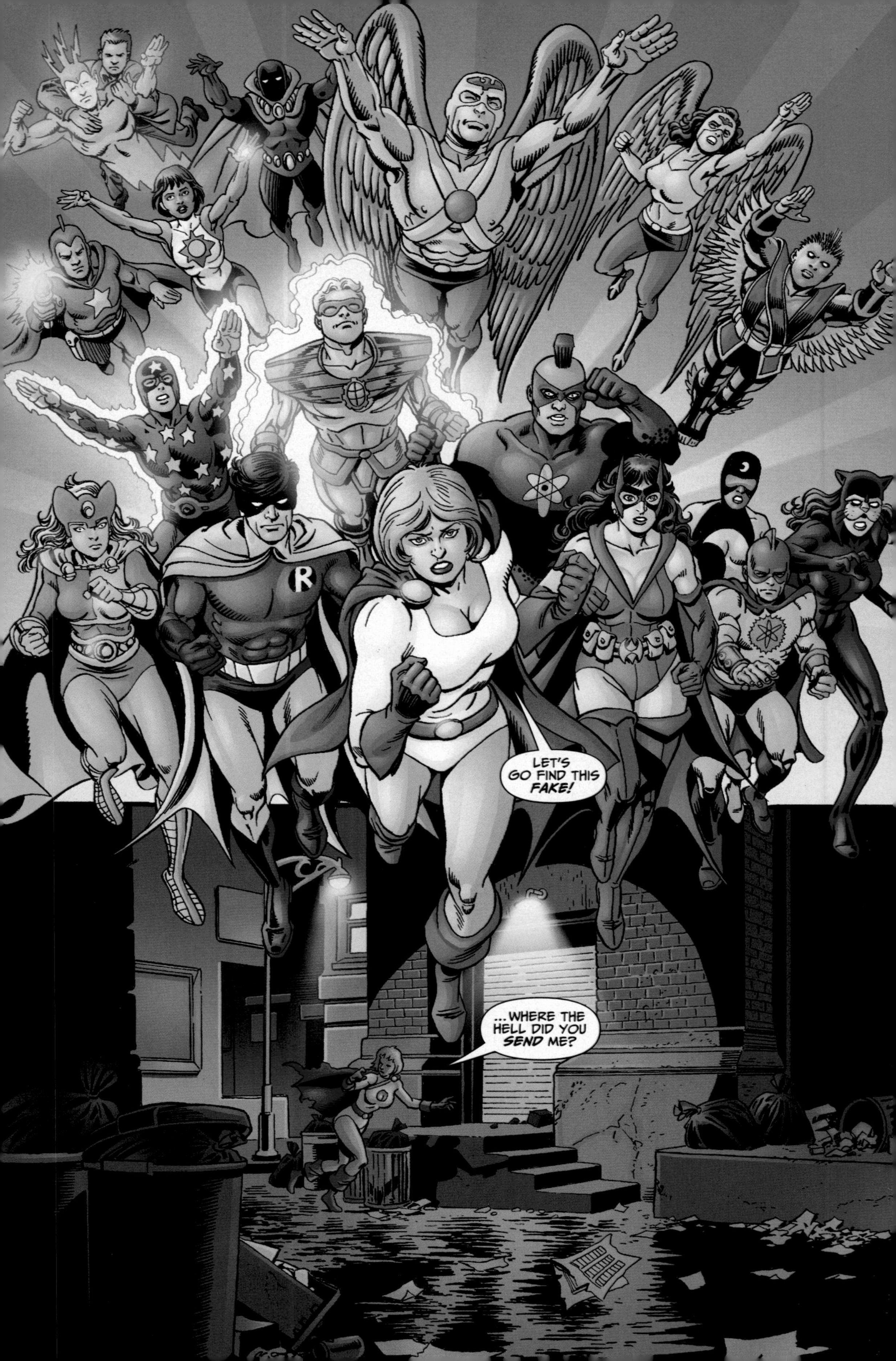
LET'S GO FIND THIS FAKE!
...WHERE THE HELL DID YOU SEND ME?

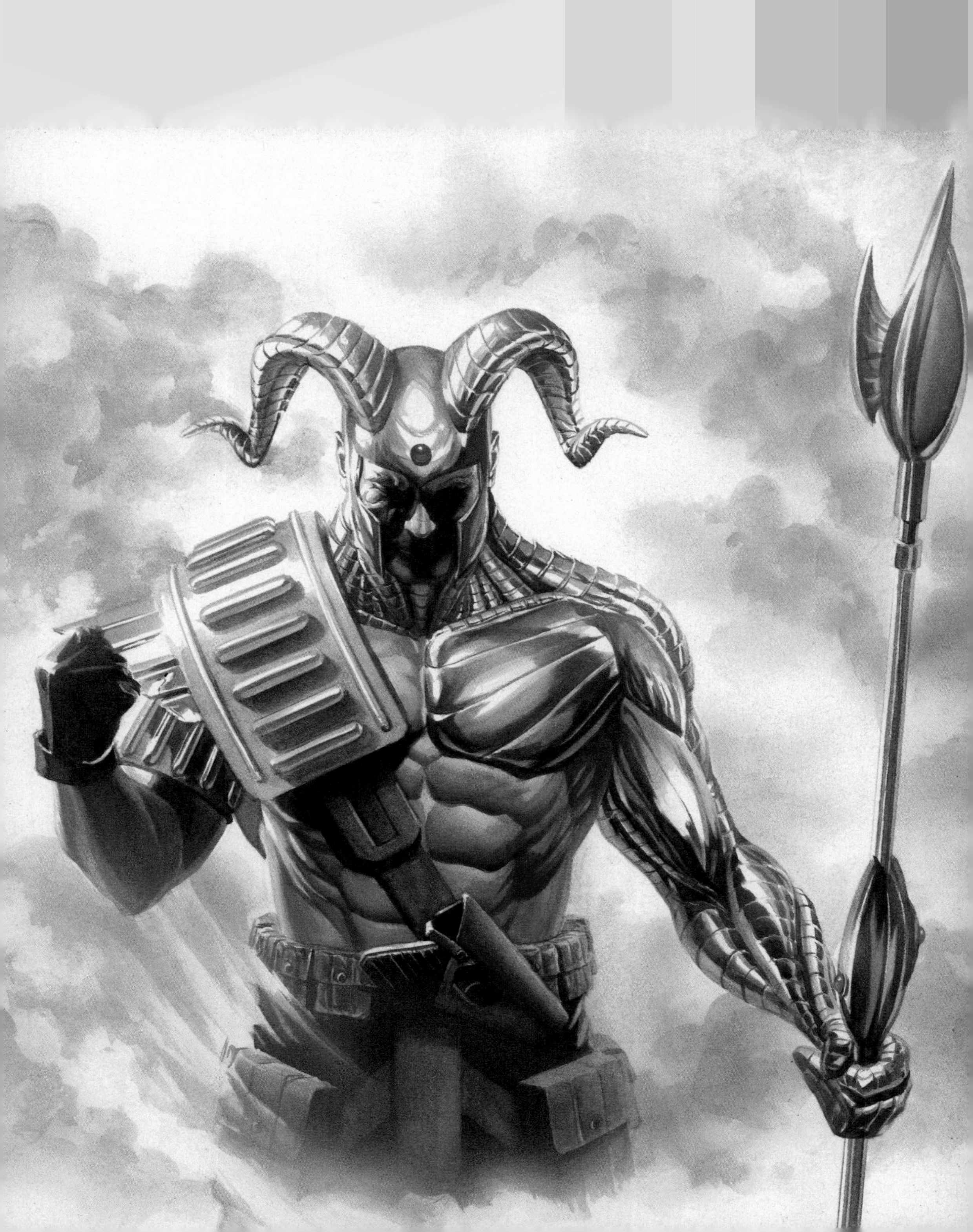

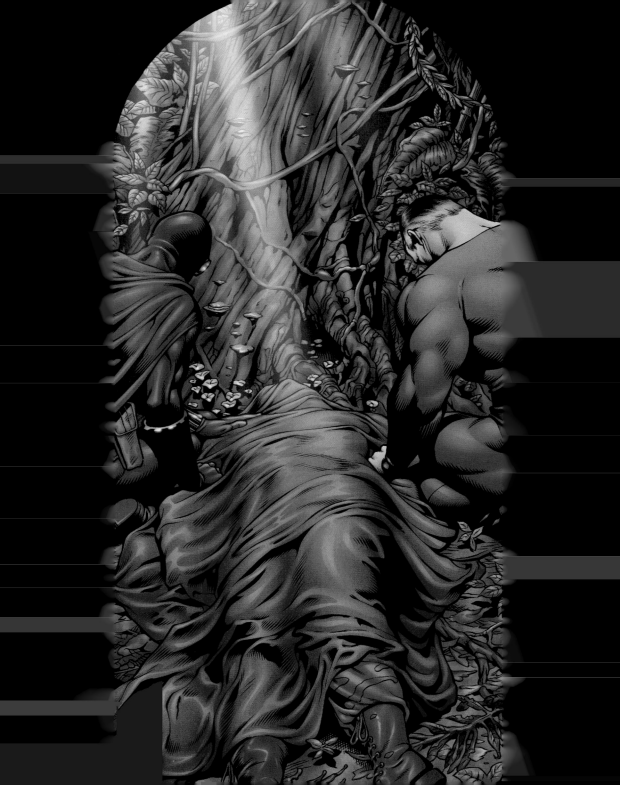

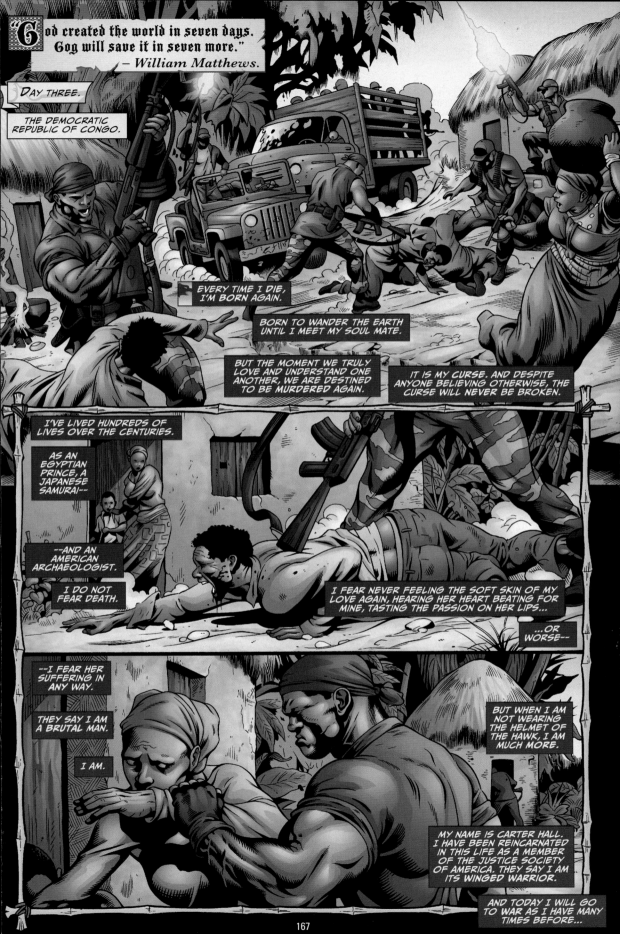

"God created the world in seven days. Gog will save it in seven more."
— William Matthews.

DAY THREE.

THE DEMOCRATIC REPUBLIC OF CONGO.

EVERY TIME I DIE, I'M BORN AGAIN.

BORN TO WANDER THE EARTH UNTIL I MEET MY SOUL MATE.

BUT THE MOMENT WE TRULY LOVE AND UNDERSTAND ONE ANOTHER, WE ARE DESTINED TO BE MURDERED AGAIN.

IT IS MY CURSE. AND DESPITE ANYONE BELIEVING OTHERWISE, THE CURSE WILL NEVER BE BROKEN.

I'VE LIVED HUNDREDS OF LIVES OVER THE CENTURIES.

AS AN EGYPTIAN PRINCE, A JAPANESE SAMURAI--

--AND AN AMERICAN ARCHAEOLOGIST.

I DO NOT FEAR DEATH.

I FEAR NEVER FEELING THE SOFT SKIN OF MY LOVE AGAIN, HEARING HER HEART BEATING FOR MINE, TASTING THE PASSION ON HER LIPS...

...OR WORSE--

--I FEAR HER SUFFERING IN ANY WAY.

THEY SAY I AM A BRUTAL MAN.

I AM.

BUT WHEN I AM NOT WEARING THE HELMET OF THE HAWK, I AM MUCH MORE.

MY NAME IS CARTER HALL. I HAVE BEEN REINCARNATED IN THIS LIFE AS A MEMBER OF THE JUSTICE SOCIETY OF AMERICA. THEY SAY I AM ITS WINGED WARRIOR.

AND TODAY I WILL GO TO WAR AS I HAVE MANY TIMES BEFORE...

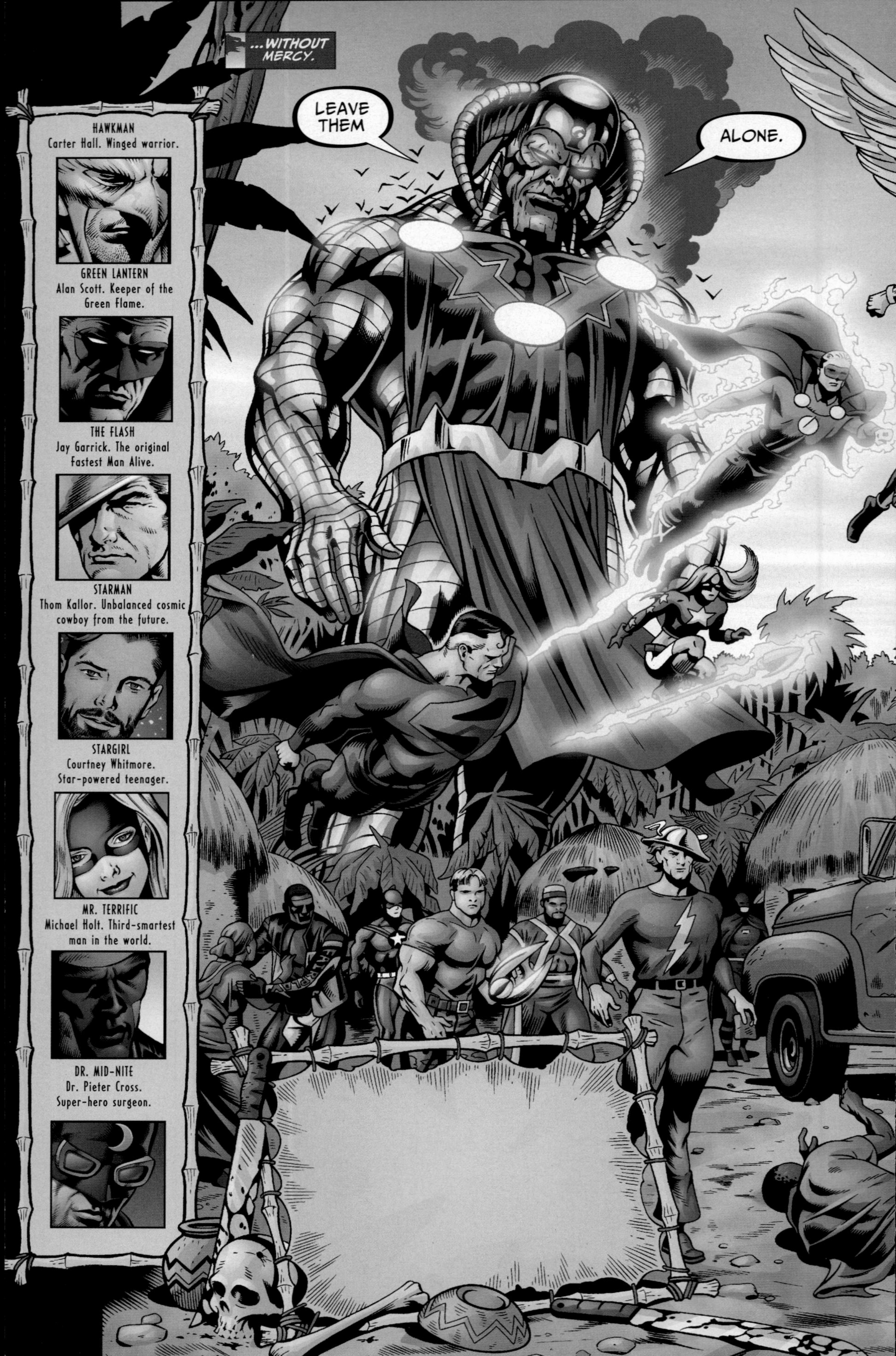
...WITHOUT MERCY.
LEAVE THEM
ALONE.
HAWKMAN
Carter Hall. Winged warrior.
GREEN LANTERN
Alan Scott. Keeper of the Green Flame.
THE FLASH
Jay Garrick. The original Fastest Man Alive.
STARMAN
Thom Kallor. Unbalanced cosmic cowboy from the future.
STARGIRL
Courtney Whitmore. Star-powered teenager.
MR. TERRIFIC
Michael Holt. Third-smartest man in the world.
DR. MID-NITE
Dr. Pieter Cross. Super-hero surgeon.

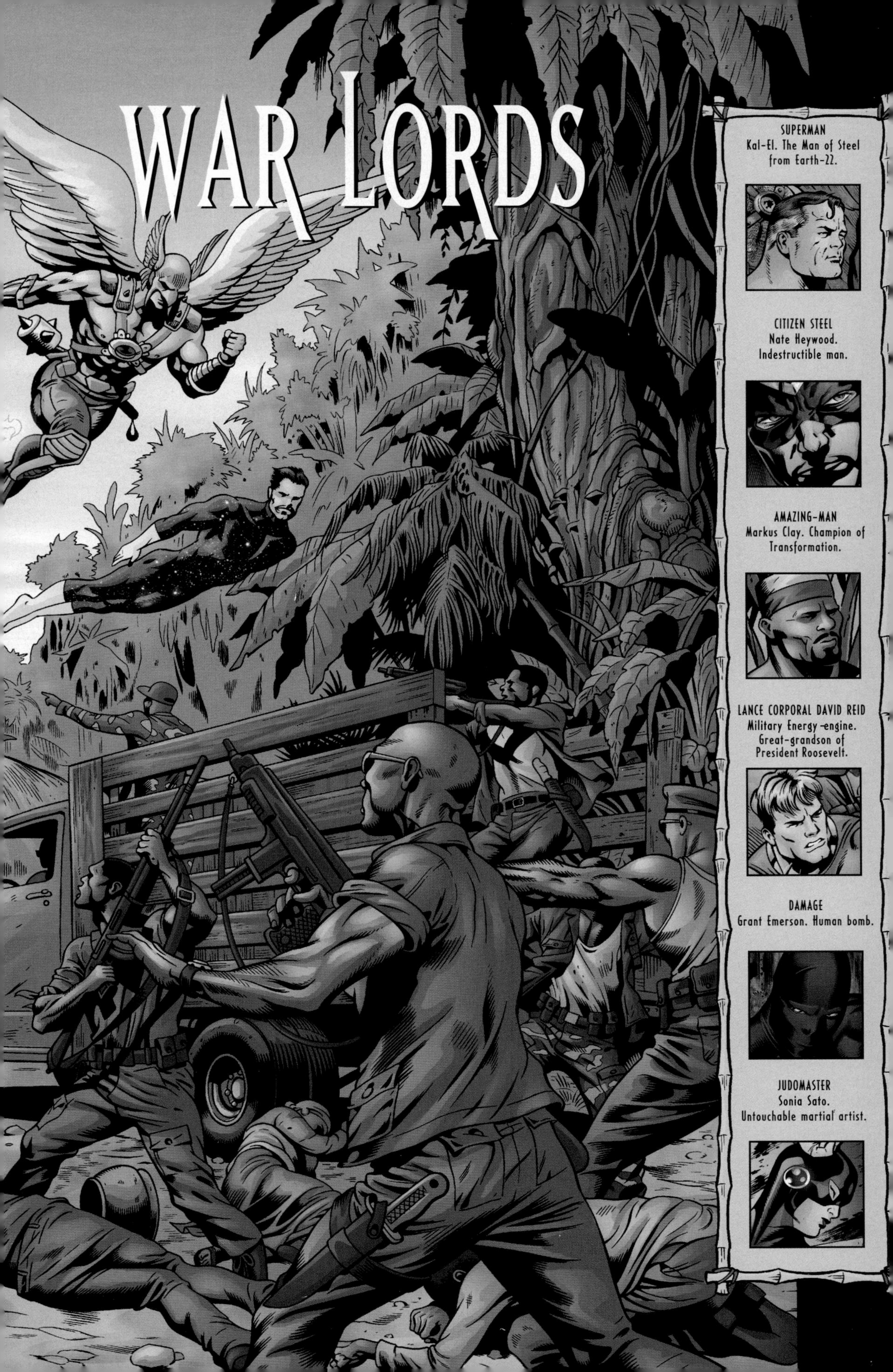
WAR LORDS
SUPERMAN
Kal-El. The Man of Steel from Earth-22.
CITIZEN STEEL
Nate Heywood. Indestructible man.
AMAZING-MAN
Markus Clay. Champion of Transformation.
LANCE CORPORAL DAVID REID
Military Energy-engine. Great-grandson of President Roosevelt.
DAMAGE
Grant Emerson. Human bomb.
JUDOMASTER
Sonia Sato. Untouchable martial artist.

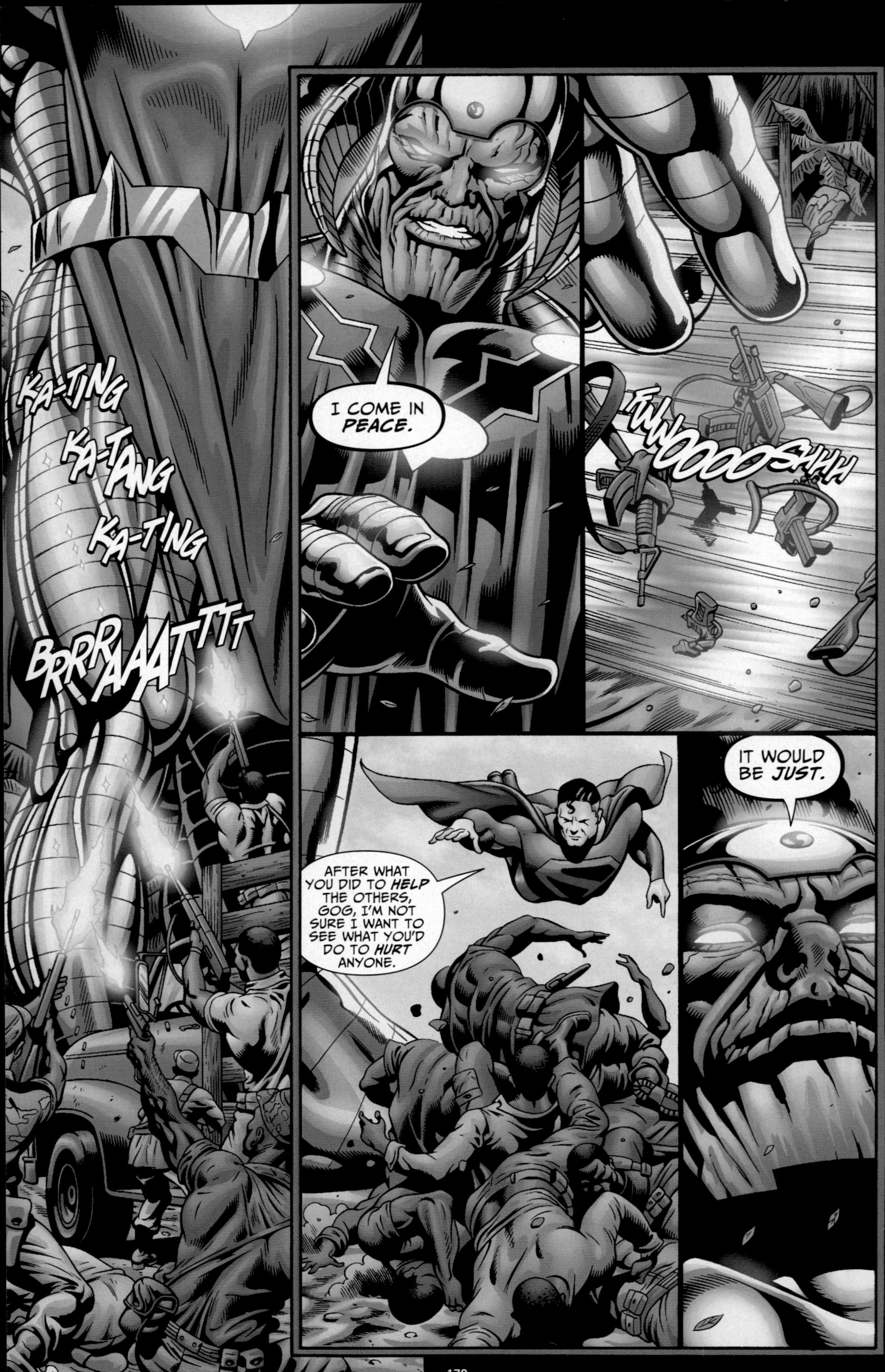
KA-TING
KA-TANG
KA-TING
BRRRAAATTTT
I COME IN PEACE.
FWWOOOOOSHHH
AFTER WHAT YOU DID TO HELP THE OTHERS, GOG, I'M NOT SURE I WANT TO SEE WHAT YOU'D DO TO HURT ANYONE.
IT WOULD BE JUST.

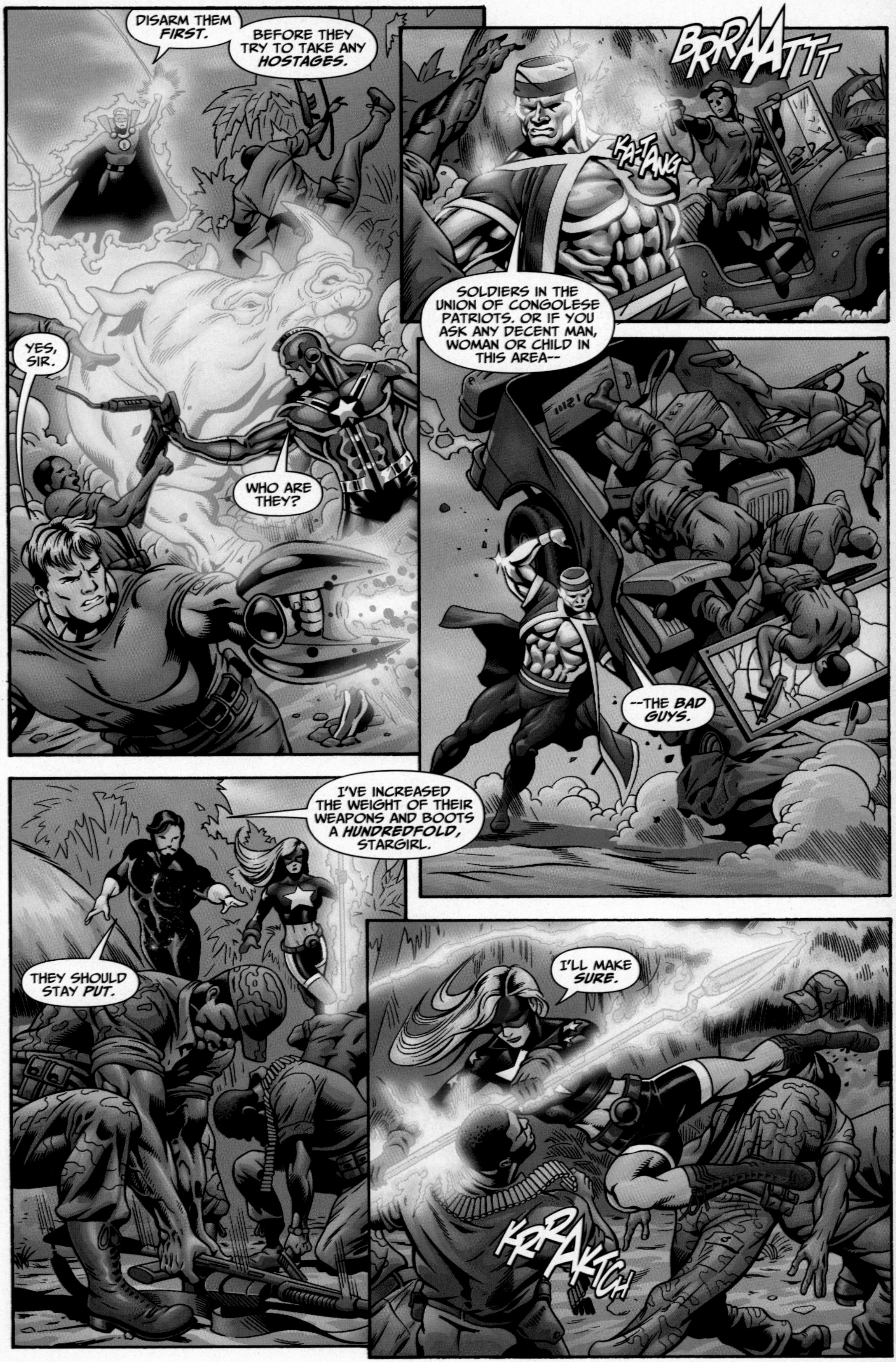
DISARM THEM FIRST.
BEFORE THEY TRY TO TAKE ANY HOSTAGES.
YES, SIR.
WHO ARE THEY?
BRRAATTT
KA-TANG
SOLDIERS IN THE UNION OF CONGOLESE PATRIOTS. OR IF YOU ASK ANY DECENT MAN, WOMAN OR CHILD IN THIS AREA--
--THE BAD GUYS.
I'VE INCREASED THE WEIGHT OF THEIR WEAPONS AND BOOTS A HUNDREDFOLD, STARGIRL.
THEY SHOULD STAY PUT.
I'LL MAKE SURE.
KRRAKTCH

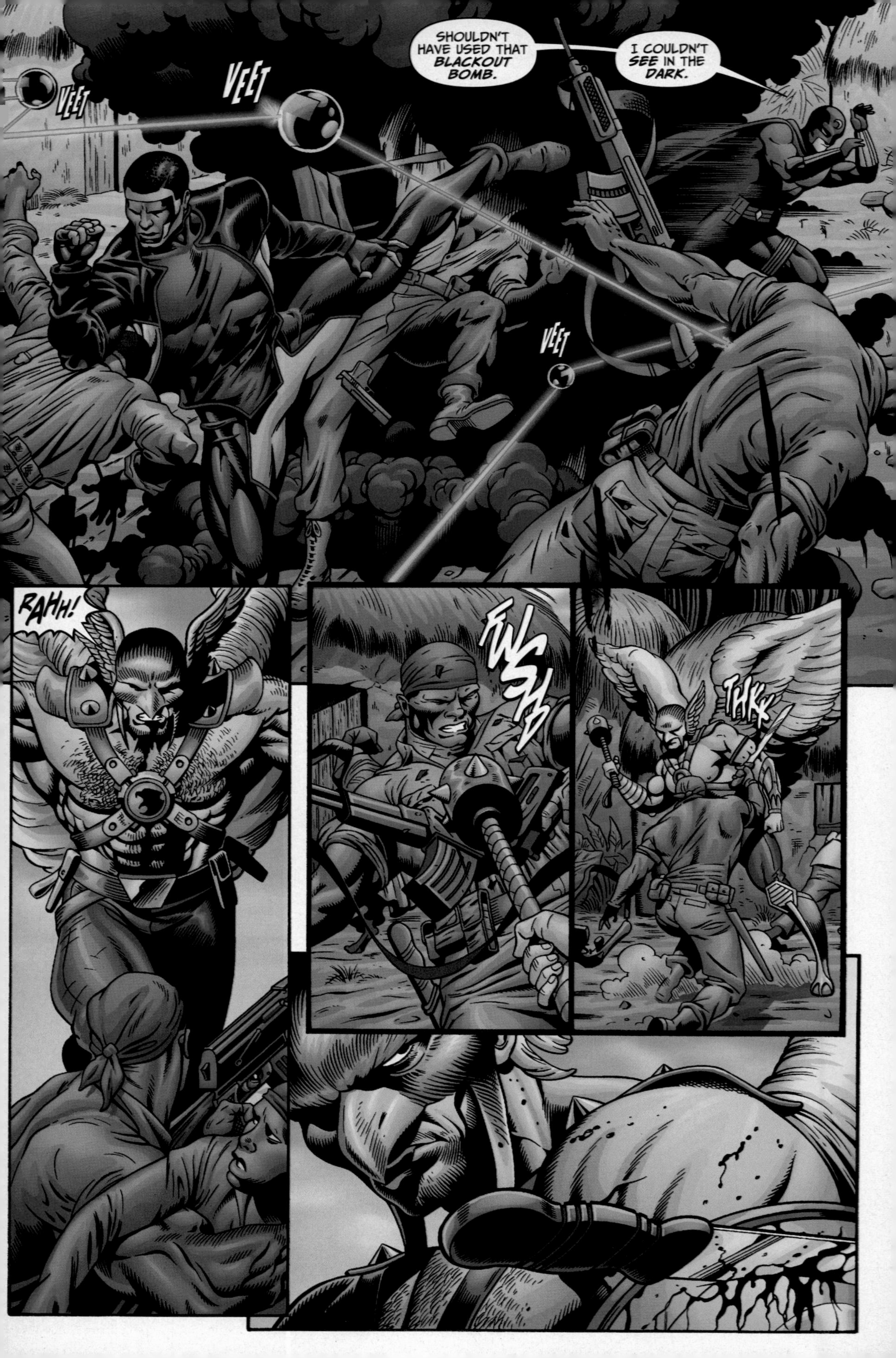
VEET
VEET
SHOULDN'T HAVE USED THAT BLACKOUT BOMB.
I COULDN'T SEE IN THE DARK.
VEET
RAHH!
FWSHD
THKK

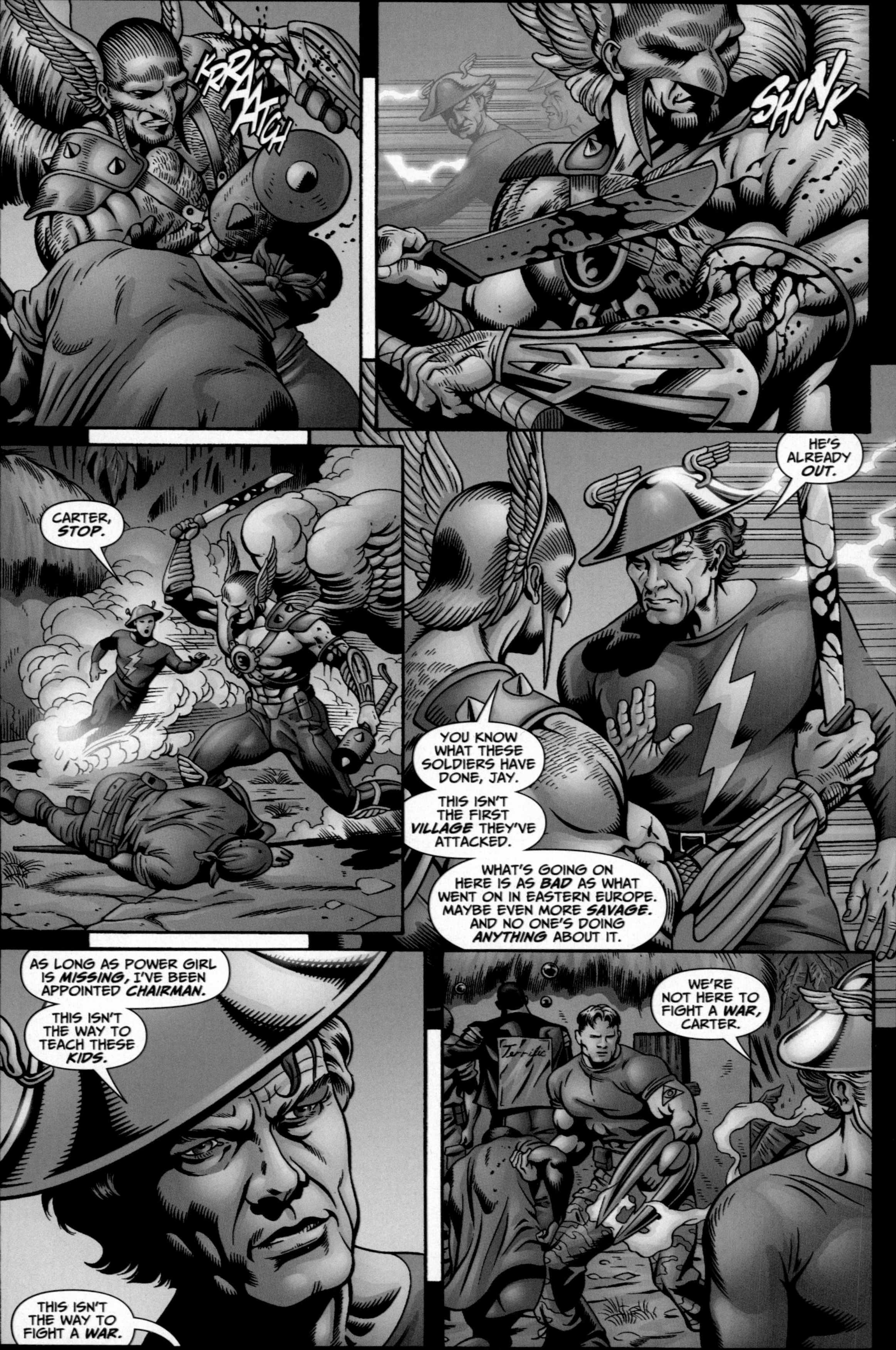

KRRAAATCH
SHINK
CARTER, STOP.
HE'S ALREADY OUT.
YOU KNOW WHAT THESE SOLDIERS HAVE DONE, JAY.
THIS ISN'T THE FIRST VILLAGE THEY'VE ATTACKED.
WHAT'S GOING ON HERE IS AS BAD AS WHAT WENT ON IN EASTERN EUROPE. MAYBE EVEN MORE SAVAGE. AND NO ONE'S DOING ANYTHING ABOUT IT.
AS LONG AS POWER GIRL IS MISSING, I'VE BEEN APPOINTED CHAIRMAN.
THIS ISN'T THE WAY TO TEACH THESE KIDS.
THIS ISN'T THE WAY TO FIGHT A WAR.
WE'RE NOT HERE TO FIGHT A WAR, CARTER.

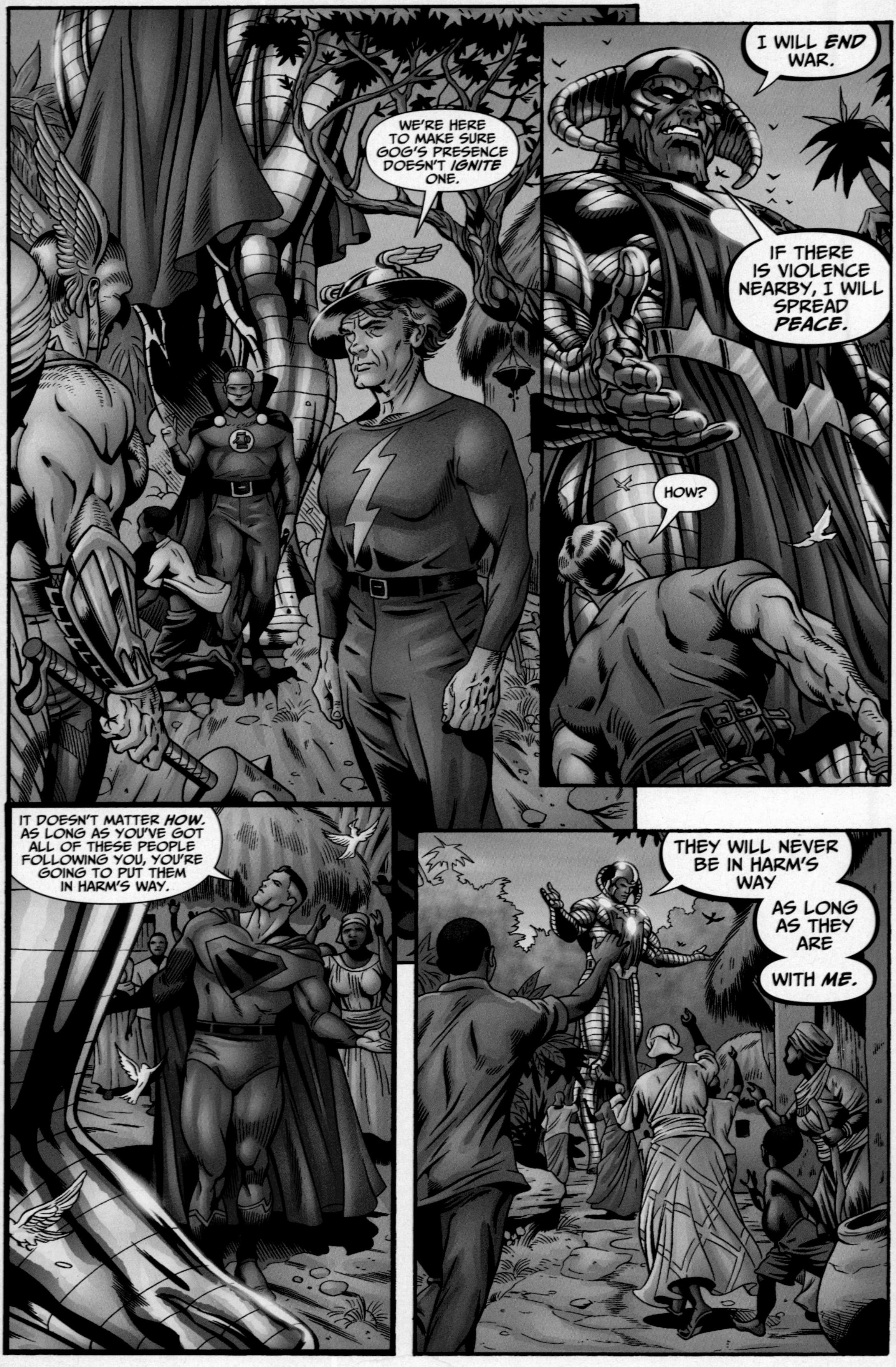

WE'RE HERE TO MAKE SURE GOG'S PRESENCE DOESN'T IGNITE ONE.
I WILL END WAR.
IF THERE IS VIOLENCE NEARBY, I WILL SPREAD PEACE.
HOW?
IT DOESN'T MATTER HOW. AS LONG AS YOU'VE GOT ALL OF THESE PEOPLE FOLLOWING YOU, YOU'RE GOING TO PUT THEM IN HARM'S WAY.
THEY WILL NEVER BE IN HARM'S WAY
AS LONG AS THEY ARE
WITH ME.

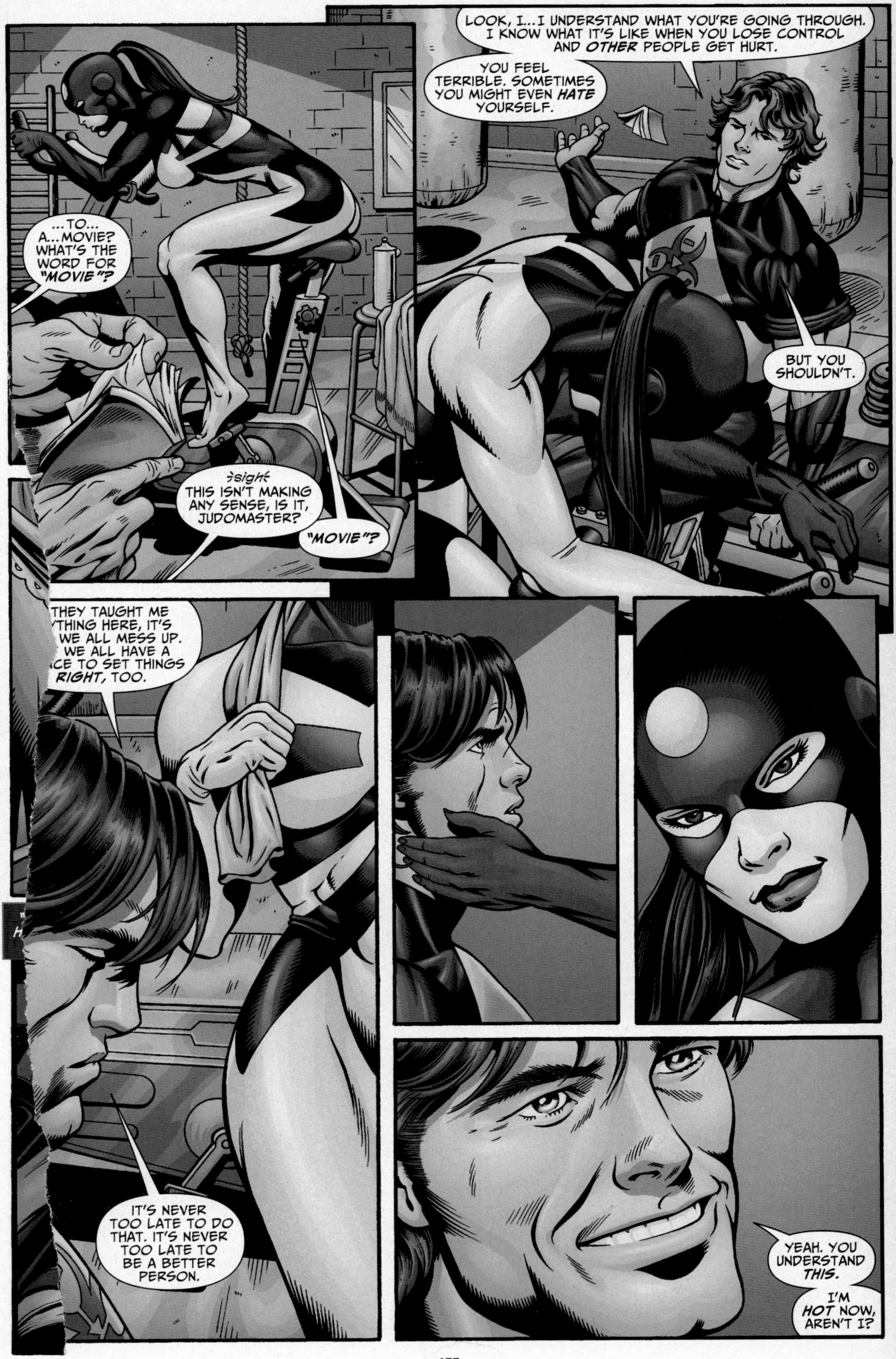

...TO... A...MOVIE? WHAT'S THE WORD FOR "MOVIE"?
sigh
THIS ISN'T MAKING ANY SENSE, IS IT, JUDOMASTER?
"MOVIE"?
LOOK, I...I UNDERSTAND WHAT YOU'RE GOING THROUGH. I KNOW WHAT IT'S LIKE WHEN YOU LOSE CONTROL AND OTHER PEOPLE GET HURT.
YOU FEEL TERRIBLE. SOMETIMES YOU MIGHT EVEN HATE YOURSELF.
BUT YOU SHOULDN'T.
THEY TAUGHT ME YTHING HERE, IT'S WE ALL MESS UP. WE ALL HAVE A CE TO SET THINGS RIGHT, TOO.
IT'S NEVER TOO LATE TO DO THAT. IT'S NEVER TOO LATE TO BE A BETTER PERSON.
YEAH. YOU UNDERSTAND THIS.
I'M HOT NOW, AREN'T I?

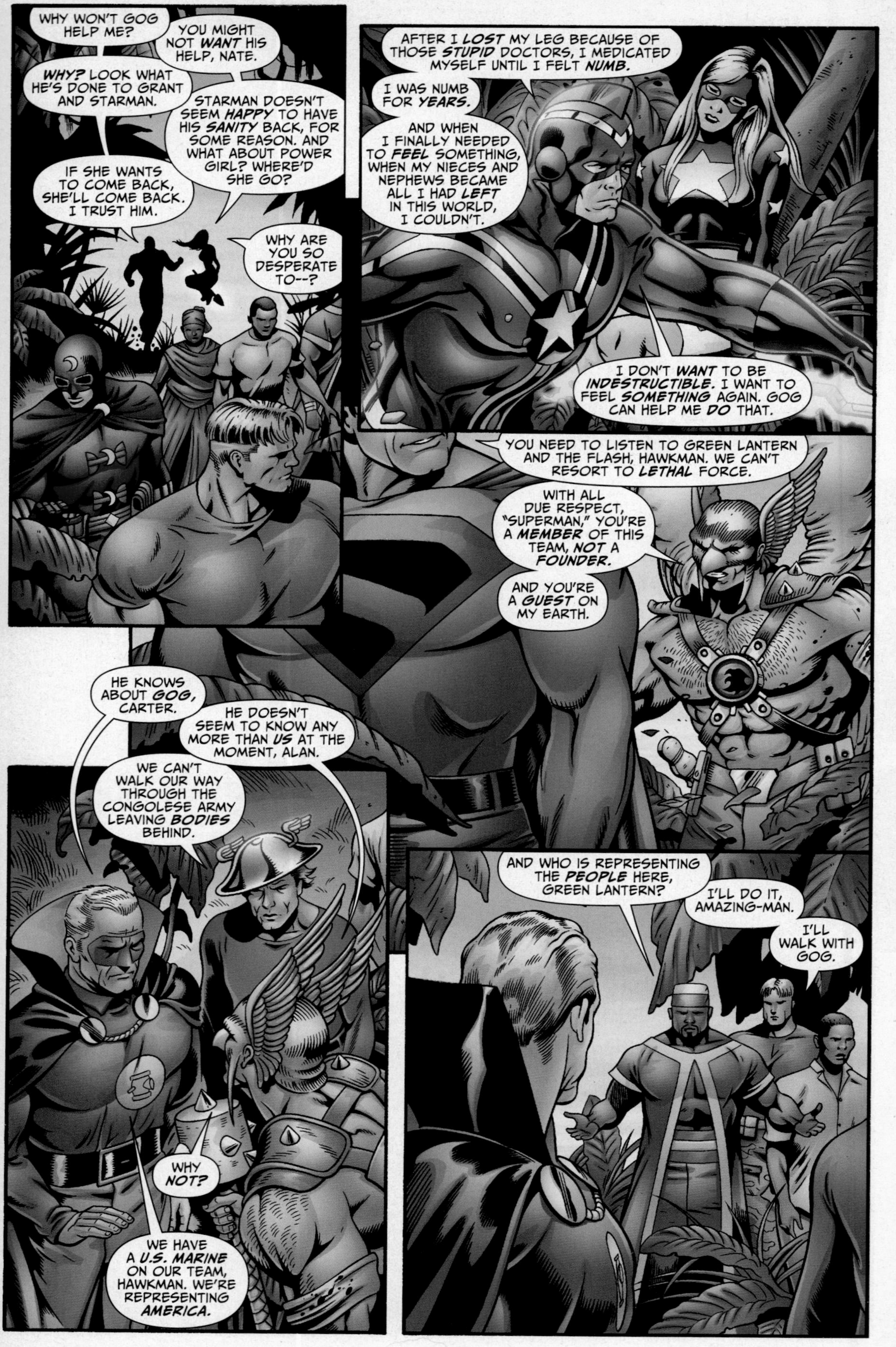
WHY WON'T GOG HELP ME?
YOU MIGHT NOT WANT HIS HELP, NATE.
WHY? LOOK WHAT HE'S DONE TO GRANT AND STARMAN.
STARMAN DOESN'T SEEM HAPPY TO HAVE HIS SANITY BACK, FOR SOME REASON. AND WHAT ABOUT POWER GIRL? WHERE'D SHE GO?
IF SHE WANTS TO COME BACK, SHE'LL COME BACK. I TRUST HIM.
WHY ARE YOU SO DESPERATE TO--?
AFTER I LOST MY LEG BECAUSE OF THOSE STUPID DOCTORS, I MEDICATED MYSELF UNTIL I FELT NUMB.
I WAS NUMB FOR YEARS.
AND WHEN I FINALLY NEEDED TO FEEL SOMETHING, WHEN MY NIECES AND NEPHEWS BECAME ALL I HAD LEFT IN THIS WORLD, I COULDN'T.
I DON'T WANT TO BE INDESTRUCTIBLE. I WANT TO FEEL SOMETHING AGAIN. GOG CAN HELP ME DO THAT.
YOU NEED TO LISTEN TO GREEN LANTERN AND THE FLASH, HAWKMAN. WE CAN'T RESORT TO LETHAL FORCE.
WITH ALL DUE RESPECT, "SUPERMAN," YOU'RE A MEMBER OF THIS TEAM, NOT A FOUNDER.
AND YOU'RE A GUEST ON MY EARTH.
HE KNOWS ABOUT GOG, CARTER.
HE DOESN'T SEEM TO KNOW ANY MORE THAN US AT THE MOMENT, ALAN.
WE CAN'T WALK OUR WAY THROUGH THE CONGOLESE ARMY LEAVING BODIES BEHIND.
WHY NOT?
WE HAVE A U.S. MARINE ON OUR TEAM, HAWKMAN. WE'RE REPRESENTING AMERICA.
AND WHO IS REPRESENTING THE PEOPLE HERE, GREEN LANTERN?
I'LL DO IT, AMAZING-MAN.
I'LL WALK WITH GOG.

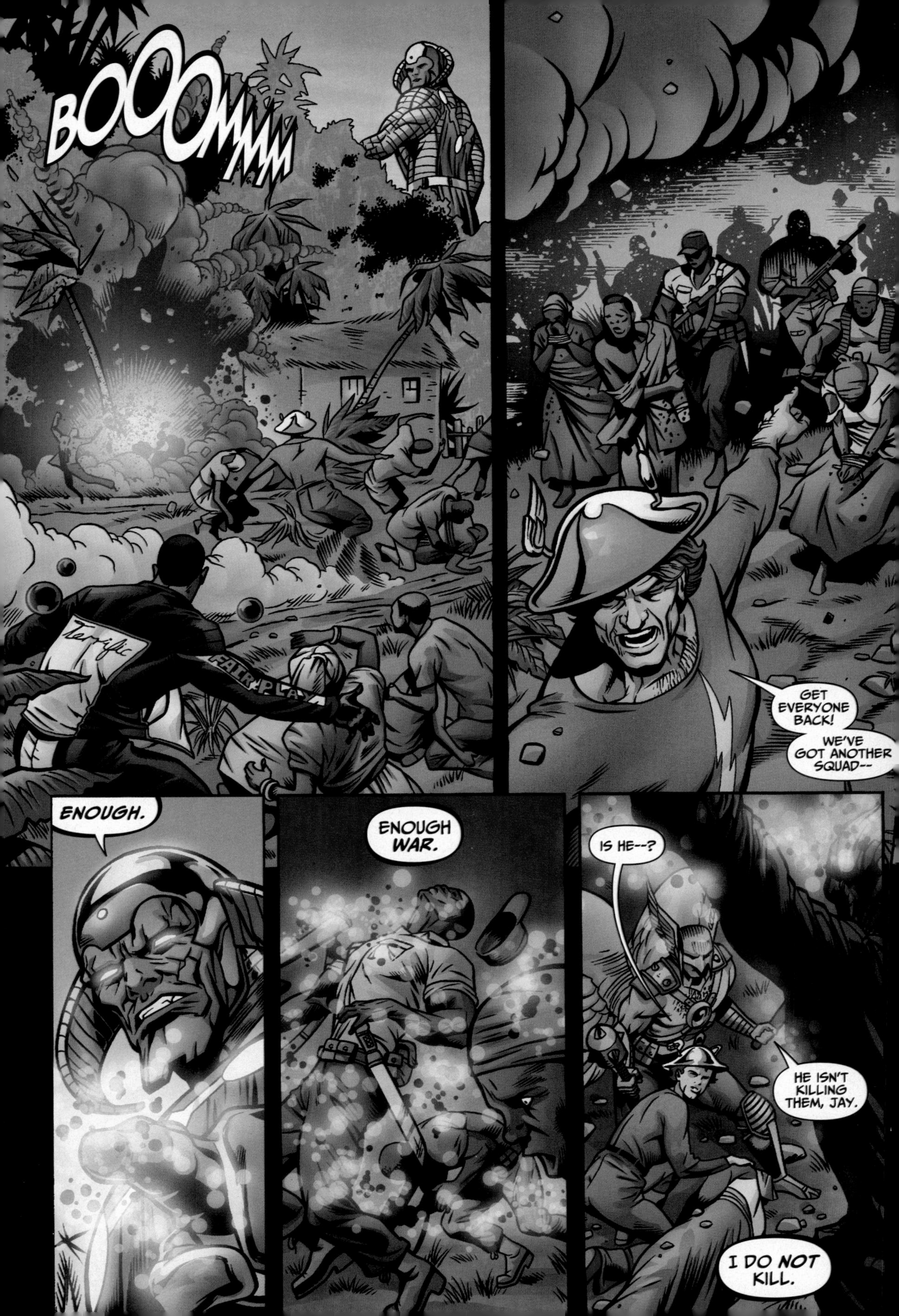
BOOOMMM
Terrific
FAIR PLAY
GET EVERYONE BACK!
WE'VE GOT ANOTHER SQUAD--
ENOUGH.
ENOUGH WAR.
IS HE--?
HE ISN'T KILLING THEM, JAY.
I DO NOT KILL.

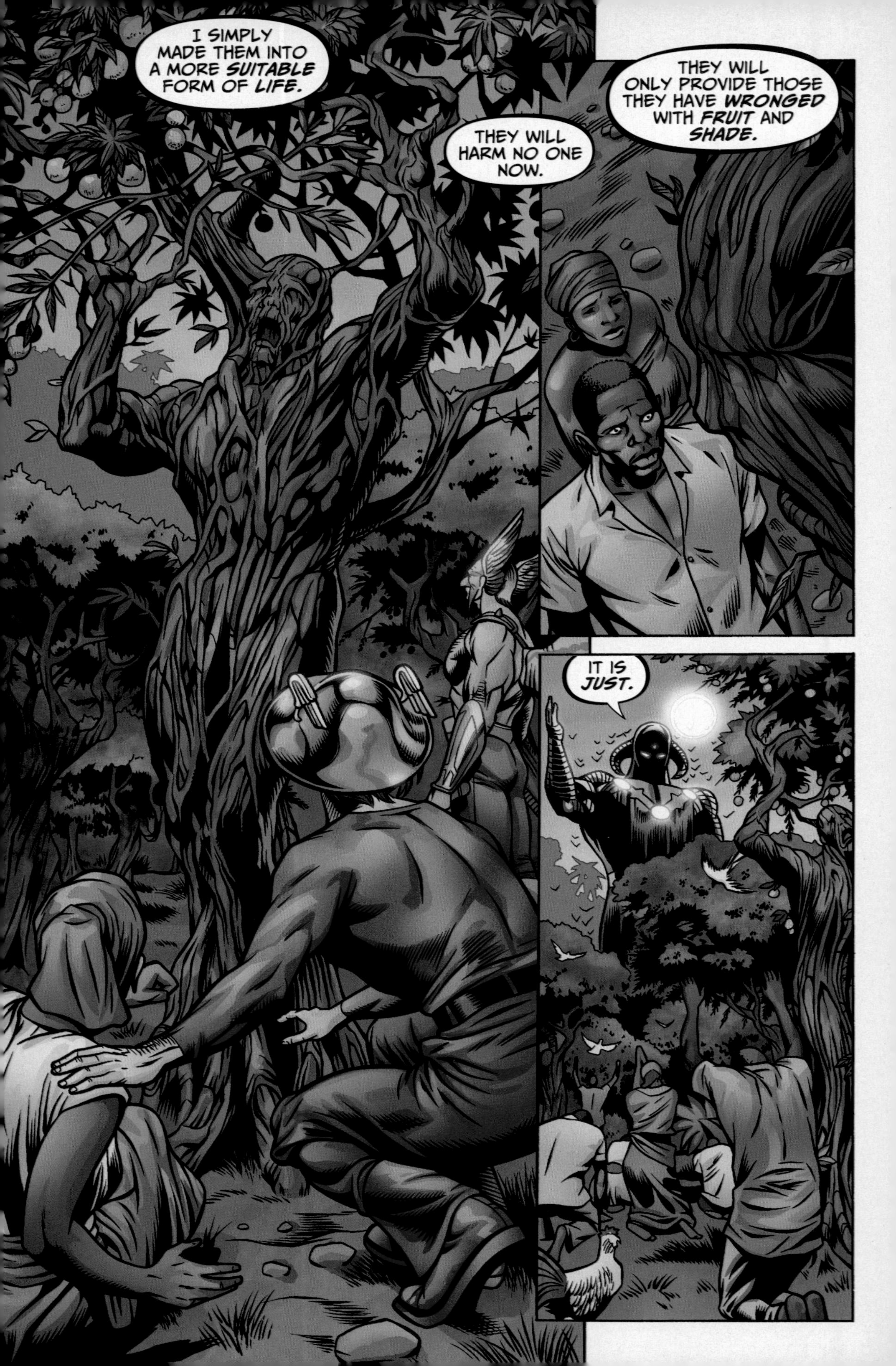
I SIMPLY MADE THEM INTO A MORE SUITABLE FORM OF LIFE.
THEY WILL HARM NO ONE NOW.
THEY WILL ONLY PROVIDE THOSE THEY HAVE WRONGED WITH FRUIT AND SHADE.
IT IS JUST.

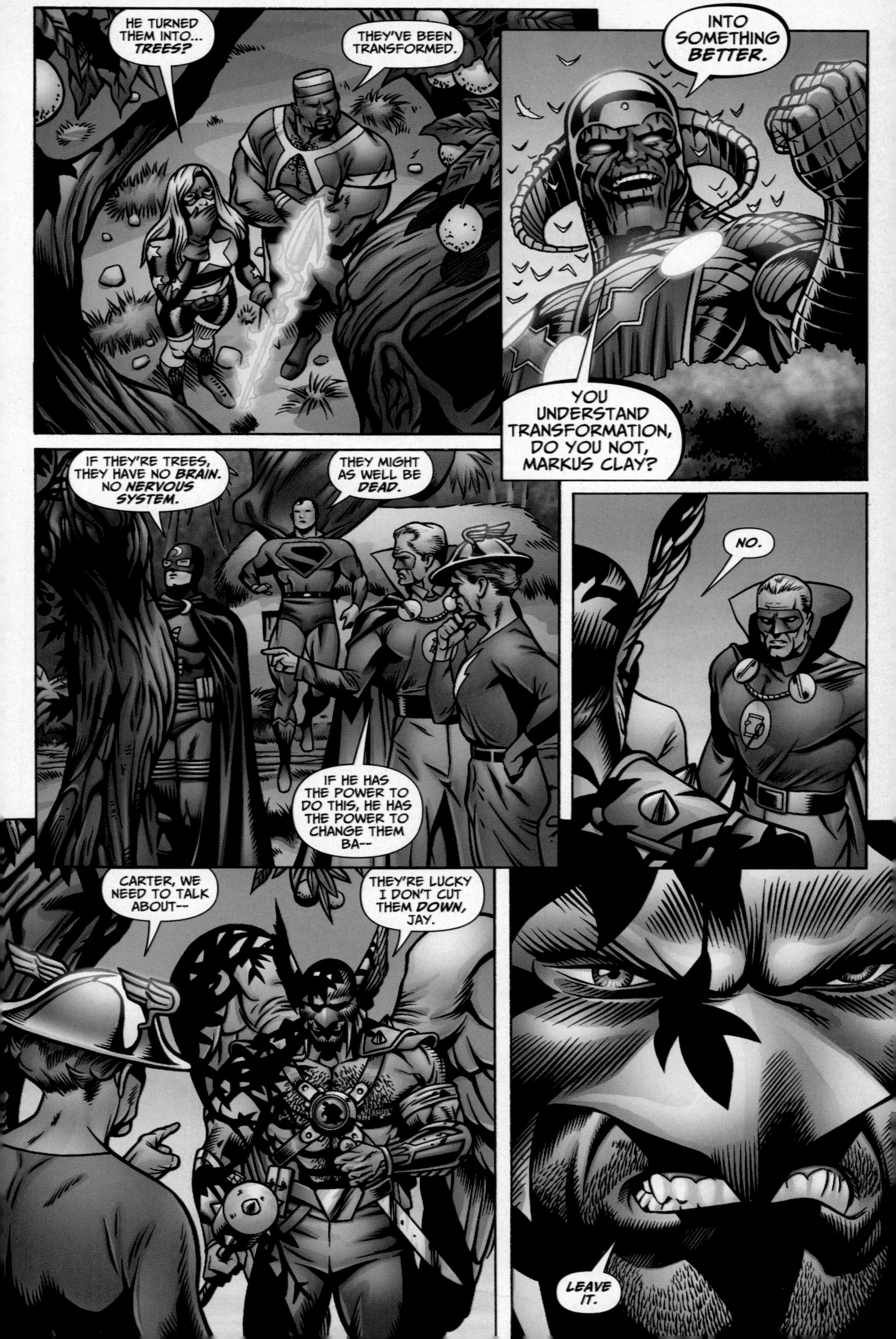
HE TURNED THEM INTO... TREES?
THEY'VE BEEN TRANSFORMED.
INTO SOMETHING BETTER.
YOU UNDERSTAND TRANSFORMATION, DO YOU NOT, MARKUS CLAY?
IF THEY'RE TREES, THEY HAVE NO BRAIN. NO NERVOUS SYSTEM.
THEY MIGHT AS WELL BE DEAD.
IF HE HAS THE POWER TO DO THIS, HE HAS THE POWER TO CHANGE THEM BA--
NO.
CARTER, WE NEED TO TALK ABOUT--
THEY'RE LUCKY I DON'T CUT THEM DOWN, JAY.
LEAVE IT.

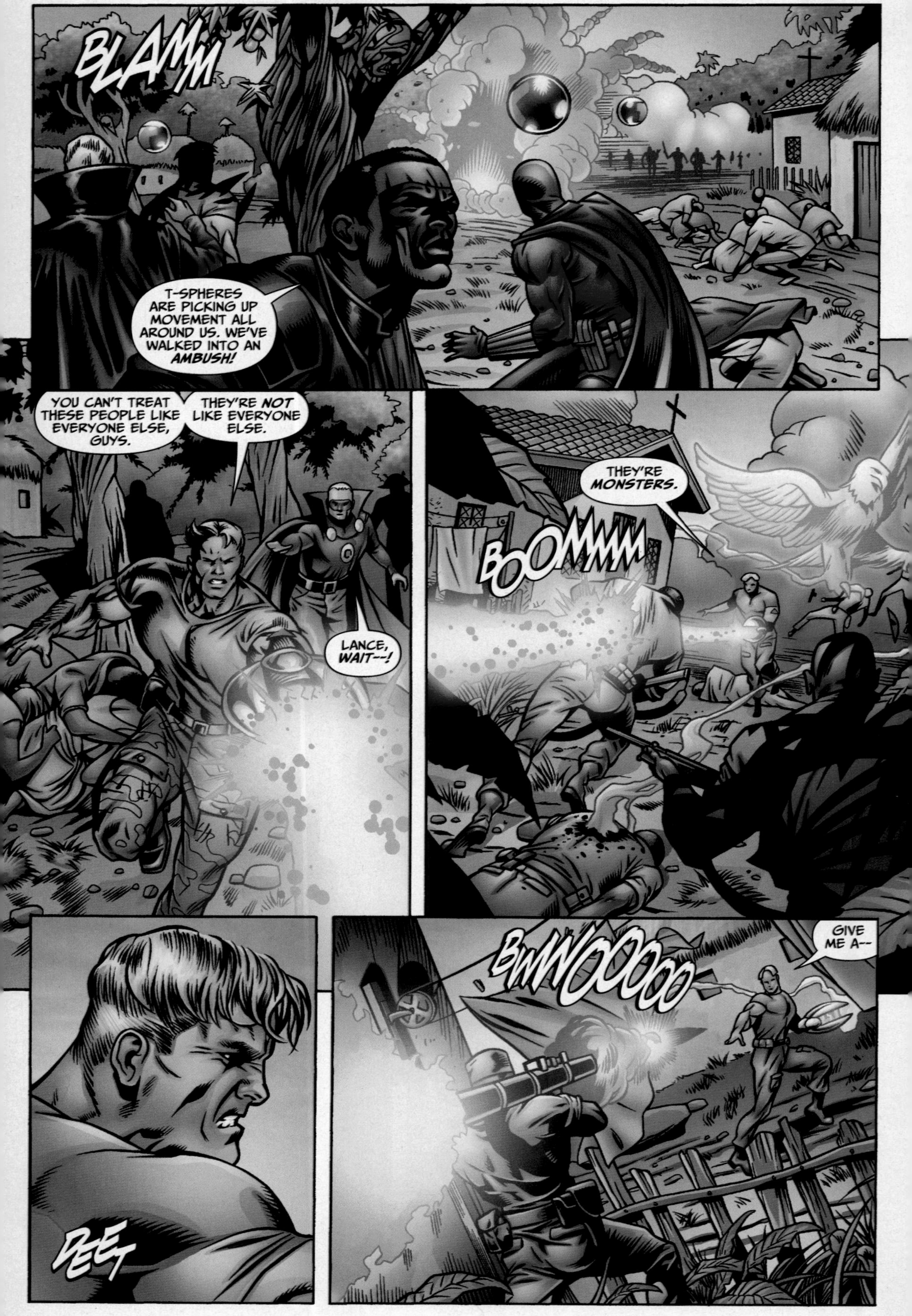
BLAMM
T-SPHERES ARE PICKING UP MOVEMENT ALL AROUND US. WE'VE WALKED INTO AN AMBUSH!
YOU CAN'T TREAT THESE PEOPLE LIKE EVERYONE ELSE, GUYS.
THEY'RE NOT LIKE EVERYONE ELSE.
LANCE, WAIT--!
THEY'RE MONSTERS.
BOOMMM
DEET
BWNOOOOO
GIVE ME A--

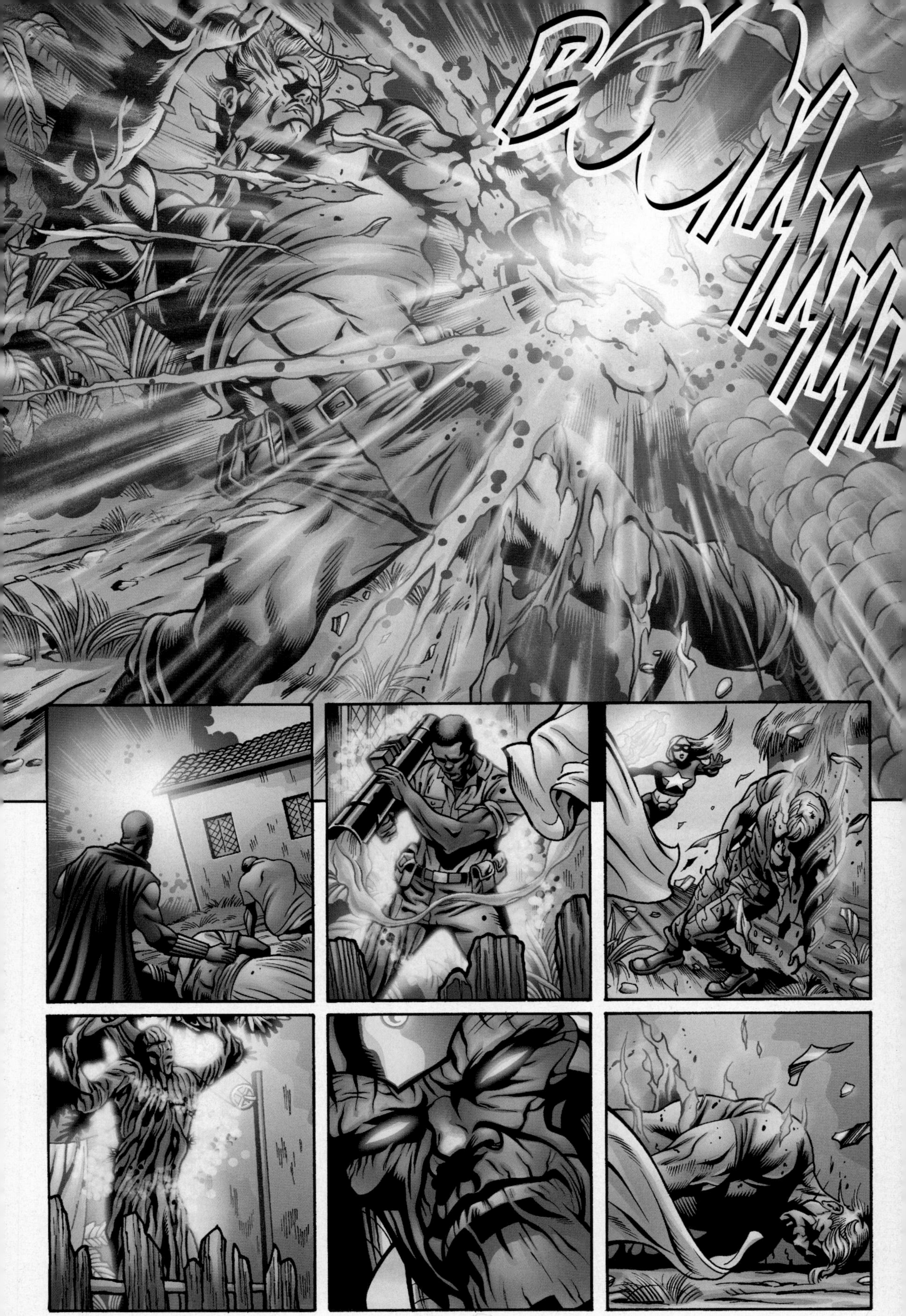

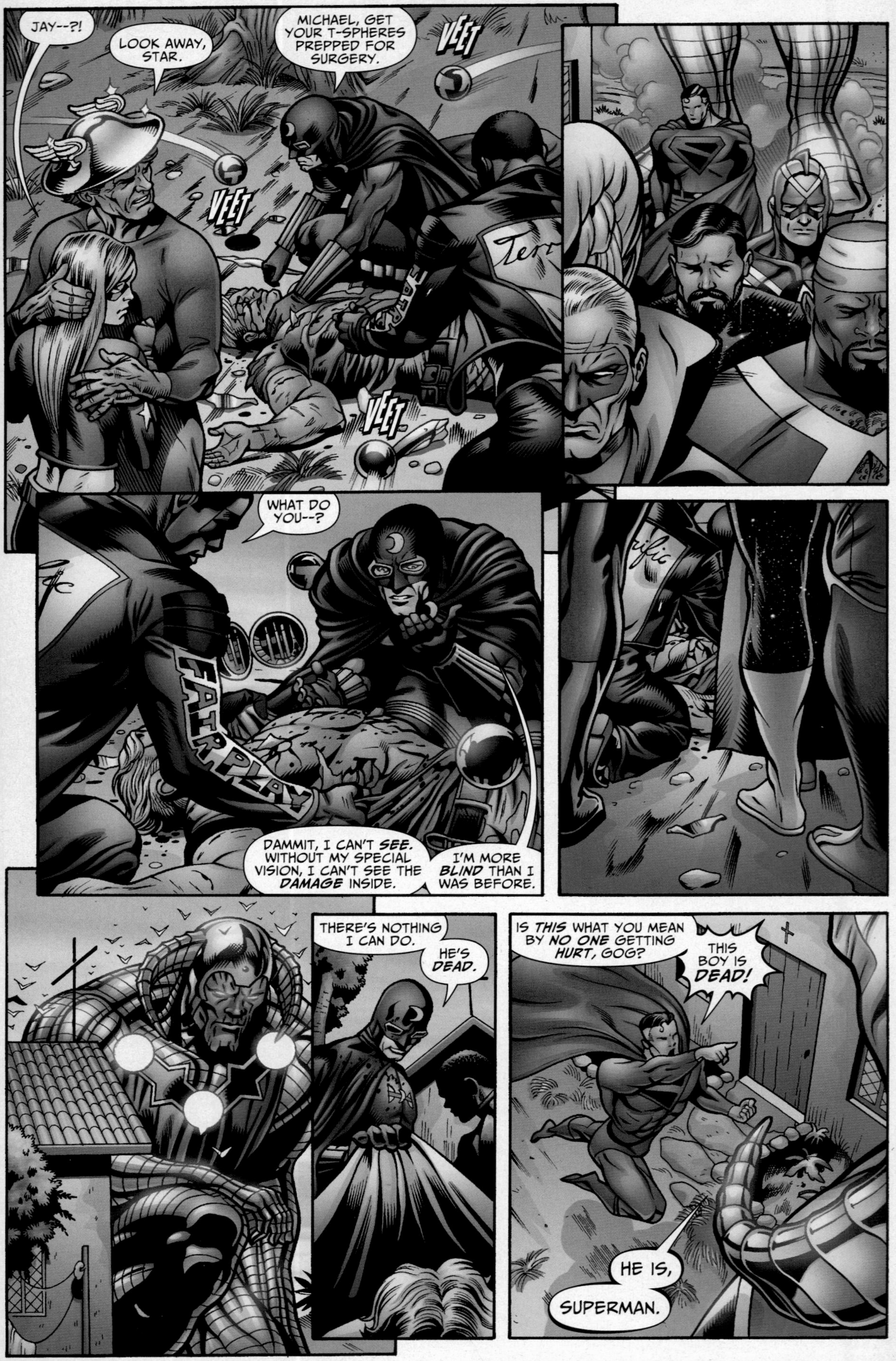
JAY--?!
LOOK AWAY, STAR.
MICHAEL, GET YOUR T-SPHERES PREPPED FOR SURGERY.
VEET
VEET
VEET
WHAT DO YOU--?
DAMMIT, I CAN'T SEE. WITHOUT MY SPECIAL VISION, I CAN'T SEE THE DAMAGE INSIDE.
I'M MORE BLIND THAN I WAS BEFORE.
THERE'S NOTHING I CAN DO.
HE'S DEAD.
IS THIS WHAT YOU MEAN BY NO ONE GETTING HURT, GOG?
THIS BOY IS DEAD!
HE IS, SUPERMAN.

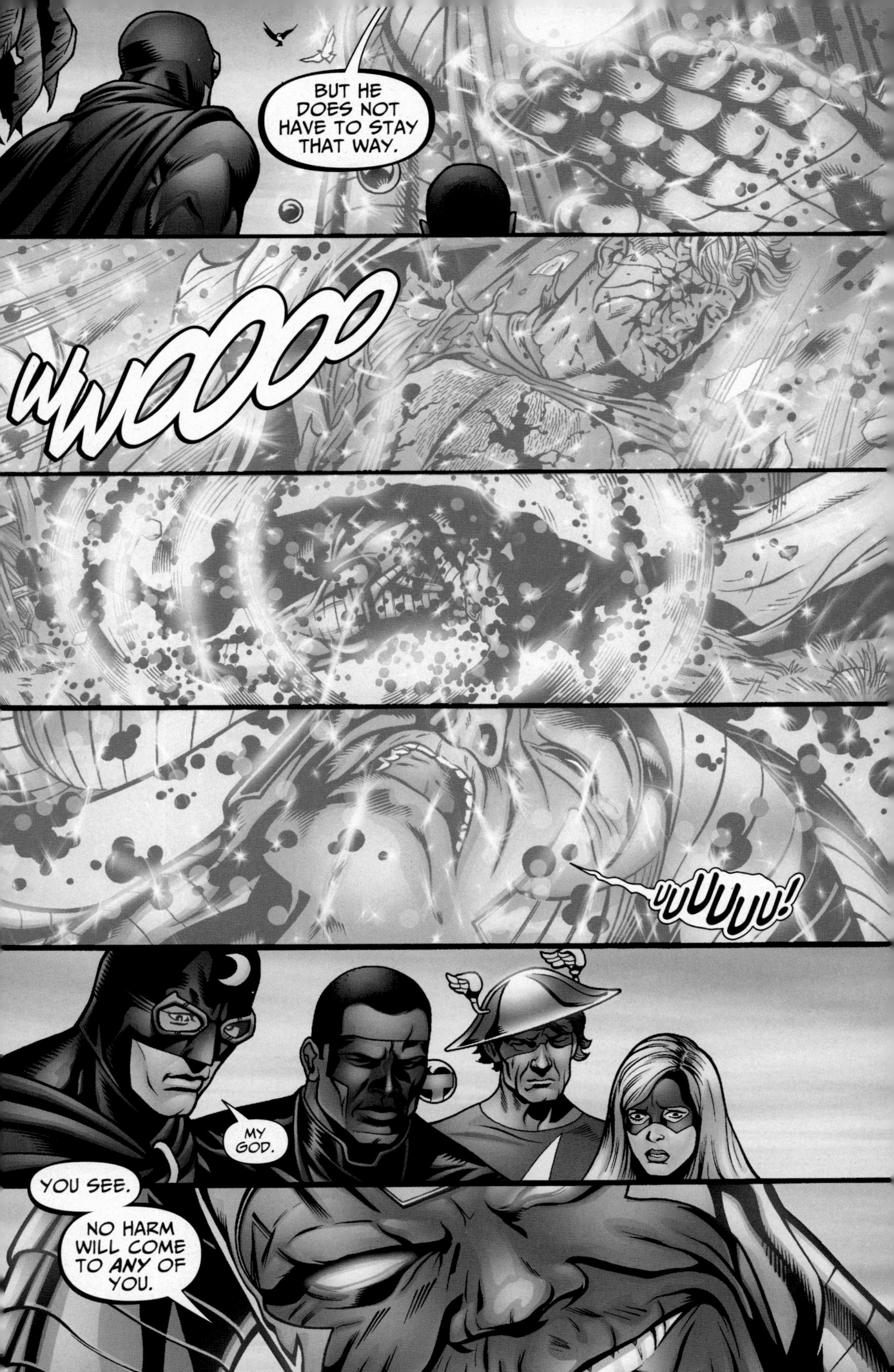
BUT HE DOES NOT HAVE TO STAY THAT WAY.
WWOOOO
UUUUUU!
MY GOD.
YOU SEE.
NO HARM WILL COME TO ANY OF YOU.

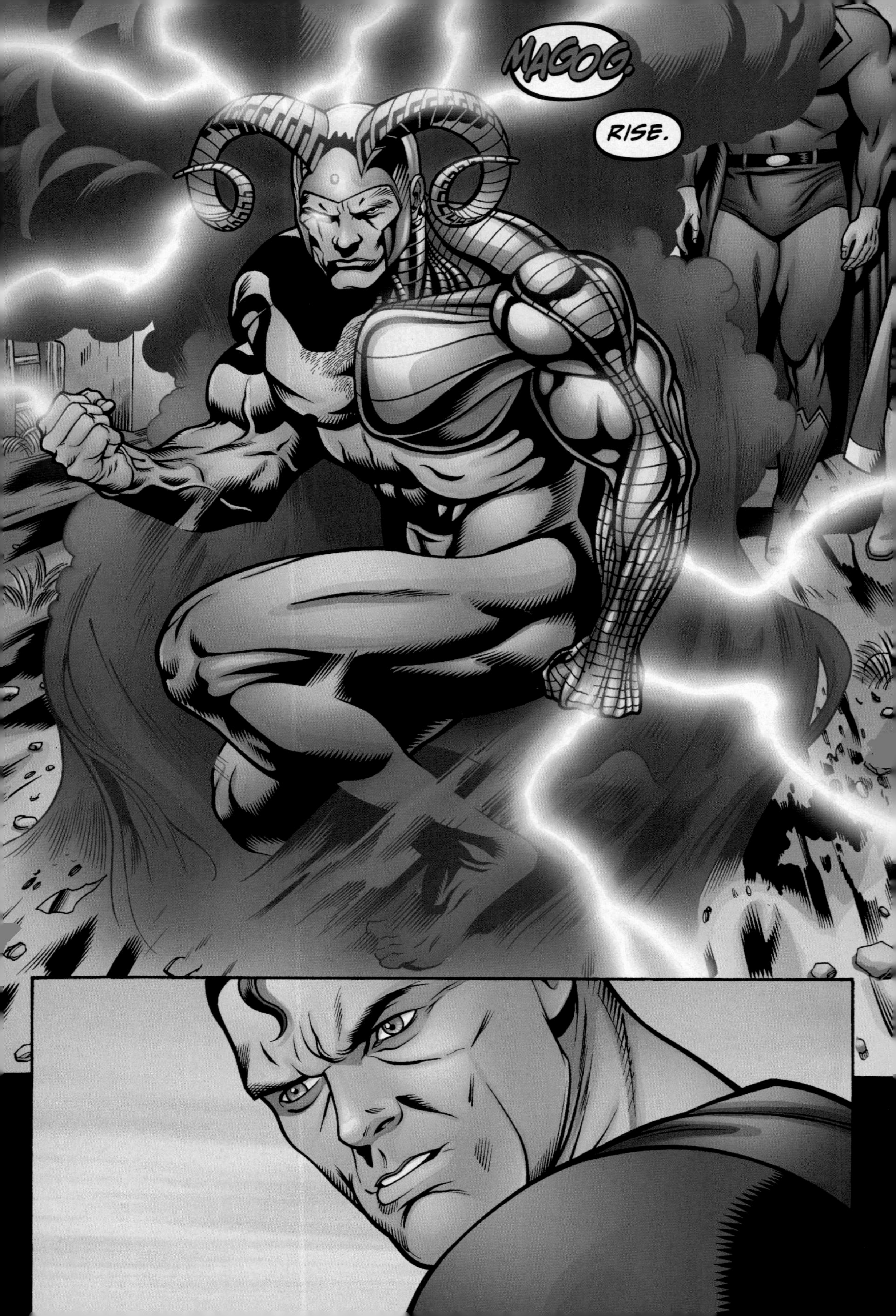
MAGOG.
RISE.

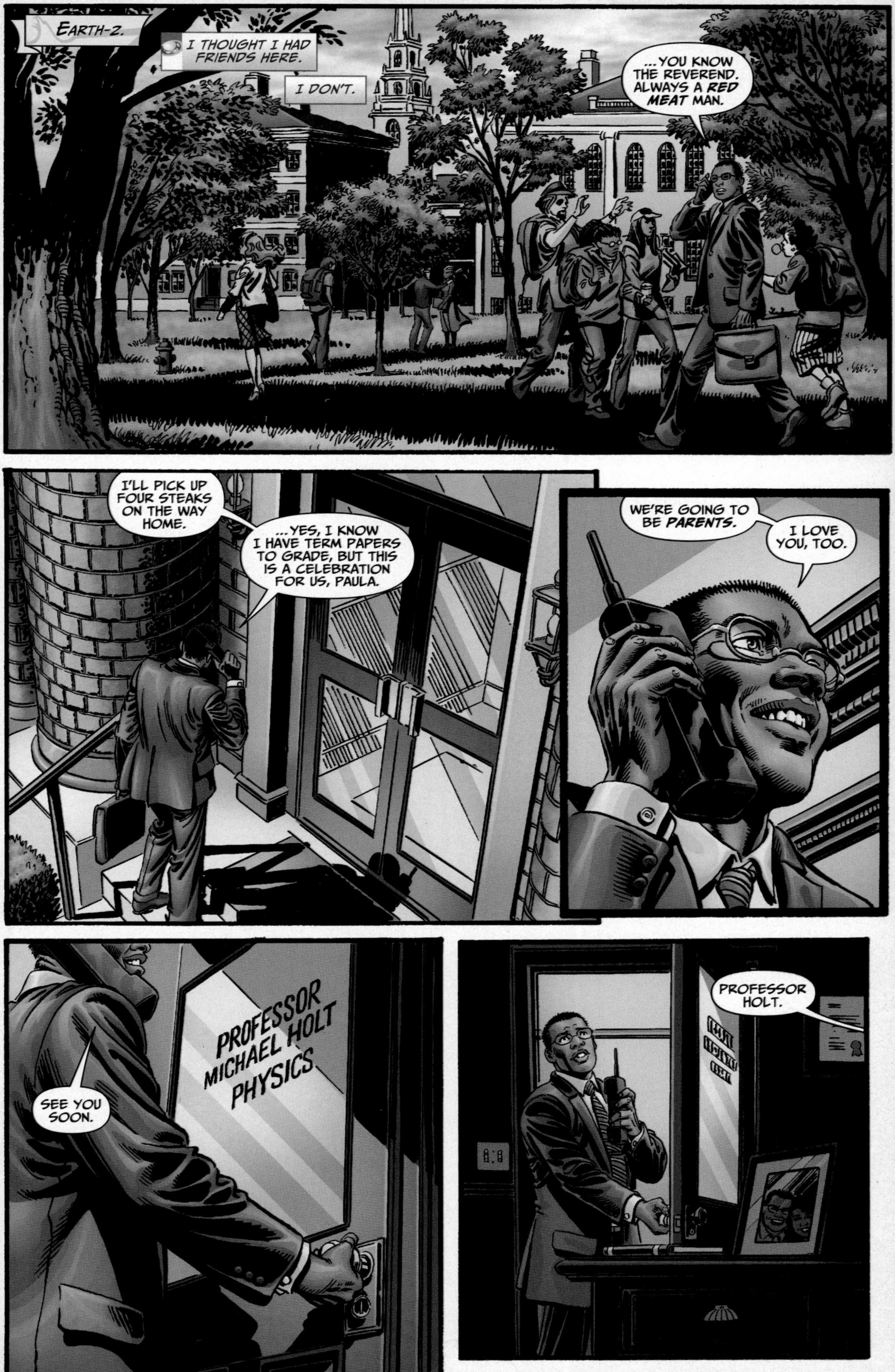
EARTH-2.
I THOUGHT I HAD FRIENDS HERE.
I DON'T.
...YOU KNOW THE REVEREND. ALWAYS A RED MEAT MAN.
I'LL PICK UP FOUR STEAKS ON THE WAY HOME.
...YES, I KNOW I HAVE TERM PAPERS TO GRADE, BUT THIS IS A CELEBRATION FOR US, PAULA.
WE'RE GOING TO BE PARENTS.
I LOVE YOU, TOO.
SEE YOU SOON.
PROFESSOR MICHAEL HOLT PHYSICS
PROFESSOR HOLT.

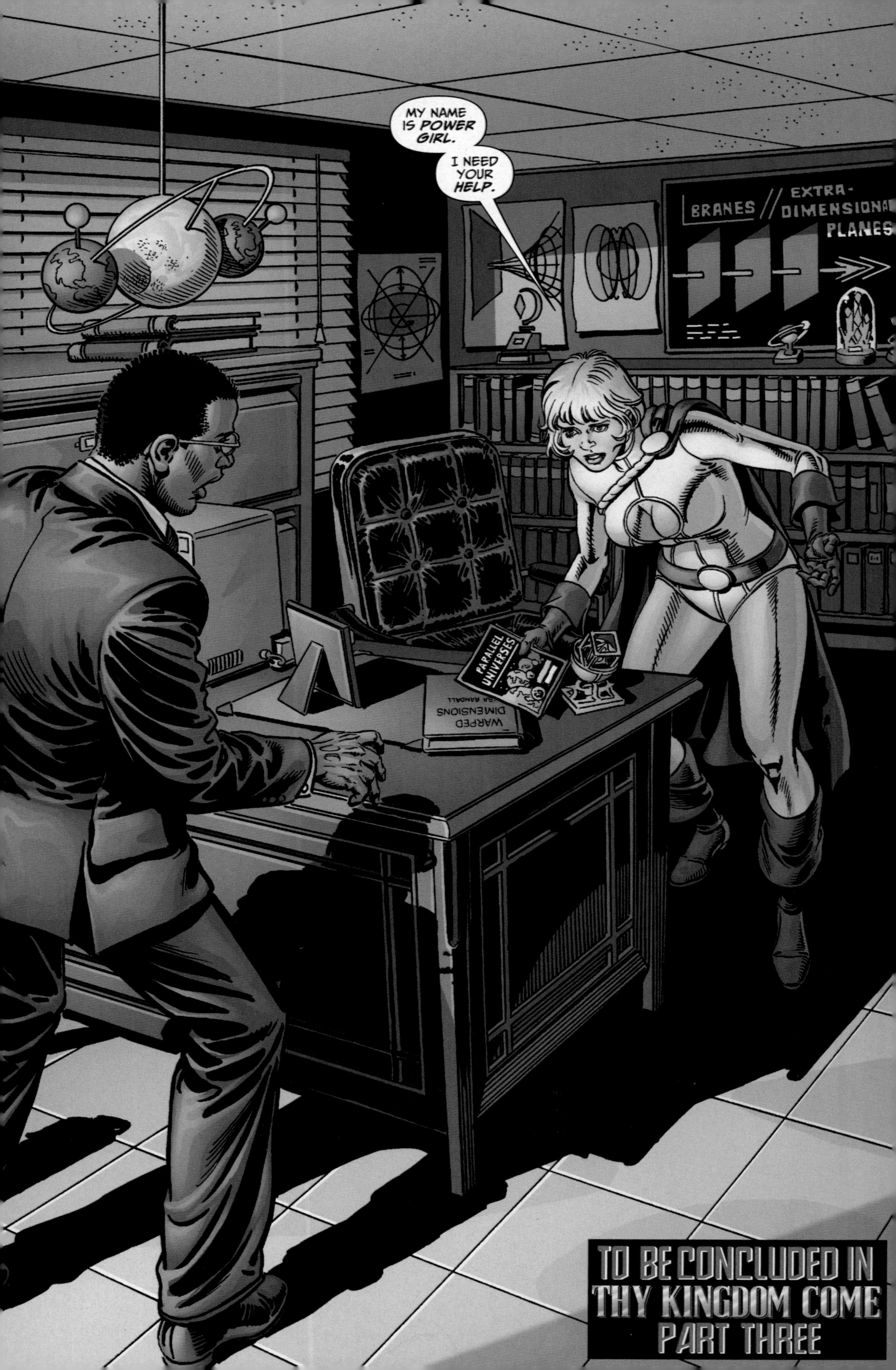
MY NAME IS POWER GIRL.
I NEED YOUR HELP.
BRANES
EXTRA-DIMENSIONAL PLANES
PARALLEL UNIVERSES
WARPED DIMENSIONS
TO BE CONCLUDED IN THY KINGDOM COME PART THREE

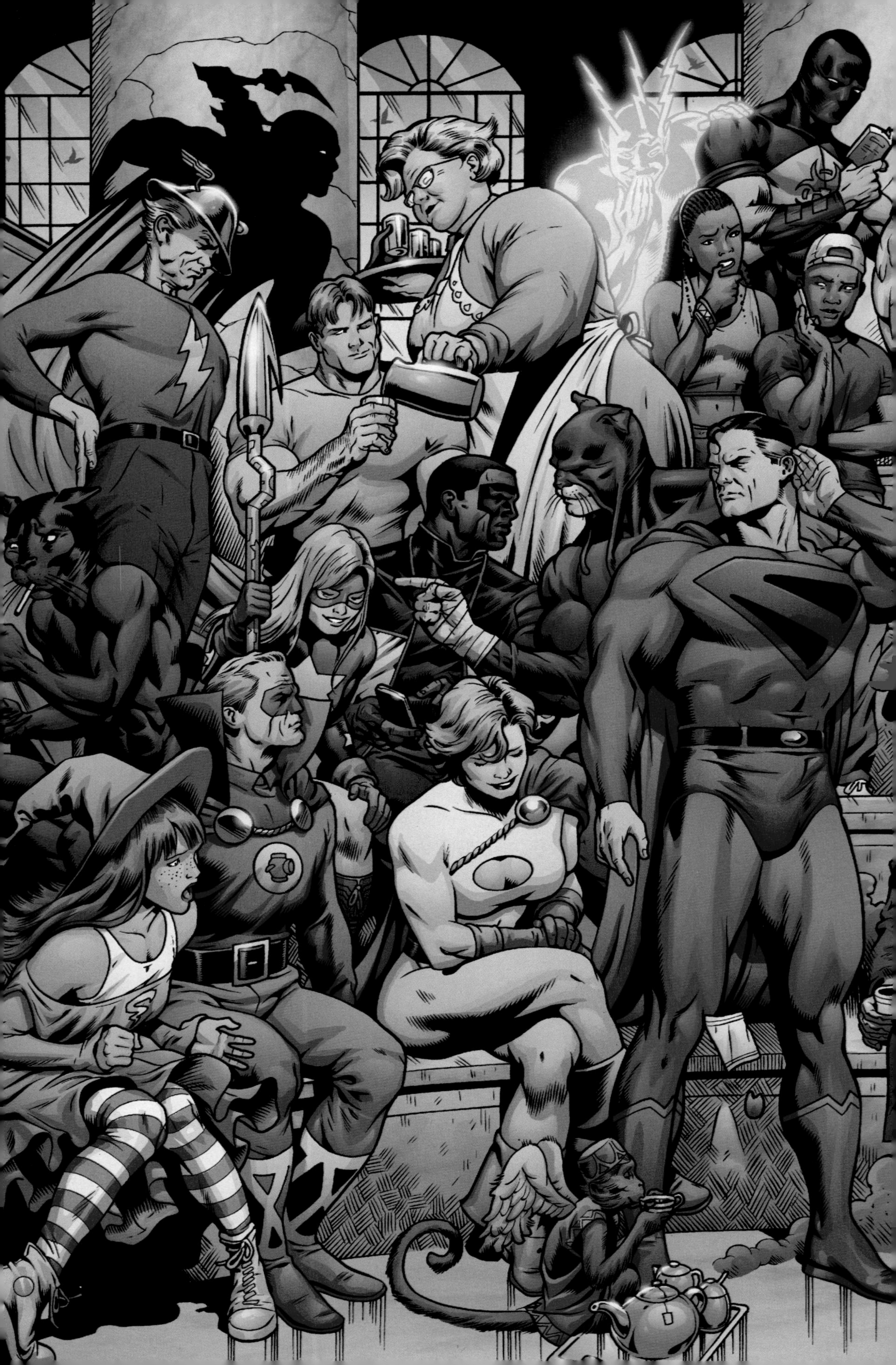

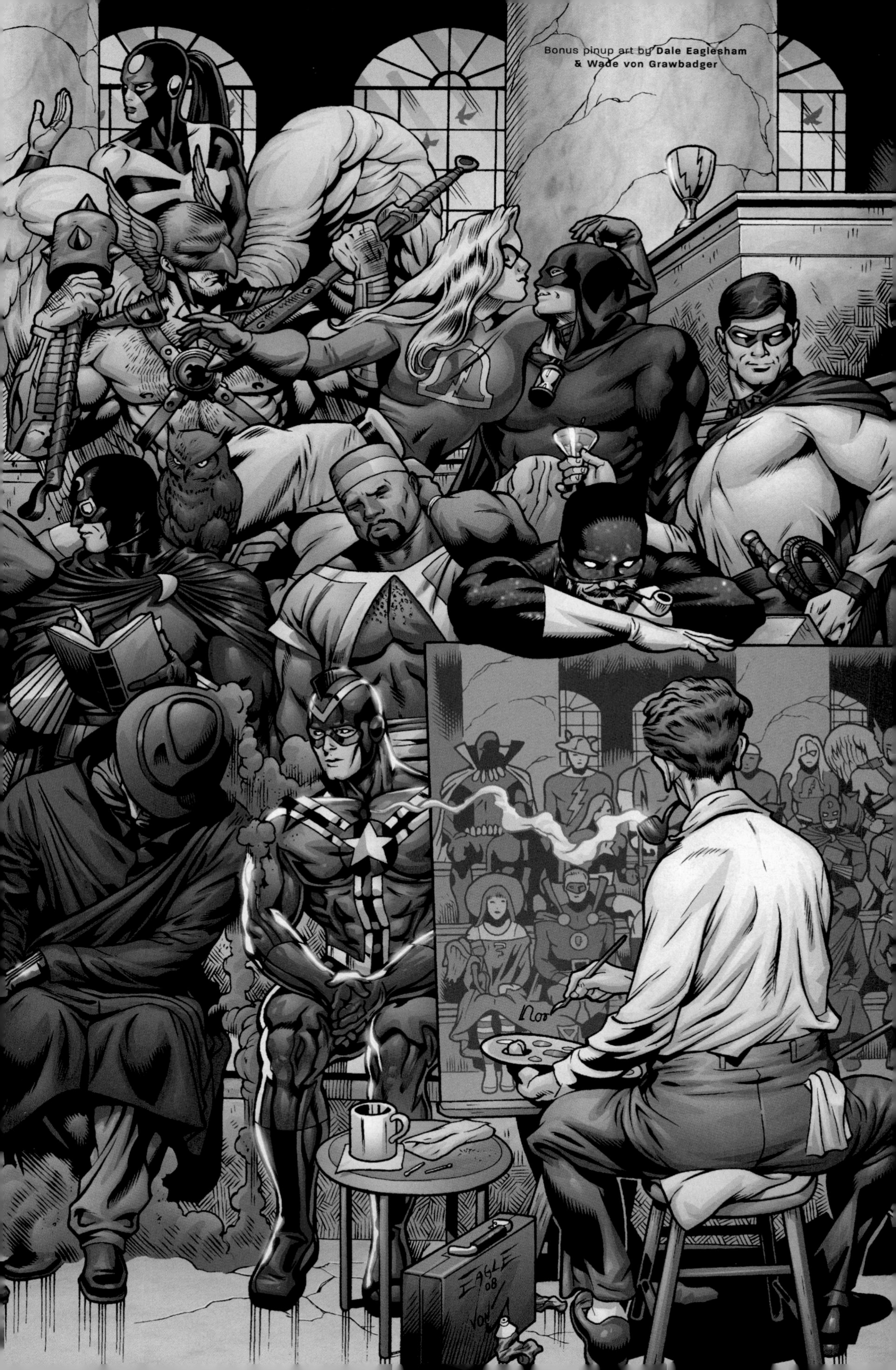
EAGLE
'08
VON
Bonus pinup art by **Dale Eaglesham & Wade von Grawbadger**